Italian and Italian American Studies

Stanislao G. Pugliese
Hofstra University
Series Editor

This publishing initiative seeks to bring the latest scholarship in Italian and Italian American history, literature, cinema, and cultural studies to a large audience of specialists, general readers, and students. I&IAS will feature works on modern Italy (Renaissance to the present) and Italian American culture and society by established scholars as well as new voices in the academy. This endeavor will help to shape the evolving fields of Italian and Italian American Studies by re-emphasizing the connection between the two. The following editorial board consists of esteemed senior scholars who act as advisors to the series editor.

Queer Italia: Same-Sex Desire in Italian Literature and Film
edited by Gary P. Cestaro, July 2004
Frank Sinatra: History, Identity, and Italian American Culture
edited by Stanislao G. Pugliese, October 2004
The Legacy of Primo Levi
edited by Stanislao G. Pugliese, December 2004
Italian Colonialism
edited by Ruth Ben-Ghiat and Mia Fuller, July 2005
Mussolini's Rome: Rebuilding the Eternal City
Borden W. Painter Jr., July 2005
Representing Sacco and Vanzetti
edited by Jerome H. Delamater and Mary Anne Trasciatti, September 2005
Carlo Tresca: Portrait of a Rebel
Nunzio Pernicone, October 2005
Italy in the Age of Pinocchio: Children and Danger in the Liberal Era
Carl Ipsen, April 2006
The Empire of Stereotypes: Germaine de Staël and the Idea of Italy
Robert Casillo, May 2006
Race and the Nation in Liberal Italy, 1861-1911: Meridionalism, Empire, and Diaspora
Aliza S. Wong, October 2006
Women in Italy, 1945-1960: An Interdisciplinary Study
edited by Penelope Morris, October 2006
Debating Divorce in Italy: Marriage and the Making of Modern Italians, 1860-1974
Mark Seymour, December 2006

A New Guide to Italian Cinema
Carlo Celli and Marga Cottino-Jones, January 2007
Human Nature in Rural Tuscany: An Early Modern History
Gregory Hanlon, March 2007
The Missing Italian Nuremberg: Cultural Amnesia and Postwar Politics
Michele Battini, September 2007
Assassinations and Murder in Modern Italy: Transformations in Society and Culture
edited by Stephen Gundle and Lucia Rinaldi, October 2007
Piero Gobetti and the Politics of Liberal Revolution
James Martin, December 2008
Primo Levi and Humanism after Auschwitz: Posthumanist Reflections
Jonathan Druker, June 2009
Oral History, Oral Culture, and Italian Americans
Edited by Luisa Del Giudice, November 2009
Italy's Divided Memory
John Foot, January 2010
Women, Desire, and Power in Italian Cinema
Marga Cottino-Jones, March 2010
The Failure of Italian Nationhood: The Geopolitics of a Troubled Identity
Manlio Graziano, September 2010
Women and the Great War: Femininity under Fire in Italy
Allison Scardino Belzer, October 2010
Italian Jews from Emancipation to the Racial Laws
Cristina M. Bettin, November 2010
Murder and Media in the New Rome
Thomas Simpson, December 2010
Anti-Italianism: Essays on a Prejudice
edited by William J. Connell and Fred Gardaphé, December 2010

Murder and Media in the New Rome

The Fadda Affair

Thomas Simpson

palgrave
macmillan

MURDER AND MEDIA IN THE NEW ROME

First published in 2010 by PALGRAVE MACMILLAN® in the United States—a division of St. Martin's Press LLC, 175 Fifth Avenue, New York, NY 10010.

Where this book is distributed in the UK, Europe and the rest of the world, this is by Palgrave Macmillan, a division of Macmillan Publishers Limited, registered in England, company number 785998, of Houndmills, Basingstoke, Hampshire RG21 6XS.

Palgrave Macmillan is the global academic imprint of the above companies and has companies and representatives throughout the world.

ISBN: 978-0-230-10836-3

Library of Congress Cataloging-in-Publication Data

Simpson, Thomas (Thomas Haskell), 1953–
Murder and media in the new Rome : the Fadda Affair / Thomas Simpson.
p. cm.— (Italian & Italian American studies series)
Includes bibliographical references.
ISBN 978-0-230-10836-3 (alk. paper)
1. Murder—Italy—Rome—Case studies. 2. Cardinali, Pietro, fl. 1878—Trials, litigation, etc.—Press coverage. 3. Trials (Murder)—Italy—Rome. 4. Sensationalism in journalism—Italy—Rome. 5. Fadda, Giovanni, d. 1878. 6. Journalism—Italy—Rome—History—19th century. I. Title.

HV6535.I83R658 2011
364.152'3094563209034—dc22 2010018835

A catalogue record of the book is available from the British Library.

Design by Scribe Inc.

First edition: December 2010

10 9 8 7 6 5 4 3 2 1

Printed in the United States of America.

per Rita

Contents

Illustrations

Acknowledgments

I thank Prof. Edward Muir for first suggesting, when I described to him the story behind the painting, *In Corte d'Assise*, that the Fadda affair would be a good topic for a book. Prof. Muir provided invaluable guidance throughout the drafting of the manuscript and the process of locating a publisher. This book would not have come to be without his generous attention. All errors herein, of course, are entirely my own.

Intensive periods of research in Rome and other places in Italy were possible thanks to the hospitality of friends Edoardo Albinati, Cristina Cieri Via, and Franco Nasi, who put me up and put up with me for extended periods of time; I hope someday to be able to repay these favors. Two great friends, Charles Matheny and Glenn Herrick, closely read early versions of the manuscript, corrected grammar and method, and encouraged me that I was on to something good. I am grateful for their skills and solidarity.

The French and Italian Department at Northwestern University has given both moral and material support for my research. Chair Jane Winston assisted me in applying for a university grant that allowed me to return to Rome for a crucial additional round of study. My colleagues in the Italian Program at Northwestern have always been the best one could hope for. I especially thank Paola Morgavi for helping me draft official letters as well as caring for animals and plants left behind during various journeys. The Interlibrary Loan office at the university library at Northwestern deserves praise for obtaining dozens of books for me.

One of the great pleasures of conducting research in Italy is meeting people who not only provide resources but also share your fascination with the project. I would like in particular to thank Luca Saletti of the Archivio di Stato di Roma, Tribunale Civile e Penale di Roma, who oversees the reading room at the Sede Succursale in Via Galla Placidia; Cristina Ivaldi, archivist at the Palazzaccio in Rome, who showed me the documentation on Raffaella Saraceni's pardon; and Silvio Biella of *Il Messaggero*, who kindly granted access to the only extant copies of early issues of the newspaper. Stefano Questioli went to great efforts to establish contacts with *Il Messaggero* after I had despaired of this possibility. I am grateful to the librarian at Casa Carducci in Bologna who allowed me to read the poet's letters and responses to the bard's poem about the Fadda trial, and to the Biblioteca Labronica in Livorno and the Biblioteca Malatestiana in Rimini for sending precious photocopies of rare documents referencing the events. I was extremely lucky to be able to spend many hours at the Biblioteca di Storia Moderna e Contemporanea and the Biblioteca del Senato in Rome, at the Biblioteche di Stato in Naples, Rome, and Bari, and a very fruitful afternoon at the Centro Internazionale delle Donne in Rome. Clara Gelao, director of the Pinacoteca Provinciale di Bari, Annalisa Bonella, Marina Pieretti, and Director Eugenio Lo Sardo at the Archivio di Stato di Roma have been very kind to grant the rights to publish the illustrations taken from their collections.

Stanislao Pugliese, editor of the Italian and Italian American Studies series at Palgrave, was assiduous in conducting the manuscript through the review process. The editorial board deserves great credit for considering a manuscript as unusual as this one. Chris Chappell and Sarah Whalen at Palgrave have guided it through editing with impressive professionalism.

The highest gratitude and appreciation goes to my mother, whose vital curiosity and enthusiasm made her an ideal person to talk to as the project carried on.

Introduction

On October 6, 1878, a war hero stationed in Rome was stabbed to death. Near the scene, police apprehended a blood-spattered circus acrobat who protested his innocence in a pronounced Northern accent. Newspapers quickly reported a link between the two men: the soldier's estranged wife, living with her family in Calabria, was said to be the acrobat's lover. Soon arrested, she too denied everything, claiming never to have heard the rumor, already bandied about in the press, that her husband's war wound had left him impotent. Several days later police in Calabria arrested a second woman, the circus company's equestrienne, alternately described as the acrobat's sister and wife.

The state's inquest carried on for eight months, heavily influenced by the dead captain's military brethren and his brother, a minor government official. The circus's stableboy, arrested together with the acrobat, died in prison after a deathbed confession. Police were unable to track down one particularly sought-after witness, a young clown. A prostitute told investigators that the clown came to her shortly before the crime and confided that the captain's wife had recruited him to kill her husband. Rumors circulated that the clown must have been murdered to eliminate a witness damning to the wife and her well-connected provincial family.

Before papal Rome joined the nation state of Italy in 1870, the secret investigative phase of a criminal inquest had been definitive in determining guilt or innocence. Under the new secular government, the investigation became merely the precursor to a public trial featuring prosecuting and defense attorneys in debate and testimony by witnesses before a jury selected from the eligible citizenry. The public trial of the captain's murderers began at the end of September 1879, with an admired government minister serving as chief lawyer for the accused wife. Court-appointed attorneys represented the two circus performers. Anticipating crowds, court officials distributed tickets to gallery seating specially built in the courtroom, but all were stunned by the swarming mass that crammed the streets, the piazza, and the ill-adapted hall of justice for a glimpse of the defendants and to hear their testimony, especially that of the black-clad, weeping young widow. Most shocking of all, the majority of the audience appeared to be women, well-dressed ones, many of them mothers with children in tow. Public fascination with the bloody and salacious crime was overwhelmed by the even greater scandal of the apparently respectable women so avid to hear every word of testimony.

The trial seized the entire nation's attention. Newspaper circulation boomed, while sophisticated weeklies built sales by denouncing the vulgar media's obsession with it. Penal experts expressed dismay at the way courtroom theatrics and leaks to journalists contaminated the dispassionate adjudication of guilt or innocence, but efforts to quell the hype only added fuel to the flames of sensation. The nation's leading poet, Giosuè Carducci, published a lacerating invective in verse against the feminine spectators in terms so harsh that a member of the defense team rose in court to defend not his clients, but the ladies of the public.

Late in the trial, with testimony over and the summaries under way, the sudden discovery of the long-lost witness, the clown, threw the entire procedure into disarray, threatening a mistrial that might have challenged the very credibility of the judicial system. When the presiding judge overruled defense objections and allowed the clown to testify, the brouhaha was so intense that the courtroom had to be cleared repeatedly. Finally, in this crucial test of the legitimacy of the widely doubted and unpopular jury system, the decision was unwavering. Two of the three parties were guilty: the acrobat was condemned to death, the wife sentenced to life imprisonment. The equestrienne was found guilty of complicity but released, judged to have acted under irresistible psychological duress. Eager to exploit her notoriety, Rome's biggest circus hired her immediately. The universal condemnation of this crass commercialization—even the *London Times* denounced it—served only to draw greater thousands representing every class of Roman society to her debut performance.[1]

At the end of the first decade after Rome became the young nation's capital, the Fadda affair (as it was called after the name of the murdered captain) became a mass convergence in which all who drew near became both performers and audience, a spectacle of distortion with no clear borders in which Italy witnessed itself, but never from an objective distance. Sparking journalism and art, as well as juridical, social, and moral discourse, the Fadda trial established a prototype of the notorious media circus trials that have played and continue to play such a visible part in the unfolding of Italy's nationhood.

The principle extant sources of information on the Fadda murder and trial consist of the following: the records of the investigation and trial in the Penal Archive in Rome;[2] contemporary newspaper coverage; bound and illustrated editions of that coverage published in the months after the trial;[3] the poem by Giosuè Carducci, "On the Fadda Trial"; an 1883 painting by Francesco Netti, *In Corte d'Assise*; journalists' and lawyers' memoirs and analytic summaries of the trial; a 2002 article on the trial by historian Angela Groppi.

This study of the Fadda affair will take different paths—some direct, some not—through the available material in an effort to make sense of the facts as they ramified and left traces in the emerging national consciousness. For a short time the Fadda murder and trial grabbed all Italy's attention, becoming a stage for national consensus, before ceding the spotlight to new distractions in a pattern prophetic of the contemporary media environment. Why did this story seize the national imagination, why did women flock to the trial, and why did men find this so disturbing? What impact, material and symbolic, did this story have on the formation of the principal social and political issues that marked national discourse in this period, such as the problem of crime, the role of the army, the Southern question, and the risk of extending democracy to vast but heretofore excluded segments of the population, including women, the poor, and the illiterate? What was the role of the press in stoking the flames of sensation? How did the new democracy's legal system turn courtrooms into theaters? How were the circus and the army played off against one another in public debate? Lastly, what access can the documentary material in the trial records provide us into the lives of the people who lived the drama?

Besides the traditional orientation of historiography to concentrate on so-called great men and events, Italian historiography in particular has been conditioned by successive waves of ideology, from liberal to fascist to Marxist. The representation of Italy's difficult, contradictory, and still unresolved process of unification has changed in order to meet the needs of the moments in which, or the movements from which, the histories themselves were being written.[4] No overarching historical paradigm has achieved undisputed hegemony, a failure reflecting a foundational weakness at the base of the nation state. The emergence of new methods in recent decades, brilliant work growing from feminist history, contributions from outside Italy, and widespread skepticism toward ideologically driven analysis have altered historical inquiry in the peninsula.[5] Despite these innovations, as recently as 2008 a leading American historian of Italy could observe that the critiques of traditional Italian historiography have not yet produced a new consensual paradigm concerning the Risorgimento or the subsequent period between national unification and the end of the century.[6]

It hardly needs to be said that this study of the Fadda murder and trial has no ambition of filling that gap; on the contrary, the Fadda affair may be of interest precisely because of its impurity as a subject. It cannot easily be said or made to serve as a lesson in historical principal. Its tawdry fascination was transient but left lasting traces, embodying an advancing wave of vulgar, raucous vivacity in public life. It was a site where North clashed with South, urban with rural, army with circus, men with women, the legal state with the real state, and the evidential with the symbolic, all during a crucial formative moment in the emergence of the Italian public sphere. Deriving from small personages and squalid circumstances, this trial was on everyone's lips because its opposing elements, deeply imbricated in exquisitely sensitive areas in the young state's nervous system, played out as an intimate but public tragedy. Through their demonstrative spectatorship, it allowed women to play a decisive role in an event that momentarily stole the scene from men in parliament and shifted attention from the halls of congress to the urban street. It briefly provided a platform for the most marginal, illiterate members of the new nation to testify in first person about their miserable lives, and it triggered a shift in the triangular relationship between government, media, and public. In his history of Italy between 1871 and 1915, Benedetto Croce cited one of the characters in our story, newspaper editor, playwright, and government minister Ferdinando Martini, who paternalistically described this postunification period of Italian democracy with the metaphor of a *commedia dell'arte* character, Arlecchino (Harlequin), "who foolishly gave his children trumpets and drums, telling them to have fun, but not to make noise."[7] The Fadda media circus and trial was just this cacophony of Italian democracy.

Immediately upon unification, the liberal regime launched a campaign of public rituals—commemorations, holidays, parades, award ceremonies, secular pilgrimages, wreath-layings—to inculcate in the populace the conviction that they were indeed Italians, sharing a codified pantheon of heroes, a single identity, a single *patria*.[8] The irresistible thrall of the Fadda trial constituted by contrast a shameful public display exposing pressures that threatened the still-fragile foundations of civil society, in particular that of the willing self-submission of women to the goal of national betterment. The trial's effect on the nation, if a single effect can fairly be distilled from such a phenomenon, was to contribute to the formation and definition of Italy as a unified people, but not to one that its founders and would-be architects had in mind or would have wished.[9] The phenomenon of widespread, intensive concentration on the trial temporarily unified the peninsula's disparate peoples into a single citizenry, in that an unprecedented plurality of the populace paid attention to and heatedly discussed the same unfolding event. But rather than reinforcing a shared consensus through which the model of citizenship envisioned by Italy's founders might take root, the trial enacted instead the ineradicable conflicts threatening the entire nationalist project. Its result, therefore, was to contribute to the creation of a collective entity paradoxically defined by the recalcitrance of its very members.

The Fadda affair is an early, formative example of the principle, by now firmly established, that we cannot separate an event from the mechanics of perception. In order to describe this phenomenon, it is necessary to alternate study of the trial itself with that of salient aspects of the context in which it took place. The structure of this book will be both narrative and analytical, stepping in for close study of texts and behaviors and stepping back to recount events that led to the production of those texts and behaviors or resulted from them. Extensive use will be made of citations not only from contemporary sources, especially from the trial archives, but also from newspapers, literature, and science. The purpose of using long citations is to go beyond merely referencing authoritative sources by allowing readers to enter into the highly dramatic rhetorical world evoked by journalists in the media, by lawyers, magistrates, witnesses in court, and even by police investigators in their reports. Because many of these sources have not been exploited in previous studies, the aim is to render a vivid sense of this particular historical moment through a gradual montage of selected pertinent texts. Performance and its necessary corollary—spectatorship—will be applied as interpretive tools to emphasize the polyvalence of texts and privilege dramatic irony and coincidence as ways of exposing otherwise invisible connections and meanings. With the advent of public trials in Rome, the predominant metaphor applied to this new social practice was that of the theatrical spectacle, and the practice was still so new that it was not merely the defendants who were on trial in a given procedure but the system itself.[10] Judges, lawyers, witnesses, jury, and public; all were quite conscious that they were wearing costumes, representing something, and performing.[11]

Examining the case, we must therefore keep in mind three overlapping forms of spectacle. First there were circus performances, both those of the Compagnia Cardinali, the family-based circus of the accused assassin that toured deep in the provinces, and those of the grand companies central to European cultural life in the capitals of that era. Second, there was the Roman spectacle of the unfolding trial, with its highly visible female audience, impassioned lawyers, tragic protagonists, and colorful witnesses. An *agon* staged by the new liberal regime, this was the democratic rite that Carducci harshly compared to the bloody rituals carried out in the ancient Coliseum under a decadent empire. Third, there was the larger spectacle of the self-formation of Italian identity, a phenomenon that took place only partly in the realm of fact and chronology but also in the dream life of millions of people who, through such dreams, were beginning to establish the foundations of a shared national consciousness.[12]

The Fadda affair is an irresistible subject that offers all the elements one could hope for in a dramatically compelling novel, movie, or opera: illicit sex, murder, deception, scandal, humiliation, vivid characters, and a trial, all set against a background of war, circus, and morbidly ingrown families. Rendering this story by applying the techniques of suspenseful narration so as to vanquish the reader, bending the tale in a ballistic arc toward the exciting climax of a jury's decision followed by an elegant denouement and a lesson learned, would certainly be a worthy endeavor. That is not, however, the aim of this study, for the simple reason that the case presents itself as fractured, its lines of causality submerged, composed of fragmentary layers, and without clear borders. Accounts of the Fadda case that choose to adopt more or less standard narrative contain the simplifications, elisions, and outright errors of fact demanded by the conventions of novelistic style, thereby manipulating the doubt and fathomlessness of lived history into fiction.[13] Precisely this kind of novelization of life characterized the journalistic treatment of the Fadda sensation as it took place and was a core reason the case exploded into the spectacle of distortion it became.

This book, on the other hand, studies not only a murder and trial but a subject that took shape in Italy's collective imagination, a cloud of sensation and spectatorship that took up residence in the emerging national psyche. The Fadda affair is of deeper interest because it evokes and prophesies the unresolved mixture of myth and substance that constitutes the weak but resilient Italian national edifice. Rather than a monodirectional narrative, therefore, this study adopts a style that might loosely be described as cubist, in that it brings forward a series of partial planes and presents them to the reader for simultaneous observation from different perspectives. Each chapter is largely self-contained and includes departures from the immediate facts of the case, but by following their sequence, the reader should accumulate a multifaceted, open perception of its impact and ramifications in the national imaginary.[14] The conventional causality of narrative is not presupposed but problematized, recognized from the outset as the dubious but hopeful construct that it is. As a subject crossing the liminal zone between public and private, what appears distantly or even randomly related may be constitutive. For example, to explore the ways journalism exploited the Fadda affair it is fruitful to devote a paragraph to the overlooked figure of E. E. Oblieght, who pioneered newspaper advertising in Rome. Oblieght had no direct connection to the Fadda case, yet his commercial innovations crucially influenced the way newspapers delivered news to the reading public. Similar indirect paths will be followed throughout this study to present a deeper, more realistic image of the complex, corrupted palimpsest of the affair. Attention will be dedicated to the changing role of the press, to the controversy surrounding the jury system, to Italy's perception of its army, and to the strange way equestrian circus manipulated and mirrored that perception. Given the painful, infected nature of Italian nationhood from its origins to the present, perhaps an apt metaphor for the technique applied here would be that of picking at a scab.

The book is organized in short chapters. Chapter 1, "The Crime and Its Coverage," presents the facts of the crime and its initial coverage in newspapers. The Fadda murder happened to occur at a precise moment when young editors were seeking subjects and formulas to engage the passion of an amorphous emerging readership. Chapter 2, "Journalism in Rome after National Unification," therefore analyzes the way journalism changed in the first decade after Rome became the young nation's capital, seizing on a newly literate public's craving to mirror itself, so as to sell papers in a new economy. Chapter 3, "Chronology of a Circus Trial," offers this study's most unusual section, consisting entirely of a sequence of selections from daily reports of the trial that concentrate especially on the behavior of the public rather than on the trial proper. The goal of this chapter is to put into dramatic relief the trial's main protagonist: its audience. The author has chosen to refrain from intervening analytically in this chapter in order to allow the choral voice of the nation's newspapers to emerge as much as possible on its own. The elements are authentic but have been selected, translated, and sequenced in chronological order; their cumulative effect should be to evoke the rich sense of life associated with historical novels. Chapter 4, "The People, the Killer, and the Weeping Widow," recapitulates the prosecution's case, discusses the jury system, and describes the beginning of the trial and testimony of two of the accused. The Fadda trial was a spectacle of media rather than strictly of journalism alone in that its representations expanded even beyond the widening confines of print and graphic journalism into the tales of street singers, the broadsides of lithographers, the dramaturgy of playwrights, the oils of painters, and the verse of poets. Thus Chapter 5, "In Corte d'Assise," discusses a variety of influential responses to the trial that took place as it was under way and shortly thereafter: those of Carducci and of Ferdinando Martini, a painting of the trial produced by Francesco Netti, several interpretations of the events in poetry, and a play. Chapter 6, "King and Quartermaster: The Battles of San Martino," jumps back in time to 1859 to describe the Battle of San Martino, where Captain Fadda received the fateful wound that led to his murder twenty years later, in a moment when the battle was being transformed into myth by a regime anxious to disseminate a sense of patriotism and national unity. Chapter 7, "To Liberate Italy from the Italians," studies the controversial status of the army in Italian public opinion, a factor that determined the intense reaction to the captain's murder and underlay the symbolic clash between army and circus enacted in the trial. Chapter 8, "Poor Giovanni Fadda," examines the intimate letters found in the trial records between Fadda, a military careerist from the Piedmont

Army, and his much younger Calabrian wife in a sequence that allows us to trace the breakdown of their marriage. Through the reading of these letters during sessions and their publication in newspapers, the trial allowed for the projection onto a national screen of a most private but recognizably middle class form of domestic suffering, adding to the affair's scandalous fascination and evincing within a family the incomprehension between North and South. Turning to a contrasting facet of the story, Chapter 9, "A New War Experiment," describes the emergence of the equestrian circus in nineteenth-century Europe as a hallucinatory sublimation of military practices, a dream reflection of war and conquest. In preparing their case, investigators were compelled to examine in detail the lives of a nomadic tribe of performers, not foreign but native to Italy, whose way of life and form of spectacle clashed incommensurably with the advancing tsunami of modern media culture. Thus the final chapter, "Characters," dwells on the circus performers, at once highly visible and socially marginal, who play major roles in the Fadda trial, actors who became passive instruments of larger forces. The aim of this book is to explore the ways conflicted and tenuous individual lives were affected by large patterns of social change, and vice versa.[15]

1

The Crime and Its Coverage

If you have visited Rome, you have probably walked these streets, although they no longer exist. The grubby, lowlife quartiere alessandrino, a neighborhood of ageless, crumbling buildings made into cheap flats and hotels to accommodate Rome's booming immigrant and transient population, once stood where today's tourists mass and traffic roars between the Coliseum and the Vittorio Emanuele Monument. As one of his great building projects, Mussolini had the quarter razed in the 1930s to create a triumphal passageway, the Via dell'Impero, through the ruins of empire leading to his balcony over Piazza Venezia, the mighty platform from which he urged his people on to glory and disaster.[1] Five thousand five hundred habitable units were destroyed, three churches were pulled down, and 85 percent of five recently uncovered ancient forums were re-covered by roadway, all to provide a ceremonial backdrop to the Duce's ambitions.[2] The seven thousand displaced inhabitants of the quarter were relocated to prefab houses on the city's outskirts, which later became notorious in their own right as the *borgate*, the desolate setting for the early novels of Pier Paolo Pasolini, focused on the unconquerable, anarchic vitality of the poor.[3]

On Sunday morning of October 6, 1878, in the Piazza of the Golden Keys, the weather was as clear and beautiful as ever, inviting the early riser to feel briefly innocent and hopeful about the future. The sun would have been still too low in the sky to strike the pavement, but the piazza was already buzzing with familiar and strange faces and tongues. In the decade between 1871 and 1881, the city's population increased from 244,000 to 300,000, consisting mostly of yokels native Romans called *buzzurri*, flowing especially from the north and Tuscany into marginal neighborhoods such as the quartiere alessandrino in the Rione Monti, where the population density tripled in a decade.[4] In 1873 a short-lived local newspaper, the *Cassandrino*, complained, "Walk the streets and you don't hear a single Roman voice. All the strangest, shrillest dialects offend your ears. The cream of Piedmont, Tuscany, the Veneto, Naples, and Lombardy is all here. The Lombards, oh, the Lombards are a regular scourge!"[5] In fact the demographic jump had begun even before unification, almost twenty years earlier, transforming Rome by now into one of those cities where few of the people you meet are actually natives.[6] Forty-five percent of the population was between the ages of 15 and 39, and men significantly outnumbered women. Many of the newcomers were uncertain as to the duration of their permanence in the new capital.[7] Crime, especially violent crime, was rife. In 1879 Martino Beltrani Scalia, a penal expert who later become Inspector General of the Interior Ministry and then Director General of Prisons, warned that "the rising tide of crime is fearsome and growing, looming over us." Citing the shocking statistics in Rome of 150 murders in 1877 and 167 in 1878, Beltrani Scalia worried that human society itself was breaking down: "Criminality in Italy demonstrates a deplorable increase, especially in crimes of blood, some of which show alarming symptoms of the violation of the most sacred ties of human nature."[8] Although he doesn't mention it by name in his study, the publication date would suggest that the author is implicitly referencing the most shocking Roman crime of 1878, the one that took place in a room overlooking the Piazza of the Golden Keys.

The barbershop was already open and Officer Giuseppe Anzella, in plain clothes, was leaning back in the chair. We can picture his face wrapped in a hot towel as he enjoyed a morning shave. As fate unfailingly decrees of such moments of simple bliss, he was interrupted. Someone was screaming for help, "*Aiuto! Aiuto!*" The policeman threw off the towel and dashed into the street with his partner, where they saw a man walking with agitated step in their direction. Reacting by training, Anzella accosted the man, slapping handcuffs around one wrist. With one arm neutralized, the man used his other to reach into his pocket for a revolver, but Anzella's partner was quick to grab it away. At that point, the officer recalled in court a year later, "The guy starts an act: 'Unhand me,' he says, 'I am from Verona and a gentleman.' 'You, a gentleman?' I say, 'You're a dirty killer; why were you running away?'" Complaining indignantly in his Northern accent at such rough handling and proudly claiming to have a permit for his gun, the man claimed to be an equestrian acrobat, a *cavallerizzo* in the Guillaume Company, the renowned circus then performing at Rome's Politeama Amphitheatre. "At that point," the policeman testified,

> I noticed he was spattered with blood. He tells me, "I was running from the killer." I yank up his other hand and say, "You're the killer, see? You're covered with blood." When he sees that, he starts squirming, trying to bring his hands to his face to lick off the blood. I stop him by slapping the back of his hand with the barrel of his gun. So he starts rubbing his hands on his clothes, but I tightened the cuffs till he said, "Not so tight!"[9]

The cry for help, as the jury, court, and crowds massed inside and outside already know, had come from a figure streaming blood, staggering several dozen meters behind the fugitive. The wounded man had stumbled downstairs and into the street still in his underclothes and slippers, to lurch, pointing with a revolver, after the one who stabbed him. One witness recalls that seeing the injured man dressed all in white, he guessed he must be a baker.

The wounded man in his underwear, a Sardinian named Giovanni Fadda, was not a baker. He was an army captain, a war hero. Or rather, it would be more correct to say that he was a war veteran and military clerk who was about to become a national hero, through a process that began with his botched murder in October 1878 and peaked during the sensational trial of his accused killers one year later. In 1859, Fadda had served under King Vittorio Emanuele at the legendary Battle of San Martino, a shining moment of Italian military glory, where he received a bullet wound that left one testicle atrophied. His symbolic destiny, the transformation from an underpaid, unhappy, cuckolded military bureaucrat into an immortal spirit of the Risorgimento, will climax epically in massive newspaper coverage and in images created and widely disseminated during the trial and after its adjournment, as its effects settled into Italian consciousness.

On the first Sunday morning in October 1878 in the Piazza of the Golden Keys, Giovanni Fadda lay on the stones where he collapsed, still pointing after his assailant. No longer able to cry out, he could only wheeze. Now even that sound turned to a rattle. The barber, the waiter, and other tradesmen in the piazza uselessly huddled around him. Blood flowed copiously from deep knife wounds in his heart, neck, and thigh. A Roman street singer's version of the tale counts no fewer than 23 stab wounds, the figure reported in the official autopsy, which determined that the first blow, to the thigh, opened the crural artery and proved to be the mortal one.[10] It is pure coincidence that Julius Caesar was said to have been stabbed the same number of times in the Roman Forum, only a couple hundred meters from where Captain Fadda now lay bleeding. The baker who ran off to the pharmacy for first aid supplies returned with bandages and iodine, but it was too late to do anything but watch the man die, his blood seeking paths through the square black paving stones. Soon he was shuttled off, speechless and moribund, to Consolation Hospital, to be pronounced dead.

The stranger with blood on his hands, still protesting innocence, was in the police lockup even before Fadda was officially declared dead. Within the hour his alleged accomplice, a tubercular horse groomer named Giuseppe De Luca, was arrested at the train station with two tickets in hand. In his testimony before the court, Officer Anzella was not speaking figuratively when he described the man he grabbed as performing an act, because he indeed had his hands around a performer. Dropping the claim of working in the grand Guillaume Circus, and dropping the Northern accent that reporters will variously identify as Romagnolo, Mantuan, and Veronese, the suspect now introduced himself as Pietro Cardinali of the Cardinali Equestrian Circus, a family-based troupe touring the provinces of Calabria, two days south of Rome by slow, circuitous train. That is, although indeed a *cavallerizzo*, he was by no means the featured star of a major European company, but rather something of a gypsy. He was lying about being a gentleman of Verona, or as the inquest reveals, he was mistaken: more likely he was a Calabrian or Sicilian bastard adopted into the circus as a child, bereft of documents to prove his provenance. Cardinali, 35, was charged with murder on October 7, as was his accomplice, De Luca, 34. The coroner's autopsy estimates the dead man's age as 35, although several newspapers give his age as 45; the latter, in this case, is probably closer to the truth.[11]

The news travels throughout the nation as fast as the telegraph lines can carry it, its rapidity surpassed only by Roman word of mouth. The Monday evening, October 7, edition of Milan's *Corriere della sera* carries on page one its regular report from the capital, "Lettere Romane" dated October 6, the evening of the murder. In its effort to trace the facts and make sense of the crime, the breathless coverage of the first days anticipates themes that will come into play as the full story emerges: "The news of the captain murdered this morning spread like lightning through the city, but, as happens in the first moments, with every possible error and uncertainty. I will tell you what I found out, having just spoken with the doctor at Consolation Hospital, where the poor captain was transported and where he died a half hour later. With the newspapers that arrive together with this present letter, you will be able to complete or correct my information."[12]

The Roman correspondent for the *Corriere* presumes that his Milanese readers will have already heard the first telegraph reports of the captain's murder, which his present piece, arriving by post via train along with copies of other Roman dailies, will fill out and correct. He then recounts the details as he has them:

> I'm assured that this morning around 7:30, Captain Fadda of the 32nd infantry, having just arisen and still in his underclothes, sitting at his writing table, heard knocking at his door—apparently he was living in furnished rooms—from a person who claimed to have a letter for him. The captain opened the door. As no one was present, and the wounded man unable to provide detailed description in the short time he remained alive, it will be very difficult to find out exactly the details of the heinous deed. It appears, however,

> that as soon as he entered, the assassin, armed with a revolver and a long, double-bladed dagger, suddenly assaulted the defenseless, half-dressed captain with the second of these weapons, stabbing at him wildly.

Compiled from the words of other reporters who have spoken with police and witnesses at the scene, the correspondent's version of the events already, perhaps inevitably, begins to introduce novelistic elements: the knocking at the door, the voice from the other side, the wild stabbing, all details that no one could verify except the dead captain and the accused killer. Constrained by restrictions against publishing information from police reports, the genre of crime reporting had not yet acquired a standard set of narrative conventions. In the heat of the moment, therefore, the reporter frames his account by drawing from the modes of crime fiction. The Roman daily *Il Bersagliere* tells readers that before being attacked by his assailant, the captain had "courteously invited him to sit."[13] The reporter for another Roman daily, *Il Diritto*, acknowledges that no one was present at the murder and condemns journalists who embellish their mise-en-scène with frills, but asserting that "it is easy to imagine by induction," he goes on to paint in dramatic colors the heroic resistance of the captain: "Although unarmed, he fought back like a lion: coiling himself around the neck of his assassin, he allowed himself to be dragged down the stairs without letting go. Surely a terrible, savage struggle, the captain made superhuman efforts to prevent the assassin's escape, while the assassin flailed with desperate blows to finish off his victim and then flee."[14]

The *Corriere* writer also reports, with due caution, the very first conjectures as to the motive for the crime: "The assassin . . . would appear to be a certain Manzi or Panzi, husband of a woman, that he apparently believed to have been seduced or tempted by Fadda. This is the current version and I pass it on with all due reserve. It's said that the police found in the murdered man's room a letter signed by this woman, the letter the killer would have used to gain access to his intended victim."

In fact, however, this letter will almost immediately be revealed to be a ruse invented by the assassin to throw investigators off the track. Instead, it will ultimately betray its creator, solidly demonstrating the crime to have been thoroughly, if stupidly, premeditated. The *Corriere* correspondent has not seen the arrested man in person, but here too he reports what he has heard from others: "He is of low condition, rather young."

Accompanying their own report, the *Corriere* offers on page two a digest of the coverage from the morning editions of three Roman dailies whose information appears more current. *La Capitale* explains that Fadda lived in a furnished apartment, served as chief accountant of the Thirty-second

Infantry, and was beloved of his landlords, who say they hadn't had such a peaceful tenant in years. The piece describes the scheme employed by the assassin to draw the captain's orderly away from the apartment, leaving the killer alone with his victim, to strike a "single, mortal blow." The *Libertà*, asserting that Fadda was around 45 (thus agreeing with the estimate given in *L'Opinione*), says the captured man is known as "Francone," a nickname whose menacing connotation will be fully exploited by the press and prosecutors, and describes him as a shopkeeper from Calabria, with "a sinister aspect, of medium height, with thick curly hair and a small black moustache." The same paper reports the arrest at the train station of Francone's accomplice, Giuseppe De Luca, whose initial interrogation has already been leaked to journalists. Referring the words of fellow officers in his regiment, the *Libertà* describes the murdered captain as having been, "a man of gentle, austere habits, alien to intrigue. He lived discreetly at home and work, and talked only about requesting leave or retirement to be able to live out his days in tranquility." Lastly, the *Corriere* cites a dispatch in the *Perseveranza*, according to which the accomplice has given the killer a different motive: to eliminate the captain so as to marry his wife, "from whom he lived separately, and who resides in Potenza. The wife is said to be very rich."[15]

By the next day's column, the correspondent for the Milanese daily is already beginning to contextualize the still scarce and unreliable evidence at hand: "The first, strange notices that spread yesterday morning about the assassination of the poor captain come to be illuminated by a ghastly light, by which we can make out the threads of one of those terrible domestic dramas so richly represented in judicial annals. In Naples, the Maceri trial is underway, in which the principal actors are also Calabrian, and that case appears sadly similar to this one of Cardinali, nicknamed *Francone*!"[16]

The reporter's first judgment on the case is that this is another familiar, bloody episode from the Southern provinces, particularly Calabria. The *Capitale* adds the detail that the bloody knife found at the scene is of a type called "*lama infallibile* [infallible blade] in the language of brigands," positing thereby an association between this murder and the Southern plague of brigandage.[17] Sifting rumors, the *Corriere* correspondent transmits what is said about the captain's wife: "It's said that she is young, beautiful, and rich, or at least very wealthy."

The woman in question, Raffaella Saraceni, will be arrested late on October 7, meaning that newspaper readers in Milan may have known of her husband's death and her imminent arrest even before she did. On the other hand, Captain Fadda's brother Cesare, a lands inspector for the government posted to the same province as the Saraceni family, read of his brother's murder from a newspaper before any friend could arrive to break the tragic news.[18] Raffaella will almost immediately be conducted to Rome for interrogation, but an anxious press remains a step ahead of the facts. The *Corriere* correspondent reports on the front page of the October 10 edition "the announcement of the arrival of the accused woman that appeared in several papers is due to a mistake, as on Tuesday evening a train arrived from Southern Italy bearing a different woman accompanied by police." The reporter also describes the emotional impact of the news of the murder on the general public as strongly influenced by the fact that the victim was a soldier: "The deep feeling provoked by the death of Fadda was certainly increased by his honored uniform, by his service to the nation, by the blood shed for Italy, by the great affection we all feel for the most patriotic institution Italy possesses: the Army."[19] Thus, even as the facts come in, the larger sociological lineaments of the murder begin to emerge—the victim as a representation of the nation of Italy, the killers as representations of the South. At the trial a year later, eloquent defense attorney Pietro Rosano will open his summary statement with poetic foreshadowing: "Ladies and Gentlemen, October 6, 1878, dawned balefully for Rome: balefully for Italy," and go on to describe the ill-fated captain: "He belonged to the Army, the most vital of our affections, the purest of our glories, the most secure of our hopes."[20] It was not merely a man who was murdered that fall morning.

On page two of the October 10 *Corriere*, an insert titled "The Wife of Captain Fadda" digests what Roman papers are saying about the accused woman. The press focuses intensely on two motifs: that she is "rich or at least very wealthy," and the degree to which she is beautiful. That she is rich appears to be accepted as a given from the outset, and admits very little degree of nuance, as though for reporters and readers there were only two possibilities: one is either rich or not. Efforts made by her defense attorneys during the trial to insist that the wife's family was not so terribly affluent after all appear motivated by the wish to disassociate their client from negative and culpable connotations her wealth may evoke in the minds of the jury and populace. By contrast, the question of Raffaella Saraceni's beauty or lack thereof invites extremely detailed inquiry. The *Perseveranza* reports her arrival in Rome on the tenth, describing her as weeping uncontrollably and dressed in black, with a long black veil, as she was transferred from the train to carriage to be conducted to the Buon Pastore women's prison. Another paper, the *Italie*, a daily published in French, offers a description of the woman passed on from an anonymous acquaintance:

> Her head is attractive and pretty; it would be beautiful in fact if only her round little face were less full; her eye is black, vivacious, expressive; her gaze betrays her southern temperament, her hair is black and abundant, her height below average; her figure rather pronounced. In sum, Signora Fadda is charming and pretty, rather than beautiful. As for her morals, they are characterized by habitual nonchalance, broken suddenly by a word or gesture a bit too lively, even perhaps indecorous; an incomplete, frankly provincial education; a certain talent for the piano, or rather a pretense of talent for the piano, such that she plays willingly at her own home or in the homes of others. That is, she is one of those women found by the thousands in the small cities. Nor does she have either the great defects or the great gifts that characterize the novel-like heroines of the Criminal Court.[21]

The French-language paper initially dismisses Saraceni as a Bovary manqué, too round, too short, and too lacking in taste to qualify as a heroine of bourgeois tragedy. This judgment will turn out to be wrong, as proven not only by the waves of sympathy she will arouse as the trial unfolds but by the publication in 1881 of the drama, "The Murder of Captain Fadda," which exalts Saraceni as the innocent victim of a self-deluding murderer and of a jury system that places undue authority in the hands of unqualified citizens too easily swayed by aggressive prosecutors.

The *Opinione* is present as she descends from her train in Rome, accompanied by carabinieri, her mother, and a lawyer, and proceeds by carriage to the convent and penitentiary of Buon Pastore, an institution run since 1615 by a women's order modeled on the Jesuits. After unification, the state had ordered the transformation of Buon Pastore from a hospice for abandoned, insane, and unruly women into a female prison, but left control of it in the hands of the resident sisters, an intermediate status that will have repercussions during the trial.[22] At the station, there are already masses of curious gawkers awaiting her arrival, many shouting invective, and a crush of press vehicles follows her carriage across the city to Buon Pastore, near the banks of the Tiber south of the Vatican. The *Opinione*'s report on Raffaella Saraceni is virtually microscopic and seems more favorably disposed than its Francophone counterpart:

> Her stature is well-proportioned, her body agile and nimble. She is rather thin. She has abundant chestnut hair, eyes black and rather pronounced, not pretty, but vivacious; the nose makes a small concave curve in the middle and bends lightly upward at the end. She has thin lips. Her extremely pallid, olive color may result from the emotional state that necessarily preys on her. The overall effect of her facial features is plain, but likeable, and from her gestures and sonorous, pleasing voice, one might take her for an artist. The long hair cascading over her shoulders gives her figure a special character. We have noted

Figure 1.1 Raffaella Saraceni, wife of Giovanni Fadda

Source: Permission granted by Ministero dei Beni e le Attività Culturali, Archivio di Stato di Roma, ASR 13/2010, Archivio Civile e Penale di Roma, Circolo d'Assise. Reproduction is prohibited.

a well-turned and slender hand. Her carriage is free and relaxed, her inner turmoil veiled by an air of self-assurance we would like to judge in her favor.[23]

In the next day's "Lettere Romane," the *Corriere* correspondent offers his take on the debate over the accused woman's appearance: "The reporters with the good luck to have seen signora Fadda, arrived yesterday in the company of her mother, are in disagreement as to the external features of that miserable creature. Some call her charming and elegant, others that she is unattractive and vulgar. It's certain that she is no beauty."[24]

Thus the newspapers from the outset seed into the public interest in the trial a debate not merely about guilt or innocence, but about Raffaella Saraceni's "esteriorità," her external appearance, the question of whether her appearance and behavior suit the role that she has taken on, or that has been thrust upon her. The degree of public repulsion or sympathy toward her, and perhaps therefore the success of her defense, will depend on her ability to play into expectations developed by the press. Disappointed in her conduct and dress upon her arrival in Rome, the reporter for the *Bersagliere* explicitly prescribes how the accused woman needs to behave in order to win over the public:

> Perhaps if I'd seen her beautiful, blooming with youth, seductive, well-dressed, in the fashion of an afflicted, desolate, great lady, I would have understood how a man might have lost his head over her, perhaps for no more than a friendly glance, a kind smile granted him, and he might have determined to commit such an atrocious crime to be able to possess her; but seeing her like that, a horrid suspicion passed through my soul: it seemed to me that, if she really is guilty, it must be a common, vulgar guilt, one that does not arouse sympathy, that does not seek to move the public and dispose it in her favor.[25]

Ultimately, through her conduct and that of her four lawyers during the trial, Raffaella Saraceni will indeed gain widespread public sympathy, although not enough to convince the jury of her innocence. She will not, however, perform the trite operatic scenario invoked by the reporter, but rather one grounded in the wrenching contradictions of her specific circumstances.

Mystique builds the next day with the announcement that Signora Fadda has hired to defend her the Honorable Diego Tajani, a minister in the new left-leaning government, and a young lawyer named Saverio Tutino, "already highly thought of in penal law circles in Rome." The woman's fate will be entirely separate from that of her presumed accomplices, Cardinali and De Luca, who will be defended by court-appointed attorneys.[26] On October 11 comes the last arrest in the case, with a charge of complicity against Antonietta Carrozza, 25, the circus company's equestrienne, initially identified as Cardinali's sister, then as his wife. She is both and neither. Carrozza too will be incarcerated in Buon Pastore from the day of her arrival in Rome until the last day of the trial. All four of the accused may face the death penalty.

Two days before the October 10 parade of vehicles and gawkers that accompanied the captain's widow from the train station to Buon Pastore, a somber procession carried her husband's mortal remains in the opposite direction, from Consolation Hospital, past the Imperial forums, up Via Nazionale, and around the train station to the cemetery of Campo Verano. Accompanied by the entire corps of his regiment, the Thirty-second Infantry, by a military band, representatives from all the regiments stationed in Rome, numerous municipal officials, and with his casket bearing an evergreen wreath offered by the city's native Sardinian community, the passage of the funeral cortege attracts extensive coverage, dwelling on the "immense grief afflicting the entire citizenry . . . the great consternation that horrible crime aroused in every citizen" and "the long roadway crowded with people."[27] For the residents of Rome, the solemn cortege bearing Giovanni Fadda's remains to his resting place cannot help but recall in a minor key the spectacular one for King Vittorio Emanuele II, that other hero of the Battle of San Martino, who had died in Rome in January. Stressing the spontaneous unity of the response to the murder, the *Avvenire d'Italia* describes how all Rome had already become expert on the crime's details: "The populace crowding the streets through which the funeral cortège passed expressed vivid scorn for the pitiless assassin, recalled with horror the details of the ferocious crime, and grieved the miserable end of that valiant soldier, who had often confronted death face to face, but never expected his life to end because of such unjust treachery."[28]

On the following day, the *Bersagliere* prints in full the angry funeral oration of a dear friend of Fadda's who appears to have drawn a striking conclusion about the responsibility for the murder. It reads, "After having faced the enemy for a just cause, he took up arms once again against that barbarous sect, the wretched legacy of an abominable dynasty . . . Death, which he had willingly faced so many times, dared not attack him face to face, but, cowardly, made use of the hand of a vile assassin to slaughter him! But it is not within the inclination of our spirit to cry out, 'Revenge!'"[29]

The orator here is using figurative rhetoric his hearers would have understood perfectly: "facing the enemy for a just cause" refers to Fadda's combat against Austria at the Battle of San Martino during the Second War of Independence in 1859; "he took up arms once again" refers to Fadda's subsequent service in the civil war against Southern brigands ("that barbarous sect") who were clandestinely supported by the deposed Bourbon rulers of the Kingdom of Naples ("an abominable dynasty"). The speaker is suggesting that Fadda's murder at the hands of a knife-wielding Calabrian was a delayed revenge killing for the national unification imposed by the North on the South, adding with his final flourish ("But it is not within the inclination of our spirit to cry out, 'Revenge!") that in contrast to the tribal code of vendetta typical of the primitive South, the evolved North lives by ideals of justice and transparent legality. In the moment of expressing his grief, the dead captain's friend betrays the psychosocial underpinnings of the crime. In his rectitude and integrity, Captain Fadda stands for progress and the young state; his opposite, Cardinali the acrobat, stands for subterfuge, primitivism, and bestiality.

On October 14, numerous papers carry the moving letter of gratitude addressed to the entire city from the captain's elderly father, a notary from Cagliari, who expresses the great comfort he has received from "the deep empathy of the citizenry, a great proof of the civil conscience of the great capital of our Italy." His perception of the public response implicitly characterizes the murder as something greater than a personal misfortune provoking sympathetic pity: it was an attack on the nation's integrity that has widely aroused the Roman citizenry's sense of patriotic solidarity.[30]

With the funeral over and the prime suspects incarcerated, the investigation moves into full swing. Cardinali, De Luca, and Saraceni are repeatedly interrogated. The police cannot implicate Raffaella Saraceni's mother, Carolina Nola Saraceni, despite a harsh report from a carabiniere in the family's hometown who dwells on her evil character and insists she must be at the root of the crime. Instinctively sympathetic to the mother, Roman newspapers tell how Carolina Nola has taken an apartment with a view of her daughter's cell in Buon Pastore. Every night, they say, she sets a candle in the windowsill as a signal of love to her daughter. Raffaella's aged wet nurse, Maria Ferraro, remains under intense scrutiny for having conveyed messages among the guilty parties, but she will finally not be included in the formal charges. Antonietta Carrozza, the equestrian mysteriously identified variably as Cardinali's sister or wife, is charged and brought to Rome. Telegrams fan across Italy demanding that local police track down the missing clown, Carlo Bertone; but one after another their hands remain empty. In January, the horse groomer and accused accomplice Giuseppe De Luca dies in prison coughing up bloody sputum after a deathbed confession contradicting parts of earlier sworn statements. Officials periodically leak juicy details to reporters, such as the one of the discovery of a poem found among the captain's letters containing a furious condemnation of an unfaithful woman.

It takes a year for the case to come to trial due to the difficulty of tracking down witnesses, as prestigious lawyers elbow their way onto the defense team, and because of the laborious task of assembling a jury. Almost all the privately hired lawyers are members of parliament. Prosecution and defense attorneys will summon Calabrian peasants and townspeople, telegraph operators from stations between Cassano and Rome, railroad men, tavern keepers in Bari, nomadic and undocumented circus performers, Roman police, bystanders, convicts, and military personnel from throughout the peninsula; almost a hundred witnesses in all. There will be the magistrates, officials who have moved to Rome to serve and feed on the government in the nation's new capital, and lawyers, most of whom come from Rome and the South. Then there are the journalists: Roman newspapers, especially the young *Il Messaggero*, staked their futures on the hype they built in anticipation of the opening of the trial (the *Messaggero* and its exploitation of the Fadda trial will be discussed in the next chapter). Last—or rather first—there are the people, the public in all its variety that buys and reads the newspapers or listens to them read aloud and attends the trial. The coming-together of all these elements around the squalid appeal of the case as it unfolds creates a great media circus in the heart of the new nation. The Fadda murder and trial especially attract two emergent forces that alter the nature of the judicial action under way. These two forces are journalism and women, that is, market-driven journalism disconnected from an overt political line and women in significant numbers as visible actors in the public sphere.

The investigative phase of the *processo* ended formally on May 18, 1879, with the publication of the "Atto d'Accusa," the official charges against Cardinali, Saraceni, and Carrozza, compiled by the investigating magistrate, Michele Finizia, and signed by the Pubblico Ministero Ippolito Rutigliano, (the state's prosecutor), whose task is to present the charges to the presiding magistrate, Pietro Giordano, who will conduct the proceedings. Rutigliano's role is to represent the prosecution's case throughout the public trial. Since 1865, it has been required that the prosecution publish its case at least eight days before the opening of the judgment phase to allow attorneys for the accused time to examine the charges and prepare a defense.[31] As it happens, however, a number of intervening events lead to postponements of the start date of the trial. It has been difficult to assemble the extremely long list of witnesses and the components of the legal teams for the defense and the *parte civile* have shifted, causing delays. Composing the jury is also a difficult, time-consuming process.

This two-page "Atto d'Accusa," to be read aloud at the beginning of the public sessions that convene at the end of September, describes the crime, details the proofs of culpability of the accused, and specifies the charges for each.[32] The parties are identified in this way: "Cardinali, Pietro, son of Vincenzo, 35 years of age, nicknamed Francone, acrobatic equestrian, born in Verona, of no fixed abode; Saraceni, Raffaella, daughter of Domenico, 25, landowner (*possidente*), born and residing in Cassano al Ionio, widow of Captain Giovanni Fadda; Carrozza, Antonietta, daughter of Francesco,

27, acrobatic equestrienne, known under the name of Cardinali, born in Catania, of no fixed abode."

Cardinali is charged with premeditated homicide for stabbing the captain to death. Saraceni is charged with being the principle agent of the killing for having used the promise of marriage to induce Cardinali to kill her husband and for supplying him with the means to travel to Rome to carry out her scheme. Carrozza is charged with complicity for having knowingly assisted the authors of the crime to prepare and carry out the murder. The cited articles of the Penal Code are listed as 522, 526, 528, 102, no. 2, 103, and 104.

From the percentage of the document dedicated to the matter, it is clear that with Cardinali's guilt virtually established, the most delicate question and biggest job of the prosecutors will be to demonstrate that Raffaella Saraceni was not only passively complicit in her husband's murder but also the principal active agent of the crime from the very beginning. This is the heart of the case: Did Saraceni merely sigh to her lover (during what prosecutors call, "moments of amorous intoxication") that, were her husband out of the way, the illicit pair would be free to legitimate their affair, or rather did she coldly conceive, plan, and assist in carrying out the murder?[33] Was Raffaella Saraceni the "principle agent" of the act?

The Atto's first paragraph asserts concisely that on October 6, Pietro Cardinali, following a premeditated plan, entered Captain Fadda's room, stabbed him repeatedly, and sought to flee. The second describes how Fadda was able to follow his attacker downstairs and point him out to police and passersby before expiring on the street. The third paragraph names those subsequently arrested: Giuseppe De Luca, stable boy; Raffaella Saraceni, wife of the murdered man; and Antonietta Carrozza, "would-be sister of Cardinali." Now follows the body of the accusation, consisting of a series of "Whereas" clauses (beginning with *Considerando*) stating succinctly the motives and proofs against each of the accused. Cardinali's guilt is indubitably demonstrated by multiple proofs, and principally by his motive: his affair with the wife of "poor Fadda" and his plan to marry her after the captain's death. The word chosen by the state's attorneys to describe Cardinali and Saraceni's relationship is *amori*, the plural form of *amore*. In the singular, the word means "love," but *amore* may have seemed to grant a certain sentimental legitimacy to the accused couple's motive. The plural instead evokes an image of sensual, promiscuous, and repeated action, of sex rather than sentiment. This characterization of the nature of the adulterous couple's relationship will be carried forward and expanded throughout the trial, exploited by the prosecution to portray the guilty pair as blinded by lust. Cardinali's guilt is further proven, the paragraph asserts, by other facts: having traveled to Rome a month before the crime to spy out the territory; statements made to his accomplice De Luca, now dead; statements to tavern keepers in Bari; and statements to his cellmate in Rome after his arrest. Material evidence for Cardinali's guilt is provided by the letter he had written as a ruse to gain entry to the captain's rooms, and by the bloody knife used in the killing; both letter and knife were found at the scene. Lastly, at the moment of his arrest, Cardinali's hands and clothes were stained with blood. In sum, it would appear a strong case.

The guilt of Saraceni, on the other hand, depends less on material evidence than on motive, and on more or less substantiated rumors reported by witnesses in her hometown of Cassano all'Ionio. The prosecutor is challenged to protect his evidence against looking like hearsay by giving it the greatest possible appearance of materiality, so he enumerates his points against Saraceni in a sequence of six numbered paragraphs. Before introducing this list, Rutigliano first devotes a paragraph to Saraceni's "common cause" with Cardinali in wishing to eliminate Fadda, thus to remove "the obstacle to their guilty love." A second paragraph describes her rancor toward her husband, due first to her anger at the alleged impotence that rendered him "a useless tool," and second to her fury that Fadda had publicly broken off relations with her by sending back her trousseau, shaming her as unworthy of him. The numbered paragraphs offer as proof the following: (1) Saraceni sought to hire Carlo Bertone, the clown known as Carluccio, to kill her husband; (2) Cardinali described the couple's plot to various witnesses, saying that Saraceni had provided him six or seven hundred lire for necessary expenses, either to carry out the act himself or to hire a killer, as well as to escape afterwards; (3) the telegrams from Cassano to Rome and back between Cardinali and Antonietta Carrozza, which use the cunning jargon of circus people to conceal their contents, but which reveal the murder plot; (4) the confession made by accomplice De Luca, witness to the amorous relations between the adulterous couple and to Saraceni's hostile remarks about Cardinali's common law wife; (5) Cardinali's words the night before the killing, which were overheard by a third tenant in the same hotel room, "Tomorrow he won't get away no matter what . . . Damn these women, look what they drive us to"; and (6) lastly, the *voce pubblica* (public voice). "As soon as Fadda was barbarously slain," the Atto claims, the *voce pubblica* of Cassano all'Ionio "arose unanimously to accuse Saraceni as the instigator of the murder of her unhappy consort."

The "principal fact resulting from the investigation," the charges conclude, is that Raffaella had "induced Cardinali with a promise of marriage to murder her husband, rendering her the principle agent of the killing." At the same time, she is also guilty of a subordinate charge of complicity for instigating Cardinali to commit the crime and for assisting his preparations, supplying him with the means to travel to Rome to carry out the act. The subtle distinction between "inducement" and "instigation" will become crucial to public debate about her degree of culpability in the murder of her husband.

In the following paragraph the prosecutor shifts his attention to Antonietta Carrozza, listing as proof of her complicity the testimony of De Luca, her relations with Saraceni, and the telegrams in circus jargon sent between Carrozza in Calabria and Cardinali in Rome in the days and hours before the murder—the contents of which were conveyed to Saraceni through the wife's aged wet nurse, Maria Ferraro. The evidence against Carrozza therefore will depend in large part on the ability of the prosecution to decipher the coded telegrams sent between the two acrobats, written in the slang of circus performers.

The prosecution's duty at the public trial will be to present to the court—the presiding magistrate and two assisting magistrates, the jury, the defendants and their legal team—and to the assembled public the testimony of witnesses who will corroborate the charges to overwhelming effect. In contrast to American courts where the prosecutor conducts the questioning, the presiding magistrate (i.e., the judge) serves not only as procedural guarantor in an Italian courtroom but also conducts the questioning of witnesses, verifying their testimony against their written depositions.

The beginning of trial sessions is postponed several times due to illnesses and changing lawyers: Diego Tajani, a controversial minister in the new left government under Agostino Depretis, has withdrawn, substituted by another minister, Enrico Pessina, an esteemed penalist of the classical school recently appointed as senator by the king. In Milan's *Corriere*, the Roman correspondent returns to the subject of the Fadda trial after an extended hiatus. In his comment published in the September 24–25 edition, he explains the reasons for repeated postponements and the motivation for the decision to begin proceedings at the end of September: "Demand for seating, already extraordinary, could become enormous after November. It is a spectacle to which the women are particularly attracted, as it is a trial that touches their sex closely and because three of the accused are women, in addition to Saraceni-Fadda's mother who, although not among the accused, will have no small part in the judicial drama. But if the president of the Assize Court had the courage, as did a colleague of his in another Italian city, to refuse women access to the courtroom, oh, what praise he would deserve!"[34]

A week before the trial opens, the media already knows that the Fadda trial will attract large crowds and distinguish itself from others for the principal roles held by women, both as protagonists and chorus. Only for a year has the testimony of women been accepted as legally probative in

Italian courts.[35] Although still excluded from sitting as judge, lawyer, or jury, and though no woman will cover the trial as a daily reporter, there is already excitement and apprehension about women's participation in this trial as defendants, witnesses, and public. Special raised seating areas have been constructed in the chamber, creating an amphitheatre effect; the red fabric used to cover the chairs evokes a theater or opera hall rather than a courtroom. A system of colored tickets in first and second class has been devised to control public access.[36] Shortly after the trial commences, a thrice-weekly satirical journal, *Don Pirloncino*, remarks sardonically, "There's not one lady who wouldn't consider herself terribly unhappy and miserable for being unable to pluck a ticket for the reserved galleries from Justice Giordano."[37]

As legal parlance became part of the journalistic lexicon, the two phases of a penal procedure come to be distinguished linguistically: the word *processo* (which would be translated into English in this context as "trial" but more literally means "course" or "process") tended generically to signify both the investigative phase, called the "written trial" (*processo scritto*) and the subsequent public, oral trial, which, when denoted separately, is typically referred to either as the *dibattimento* ("debate" or "discussion") or the *dramma giudiziario* ("judicial drama," as in the citation above).[38] Formerly, under the papal government in Rome, the expressions *processo* and *processo scritto* had been virtually synonymous, because the investigative phase determined guilt or innocence such that the final hearing before a magistrate functioned merely as a confirmatory formality. Now, with the introduction of the jury system and public access to trials, what was once a formality became instead a debate, a discussion, a drama, and a spectacle. The principle mirror of this spectacle is the newspaper. The next chapter will explore the evolution of the newspaper industry in Rome and its exploitation of the Fadda trial to meet the appetites of a new audience.

2

Journalism in Rome after National Unification

Journalism changed in Italy in the decade after the capital moved to Rome, concurrent with the massive descent into the city of government operators, bureaucrats, financiers, small businessmen, and the wishful employees who flocked to serve them. Initially established in Turin where the Savoy monarchy was based, the capital of Italy moved first to Florence in 1864 and finally to Rome in 1871, immediately after the pope's forced capitulation of his temporal power over the city. Numerous newspapers either transferred there from the previous capitals or came into being, bearing such names as *La Capitale*, *La Riforma*, *Il Diritto*, *Il Popolo Romano*, *La Libertà*, *La Concordia*, *La Nuova Roma*, *L'Opinione*, *Roma*, and *La Frusta* (these titles might be translated, respectively, as "The Capital," "Reform," "Law" or "Right," "The Roman People," "Liberty," "Concord," "The New Rome," "Opinion," "Rome," and "The Whip"). Organs of the various factions in the new liberal state, these lay papers competed with dailies oriented around the Church. *L'Osservatore romano*, "Voice of the Holy See," had been founded in 1861, but newer Catholic newspapers included *Il Divino Salvatore*, *Il Romano di Roma*, *La Voce della Verità*, *Il Conservatore*, and *La Fedeltà* ("The Divine Savior," "The Roman of Rome" or "The True Roman," "The Voice of Truth," "The Conservative" or "The Conserver," and "Faith,").[1] Virtually all the lay papers embodied a specific political line or still more narrowly that of an individual political leader.[2] The content of newspapers consisted less of what we have come to call news and more on partisan commentary on events in parliament, the new state's foreign relations, and on accords and ruptures between the various liberal state affiliations.[3] Party leaders in the national government had no mass constituency in the general population, no organizational structure in the provinces and neighborhoods. Newspapers were thus their primary organ for propaganda and mobilization, a way for the parties to claim to address their constituency while in fact seeking one.[4] Newspapers functioned as a rhetorical, promotional arm of the new state apparatus and were partially funded from the state coffers, whether openly or under the table, or by factional leaders with their private fortunes.[5] Even before Rome became the capital, Minister of Public Education Angelo Bargoni in 1869 declared the duty of newspapers to be a form of missionary work among the largely unknown populace, with reporters serving as apostles of the religion of secular liberalism: "A newspaper must be an act of priesthood, the work of apostles."[6] A newspaper was also a vehicle of urbanity. An 1863 drawing room comedy by Ferdinando Martini, the Florentine editor who will later publish Carducci's poem on the Fadda trial, contains this bit of repartee between the protagonist and his journalist sidekick:

> Giovanni: (*smiling*) What is man!
> Ettore: By Plato's definition, a featherless biped; by mine, an animal that reads newspapers.[7]

This play, titled *The New Rich*, won a government-sponsored literary prize; Ettore's line is clearly intended to trigger a self-congratulatory laugh in its urbane audience, sophisticated elites able to catch on the fly its classical reference, allusion to Darwin, and the self-mocking image it sparks of a newspaper reader.

With such a numerically restricted readership, sales were necessarily low, with distribution limited almost exclusively to subscribers.[8] Given the high costs of printing and paper, profits were hard to come by. Of the five-cent cost of an issue, half went to street sellers or postal costs for subscribers. Paper cost one cent per issue. Typographers were highly specialized and comparatively well paid, receiving an average salary of 3.50 lire per day, better than carpenters, builders, and railroad workers.[9] Other necessary expenses left editors generally with between .5 and .9 cents per copy for writing and composing the paper, virtually excluding any hope of profit.[10] Most of the papers that originated in Rome or transferred there in the first decade after it became the capital were structured on an ideological or political model rather than a business one, so making a profit was not the primary goal. Not only did they not succeed in selling enough copies to recoup their costs, however, they also discovered that the Risorgimento ideals they wished to disseminate among the Roman populace did not, in the words of a principal historian, "have much force of penetration."[11]

The term *figlio d'arte* (son of the trade), applies to any son who follows his father's profession, especially when that profession entails the use of one's hands and requires the absorption of an oral and corporal tradition of trade practice. Luigi Cesana was a *figlio d'arte*, son of Giuseppe

Augusto Cesana, one of the creators of the newspaper industry in Rome.[12] The younger Cesana started working for his father's daily, the *Corriere italiano*, when he was 15; by age 19, the son had become managing editor of his first newspaper. *Il Fanfulla* was a new concept daily originally proposed to Cesana père by nobleman Francesco De Renzis, captain in the Piedmont Army, playwright, and theatrical impresario. De Renzis imagined a paper "written with brio from top to bottom, without the aid of scissors, refined, witty, vivacious, pleasant to read; tied to no party, free of encumbrances, able to speak its mind to all, temperate but frank, slave to none."[13] De Renzis was unable to carry his proposal forward personally, encumbered by a two-month forced confinement in Alessandria, a result, rumors said, of becoming too familiar with an actress who was also known to frequent the king.[14] Freer to act autonomously than De Renzis, the elder Cesana adopted the idea, assembled an editorial team, named his son as administrator, and the first issue of *Il Fanfulla* came out in Florence in the summer of 1870.[15]

Exploiting connections, the younger Cesana managed to attract commitments from 1260 subscribers even before the first issue appeared. He built on the initial promise of *Il Fanfulla* by hiring skilled writers, including Carlo Lorenzini, who had already adopted the pseudonym Collodi but who would not begin publishing his famous *Pinocchio*, released in serial form, until the end of the decade. Common among journalists, the use of pseudonyms was a vestige of the eighteenth century when noblemen used false names to hide the shame of labor in the public sphere, and from the Arcadian academies of the seventeenth century, where noble esthetes invented fantastical Greek epithets for themselves. A decidedly curious and anachronistic practice, pseudonyms often evoked a rustic or playful literary mask (Collodi adopted the name of his mother's hometown, while another *Fanfulla* writer, following perhaps both Sterne and Shakespeare, dubbed himself "Yorick, Son of Yorick"), while hinting that the identity behind the humble mask was of noble blood. Ferdinando Martini, for example, was the son of a Tuscan marquise and a successful dilettante playwright who signed his plays *anonimo fiorentino* (anonymous Florentine). When he was orphaned at 19 and found his patrimony to have been squandered by his artistic father, Martini's budding skills as playwright, journalist, and teacher suddenly became his means of sustenance.[16] Now independent entrepreneurs, any blue blood in these writers' and editors' veins was rapidly thinning. Investment capital was scarce in such an adventurous industry. Competition between rapidly proliferating dailies (in Milan there were as many as fifty operating simultaneously; by 1885 there were 199 in Rome), provoked initially by factional politics, became bitter under the Darwinian pressure to survive in an increasingly crowded market.[17] This generation of journalists was creating the voice of the middle class of the new Italian state, committed to a progressive, positivist principle of objective truth combined with a need to make a living from their labor.

Financing behind *Il Fanfulla* balanced between the patrimony of one of the paper's directors, Piacentini, and the capital of a crucial but little-studied figure in the history of liberal Italy. E. E. Oblieght (names given variously as Ernest, Eugenio and Emanuele, the surname also given as Obleight) was a naturalized Italian, Hungarian Jewish entrepreneur who published *Storia di un burattino*, the first form of Pinocchio, and financed the Vesuvian funicular railway (the one celebrated in the song "Funiculi, Funicula.").[18] In 1870, in order to achieve the independence envisioned by De Renzis, the younger Cesana contracted to Oblieght the right to carry advertising on the fourth (and last) page of *Il Fanfulla* for 24,000 lire per year. An innovative pioneer in both commercial and classified advertising, Oblieght will, through the course of the decade, come to gain outright or de facto ownership of numerous newspapers of opposing political camps, such as the staunchly right-wing *L'Opinione* and the oppositional, left-leaning, Southern-oriented *Il Bersagliere.*[19] During the same period as the Fadda trial in 1879, Oblieght appealed to the government to permit him to open a telegraphic agency in competition with the Stefani Agency (which Oblieght claimed to be influenced by France), but *La Capitale*, an organ of the democratic parliamentary left opposed the cession, charging that too much influence would fall into the hands of a media magnate whose patriotism as a mere naturalized Italian was perhaps not to be trusted.[20] *Il Messaggero* (in which Oblieght was a shareholder) disagreed, favoring what it described as Oblieght's public-spirited effort to expand the people's access to news.[21] In 1882 Oblieght found himself at the center of an international scandal when he attempted to sell his six dailies to a Franco-Roman bank in Paris, Fremy-Bontoux, connected with clerical circles, purportedly with a secret contract stipulating that the papers all maintain a political line agreeable to the new buyers. Non-Oblieght papers, including Milan's *Corriere della sera*, *Il Secolo*, and Rome's *La Capitale*, made a national issue of the threat represented by Oblieght's media monopoly and succeeded in compelling him "to retire from the scene."[22]

Despite the *Fanfulla*'s relative success, tension between old and new capital and right and left politics soon sparked the young publisher's decision to establish a new kind of newspaper, one that could survive entirely on profits from sales and advertising.[23] Cesana's new idea is *Il Messaggero*. From its inception Cesana experimented with diverse strands of the new, combining advances in telegraphy and typography with cheaper modes of distribution to meet the exigencies of an audience that still had little consistency but that the publisher believed must be out there, somewhere.[24] Similar experiments were taking place at the same moment in other major cities in Italy, where publishers were implementing innovations from Paris, London, and New York.[25]

To begin with, Cesana conceived his paper under the sign of "scrupulous impartiality."[26] The first four issues of *Il Messaggero* are distributed as free samples to all subscribers to *Il Fanfulla* during the third week of December 1878. Regular publication begins on January 1. Introducing *Il Messaggero* to the public, Cesana identifies three unprecedented issues of concern to his readers: time, thrift, and access. "Not everyone can read multiple newspapers," declared the editor in the first, free sample issue of December 16, acknowledging in a single phrase that potential readers have limited time and an abundance of choice. *Il Messaggero*, therefore, proposed to serve as *il giornale de' giornali* (the newspaper of newspapers), "to report all the opinions on every issue, all the news on every event."[27] By exploiting advances in telegraphy, which made it economically feasible to gather reports almost immediately throughout the nation, *Il Messaggero* promised to offer its readers "every day, the reports of the entire Italian press on the issues and events of the day, completely or in part, according to importance and available space." Journalistic objectivity, Cesana's "scrupulous impartiality," would thus be expressed as total inclusivity, limited only by space and a still-undefined criterion of importance. The strategy was to supersede competitors through democratic-spirited universality; the publishers imagined potential consumers thinking, "Why buy one partisan newspaper, when I can buy them all for the same price?" On January 24, the editors further clarified their mission: "By collecting the articles of the most authoritative newspapers—clerical, liberal, progressive, radical, republican—by presenting every position, from the moderate to the revolutionary, in a genuine, original form, [*Il Messaggero*] epitomizes within its columns the movement of ideas in Italy."[28] In the execution of this ethos, *Il Messaggero* and similar dailies throughout the nation began to circumscribe the identity of an amorphous new entity, middle class Italy.

The idea is visionary, the staff young and skilled, production and distribution innovatory. But daily sales stagnate at about three thousand. Something must be missing in the formula. Cesana notices that readers skim over parliamentary debates and dwell instead on the bulletins from Naples covering the Passanante trial. On November 17, 1878, as the young king, Umberto I, and his popular wife, Margherita, rode a carriage through Naples, a cook named Giovanni Passanante rushed out of the crowd and slashed at the king with a knife. The prime minister, riding in the same carriage, threw his body in front of the king, taking the blow in his thigh. Passanante was condemned to death on March 7, 1879. Three weeks later the king commuted the sentence to life imprisonment.[29] The telegraph allowed

Il Messaggero to receive daily reports from the trial in Naples, which at first they published in a back section devoted to short clips from the hinterlands. But readers eagerly followed the trial's daily developments and responded favorably when editors added color and drama to the reports with descriptions of the appearance and behavior of the defendant and other protagonists. Apparently, people were less interested in the political and legal ramifications of the event than in the human drama of it. Budding technologies for the mass production of illustrations fed this taste, allowing printers to publish broadsheets and flyers with engravings of Passanante's assault on the king, the queen's dismay, and the heroic intervention of the prime minister.

Once the Passanante trial ends, Cesana needs a new one with similar characteristics to incite public interest. He finds one close at hand: the upcoming Fadda trial. The day after the Passanante verdict, the first column of the March 8 *Messaggero* announces, "The Passanante trial will have demonstrated to our readers that Il Messaggero kept its promise, despite the high expense, of giving an accurate telegraphic rendering, more diffuse than any other newspaper . . . Next, Il Messaggero will offer the most exact coverage of the trial following the tragic murder of Captain Fadda."[30]

For the *Messaggero*, the murder of Captain Fadda is a godsend. From this date, Cesana jettisons the project of creating a "newspaper of newspapers." Instead, the *Messaggero* will devote intensive coverage to "cronaca locale" and especially "cronaca nera"—that is, local reporting and crime news. It's a formula that will prove successful in other European capitals: in 1888, coverage of Jack the Ripper will bring Lloyd's *Weekly News* in London to a peak circulation of almost two million copies.[31] In Milan, an ex-lawyer named Carlo Romussi, writing for *Il Secolo*, made a name for himself by going in person every day to city hall, police stations, courts, hospitals, theaters, and anywhere else people gathered. Rather than being a "journalist," Romussi was a "reporter"; a peer recalled him as standing out from his gentlemen fellows because he only rarely wore gloves.[32] Cesana applies the formula to Rome. An early historian of the era remembers,

> No one in Rome could slip on the sidewalk, steal a handkerchief, harass a woman, not pay the tram, without the *Messaggero* printing it as news. The secret is to name lots of people (because everyone named will buy the paper) and describe scenes with the precision of a medieval book illuminator. But when a crime comes along, the murder, the dozen knife wounds, or the complicated deception, then it's no longer mere reporting; it's Alexander Dumas.[33]

The Fadda trial offers in spades everything Cesana's *Messaggero* needs. Since the murder happened locally and the trial will be held in Rome, the Fadda story carries the further advantage of savings on telegraph expenses, a factor of no little consideration; the paper can sell its eyewitness reports, sent via telegraph, to newspapers throughout the nation who can't afford to send one of their own reporters to the trial every day.

The start date of the Fadda trial will be postponed as the investigation widens to include more witnesses and shifting legal teams. But in an early and successful experiment in hype, the editors seize on the delays to promote their upcoming coverage and build public anticipation of the trial. The March 8 issue already features the news that the defense attorneys for the two female defendants are holding meetings that day with their clients in Buon Pastore. The next day's issue carries a piece planting seeds of future suspense: "Word has come of a poem found among the papers of the poor captain assassinated by his wife's lover. This poem, written by Fadda to his wife, contains an entire intimate drama; it is a mysterious summary of what preceded the fatal, bloody outcome." The text of the poem follows, but lest the reader lose interest in the trial—given that the paper has already reported who is guilty—editors direct readers toward the drama of the judicial process: "But Justice, according to what we are told, has not been able to gather definitive proof against her (the accused wife). All it has is fragments of evidence, more or less substantial. Before the Assize Court, the drama will unfold entirely in the full light of the sun."[34] The performances of star lawyers, especially the defense team for Raffaela Saraceni, will constitute one of the main dramatic threads of the Fadda story.

Pursuing this new strategy, Cesana releases one of his original directors to bring in a new one a year younger than Cesana himself. Genoese schoolteacher, lawyer's clerk, copy boy, Luigi Arnaldo Vassallo, 26, published his first paper while still in his teens: an antiroyalist broadside whose name varied among *La maga*, *Il mago*, and *La strega* in efforts to avoid continuous censorship. Between Genoa and San Remo, in the decade between 1869 and 1879 he worked for no fewer than five newspapers (serving in functions from publisher to billposter), published a novel, and nearly died in a duel sparked by a dispute between two leftist political factions. Sent to Rome first as correspondent for a Genoese paper, he briefly directed a short-lived newspaper named *Lo Squillo* before being hired by Cesana in March 1879.[35] Like Romussi in Milan, memoirists will later recall Vassallo as the first Roman journalist to be called a "reporter," a comparatively early example of an English term being adopted to describe a social function for which there is not quite the right word in Italian.[36] Foreign borrowings such as "leader" and "killer" cannot be far behind, more words seized from

English by Italian newspapermen, especially by composers of headlines, to fit restricted column space, and for their punch.

Shifting among three pseudonyms (Macrobio, Gandolin, and Elio Staleno), Vassallo is also a graphic craftsman. He will pioneer the use of an economical illustration technique called the *pupazzo* by making drawings on white lead spread onto pear wood, which are then incised, inked, and inserted between lines of text.[37] Starting at *Il Messaggero* in March, Vassallo uses the *pupazzo* to introduce a new daily feature, the rebus, a graphic puzzle that invites readers to decode a sequence of images into words or word fragments that can be recomposed into a familiar proverb. Ancient in origin and complex as a phenomenon of linguistic metamorphosis, at once popular and secret (they make the participant into an initiate looking past appearances to solve mysteries), the rebus proliferates in cultural periodicals in postunification Italy.[38] Vassallo's first, primitive rebus appears on March 31; but from April 12, it becomes a daily feature of the paper, its graphic sophistication progressing noticeably from week to week. A rebus presupposes a certain pictorial and cultural initiation on the part of a reader, who must be able to distinguish, for example, a head symbolizing "monarch" from one symbolizing "prime minister." The solutions are given at the bottom of the following day's puzzle, and consist mostly of proverbs reinforcing good common sense such as "he who is healthy is wealthy," "the worst wheel is the one that squeaks," and "he who sleeps catches no fish." Rebuses and similar games in a genre that will soon be named *enigmistica* turn the reader-participant effectively into the subject of the paper, while presupposing that the player possesses the small, discrete chunk of leisure time, the particular kind of attention, that the game requires. From this same graphic technology, followers will later invent the means for headlines and graphics to stretch over multiple columns.[39]

Vassallo's rebuses exemplify a principle of interactivity that distinguishes *Il Messaggero* from the earlier generation of newspapers in Rome. For Cesana's paper, it is as though the public itself, rather than events in parliament, were the subject of every day's issue.[40] He introduces recurring features that humorously highlight problems of everyday life and the ingenuity of common people, expressed in language using slang and dialect, such as *Le volticelle di ricotta* (ricotta ceilings) about substandard building practices during the construction boom and *Gli incertarelli de li vetturini* (roughly, "dicey times for carriage hacks") about taxi drivers cheated by dishonest customers.[41] He appeals to readers to bring in news articles, offering fifty cents per item upon verification.[42] With his financier Obligeht, Cesana starts running classified ads at a word-by-word rate. He announces that *Il Messaggero* will not carry theater reviews because his readers can't afford the tickets.[43] The paper's slogan becomes "Peace, Order, Labor, Common Sense."[44]

In practice, the editors will soon rationalize that the principal of common sense is affirmed by intensive journalistic exploitation of its opposite. Readers, it turns out, have a huge appetite for stories that reveal the horrors of human behavior and psychology. By contrast, the approach of the dailies representing Risorgimento-era political parties rooted in the North begins to seem paternalistic, even colonialist. The traditional dailies will either learn to compete with the *Messaggero* or die out. Others succeed by positioning themselves polemically against it: credit for the early success of Ferdinando Martini's high-toned weekly cultural insert in the *Fanfulla*, "*Fanfulla* della Domenica," is attributed in part to Martini's condemnation of the *Messaggero*'s opportunistic exploitation of the vulgar Fadda trial in order to sell papers to the less-cultivated classes. Unconcerned with ideological contradiction, Obliegħt was a principal financier behind both papers.[45]

While serving also as editor, Vassallo is assigned to apply his pictorial imagination to daily coverage of the Fadda trial.[46] In the newspapers that spring up when the national capital moved to Rome, many of the first reporters sent out to cover local stories had little preparation. In a memoir, journalist Diego Angeli remembered, "In those often makeshift journalists, there was a lot of ignorance, huge arrogance, and fear that someone else would come along and take away the job they'd so easily created for themselves. Being a journalist meant being a scapegrace and an idler."[47] Vassallo is different. The hours he keeps are those of a workaholic: "Leaving the editorial offices very late, he went home to his studio, and when dawn came he was still there studying, taking notes, doing research, because his stories didn't merely lay out the facts, they contained historical, literary, sometimes even scientific erudition which he procured through great effort, robbing his sleep."[48]

Vassallo's Fadda trial coverage is assiduous. He seems to be the first at the court every morning and expresses annoyance when sessions start late or recesses go on longer than scheduled. He is as erudite and eclectic as he is hardworking, often changing register and making literary and historical allusions that are humorous rather than ponderous. What most sets his coverage apart from competitors, however, is that rather than narrowly covering the events of the trial proper, his attention focuses on the larger spectacle.[49]

As the September 30 trial date approaches, the *Messaggero*'s daily circulation jumps. Having hit the maximum capacity of his original printer, Cesana must hire an additional print shop to meet a booming demand coming not only from the city but also from the surrounding provinces. The growing public interest in the trial, and the *Messaggero*'s status as self-declared leader in its coverage, become momentum-building elements in the expanding story.[50] With four days remaining before the trial convenes, the editors begin warning the public that there may not be enough copies to go around: "In response to orders coming from news vendors in the provinces, the print run of the *Messaggero* threatens to take on such proportions that we may not be able to satisfy demand. We expected an increase in circulation, but we never would have dreamed of doubling it from one moment to the next."[51] To keep ahead of circumstances, Cesana turns to Obliegh for an additional loan of 75,000 lire. By the end of 1883, the *Messaggero* will be selling 60,000 copies per day in two editions: one published at 8 p.m. to be sent outside Rome and a local edition that comes out at dawn.[52] By comparison, another leading Rome daily, *La Riforma*, reached a peak circulation of 7,000 before folding in 1874, and *Il Diritto* managed a maximum print run of 12,500 in 1881.[53]

Who is buying *Il Messaggero* in increasing numbers and why? Demographic statistics suggest that a significant portion of the paper's success depended on newly literate readers freshly arrived in the capital. The 22 percent increase in population in Rome between 1871 and 1881 is still more striking considering the rising mortality rate of the aging native population.[54] Young workers and jobseekers crowded into marginal neighborhoods such as the Rione Monte, increasing density and provoking the spike in rents that Captain Fadda complains about in letters to his wife. In the same decade, the working population of the city increased from 54.5 percent to 62.9 percent. Most new workers arrived in the city essentially without skills; those whose literacy consisted of more than being able to write their own name enjoyed an immediate advantage in finding office work in public administration, commercial trades, transport, insurance, or banking. Salaries were low. An assistant secretary might make a median of 115 lire a month, a figure to set against Fadda's struggle with his Roman landlady, who first demanded a rent of two hundred lire a month for three rooms, before being talked down to ninety. An article in the April 1880, *Messaggero* denounces the poor pay of clerks, noting that a vice secretary makes less than a cobbler. The five-cent price of a daily paper, however, would have put it within the reach both of the secretary and the cobbler.

It is generally held in the folklore of Italian journalism that newspapers are purchased and read less in the home than in the local café, so that a single copy of any given daily is perused by many readers who haven't paid for it. In an era of high illiteracy, a fair share of newspaper reading in Rome would have taken place aloud, for the benefit of multiple listeners. For example, the Fadda trial's surprise witness, Carluccio the clown, testifies in court that he had heard of Pietro Cardinali's arrest from the newspapers. When the interrogating magistrate points out the apparent contradiction that since Carluccio has admitted to being illiterate he could not have learned of Cardinali's arrest from reading a newspaper, Carluccio clarifies by saying he had heard the paper read aloud in a café. Further, as an issue passed from reader to reader, a day's edition was not necessarily useless to read once the next had come out. When his breakfast is interrupted by a strange visitor on October 6, there are three periodicals on Giovanni Fadda's parsimonious dining table: the October 4 edition of *Il Diritto*, the October 1 edition of *La Libertà*, and the September 24 edition of *Il Buonumore*.[55] These two details of orality and perdurability reveal neglected channels through which the journalistic principles of factuality and currency colonized popular imagination.

Dominique Kalifa has argued that crime reporting and trial coverage, combined with the serial novels carried daily in newspapers, were "prime instruments of a silent revolution which saw the masses achieve literacy and the habit of reading."[56] In postunification Italy for the first time, the handy dictionary comes into use; smaller in size, affordable for the better middle-class families, oriented toward modern usage, and designed not for the scholar but for the "common" reader and writer. Captain Fadda kept just such a volume on his worktable in his apartment, a tool of his trade as accountant, drafter of letters, and writer of reports. Based on contemporary Florentine, the *Novo vocabolario* by Giorgini and Broglio, published between 1870 and 1897, was designed to both instruct and homogenize its audience; its aim was to relegate all other idioms of the peninsula to the status of dialects.[57]

Kalifa concentrates especially on the contamination of genres taking place in newspapers and popular novels, and thus in the minds of their readership: "The often ambiguous presentation of many novels contributed to confusion about their status: reportage or fiction? Conversely, much crime news is frequently hereafter termed 'romans.'"[58] As the example of Vassallo shows, the same writers moved between genres, publishing novels while working as reporters, deriving fictional plots from actual events, and casting real events in dramatic terms, much as Francesco Netti and other *verista* artists depicted current events in the pictorial codes of history painting, or conversely, painted mythical scenes in an anecdotal or documentary style. Neapolitan writer Matilde Serao identically transcribes dialogues, first published in an ostensibly fictional short story, into a factual journalistic piece on the harsh lives of female telegraph operators.[59]

The confusion of fact and fiction under the banner of common sense appears to have been particularly extensive in the handling of foreign news. In a lively passage in his memoirs, Cesana père justifies his conduct as he confesses to an extended episode of outright fabrication of reporting on the Franco-German War shortly after the launch of *Il Fanfulla* in mid-1870.[60] When tensions broke out along the Rhine between France and Prussia, the paper wanted to send a special correspondent to cover the conflict. By a stroke of fortune, a millionaire friend was curious to witness the war at firsthand and offered to tour the battlefields, sending dispatches back to Florence at no cost to the paper. The paper was thrilled to be able to offer eyewitness coverage. Problems arose, however, when numerous readers expressed doubts about the authenticity of the reports coming back from the front. Because their wealthy correspondent demanded anonymity, *Il Fanfulla* editors were unable to demonstrate the actual dispatches they were receiving, and their reticence in the matter seemed to confirm public suspicion. As the situation between France and Prussia grew ever more dramatic, the dilettante reporter suddenly became ill and returned to Italy. Now the abrupt cessation of eyewitness reports would seem proof that the paper, caught out, had hastily terminated their fictionalized coverage of the real war. At an editorial meeting called to resolve the problem, Yorick arose and offered to cover the battlefield, without, however, leaving his desk in Florence. In answer to his colleagues' objections, Yorick said, "Eh, my friends, if the public wants to be deceived, then let's deceive them to keep them happy; I'll cook them up some coverage that will leave them licking their fingers." The experiment, as Cesana recounts it, couldn't have turned out better:

> So would you believe it? The test went so well that the same friends who had been accusing us of tricking the public were the first to come tell us, "Now this is real coverage . . . You can really see the reporter on the scene, he witnesses the events and calls them the way they really happen . . ." I have to say that Yorick fabricated letters that were a wonder! And he wove them with episodes, with battles partly invented from the ground up, but with such verisimilitude that they drew in even indifferent readers and fooled the most suspicious. For the rest, he took advantage of official French and German bulletins and telegrams published by the foreign press . . . Our correspondence from the field was read with such interest and granted such credibility that foreign legations came to ask us for more details about this or that event.[61]

Cesana closes his story with six paragraphs of jovial rationalization for his newspaper's fraudulent, fictional coverage, calling it "nothing but a simple venial sin diluted in a few dozen articles, in such small doses as to be considered homeopathic." He then places any blame squarely where he believes it belongs: "In the end, *Il Fanfulla* wasn't the first to resort to this solution, and it won't be the last. But whether first or last, who forced it to commit the horrible crime? Who dragged it by its hair into delinquency? It was Signor Public, who—as I have said—insisted on being deceived."[62]

In the story immediately preceding this one in his memoir, Cesana describes an occasion of altering his paper's editorial position against Germany in response to a private appeal from a government minister, Quintino Sella.[63] Bending to the wishes of the authorities and self-censorship in anticipation of their objections were nothing new in Rome, but this account of *Il Fanfulla*'s invented war coverage may be one of the earliest examples in Italian journalism of the principle of giving the public what it wants.

As Cesana rightly asserts, this will not be the last case of such practice. While working as a novice reporter under Vassallo for *Capitan Fracassa* in the early 1880s, young Edoardo Scarfoglio was assigned to provide eyewitness reports of news events that he experienced only via telegraph. As he remembers it in his memoirs,

> O blessed war in Tunisia, that I reported without so much as a map! I took the telegrams from the *Temps* and turned them into three columns of fantastic prose, inventing a geography full of savages, dusting off the most clichéd and crazy oriental rhetoric, minutely describing battles of which I knew no more than the number of dead and wounded, giving it a form only the most insane depravation of fantasy can concoct. One day I translated a description of market day in Tunisia from a novel by Belot, *Le Roi des Grecs*, and ran it: that atrocious prose was reprinted in every newspaper in the Kingdom of Italy. Another time, to give an example of the language of the Krumiri, who speak Arabic, I printed a fable in an African language of the Zambezi region; not a single Orientalist in Italy protested.
>
> Vassallo was delighted: "You see?" he said.[64]

The practice Scarfoglio describes here was as fundamental to this era's journalism as fact checking is to today's. Reducing words to a minimum, the Stefani news service would wire only the most succinct and truncated notice of events from capital to capital. It became the task of writers in editorial offices to flesh out all that was not said in the bare telegraphic notations, inventing, for example, on a report from Paris of a heated parliamentary session, "the impressions produced by the various speeches, the interruptions, the vivacious incidents, the tumults, everything that forms the vital and particular character of the session."[65] A colleague remembered Vassallo as particularly brilliant at this operation: "He took Stefani and renewed it, restored its youth, gave it that color, that freshness, that feeling, by which the cold, unsewn rendering became, under his hands, a work of art."[66]

As formulated by Jürgen Habermas, speaking especially of the cases of France and England a century and more before the Fadda trial, the modern public sphere takes shape as consumers of printed paper develop into a reasoning public, whose collective discourse leads to the open exposition of truth.[67] Scarfoglio's whimsical reminiscence does not consider that within three years of his cub reporter apprenticeship, Italy will invade Africa armed for battle with a complex of ideas more imaginary than actual. When five hundred Italian troops were ambushed and massacred at Dogali (in present day Eritrea) in 1887, Prime Minister Depretis was unable to find a map of Africa in any bookstore in Rome.[68] Because geographers learned that the city of Asmara, in Ethiopia, was at 2,400 meters altitude, Italian troops were sent there equipped with ice pitons. The first civilian governor of the Italian colony in Eritrea, from 1897 to 1907, was Ferdinando Martini, who began his career as a playwright, then became a journalist, and finally a government minister.[69] In practice, the realist discovery of factuality and the bourgeois insistence on common sense trigger frenzied contamination of the actual with the fantastical in a setting where success and survival are increasingly determined by stimulating and feeding the public's appetite. That is what the new reading public demands, the mirror against which it regards itself.[70]

The day after the Fadda story broke, the *Italie* had already described the murder's web of intrigue as *un veritable roman*—that is, as a novel of the same genre as the serial novels running below the fold on the front page of almost every daily paper.[71] As the trial began a year later, *Il Messaggero*'s rival, *Il Bersagliere*, prefaced the nine columns devoted to the first day's testimony by explaining it intends to offer a *verbale artistico* of the proceedings.[72] The expression is an oxymoron: a *verbale* is the legally binding, official minutes of a meeting, session, or hearing, which must be rendered with utter objectivity. The adjective *artistico* negates the noun it is called upon to modify; but the combined term perfectly identifies what might be called the field of irritation enveloping Rome's new urban readership. Reports from the colonies patched together from promiscuous sources are presented as fact; young journalists seeking a name inflate telegraphs from European capitals; proceedings in the Assize Court are distilled artistically using the codes of fiction. These practices are constitutive elements of the Italian public sphere as it takes shape after national unification.

The public also wanted pictures. A *Messaggero* competitor, *La Libertà*, opens its Fadda trial coverage with its first use of a lithographic engraving to illustrate a news story, side-by-side portraits of Saraceni and the husband she murdered.[73] Both images are clearly derived from the photographs in the possession of the investigating magistrate. The second day's coverage features similar portraits of Cardinali and Antonietta Carrozza. In illustration for mass publication, there is not yet the distinction between the "real" of photography and the "imaginary" of engraving. The same technology with the same graphic style was applied by the same typographers to provide illustrations for children's books, broadsides, pamphlets carrying true or fictional accounts or poems of bloody acts of murder and rape, and news featuring pictures of important people.[74] Immediately upon the end of the trial on October 31, Edoardo Perino, a Piedmontese publisher transplanted to Rome, sells Vassallo's Fadda trial coverage as a soft cover volume with illustrations at a price of 1.5 lire; advertisements for the book begin to appear in the *Messaggero* several days before the verdicts are determined.[75] The cover image shows the crowded courtroom, defendants in profile at center surrounded by carabinieri, and the gallery overhead where young women pose prettily. Fadda, Cardinali, Carrozza, and Saraceni are all pictured in separate illustrations. By November 7, a new series of advertisements announce the imminent release of a second edition of twenty thousand copies.[76] The fact that today only two or three copies of these hastily produced volumes remain in the collections of the entire Italian national library system testify simultaneously to their low literary status and to the way they must have been devoured and consumed by their voracious readership.

A still more abundantly illustrated compilation of trial coverage is published at the same time by Perino competitor Giovanni Bracco, titled *Processo Fadda illustrato*, also advertised in Roman dailies on the penultimate and concluding days of the trial.[77] Written by lawyer-journalist Nicolò Coboevich of the *Bersagliere*, the Bracco volume contains no fewer than twenty-four full or double-page illustrations. Signed by "Marchetti" and drawn in a style simpler than the Perino edition, there are individual portraits of each member of the distinguished Saraceni defense team, beginning with the most illustrious of all, Senator Enrico Pessina. Two officers of the court are represented, the head magistrate and the public prosecutor, as are Cardinali's and Carrozza's defense lawyers, Fadda's brother Cesare, and parliamentary deputy Professor Ponsiglioni, representative for the *parte civile* (the Fadda family). Besides the portraits, the artist also renders highly dramatic moments of the murder.

The investigative phase is represented with an image titled "Police Delegate Michelangelo Chiodi arrests Raffaella Saraceni," while the trial itself merits several impressive double-page scenes: "Saraceni conducted from her carriage into the hall of the Assize court," "The crowd as it bursts into the Palazzo Filippini at the beginning of the session." Three particularly colorful witnesses merit portraits: "Maria Ferraro (*Mamma di latte*), accused of perjury, appears for the second time before the court," and surprise witnesses "Carluccio" and "Bergamuccio," both so famous that they are presented with their nicknames only, with neither last name nor descriptive caption.

Figure 2.1 Pietro Cardinali assaults Captain Fadda in his apartment

Source: Illustration from *Processo Fadda illustrato, dibattimento alla Corte d'Assise di Roma dal 30 settembre al 31 ottobre 1879*, Bracco Editore, 1879.

The three accused parties are of course represented in the Bracco edition. Curiously, variant editions of this text, otherwise identical, offer two different representations of Raffaella Saraceni. One is a sympathetic three-quarter rendering of her face, clearly taken from the photograph in the investigative records. In the other she is seen close up in stark profile,

Figure 2.2 Fadda revives momentarily, and with superhuman effort follows his assassin, reaching the street in time to point him out to neighbors and passersby

Source: Illustration from *Processo Fadda illustrato*

weeping large tears. The edition containing the more neutral portrait regrettably lacks a title page, making it impossible to know if it was the first or second edition of the publication. Did the weeping portrait replace the photographic one for the second edition, subsequent to the guilty verdict against her and the upswelling of public sentiment in her favor?[78] Cardinali and Carrozza are both shown in circus settings, with Cardinali seen backstage, whip in hand, waiting to go on. In the background his female partner, Carrozza, leaps on a horse. In another image entirely dedicated to Carrozza, she prepares to mount a demurely smiling white horse. Rather than using a stirrup, she places her raised foot on the back of a clown, who is kneeling on all fours and looking up at her upraised leg with an equivocal smile. There is something Picasso-like in this image of the woman's radically simplified face as she looks away in absolute profile, with the sensual roundness of her limbs, the companionable horse, and the agitated presence of the clown—a surface guilelessness undermined by strangeness at every turn. Of special note is the penultimate image, a double-page portrait of the journalists "L. A. Vassallo, Director of *Il Messaggiero*, Advocate Nicolò Coboevich, correspondent for *Il Bersagliere*," with a caption in parenthesis, "(to render this publication more complete, we also offer portraits of two of the principle reporters of this celebrated trial)." The era of journalistic pseudonyms is effectively over; the media are inextricably within the story as much as any other actor.[79]

A Roman satirical paper, *Don Pirloncino*, will express this contaminated atmosphere in an image of the Fadda trial included in an end-of-year composite graphic titled *The Sunset of 1879*. The picture shows two men with dazed expressions sitting side by side at a table. One of them is dressed in a lawyer's toga and cap; the other, rather resembling Vassallo himself, is identified as a journalist by the caption, "Lawyers and Journalists." On the table, an inkstand holds two quill pens; unfurled below it and curling off the edge of the table, a scroll reads: "Fadda Trial, RECLAM." This last word, drawn from French, refers to the clanging atmosphere of publicity and promotion that characterized the Fadda media circus, for which the satirical paper considers the press and the legal profession together to be responsible.[80]

The serial novel running below the fold in *Il Messaggero* during the run-up to the Fadda trial, *Il medico strangolatore* (The Strangling Doctor), recombines murder, trials, and science that borrow settings and terminology from concurrent local news. Despite sometimes violent, horrific

Figure 2.3 L. A. Vassallo, Director of *Il Messaggero*, Lawyer Nicolò Coboevich, correspondent for *Il Bersagliere*, (to render this publication more complete, we also offer portraits of two of the principle reporters of this celebrated trial)

Source: Illustration from *Processo Fadda illustrato*

content, it was a commonplace that the serial novel was included to appeal to the female readership. In its front page, end-of-year message, "To Our Readers," Milan's *Corriere della sera* of December16–17, 1878, devotes special attention to the women readers: "As for our serial novels, our female readers can see that we make efforts to give them a copious, varied selection . . . the novel will NEVER be left out, not even on days when we publish other kinds of appendices." In the same piece, the editors promise a new literary supplement, saying they intend it to be "in itself a little work of art, that can be read with profit and delight also by those not specialized in literature, and particularly by the ladies." In addition, "The Marchesa Colombi will give us articles on fashion and feminine affairs."[81] Demonstrating its commitment to female readers, the *Corriere* made it explicit that the serial novel, with its often-sensational contents, was a particularly feminine province of each day's issue and one to be granted unfailing priority. In the *Messaggero*, the opening sessions of the Fadda trial begin on the front page and continue on the inside, so overwhelming the available space as to push the usual reports on government affairs entirely out of the paper. But the serial novel retains its space, as does the daily feature containing jokes, funny stories, and supposedly overheard conversations, titled *Valigia delle recenti corbellerie* (Valise of the most recent foolishness). The rebus, too, is indispensable.[82]

As the reporter for *La Libertà* vividly describes the raucous scene surrounding the arrival in Rome of Carluccio, he addresses his readership in the feminine, "mie buone lettrici," acknowledging thereby that his readers are predominantly women.[83] During the same period, Rome's *La Capitale* is running a serial novel titled "Original Sin" while *Il Pungolo* in Naples is offering "The Judicial Drama." Both these titles, together with *Messaggero*'s "The Strangling Doctor," would have been conceived with female readers in mind. Thus, the contamination of domestic fiction, with its blood and bodies, into the space previously occupied by dry political commentary was perceived as a female irruption into the liberal public sphere as it had been conceived by the founders of the Italian state.

It is by no means unusual that despite the scandalous phenomenon of massive female interest in the Fadda affair, very few women were actually given the chance to express a woman's, much less a feminist's, view of its events. The silence in print of the leading women writers of the day suggests that they chose to stay wide of the topic. Nevertheless, by publishing in reduced and excerpted form several letters to the editor from women, Rome's newspapers reinforce their formulation of the intense and particular obsession of women with the Fadda affair. In most cases, these letters take the form of protests against male presumptions about women's behavior. In late October, the journalist covering the trial for the thrice-weekly

Don Pirloncino cites a letter from a female reader who has objected to his recriminations against women's interest in the trial, in which she accuses journalists and other writers of having habituated females to immorality through their novels and plays set in law courts.[84] During the same week, the *Messaggero* publishes the greater part of a letter from a reader who signs anonymously but claims to be a countess, who has written to object to the rhetoric used by one of the prosecuting attorneys during his summation, who had delivered a florid address on the power of love to level all classes, such that a wife from a wealthy family would submit to a vulgar saltimbanco.[85] On the contrary, the countess insists, true love may only take up residence in the most select and noble spirits, never in hearts corrupted by lust. With this, the lady writes, "I intend to protest in the name of all the ladies who are conscious of their position and know to respect themselves, thereby imposing respectful treatment from men."[86] Another letter insists, similarly, that the women who attend the trial are not society ladies at all but members of the lower social orders: "Ballerinas and three or four ridiculous women with neither heart nor culture."[87] Although written as protests against the dominant modes of representing the Fadda trial in the media, once they are excerpted and reframed by those same media, the letters from women serve in effect to reinforce the representation of women's obsessive fascination with every aspect of the trial.

From the beginning, the *Messaggero* has promised its readers "scrupulous impartiality." With this expression, Cesana means that his paper will not bespeak a single, narrow political or parochial faction. Cesana's impartiality expresses itself as a negative value by explaining what it is not: "The *Messaggero* is not a newspaper of the Right, The Left, or the Center . . . We think there is room enough between one party and another for an impartial press that comments on the facts with good-natured common sense . . . We are neither of the Right nor the Left; after all, since times have changed, the ancient principles of these two parties no longer have any reason to exist."

With this credo, the *Messaggero* claims the empty space between partisan positions. Into this vacuum rush the appetites of an agglomeration of people Cesana defines, again, by what they are not: the "middle class," the category of those who are neither ensconced in power nor lost in illiterate anonymity. His newspaper "does not pretend to be the voice of the nation, but to manifest opinions which are shared by a noticeable majority of the public."[88] Notably, this credo underlines the alienation of "the nation" from "the public."

The *Corriere della sera*, founded in Milan three years before the *Messaggero*, takes similar pains to distance itself from previous models of journalism tied to governing factions, but identifies itself ideologically much more specifically than the Roman daily will—countering an initial list of negatives with an even more extensive list of positive attributes:

> The Corriere della sera, as is known, is not the organ of a businessman, nor of an editor, nor of a politician, nor of a group of politicians. It is the property of a society of Milanese citizens who intend for it to be a representative of the opinions of a very large number of persons who favor the unity of Italy, liberty, order, good administration, the greatest material wellbeing, and peace and concord among the various classes, and at the same time has no direct interests in the government, and doesn't care whether the State is governed by these or those or yet other men, as long as it is governed honestly and prudently.[89]

The *Messaggero*'s program is more elusive than that of the *Corriere*: In place of archaic class, political, or religious partisanship, Cesana proposes betweenness; in place of ideology, opinions grounded in a shared consciousness he names as good-natured common sense. The instability of betweenness and the relativity of common sense are revealed in the preferred reading of this new public, whose consistency is still too tenuous to enjoy the hegemony of which Cesana's *Messaggero* is an engine. Specifically addressing the case of Italy, Benedetto Croce will define this public not in terms of its economic stability, but in terms of its unachieved aspiration: "The so-called 'middle class' is not an economic class but an ideal, or rather an ethical one, an ethical-political class."[90] Describing a similar phenomenon in Paris a century earlier, an Italian legal historian has made an observation equally pertinent to the way Roman dailies constituted a *ceto civile* in 1879. Like the popular collections of causes célèbres in prerevolutionary France, the *Messaggero* "mixed diverse levels of culture and social practice onto the same plane and same tone, offering itself to a plurality of readers, many of whom did not aspire to other literary genres. The uniformity to which the distinct social and cultural spheres were drawn constructed a relatively autonomous mental space, producing in turn a certain homogeneity: the work thus created its own audience more than it reflected a trend in public taste."[91] The contamination of journalism with modes of fiction thus coincides with, as it contributes to, the emergence of a new reading public in Rome, hungry for the spectacularization of the text.[92]

Similar contamination is taking place in law and science. The introduction of open debate and the jury system in Rome in the early 1870s have altered the role of lawyers, who now must reinvent themselves as actors capable of swaying a mixed audience of judges, colleagues, jury, spectators, and the press. The defense team for Raffaella Saraceni contains star attorneys who know how to combine oratorical flash with procedural skill, who engage in repartee with defendants and judges, and who can draw tears or hilarity from listeners with the turn of a phrase. The most outstanding of these at the Fadda trial, by public acclaim, was Enrico Pessina's young protégé, Pietro Rosano, who had established and run a theatrical journal in his native Naples before turning to law.[93] In the realm of science, similarly, the advent of the social sciences eclipses the figure of the disinterested gentleman sage and summons that of the entrepreneur. As the case of Cesare Lombroso exemplifies, scientists emerge as frontline soldiers in the patriotic war of civilization against atavistic savagery, and even the irrefutable, statistical proofs of positivist objectivity will depend on a pronounced element of showmanship.[94]

First-generation literates are eager to pay five cents a day for concision, novelty, suspense, and grand themes drawn from miserable episodes of daily life.[95] Most influential Italian authors of the second half of the nineteenth century devote at least part of their career to journalism: Edmondo De Amicis, Matilde Serao, Igino Ugo Tarchetti, Salvatore Di Giacomo, Federico De Roberto, Luigi Capuana, Emilio De Marchi, and L. A. Vassallo. Conditioned by the need to make a living through their writing, they continuously cross the line between fiction and reality, applying journalistic techniques to literary writing and casting local crime news and trial reporting on a dramatic scale previously reserved for historical and literary writing.[96]

Crime news and trial coverage for the new readership demand particular abilities, especially skills in "the definition of characteristics, personalities, settings. Free-hand sketches composed of a few incisive elements, realistic and subjective at the same time."[97] Anticipating cinema, *la capacità di osservazione* (a talent for observation) unifies the styles of writers as ideologically opposed as De Amicis and Tarchetti and sensibilities as contradictory as Serao and Valera. "Above all," writes editor Dario Papa in 1880, "journalists must write clearly. Insisting that they be pure in their language, exemplary in their style, would be like demanding that a miller not be white with flour."[98] Papa here contrasts immediate, clear, direct communication with literary purity and exemplarity, legitimating the use of multiple rhetorical and linguistic registers to reflect a faceted reality to a motley audience.

Reporting the Fadda trial, Vassallo alternates comedy with tragedy, celebrates and condemns the circus atmosphere, parodies and seconds the dignity of the court, and is alternately bored and enthralled by the drama unfolding around him. He both reports and entertains, supplying prurient shivers but accommodating as well the moralists reading to be scandalized. Indulgent, rigorous only in his nonaffiliation, he provides ways for readers to play every role in the drama. For new readers in a society still largely grounded in Counter-Reformation Catholicism, just learning to be secular, Vassallo's coverage of the Fadda trial implicitly proposes a model of how to negotiate between moral principle and the contaminating influences of modern urban life. Dismay at the trial's thrall over women came not from the Church, for whom precipitous moral decline was simply the logical consequence of the secular forces' seizure of the pope's temporal power. In 1871, Pius IX wrote to Vittorio Emanuele that Rome had become the capital not of Italy, but of "disorder, confusion, and impiety."[99] The newspaper of the Vatican, *L'Osservatore romano*, charged the liberal press with crying crocodile tears over the "indecorous curiosity" of women about the Fadda trial, asking, "Who gave birth to this disgrace? Who converted the sacred temple of justice into a theatre? . . . Is it not you, liberal gentlemen journalists?"[100] The Church, that is, took a certain grim satisfaction in the moral decline represented by women's fascination with the Fadda affair. Rather, it was the guardians of the moral rectitude of the new liberal state, such as Carducci and Martini, who found women's passion for the trial so threatening.

To what degree can a free citizen come in contact with degrading human commerce without being compromised by it? The conflict was by no means new in Italy, as it can be found at the base of the Franciscan revolution of the thirteenth century as well as in the canonical Renaissance treatises of Machiavelli and Castiglione. But the context here and Vassallo's solution, his engagement channeled by urbane detachment, are radically new. The moral imperatives are never resolved; they simply shift from foreground to background and back again, competing for attention with every other element in an interminable pageant of display. As with E. E. Oblieght's simultaneous controlling interest in politically opposed dailies, ideology does not disappear: rather, it becomes intensely commodified, jostling for attention in the mediatic piazza.

The decision by newspapers to traffic in truculence while claiming to act as a beacon and engine of national progress forced them inevitably into a zone of ethical and moral ambiguity. In its November 9–15 issue, the *Emporio pittoresco*, an illustrated weekly offered free to subscribers of the Milanese daily *Il Secolo*, summed up the sensation of the Fadda trial for Italy as a people, saying, "We have made a dolorous spectacle of ourselves," accusing particularly the newspapers of complicity for feeding, and leading, public voracity for scandal:

> A great mess of filth mixed with blood, in which an adulteress, a murderous *saltimbanco*, their go-between, and a clown thrashed about, convulsive and shameless, held Italians spellbound for a long time, anxious to see, to hear, to rummage in that horrid mixture of shameful abjection and crime . . . On one hand, the newspapers satisfied the diseased curiosity, while on the other, they stigmatized those who took pleasure in that repulsive social plague.[101]

Against charges such as these, a reader's letter to the *Corriere* at the end of the Fadda trial provided the paper's editors with the chance to justify and reconcile their conflicting obligations. The long letter and longer reply appear on the front page, as though presenting a major statement of policy on a subject at the forefront of readers' minds. Waving in one hand the banner of common sense, the newspaper must accommodate the public craving for its opposite by providing intensive coverage of scandalous crimes and trials. On the other, under the banner of progress, it must carry on its "work of apostles":

> A subscriber from Modena, Professor Gibelli, renews his subscription and adds this note: "Allow me to plead with the diligent Editors to respond to a request. For some time, thanks to the Fadda trial, half of every issue is dedicated to news of crimes and unspeakable acts of every kind, a true and terrible disgrace of our unfortunate nation. But at least once a week, wouldn't it be possible to publish an issue virgin of shame? An issue like a Divine truce? One issue per week with a fig leaf over the shocking shamelessness and violence of Italy? For my part I assure the Editors I would be very happy, because at least once a week I could read the whole paper, whereas for some time now I limit myself only to the first page . . . the rest is almost entirely filth."
>
> Between the lines of this letter, we think we discern someone kidding. Certainly, we would like to give our esteemed subscriber the satisfaction he desires, but doesn't he agree that by so doing, we would fail the first duty of journalism, which is to display the world just as it is, as faithfully as a mirror? An American journalist, whose paper is long on news and short on commentary, said, "an article of commentary is a man speaking to other men; but the news is Providence itself speaking to mankind." A conscientious newspaper has the duty to transcribe the discourse of Providence without adding or subtracting a single syllable. Truth is always healthy, and we can already see that telling the story of these atrocious crimes is having a good effect. By now everyone is concerned about the reawakening of evil instincts that seem to be leading us back into barbarism; everyone feels that we must put a brake on the audacity of evildoers, that not only the Government but every single citizen must occupy himself with this crisis. This sentiment still hasn't been translated into action, but it has been born, and we are dedicated to keeping it alive.[102]

With this sort of self-analysis of their coverage of the trial, the "diligent Editors" make an effort to distill the principal social themes generated by the Fadda case into an exemplary lesson of moral benefit for the public. The genteel subscriber cites the Fadda trial as the prime instance of that "true and terrible disgrace of our unfortunate nation," an expression that echoes statistical reports on what was termed Italy's "sad primacy," leading Europe in the number and virulence of violent crimes. Professor Gibelli remonstrates against the *Corriere*'s practice of disseminating vulgarity, but behind his appeal to paste a fig leaf over shame stands the more serious charge that newspapers multiply crime and worsen social degeneration by reporting it so avidly. In the same year as the Fadda trial, Cesare Lombroso published *On the Increase in Crime in Italy and How to Stop It* in which he charged, "Making criminal trials public, and expanding their publicity by the thousands through the press, renders the criminal a spectacle to himself and others little different from him, and what's worse, also to uneducated people not yet intent on crime, but who enviously see another path open to that goal which both small and great men so often aspire to: being talked about."[103]

As evidence, Lombroso adduces his personal experience: "All the criminals I visited during or after their public trials always asked me how the newspapers were reporting on them," and goes on to list French and Italian copycat crimes inspired by media coverage of brutal murders. He distinguishes between responsible newspapers and their disgraceful brethren, those "truly criminal diaries, who dip their pen in the most putrid filth of social wounds for no other reason than for shameful profit," but charges that the respectable press also contributes gravely to the problem by devoting "only one line to the verdict and a hundred to the crime."

By responding to an opportune letter to the editor, the *Corriere* demonstrates its beholden-ness to the paper's true director, its ideal reader: that is, of course, the gentleman from Modena, not Lombroso's criminals in prison checking their notices or the unlettered masses craving fame. The faithful mirror momentarily makes a spectacle of the concerned citizen, who happens to be captured at the moment he renews his subscription. Taking the occasion to defend its practice, sanctioned by sales, of publishing lurid and lubricious stories in exquisite detail, the editor insists that the *Corriere* is doing God's work, combating the return of atavistic barbarism to usher in an era of American-style self-help, hygiene, and progress.

Whatever might be the influence of mass media and its content on the morals of a nation, certainly the most pronounced effect of the Fadda affair, as disseminated by telegraph, handbill, newspaper, and street singers, was its contribution to the forging of a national community, however self-divided, as the diverse and scattered peninsula was momentarily united through the press by its common enchantment by this single, suspenseful event. Midway through the sessions, the Neapolitan daily *Il Pungolo* marveled that the trial "has achieved the miracle of impassioning all Italy, creating, even unto the most distant corners of the peninsula, angry district attorneys, brashly contentious lawyers, a spontaneous generation of bawling *rabulae* and hairsplitters who make orations in the street or from the rostrum of a café table . . . this trial has for the past half-month become the obligatory theme of every conversation."[104]

The *Bersagliere* went further, contrasting the general apathy of the population toward issues of national affairs and economy with its detailed, exhaustive knowledge of the most arcane details of the Fadda case: "Just imagine if, tomorrow, Italians were granted the right to express their opinion on the guilt or innocence of Raffaella, Widow Fadda: you can bet a hundred to one that no one would miss out on the call to have their say, and everyone would be fully informed of the most minute circumstances of the trial sessions."[105]

Two weeks after this comment, following the sensational discovery of the crucial witness, Carluccio, the *Libertà* remarks on the way the citizenry, through the audience present at the trial, feels a personal involvement in the outcome far beyond their participation in political affairs: "The audience is no longer the impassive spectator that the law imposes . . . Every café table is a judge's bench, every modest citizen is an improvised commentator on penal procedure, every gathering a courtroom where the innocence or guilt of the accused is weighed, aired, judged"[106]

Through its relentless feeding of the public appetite for Fadda news, the press transforms Rome in the national imagination into something like the central piazza of all Italy. Commentary runs thick with the combined words *tutta* and *Italia* (all Italy). On the first day of the trial, "the representatives of newspapers of all Italy had faithfully taken their places, ready to transmit instantly the echo of this trial into the most hidden corners of the peninsula," reports the *Don Pirloncino*.[107] The *Diritto* remarks on how "this singular drama arouses such fabulous interest not only in Rome, but in all Italy."[108] The newspaper-reading public and nonreading listeners scattered in cafés and homes throughout the nation come to be identified with the noisy Romans who gather to gawk at the most dramatic moments of the unfolding spectacle; first they line the streets along Fadda's funeral procession, then they mass to witness the arrival of the accused widow at the central rail station, and most of all they crowd the piazza outside the courtroom for the entire, unseasonably hot October that the trial carries on.

Trumpeting the national obsession with the case, the Roman press inevitably places itself at the center of the phenomenon. The *Bersagliere* describes "the furor with which newspapers carrying the trial reports are read and devoured," and boasts, "Last night, more than a thousand people gathered outside the Caffè del Parlamento and in Piazzetta San Claudio, waiting for this newspaper to be put on sale," while the mass in the piazza outside the court every day is regularly portrayed by journalists as composed of groups clustered around newspapers, dissecting and hotly debating the most recent reports.[109] This specular distortion characteristic of the media, whereby the media measures the importance of an event by how much media it generates, is an inextricable problem of the Fadda affair as it takes up residence in the formative national consciousness. Why does this murder matter? Is it meaningful to the young nation, or is it merely a short-lived bubble of hype blown up to sell copies, a mass distraction devoid of substance or import? And if there is some urgent social problem exposed here, has the ugly crime itself revealed it or is it rather the phenomenon of women's attendance at the trial that shows something's gone awry? Or further, is there a new social menace neither in the crime nor in the trial but in the new power of the media to whip up such frenzy over a trifle in a populace poorly prepared for citizenship? Answers to these questions are no more probative or convincing than the *Corriere*'s claim that its Fadda coverage has advanced progress by raising public awareness of the menace of crime, except to the degree that they momentarily seize attention in the debate.

3

Chronology of a Circus Trial

This chapter steps away from historical analysis to present in chronological order a selection of the newspaper reports of the journalists who followed the Fadda trial's daily sessions throughout its monthlong duration and dramatized it for the national public. By widening their perspective beyond the strict determination of culpability, reporters covered the trial less as a legal procedure than as a social spectacle in which the spectators themselves played a crucial role. At the center of attention stood women, whose visibility itself became the news, the sensation, and the scandal that the invariably male gaze attended the trial to report on. The aim of this chapter is to provide readers an unalloyed experience of the rhythms and rhetoric of the coverage as it developed day by day, so as to witness how the trial proper became a backdrop to a much larger social phenomenon, calling for a variety of modes of narration. Unassisted by commentary, the chosen selections convey directly and vividly the attraction of the trial as it built breathlessly toward the climax of the jury's decision. Most prominent, for their mordant wit, are the observations of Luigi Arnaldo Vassallo, reporter for Il Messaggero, widely recognized as the leading chronicler of the trial. Vassallo's sexism stands out for its libertine insouciance but differs little in substance from that of his fellow journalists.

September 30

"At 9 a.m., the foyer, the hallways, the courtyards of the Filippini are swarming with a silent but restless and impatient throng. Twenty or so guards, another twenty carabinieri, and various city police maintain order, pushing back the mass that wants to invade all the entrances into the Assize Court. Only those with special invitations are allowed to cross the barrier and pass into the courtyard leading to the courtroom, where the witnesses also wait to be called. Outside the closed doors that open onto the plaza of the Chiesa Nuova, there is almost a mob, shouting with frenetic impatience, pounding on the doors as though to beat them down and penetrate violently. The bailiffs, guards, justice officials, doorkeepers, and attendants run hurriedly to and fro looking dazed, as though they can't take any more. At the bottom of the stairs that lead to the reserved galleries crowd a great quantity of ladies, both young and old. Many are dressed in mourning colors, but others sport white satin hats whose gay hue, in the midst of all this emotional squalor, is distinctly off-key" (*Il Messaggero*).

"The reporters nose around among the various groups. There's Wood of the *Times*, briefcase under his arm. There's the *Daily News* correspondent, looking more diplomatic than ever. The reporter for the *Tagblatt* is wearing a white tie, testifying to his modest and pacific intentions. Then there are some spurious journalists, who have suddenly sprouted like mushrooms, representing unlikely gazettes, certainly outside the grace of God" (*Il Messaggero*).

"Suddenly we begin to move. The crowd of invitees, pettifoggers, dilettantes, reporters, launches into the corridor lined with guards leading to the courtroom . . . Everyone grabs for a space, pitiless toward neighbors and friends" (*Il Messaggero*).

"The witnesses for the prosecution and defense are brought in and introduced to the court. There are 94 in all, of whom 80 for the prosecution and 14 for the defense. Every social condition is represented. Women of the people, high society ladies, gentlemen and poor, soldiers, lawyers, equestrian acrobats, circus clowns; every age, every nation, every social status" (*La Capitale*).

"Other than the two galleries added to accommodate reporters, a loggia has been raised over the main door for ticket holders. Although the court anticipated using all space possible both above and below, there is more demand than space, in fact the ladies alone would more than fill all the seats available. Curiosity is traditional in women, but for this case—so full of dramatic, romantic shadows—there is a sort of fanaticism. The gentle sex exercises all its potent influence to obtain seats for this grand drama. Quite a number of stars of the aristocracy will sparkle in the marble loggias on the right and left over the judges' bench" (*Corriere della sera*).

"This is a trial that will pass into the annals of law with the adjective 'celebrated.' The first session drew an immense crowd. At precisely 11 the court was called to order. The accused were conducted into the courtroom with the public crowding along where they passed. In the blink of an eye the courtroom fills with people. The press gallery is overflowing, and in the reserved area, the lovely sex, despite being warned away, is extremely numerous" (*La Libertà*).

"The audience manifests its indignation for such cynicism with a murmur.(*Corriere della sera*).

"The guards who man the barrier between the first and second courtyards, allowing passage to the press, judges, invited guests, and witnesses, are soldiers of the 32nd Infantry Company; precisely the regiment to which poor Captain Fadda belonged" (*La Capitale*).

"Various modifications have been made to the courtroom in order to accommodate the many requests for reserved seats. Beneath the arches of the vestibule a suspended gallery has been set up, covered in red fabric. That red contrasts strangely with the severe appearance of the judges' bench. An additional reserved gallery has been constructed above the postergale of the courtroom. Three rows from the reserved seating have been set aside for witnesses who will be called to testify . . . Outside the court, a huge crowd awaits the departure of the accused" (*La Capitale*).

October 1

"If the expression weren't out of place, I'd say that the courtroom has quite a festive air" (*La Libertà*).

"The ladies pull out handkerchiefs and we can see tears of compassion stream from their eyes" (*Corriere della sera*).

"Curiosity is more intense than ever. In the plaza, there is so dense a mass of people you would think they were passing out free bread. If precautions hadn't been taken to limit entrance, many people would have been crushed against the doorjambs. On the steps of the Filippini church, knots of people read and comment on the numerous and varied versions of the facts that have come out in the papers . . . There are many women mixed among the crowd, and what is still more strange, many of them have brought babies and children along . . . At 10:30, the courtroom was packed. The number of ladies in the gallery has grown. Many are dressed elegantly and with coquettishness. Quite a show, indeed . . . In the meantime word arrives that a chocolatier with a shop in Piazza di Pasquino has had a heart attack as he watched the proceedings from the gallery. He was carried into the corridor and died there, unable to speak a word" (*Il Messaggero*).

"The same mass of people again this morning. The courtroom is packed full. Many ladies, married and not, in the galleries reserved for them . . . It's superfluous to add that the witness's testimony is received with an extremely meaningful murmur in the audience . . . Because this woman's testimony is so important, the silence and concentration of the audience become imposing" (*Corriere della sera*).

"Although the police and army troops are able to impede any too vivid emotional fluctuations among the public lucky enough to have entered the hall, they cannot prevent the threatening rumble, like the sound of a waterfall, that accompanies the questioning. It is the extraordinary crowd out in the piazza, struggling at the entranceway . . . in the same way that drops of water and brooks form into rivers, all that murmuring united together forms a fracas as great as the potent voice of a hurricane" (*La Libertà*).

October 3

"The crowd has not diminished; on the contrary, in the hallways people bump, press, push shamelessly, because the guards don't allow them past a certain limit. Everyone knows they can't get through, but they jam in just the same, hoping for who knows what . . . The standing room audience (so to speak) chatters at the top of their voices, a frenzied humming of observations and opinions. Court guards stand in the middle of the crush trying their best to keep control . . . The audience notices that Saraceni is listening and cries less frequently . . . 'Summon Signor Guillaume!' orders the presiding judge, and the public expresses a murmur of good humor" (*Il Messaggero*).

"In the upper gallery there is some commotion. Due to the heat and the crowding, a lady has fainted. She is taken out to breathe some fresh air and quickly regains her senses" (*La Capitale*).

October 4

"The audience is becoming accustomed to the show. They no longer arrive, as the saying goes, before the firemen. The loggias and raised seating in the galleries are slowing filling up. The majority (I'm sorry to report, for my *ultra*-moralistic colleagues) is always ladies. Needless to say, the space set aside for the mass public, those without privileges, is always packed with a noisy crowd which endures a steam bath of a good five or six hours, with a tranquility, a stoicism, that makes you ponder. At the moment the accused enter, instead of pointing my binoculars at their cage, I aim it at the audience. Truly a curious scene. Hundreds of heads all converge irresistibly toward a single point, as though helplessly drawn there. Their eyes strain, they squint to see better; but to see what? . . . The audience laughs . . . 'He fled together with a man named Bergamusci, six or seven days before the company left town. They left because Francone beat them, plus they had some debts.' 'How much did they owe?' 'Three dollars.' (*Loud hilarity from the indebted class*)" (*Il Messaggero*).

"Celebrated trials often arouse extraordinary interest—the ladies attend and sometimes, so as not to miss even one moment of the strange performance, they bring along provisions, as though they were at a picnic.

Curiosity on these occasions manifests itself in the ugliest of ways" (commentary in *La Capitale*, drawing from the trial an argument in favor of legalizing divorce).

October 6

"Despite yesterday's vacation, the public's interest seems rather to grow than decrease. Masses await the arrival of the defendants, masses await the opening of the courtroom, masses in the corridors, masses everywhere. The arrival of the coach carrying the accused provokes the usual whistles and yells . . . Cardinali watches the crowd, sneering . . . A surge of attention in the audience . . . Prolonged murmuring in the galleries and standing area . . . The anticipation is immense . . . The contradictions and new claims made by Ferraro provoke explosions of disgust from the listeners, angry at her devious answers. Murmuring reaches such a point that the prosecuting attorney, Cavalier Rutigliano, asks the Court to incarcerate the witness for false testimony" (*Epoca*).

"The scene is the same as the day before yesterday. The crowd is just as large, if not larger, than Saturday's . . . In the judge's gallery, the leonine head of Pietro Cossa pokes out; he won't find any analogies between Saraceni and *Messalina*, at least not physically . . . Cardinali forces himself to laugh. The audience reacts . . . A gentleman with a black moustache, a white vest, a starched white cravat, ash-grey silk gloves, flower in his lapel, a *pince-nez* on his nose, appears in the judges' gallery wearing a snappy straw hat. The presiding judge gives the irreverent spectator a vicious stare. A bailiff runs to the gallery to tell the man to remove his hat . . . The audience laughs at this statement, because the witness has the shameless nonchalance of an old lawyer, to say the least" (*Il Messaggero*).

"Today in the reserved seating there is a distinguished audience. Poetry is represented by Pietro Cossa, war by General Merzliack, and the musical arts by *prima donna* Orsolina Picconi Pierangeli" (*La Capitale*).

October 7

"The public turnout at the Filippini cannot even be compared to the crowds of previous days . . . Senator Giovanni Prati, the illustrious poet, can be seen in the reserved galleries . . . The ladies are present in much greater numbers than yesterday and the day before. Interest in this trial grows ever greater . . . In the courtroom, continuous, animated arguments are taking place . . . The concentrated attention of the listeners is indescribable, all hang from the lips of this Calabrian peasant woman. All crane their necks, stand on tiptoe, squint their eyes . . . The noise coming from the public is the clearest and most eloquent proof that Cardinali's guilt is held to be abundantly proven . . . Huge reaction from the audience" (*Corriere della sera*).

"It is 11:00, but the galleries—who knows why—are less crowded than yesterday. Today, over the court reporter's desk we can see Giovanni Prati with his handsome, artistic head, its wavy gray hair combed with his usual diligence. What noble things you have created, senator! And what petty miseries, what cowardice and abjection will you see file before your eyes. Here, there is no *ideal.* In the middle gallery over the door, standing very tall, a young foreign priest is jammed in with the ladies, avid for the strange sensations that arise in the Criminal Court. Look how he chatters with his neighbors up there! Just imagine what they're saying! He is a young priest, with thick, curly hair. Is he able to comprehend the psychological reasons of this social drama? Is he allowed to understand them? Who knows! In the next gallery, there is a thin, pallid young lady dressed in light gray. Among the shadows of the gallery, she looks like a ribbon of sky. And you, young lady, what are you looking for? What emotions do you hope to feel? What pathetic pages do you wish to leaf through in the mysterious book of life? Vivacious murmuring in the audience . . . In the presiding judge's gallery, two charming, elegant ladies have appeared, dressed in white. In the opposite gallery, one can make out a lady all in black, with aristocratic refinement and impeccable taste . . . The session is suspended for the usual ten minutes. The ten minutes become twenty, then thirty, and threaten to pass even forty. The natives of Cassano all'Ionio, seated in a row in the courtyard, act as though gathered at the main café in their little town, intent on hearing all the most important gossip of the day. The canon smokes a clay pipe with an extremely long stem, then passes it with charitable courtesy to a neighbor. The photographer is repeating to a curious throng his story about what he heard while pretending to sleep in the same room with Cardinali and De Luca. The wife of the tavern keeper and others who live on the Plaza of the Golden Keys are painting in vivid tones the scene of the arrest and other happenings" (*Il Messaggero*).

October 10

"In the meantime, we notice a reaction against the excessive interest, ephemeral and artificial, given to this trial, and we predict that if it goes on very long, it will end in indifference unless new revelations and surprises come forth" (commentary, *Corriere della sera*).

"Like a landslide, the crowd precipitates headlong into the courtroom . . . The curiosity of the audience is indescribable . . . the exclamations, the conversations, the murmur of the crowd renews itself" (*Corriere della sera*).

"At twenty minutes before 11, the sacramental hour when the session is to begin, the galleries are already crammed, the standing areas packed with a motley, excessively noisy crowd. There is an interminable buzzing that makes one's head big as a balloon. The gallery over the judges' bench is crowded as usual with elegant ladies, among whom I note several aristocratic grand dames who couldn't resist the prick of curiosity, though it would displease them greatly if word got out. There is a lovely little figure in a gray dress with black lace around her neck, setting off the pearly pallor of her diaphanous, delicate complexion. Capricious chestnut locks sprout from beneath a little black hat with a white plume, perched on her head with studied indifference, and confer extraordinary vivacity to the character of that head. Tell me, madam, or young lady, with your fanciful eyes, don't you feel a desire to breathe less impure air? Believe me, when you leave here today, you'll find yourself less satisfied than you imagined this morning as you prepared your toilette! A curiosity: over the parapets of the galleries poke little blond or chestnut heads of children, even babies. I would wager none are more than four years old. Let's hope we see their nannies tomorrow . . . In the judges' gallery I spot the olive profile of an attaché from the Japanese embassy" (*Il Messaggero*).

October 11

"The little people have earned themselves a star for good behavior, having ceased to revile the defendants as they arrive at court. This is due also to the measures taken by Inspector Diego Vallisnieri, stationed permanently at the court to direct and oversee police services" (*Corriere della sera*).

October 13

"The hearing begins at 10 a.m. The apostles of the press, unaccustomed to observing mass at such an early hour, arrive late. The accused, however, demonstrate a punctuality that truly honors . . . their jailers. Nor are the curious, ladies and men, any less punctual. The galleries are always filled with ladies. Over the judges' bench, there are quite a number of very pretty ones as usual. I note a gray and coffee outfit with a Rubens cap set at a jaunty angle, a mass of chestnut curls over her forehead, and two naughty, criminal eyes" (*Il Messaggero*).

October 14

"It is 10:15, but only the court reporter has appeared. There is the usual display of provocative *toilettes* and anxious binoculars, in the galleries the crush of ladies is greater than ever. The moralists continue preaching in the desert. In the judges' gallery, older ladies are in the majority. Their curiosity has come late. Today's session promises to be very entertaining, a six-hour address to the jury, enough to bring on apoplexy! And just think, this is only the first of at least twenty to follow identically. Some of my colleagues turn gray by the day" (*Il Messaggero*).

"The reading aloud of these letters makes an enormous impression on the audience; I leave it to readers to imagine the comments. There is a murmur, or rather a generalized noise of agitated voices. In the galleries, the silvery voices of the ladies rise over the baritones of the so-called stronger sex . . . When prosecutor Lopez stands, a religious silence descends over the crowd . . . Sensation among the listeners, voices raised . . . The terrible oration comes to an end. The effect of it is huge, especially in the galleries where the feminine element predominates. The public is excited" (*Epoca*).

October 15

"Since the session is to begin at ten, there is time to stroll in the courtyard until ten thirty, smoking a cigar and speaking ill of my friends. A pretty young lady walks by, dressed in black. She is in such an advanced state of interest that someone exclaims, 'She must be in her tenth month!' In fact, it appears the matter may well be resolved during today's session. Nature demands equilibrium. One person has died in the galleries, so it is only right that another be born. But it would hardly be consoling to find on your birth certificate, 'On this date in October, in the hall of the Criminal Court in Rome . . .'" (*Il Messaggero*).

October 16

"It's impossible even to compare with past days the throng crowding into the courtroom today. Until today there has been a considerable number of people; this morning there is a multitude *sine fine* of human beings squeezing in on one another. They push, they curse one another, they cry out in pain and anger. Up in the galleries they must be extremely uncomfortable. Humidity, a Senegalese heat suffocates us . . . A powerful sensation throughout the audience. The ladies dry eyes stained with tears of compassion" (*Epoca*).

"The ladies are by far the majority, and ever since the press stigmatized their presence at this wretched spectacle, their number—a touching proof of the omnipotence of the fourth estate—grows by the hour" (*La Libertà*).

October 17

"The police security force seems to be increasing. Not that they fear riots, but the ever growing public turnout could lead to problems that are best impeded and prevented . . . The echo of his words has not yet ceased and already, from every part of the courtroom, arises an incredibly eloquent murmur that affirms with utmost clarity that Cavalier Rutigliano has performed his duty in a most worthy manner" (*Epoca*).

October 18

"Ranzi, Cardinali's defense attorney: 'If it were necessary to try every man who has illicit relations with married women, and if the women had to appear in court as well, we would need a courtroom as large as all Rome.' Hilarity. All gazes turn to the ladies present in the court" (*Epoca*).

"The usual recess. It's raining. Instead of strolling in the courtyard, the witnesses gather in the little room off the hearing room. Every mouth from Rossano, Castrovillari, Cassano all'Ionio, not to mention the two from Bari, curses the trial, the defendants, the lawyers, and only out of profound respect for justice and its representatives, the police, are the judges themselves spared the same imprecations. At least, not out loud . . . The fact is that all these poor people are due our greatest sympathy. Many among them, in order to serve as witnesses here in the capital, have subjected themselves to that public, universal, civil institution which we nevertheless call private debt. Show compassion, Presiding Judge! Some of these poor devils have been forced to spend (prodigious sum!) hundreds of lire that they do not possess. Others are dipping deeply into life savings. From Cassano, from Corigliano, from Castrovillari, feminine voices are calling home their fathers, their brothers, their husbands! It's a catastrophe" (*Il Messaggero*).

October 20

"The Court has been moved at my few but deeply felt words of yesterday. As soon as the session opens, the presiding judge delivers the comforting news that a fair number of natives of Cassano all'Ionio are to be released. The little jeweler, Minervino, is so overjoyed he can't contain himself" (*Il Messaggero*).

"The brilliant address by attorney Palomba provokes expressions of approval from his colleagues of the bar, in the gallery, and throughout the courtroom" (*Epoca*).

"Saraceni weeps uncontrollably. Her lawyer Tutino's address has lasted almost three hours. The young attorney spoke to the minds and hearts of the jury with all the fire of youth, seeking to transplant his own authentic, deep conviction of the innocence of his client" (*Il Messaggero*).

October 21

"Attorney Rosano, defense for Saraceni: 'Granting just for a moment that she were,' the orator exclaims, throwing an inquisitorial glare up at the ladies' gallery, 'Granting that she were unfaithful, how many women would dare throw the first stone at her?' Murmuring and confusion in the galleries, prolonged laughter among the crowd . . . Universal amazement translates into an *oooh* and vivid agitation among listeners to the debate. The emotion that takes possession of those present in the Filippini at the arrival of this surprise is indescribable" (*Epoca*).

"A murmur of amazement, of dark surprise spreads through the auditorium . . . A hellish noise fills the hall. Carluccio has stirred up a hornets' nest" (*Il Messaggero*).

October 22

"What a mass of people! What a crush! What confusion! The indignation of the public has reached paroxysm . . . At this point the scorn of the audience bursts all bounds. There is a universal scream of condemnation, terrible and impressive. The session is briefly interrupted. Once calm and order are reestablished, the questioning of Carluccio continues . . . A new and even more clamorous explosion from the crowd" (*Epoca*).

"It's a regular frenzy, a delirium! The throng is tumultuous, they scream, they clamor, they shove, they crush. A regular house of devils. Have they all gone mad? Colossal curiosity, as though Pinta had come yesterday to say: Ladies and Gentlemen! A ten minute intermission, and I announce for tomorrow the debut of the unique, famous pagliaccio, Carluccio, with his remarkable, never-before-seen tricks! The plaza of the Chiesa Nuova is jammed with people. The door of the Filippini monastery is shut hermetically and defended by a sizeable platoon of guards and *bersaglieri*. The ladies are granted the special favor of entering the galleries. But since even they are guilty of a lack of calm, it happens that many lose their jewelry, which, after the furious charge, is gathered up by police officials . . . I cannot describe how crowded it is. In a space that would barely accommodate ten foot-soldiers without their packs, there are at least fifty ladies. Aristocracy, diplomacy, parliament, it's a curious mixture . . . We are suffocating! Behind the judge's bench, there is a file of magistrates, ministers' deputies, lawyers, professors, who knows what. Sooner or later someone is going to take a seat in the defendants' cage. All the puritans, all the moralists, all those who flee from these spectacles, even they pray to Jesus with joined hands for a tiny space to stand . . . through a side door can be seen the head of the Honorable Martini, Zeppa, Delvecchio, and other congressmen. In the loggia, I even spy Honorable Di Belmonte . . . Five or six reporters are sitting on the floor . . . Carluccio enters. All are on their feet, journalists, lawyers . . . some even stand on chairs . . . A near riot takes place in the audience, so that it's almost impossible to continue the session. The presiding judge orders the court cleared . . . The public again protests, so the judge orders the courtroom cleared a second time" (*Il Messaggero*).

October 23

"This morning the crowd is more compact than usual. They are hungry for sensational scenes. Some predict a scandal that will require another session to be called . . . At the arrival of the judges, all chatter, every sound stops . . . At these words, a near riot erupts. From all sides come cries, protests, gesticulation. It feels like the Tower of Babel, so great is the confusion" (*Epoca*).

"The usual throng jammed in all the corridors. At 11, the galleries are already packed. I note with great satisfaction that today the ladies are all, or almost all, pretty, but the majority are all over twenty-five . . . or even twenty-six. At noon, the door opens and a mass of people rushes headlong to take places in the part of the courtroom reserved for the public" (*Il Messaggero*).

"Today the court officials have taken steps to see that the platform reserved for the press and witnesses has been cleared of the usual intruders. In the reserved seating as well, one notes that the rows of little stars, angels, and cherubs have been thinned out. After the crush yesterday that made it impossible to write, to hear, even to breathe, it's a true comfort. Greater parsimony has been employed in the distribution of tickets" (*La Capitale*).

"The public is no longer the impassive spectator required by the Law. Impassioned, as though personally involved in the matter at hand, it stirs at every declaration Carluccio makes against Saraceni and Carrozza, it murmurs when he contradicts himself in some detail, it shudders when the contradictions between Carluccio and other witnesses and the accused cloud over previously explicit testimony" (*La Libertà*).

October 25

"2 p.m. The hall is already packed with people . . . Many ladies in the judges' gallery. I note that their predominant color is light *havana*, very light . . . The presiding judge asks Trebisondo whether, when Cardinali spoke those words to Carluccio, there was anyone else present. 'Yes sir,' answers Trebisondo, 'There was Carluccio and the horse.' (*grand hilarity in the courtroom*)." (*Il Messaggero*).

October 27

"The carabinieri bring in the defendants. Cardinali has an, 'I couldn't care less,' air about him that chills the blood. He seems to feel that he's the judge and the public is the defendant" (*Epoca*).

"10 a.m. Despite the morning's cool weather, all the ladies are at their places in the various galleries. In this part of the audience, among which I admit to certain predilections, I note some ladies belonging to the British colony. Today the look is less *havana* than the day before yesterday; the predominant color is Bismarck red . . . Through a door to the judges chambers I see the likable figure of Don Leopoldo Torlonia . . . The orator says, 'After the defense of Saraceni given by my illustrious colleague, Mr. Rosano, public opinion had shifted favorably toward my client. There was no doubt that a negative verdict would have returned that poor woman to her family and redeemed her honor, which a stroke of fate dragged to that chair of ignominy'" (*Il Messaggero*).

October 28

"The session is about to begin. The hats, the feathers, the gowns of the ladies quiver" (*Epoca*).

October 30

"Today will be a battle: the Honorable Pessina will speak. The ladies are extremely numerous. It's only natural. Today Pessina will defend a woman like them; a woman who has sinned, true, but who sinned for love (whether platonic or not little matters) . . . The anticipation for Pessina's oration is at the maximum degree. The courtroom is crammed to the gills . . . His eloquence is enchanting; he draws us along, all hang from his lips . . . continuous, incessant responses of agreement . . . The public explodes in unanimous, raucous applause. The presiding judge vainly rings his bell, finally he orders the courtroom cleared . . . Applause erupts, resounding, immense. Commotion throughout the court, near delirium. Everyone who can get close to Pessina embraces him, they suffocate him with hugs. He can't go on anymore. He is truly spent" (*Corriere della sera*).

"Waves of approval. Mr. Rosano tenderly kisses his colleague . . . During this brief interval, a brave policeman, officer Neri, arrests five or six pickpockets in the courtroom who were amusing themselves by lightening the pockets of the audience" (*Il Messaggero*).

October 31

"The hall is so crowded that people are breathing air that is literally rarefied" (*Il Messaggero*).

"The throng cramming itself into the courtroom today is truly, without exaggeration, immense. Never before has this been seen" (*Corriere della sera*).

4

The People, the Killer, and the Weeping Widow

The Fadda trial begins at 11 a.m. on September 30, 1879, in the Palace of Justice in Rome. Adjacent to the Chiesa Nuova on what is now Corso Vittorio, the courthouse, called the Palazzo di Giustizia dei Filippini, was begun in 1637 by the great baroque architect Francesco Borromini. The building's original purpose was to provide a total environment for the Filippini, a Franciscan order named after their founder, Saint Filippo Neri. Borromini's design included both public and private spaces, housing, a sacristy, a refectory, library, a clock tower, and a spacious recreation room (*sala di ricreazione*) with a large fireplace. The revolutionary, fluid façade of the Filippini was justified by the architect as being inspired by "the human body, with open arms, as though embracing everyone who enters."[1] In 1871 the new Italian state, having moved its capital to Rome and in urgent need of space, confiscated the Filippini from the Church and turned it into government offices. In 1874, the largest hall in the building became the Criminal Court (the Assize Court) where the young nation meted out justice, demonstrating its probity, moral discipline, and mercy to transgressors and the public at large.[2] In the last busy days before the trial, workers hurried to complete the raised seating platforms ordered by the president of the court to accommodate the press and spectators. Two classes of reserved tickets were available, the most prestigious of which to be distributed strictly by the president himself.[3]

From early in the morning, agitated gapers crowded the plaza in front of the Filippini awaiting the arrival of the coaches holding the accused. For days the entire city had been plastered with competing handbills promoting the coverage of the trial by each of the principal papers.[4] Two days after sessions convened, with a self-reflexivity typical of the media's heated attention, *Il Bersagliere* described how the trial was monopolizing street life in the capital:

> The Fadda Trial has fascinated the public, as evidenced by the furor with which newspapers carrying trial reports are being read and devoured, and people avidly buy the illustrations on sale. Throughout the city, all you hear are hawkers crying out "the trial of Captain Fadda!" His portrait has been made in a thousand versions and sizes, the traveling vendors carry it on their arms, screaming "Captain Fadda's portrait" at the top of their lungs, some of them stating it baldly as, "Captain Fadda for one cent!"[5]

Finally the protagonists are to stand publicly before the nation in a hall of justice. Pietro Cardinali and Antonietta Carrozza arrive first in the prison transport. Widow Saraceni then enters the piazza, descending alone from a private carriage. The "little people," as the *Corriere* reporter terms them, those without the fortune or connections to have obtained tickets, form a kind of gauntlet; they hoot and catcall at the accused as they pass from carriage to courtroom. Amid the mass bearing down, journalists feverishly take notes on the appearance and conduct of the defendants.

From the trial's opening session, *Il Messaggero*'s descriptions of the protagonists mix key physical traits and dress with implied moral summary of the subject's character. As reporter Luigi Arnaldo Vassallo prepares readers for the extended drama to come, his introduction of defendant Cardinali at the trial's opening session develops from intense attention to fashion into a conclusion about the accused murderer's deep superficiality:

> He dresses rigorously in black. Even his shirt collar is bordered in black, the shirt being the only thing white in his appearance. His head is covered with a low black hat, from whose narrow folds emerges a wave of black hair carefully done up with that special cut we see in operatic baritones out on a spree. His physiognomy is intelligent but most of all theatrical. He looks like one of those stage extras or role players who ape the behavior of the great star. His complexion is florid and his lips vermillion.[6]

Next the reporter comically details Cardinali's codefendant, equestrian acrobat Antonietta Carrozza, so as to deflate the popular stereotype of female circus riders as brazen amazons.[7] Whereas his description of Cardinali derived from figures of theatre, his reaction to Carrozza depends on figures of class:

> She looks simply like a maid for a good family. No one would take her for a tightrope dancer. Rather, she looks prematurely aged, an appearance of bigoted high-mindedness. Copious chestnut hair combed with pointed coquettishness. She wears an olive green dress of decidedly questionable taste, livened with lighter-colored ribbons. She wears one of those little black veils from Milan, the kind so popular among serving girls. She appears ashamed, but indifferent. Her step is firm although her walk somewhat awkward.[8]

Figure 4.1 Pietro Cardinali, *cavallerizzo*, accused assassin

Source: Permission granted by Ministero dei Beni e le Attività Culturali, Archivio di Stato di Roma, ASR 13/2010. Archivio Civile e Penale di Roma, Circolo d'Assise. Reproduction is prohibited.

Vassallo knows that the center of everyone's attention is the last defendant, Raffaella Saraceni, the adulterous wife, too complex and mysterious a character to be summarized at the outset. Accordingly, he describes not only her appearance, but her entrance, her arrival in a private car surrounded by a crush of gawkers shouting invective, a moment that will merit a two-page illustration in the *Processo Fadda illustrato*. The three are ushered into a room off the courtroom. Guards allow the crowds to pour into the corridors, but push them back against the walls to allow the defense attorneys, all in black, to proceed down the hallway for a final conference with their clients. When the lawyers emerge, Vassallo reports, "They appear graver, moved." The reporter seizes on one of them who he describes as "a friend of mine." Their dialogue focuses the suspense:

> "Well?"
> "What?"
> "Signora Saraceni?"
> "She is in a state to inspire the deepest compassion; I am deeply moved."
> "What did you say to her?"
> "Come now, madam: Courage. This is the supreme test. Now more than ever you must have courage."
> "And she?"
> "All she can do is weep."[9]

The door opens to admit the defendants into the courtroom. Cardinali passes first, with his head high and staring frankly back at the eyes fixed on him. Now two carabinieri emerge,

> and behind them, a lady dressed in black; bent, almost doubled over. She wants to be half the size she is . . . but what half? To be a bug, an ant, to withdraw from all those hundreds of eyes fixing her with their intense, shameless, embarrassing stare. It is Signora Fadda. It is Raffaella Saraceni. Shattered, worn, thinner, aged, made uglier by physical and moral suffering. She can do nothing but weep, nothing but sob, knowing all this will go on for days and days. Her nose is red, her eyelids and eyes sunken into black circles, her lips wet, swollen, trembling. She is dressed in mourning, with a small black tulle hat not without elegance. Her hair is worn with great simplicity, although we can see she has long hair gathered at the nape of her neck. She wears black gloves, which set off the pallor of her complexion.[10]

Vassallo's description of the weeping widow is too detailed to conclude with a summary of her character, which would in any case deflate his readers' need to follow his coverage every day in search of an answer to the case's central mystery: How could she do it? How could a married woman be so morally depraved as to kill her husband? In contrast to his representation of the circus performers, that of Saraceni already evinces a certain degree of sympathetic identification. The reporter's description of the wife contrasts with that of her husband, the murdered soldier:

> Captain Fadda was not classically handsome, but he was extremely pleasing to look at, with an open, noble, jovial physiognomy. Eyes deep and vivacious, with laugh lines at the corners that denoted his jocund, expansive nature. A moustache, neither too long nor too pointed, shadowed two vigorously pronounced lips, the lower of which did not lack sensuality. Prominent cheekbones and an energetic chin conferred patent courage upon those masculine lineaments. The captain's head slightly inclined toward his left shoulder, as of a man who is sometimes pensive and meditative. All in all a noble, agreeable aspect.[11]

The most pronounced difference between the description of the captain and that of the trial defendants is the use of the past tense. Fadda is dead and Vassallo never knew him, but in effect his ignorance of the man facilitates the portrait. The description can only have been taken from the photographic visiting card, set in an oval frame measuring five by seven centimeters, found in the captain's room after his death.[12] In an early example of a practice today termed "leaking," the photograph must have been offered up for observation to reporters and newspaper engravers by the investigating magistrate.[13] The writer never met the captain and never saw him. The testimony given in court by Fadda's orderly, his military fellows of the Thirty-second regiment, his brother, and a female acquaintance, and the image of the man that emerges from his own letters, suggests that Fadda had virtually none of the characteristics attributed to him by Vassallo: his friends do not describe him as open, noble, jovial, vivacious, expansive, vigorous, sensual, energetic, pensive, meditative, noble (as Vassallo repeats), or agreeable. On the contrary, Fadda's injury, his military nomadism, poor pay, and the collapse of his marriage had left him a solitary and depressed man who was waiting only for retirement. During the trial, a military acquaintance who knows him from Sassari, in Sardinia, says that Fadda was called *il capitano contabile* (captain accountant).[14] His conduct at the Battle of San Martino would indeed confirm Vassallo's assertion that the captain was courageous. But here the journalist is interpreting a photograph, believing that physiognomy reveals character and that photography reveals truth, two articles of the positivist faith so influential to his generation.[15] The apparent factuality of the photograph has been construed to elevate the dead captain onto an ideal plane of virtue and nobility of character.

Once the court is called to order, the first task is the seating of the jury, consisting of a panel of fourteen citizens. Receiving four lire per diem for

Figure 4.2 Giovanni Fadda, wearing the medals obtained for heroic service at the Battle of San Martino

Source: Permission granted by Ministero dei Beni e le Attività Culturali, Archivio di Stato di Roma, ASR 13/2010. Archivio Civile e Penale di Roma, Circolo d'Assise.

their service, it will be their duty to attend every session as long as the trial continues, follow the testimony of the three defendants and nearly a hundred witnesses, listen to the summations of the prosecution, the six lawyers for the accused and two for the *parte civile* (i.e., lawyers hired by the Fadda family to argue for conviction), take their instruction from the president of the court, and finally decide whether to convict or acquit.

That normal citizens—or rather, those of the enfranchised 2 percent of the total population with the right to vote, and thus potentially eligible to serve on a jury—were capable of dispassionately determining a matter so historically, philosophically, and scientifically complex as legal culpability was not at all a matter of public consensus. Enrico Pessina, the respected jurist, government minister, and firm supporter of the jury system who led Raffaella Saraceni's defense team, had acknowledged in a discussion of the issue in 1868 that "in Italy, the jury was not unanimously desired" and that it was "a great problem."[16] By 1874, Justice Minister Pasquale Stanislao Mancini, in proposing another in a sequence of reforms of the controversial institution, observed that many magistrates believed that "the time of the jury has passed, and it needs to be thrown out like an old, torn suit."[17] In an unsigned editorial published in the January 11, 1874, issue of the conservative daily *La Perseveranza*, the editor takes up the debate, identifying one particularly pernicious effect of the institution: "It is universally lamented that the criminal courts are very often converted into a theatre, which people flock to in search of large, powerful emotions, to witness a struggle and judge the oratorical strength of the actors in the judicial drama. We already have too many *circenses* to have to go seek them in the criminal courts. To turn the administration of justice into a public spectacle is not the best way to educate the populace."[18]

The paper's position on the matter is widely shared, and not only among its dwindling readership, the staunch supporters of the *Destra* (the Right), that first generation of liberal patriots who guided the young state from its establishment in 1848 until their defeat by a rising *Sinistra* (the Left) in the elections of 1876. Neither is the editorialist simply adopting the easiest available metaphor when he describes trials as having degenerated into a form of theatre. No longer, the author complains, is a trial a matter of determining the truth, but rather of "exciting the feelings and moving the spirits of the jury and the audience," of shifting the attention of the trial from the facts and the actions of the accused to the sentiments of the public.[19] On March 19, an unsigned article in another daily, *La Nazione*, expresses similar sentiments: "Whenever a jury is involved, it becomes a matter of the unknowns of moods, of passions, and of the variety and variability of human emotions."[20] In a memoir, a lawyer of the era remembers that once public, oral trials were imposed over the written, private proceedings heretofore conducted in the Papal States, young lawyers from the North, skilled in oratory, swarmed into the capital and threatened the livelihoods of the traditional Roman attorneys, who were still unpracticed in the art of swaying a jury.[21] Written trials had been considerably more arduous, according to the memoirist, because they required reflection and study, in contrast to the verbal improvisations that came with public proceedings.[22] "The piazza was propitious for the newcomers," he recalls, using here the term "la piazza" to apply to the courtroom a term of commercial and theatrical trade slang.[23]

During the Fadda trial, the lawyers' final summations, each of which goes on for hours and some of which stretch across three days of sessions, are regarded by legal colleagues, jury, public, and press as rhetorical arias to be rewarded by applause or ovation. One of the trial's ambitious young attorneys, Tommaso Lopez, rose to celebrity in legal circles precisely for his bravura in the open court and his impeccable elegance. The *Diritto* described his voice as "a steel blade that cuts with slow and measured blows."[24] The paper's greatest oratorical praise was reserved, however, for Enrico Pessina's Neapolitan protégé, Pietro Rosano, whose eloquence was said to seduce like a siren: "The thoughts, the phrases pour forth from his lips like iridescent globes of crystal." Vivacious, troubled, and religious, Rosano had founded a theatrical journal in Naples before turning to law.[25] For the summation that closed the trial and provoked near bedlam in the court, Rosano's mentor, Senator Pessina, was described by a colleague as "Michelangelo reborn."[26] On the other hand, the lead prosecutor, Pubblico Ministero Ippolito Rutigliano, was thought to have weakened the state's case by resorting to "tears, sobs, trembling and convulsions."[27] "Perhaps a day will come," complained the author of a study of forensic eloquence almost three decades later, "when the criminal courts will no longer be theatres crowded with audiences who go to listen to lawyers as though they were tenors."[28]

Following the French model, juries composed of citizens had been imposed in courts on the Italian peninsula during the wave of democratic fervor that established representative government in Piedmont in the spring of 1848. That same revolutionary summer, juries were introduced also in the Kingdom of Sicily and in Tuscany, only to be withdrawn during the subsequent repressive reaction, but definitively reimposed with the achievement of national unification. Initially, citizen juries were called only in cases pertaining to acts of the press (although the short-lived Roman Republic of 1849 had decreed the presence of juries in all criminal cases).[29] By the patriot founders of these liberal governments, the institution of the jury was held to be even more essentially determinative of a free state than the parliamentary system itself. Born from the bourgeois distrust of a magistracy regarded as a servile instrument of the monarchy, the people's jury, promoted by Prime Minister Camillo Benso di Cavour as a cardinal institution of the liberal order, became one of the most secure convictions of the new ruling class.[30] Like many of the beliefs of these patriots, it was a political principle, an ideal rather than a popular demand. A citizen panel was especially called for in cases involving legal action against the press because, whereas culpability in crimes against property and persons required detailed knowledge of penal codes and legal theory, the criminality of actions of the press was necessarily a matter of public opinion rather than legal deduction or demonstrable fact. As one jurist explained in 1853, crimes of the press "receive their essence and definition from public opinion."[31] Because press crimes were fundamentally political, culpability could not fairly be judged by the magistracy, an arm of the very institutions of power most likely to be the object of press denunciation, but only by representative citizens who, "in full independence of political power, interpret public opinion."[32] By 1852, however, the government of Massimo D'Azeglio had already proposed a law reducing the authority of juries even within that narrow purview.

From the beginning, the ideal of popular participation in the judicial process conflicted with efforts to limit participation to an intellectual aristocracy. At first juries were selected by lottery. In practice, two problems soon emerged: the first was that the majority of qualified electors had neither the political nor juridical culture sufficient to perform their task adequately. Citizen juries were likely to be either incapable of understanding the legal issues or politically unreliable. In 1863 a government minister called for the ending of the jury system, complaining about "these jurors who come from the villages and can barely read and write," with the result that "the perturbation of spirits is already appearing in many forms, and public restlessness is already translating into public opinion."[33] The minister's comment reveals his concern that ignorant jurors, suddenly granted judicial authority, might be manipulated by republican or socialist rabble-rousers. Responding to this worry, Enrico Pessina's defense of the jury system in his 1868 discourse justifies the institution neither as a democratic principle nor on the basis of its efficacy, but rather as a teaching tool, an instrument for educating the populace in how to assume its democratic responsibilities over time: "Complain as much as you like against the people's jury. [But] It is a potent instrument of progress because human nature most loves what it participates in with its own activity. The multitudes acquire greater awareness of justice, and better identify with it, the more they are called to serve as its operant organ."[34]

Although Cavour expressed his unconditional support for the principle, he worried that the decisions of juries might give expression to public opinion at odds with his government's foreign policy. Shortly after the Italian revolutionist Felice Orsini threw three bombs at French emperor Napoleon III in 1858, a newspaper editor in Turin published an article in which he attempted to explain the rationale that might have driven the would-be assassin to his act. Cavour was outraged by the article, believing that it threatened his government's delicate relations with France, and insisted that the editor be brought up on charges of undermining the state. He assigned a commission to reform the jury selection process so as to guarantee the quality of jurors and avoid the permeation of republican sentiment into the judicial process. No longer would the panel be chosen by lottery from the outset; instead, regional administrators conducted an increasingly complex selection process that sifted eligible electors so as to guarantee an acceptable level of probity in juridical proceedings, as well as to avoid political embarrassment. The lottery system was reintroduced at a final phase, once the reliability of the participants had been verified. The next year, however, as patriotic fervor grew and Piedmont expanded eastward, the jury system was extended beyond press crimes to all criminal cases.[35]

The second logistical problem confronting the application of juries to the Italian court system was that the ideal constituents of the public jury, those bourgeois with high levels of education and discernment, did everything in their power to avoid serving.[36] Legal experts published booklets purporting to offer helpful guidelines to citizens called to serve on juries, but at least one such volume contained an appendix detailing how to obtain exemption.[37] In a study of the bourgeoisie in Naples between 1860 and 1880, Paolo Macry devotes a delightful paragraph to the excuses proffered by Neapolitan elites to recuse themselves from jury duty, including deafness, gout, arthritis, incurable asthma, eye diseases, "intestinal catarrh," hemorrhoids, urinary problems, "cerebral apoplexy," nervous palpitations, vertigo, claustrophobia, a phobia about hearing accounts of passion and crime, excessive corpulence, "habitual somnolence," and that of one potential juror who flatly affirms that "it is simply impossible for him to listen to discussions in the criminal court."[38]

The last reform efforts before the Fadda trial, those approved under Mancini in 1874, attempted to raise the quality of juries by introducing twenty-one categories of eligibility for service, including ex-parliamentarians, teachers, professionals, public functionaries, authors of literary and scientific books or of other works requiring "ingenuity," and directors of public agencies or banks. Such individuals, it was presumed, would be reliably capable of discerning facts and resisting the siren call of trial attorneys playing on their sentiments. Once it was calculated that the sum of jurors deemed eligible according to the proposed criteria would supply only 11,000 of the 30,000 needed nationwide, a final category was added to include a much wider range of simple taxpayers. Now anyone who had paid a certain amount of taxes, including tradesmen and small merchants, would have the power to judge the guilt or innocence of their fellow citizens. The addition of the last category succeeded in filling the jury rolls, but contaminated them by admitting the poorest electors, who were felt to be characterized by "instability and uncertainty of opinion and sentiment or by convictions not firmly rooted in tradition, and tendentially favorable to the opposition parties."[39] Within two years of Mancini's reform, in fact, those newly enfranchised poorest electors, many from the South, had swept the Left into power. Cavour's liberal ideal of sober deliberation was stained at the outset by the disruptive proliferation of a social spectacle that appeared to know no bounds.

Despite these democratizing reforms, the jury constituted for the Fadda trial appears to have been composed from among the more select elements of the Roman bourgeoisie in the immediate postunification period. The trial archive contains a list constituted one week before the trial of the names and professions of the forty qualified jurors and ten *supplenti* (substitutes) from whom the court will select those who will ultimately determine by majority vote the guilt or innocence of the three defendants. Of these forty, at least thirteen work in various government offices, while five more are themselves lawyers or degreed in law. There are three pharmacists, two engineers, a surgeon, an agronomist, and one who registers as degreed in philosophy. Three in the jury pool who list no profession may have considered themselves of noble rank. Three others identify themselves as *possidenti* (landowners) but only two in the list have qualified as mere *contribuenti* (taxpayers). There is a single shopkeeper, while another calls himself a licensed broker. Two are pensioners, one of whom is retired military.[40]

At the beginning of the trial's public sessions on September 30, after the accused and the public have been seated, the judge admits 33 jurors into the hall, a group distilled from the eligibility lists divided into *ordinari*, *supplenti*, and *complementari* (ordinary, substitutes, and complementary). The judge reads the potential jurors their responsibilities as described in the reformed laws of 1874. The three in the group who raise the number to 33 are released. Then the public is ordered out of the hall, and behind closed doors the names of the thirty are placed in an urn, from which the names of the fourteen who will serve in the present trial are drawn. During this process, the prosecution rejects eight names while the defense rejects seven. Of the final 14, half work in various government ministries (including the one selected as foreman). One is a shopkeeper and one is a telegraph operator.[41]

Now the public is readmitted into the hall. As Vassallo describes it, "Everyone seizes their own place with no pity for neighbors or friends."[42]

The names of the 14 jurors are read aloud; the remaining 16 are definitively released. Each juror is required to swear with his right hand on the law book containing the trial procedures. The decision of guilt or innocence will ultimately be made by 12 jurors, while two attend along with the others but serve as substitutes, only voting in case a regular juror is unable to continue to the end of the trial.

The lawyers have taken their positions, six for the defense at a front table, and behind them the two of the *parte civile*.[43] The panel of three judges has been seated; to their side, the prosecutor. The jury has been installed. The press boxes above are so packed that those who are not standing are sitting two to a chair. All the above mentioned are men. The accused have been admitted and led to the *gabbione*, the risers surrounded by a barred railing, where they sit. Within the *gabbione* stand four carabinieri while three more stand just outside it. Cardinali sits on the lower bench in front, the two women side by side on the higher bench behind. Above and around the men sit the women who have procured tickets, many of them wives of magistrates, lawyers, and parliamentary deputies or society ladies with the necessary access. Women are also mixed in among the lower class of standees who have been admitted on the ground floor. Every available inch of space is filled and the room is already far too warm for comfort. Spectators squeeze in so close to officials and defendants that people can smell one another. There is some debate in the press whether women actually constitute the numerical majority of the audience, or whether it merely appears that way because they are so much more noticeable than the men.

The judge reads the formal charges, then explains them succinctly in simple words to each of the defendants. Now the witnesses are summoned into the courtroom and their names are read aloud: 12 for the defense, 82 for the prosecution. When the names of two members of the Fadda family are called, that of Giovanni's aged father, Giuseppe, and his younger brother, Cesare, the public reacts with loud murmuring and craning of necks. Several witnesses are missing, a matter causing a short delay. Once accounted for, the witnesses are released to the rooms in which they will wait to be called, those for the defense held separately from those for the prosecution, with communication between the two groups forbidden.[44]

The official minutes taken by the court reporter, the *verbale*, describe the sequence of trial procedure but not the testimony, neither that of the witnesses nor the accused, and not the words of the lawyers' final summations.[45] Because full trial transcription is not yet a part of standard procedure, the record of testimony that takes place in the courtroom from this moment to the passing of the sentence remains entirely in the hands of the press, particularly of Vassallo of the *Messaggero* and Coboevich of the *Bersagliere*, whose reports will be published daily, then collected and sold in inexpensive books as soon as the trial ends. The two journalists' versions purport to transcribe exact testimony, but they vary significantly, especially when trying to follow the twists and turns of Pietro Cardinali's contorted denials. In fact, once past their agreement on the exact wording of Cardinali's initial, one-word rebuttal of the charges against him (*affatto*, a decisive "not at all"), the two versions, as well as those of other newspapers present, never report precisely the same questions and answers. They also differ widely in their renderings of all the lawyers' final summations.

As the trial is about to begin, Raffaella Saraceni sits with lowered eyes, her chin leaning on her hand, holding a white handkerchief. She dabs at her eyes and mouth, blows her nose, and returns to the same position, "immobile," Vassallo says, "like a figure in a painting." Antonietta Carrozza looks here and there "as though she doesn't know what to look at," her arms crossed. Cardinali, on the other hand, makes a show of indifference. His gaze fixes on the president of the court, then passes to the public, "with a slow movement not without dignity." This is the last time that Cardinali's conduct will be granted any dignity by either reporter. Once he opens his mouth, in a few moments, he will become a figure of open derision and a source of laughter.

The accused are summoned to rise and identify themselves. Saraceni weeps while the others remain silent. As the imposing spectacle of the Assize courts begins, even Carrozza is finally moved: tears falling on cheeks red with emotion, she dries her eyes with a red and white striped handkerchief and adopts the same pose as Raffaella. Here Vassallo inserts another artistic simile: "They seem two figures from Pinturicchio, one modeled on the other." His allusion to the Renaissance painter of delicate, ethereal madonnas is pointedly ironic.

The first three days of the trial are devoted to the testimony of the three defendants, the first day and a half to Cardinali alone. He stands, responding with a firm denial to the judge's first question of whether he killed Captain Fadda. Referring to the depositions taken during the investigative phase, the judge begins to question Cardinali about the motives for, and the steps taken during, his trip from Calabria to Rome at the beginning of October in 1878. To the apparent surprise of the judge, Cardinali's answers differ from those he had given under interrogation: Coboevich's report identifies at least 15 moments when the judge points out to Cardinali that his testimony in court directly contradicts previous statements made under oath. The defendant also astonishes the assembled audience: Coboevich's account is densely scattered with eighteen parenthetical insertions, "(*Ilarità*)" or "(*Sensazione*)," indicating moments when remarks by the acrobat or reactions by the judge provoke hilarity or sensation in the courtroom.

Cardinali departed from Corigliano Calabro on September 29. He had stated to investigators that subsequent to a fight with his two brothers, he quit the company to seek to join the Fassio circus in Naples. In court, instead, he now claims to have made peace with his brothers, and went to Naples to hire new artists for the company, except that when the train stopped in Caserta, he learned that the Fassio company was no longer in Naples and so decided not to go there but to Rome instead, where the Guillaume Circus was playing. When the judge points out the contradictions in his testimony, Cardinali answers variously either that the investigator misunderstood him or that he was in such a state of distress in prison that he didn't know what he was saying. He charges that the investigating magistrate told him, "You assassinated the captain, and I shall assassinate you," and when the public responds loudly to this statement, he turns to them to answer, "That's right, ladies and gentlemen, and the prison custodian can prove it." Unfortunately he mispronounces the word for "custodian," and his audience responds with another wave of derisive laughter.

As the judge proceeds to question Cardinali about his trip to Rome, the defendant responds with contradictions: he denies having traveled together with his accused accomplice, the stableboy De Luca, asserting that mere chance found them together on the same train. The key damning moments of the trip center on the two men's stop in Bari, where Cardinali is said to have made incriminating statements to a tavern keeper and his uncle (the Forleo and Genghi named in the *Atto*), and the stop in Caserta before proceeding to Rome, where Cardinali is alleged to have paid a clerk to write the letter that was found, bloodstained, in the captain's apartment after the murder.

In Bari, the two men went to an *osteria* (a tavern serving simple meals) run by an acquaintance, a young fan of Cardinali's who kept a photo of the acrobat pinned to the wall in his inn. Forleo and his uncle, Genghi, have testified to police—and will soon repeat their testimony in court—that Cardinali showed his hosts a photograph of a woman and said that he was in love with her, the well-to-do wife of a captain, and was going to Rome either to find someone to kill the captain, or to do the job himself. According to the young innkeeper, Cardinali attempted to recruit him to carry out the murder or find someone in Bari willing to do it, promising 120 lire; brandishing a long knife, he had pressed its point against the innkeeper's chest.[46] The young man refused the offer, telling Cardinali, as a point of civic pride, that, "In Bari, when someone has too much wine he might stab someone, but never for money." The tavern keeper had later learned of the murder when a carabiniere in his tavern happened to read aloud a newspaper article reporting the crime. Cardinali denies the story, calling it a calumny directed against him by the innkeeper, with whom he had quarreled.

Proceeding by train toward Rome, the prosecution case asserts that Cardinali and De Luca arrived in Caserta on October 1. The station's *guardasale*, the watchman, has deposed that Cardinali approached him and gave him a cigar, asking if he would write a letter as part of a practical joke. They retired to the third-class waiting room, where the acrobat dictated a letter that read, "my dear Giovanni, I beg you this evening not to come because my husband found out that you came to my house, and he swears he'll take my life and yours and says he wants to show the Roman dagger. I advise you to let some time pass before you come again. Do it for my love for you, and I beg you not even to pass by because he will find out. I embrace you to my breast and say I love you to death, your dear Teresina Panzi."[47]

This letter was found in Fadda's rooms, its envelope bearing bloody prints that match the high riding boots Cardinali wore throughout his sojourn in Rome. The prosecution argues that the murderer had composed this letter with a double purpose: to use it as an excuse to gain access to Fadda's apartment, then to attack him as he read it; and to leave it at the scene of the crime as a red herring to throw investigators off the track. In answer to this accusation, Cardinali explains that it was not he but De Luca who dictated the letter to threaten a man he believed was courting his wife. When the judge points out that De Luca's wife is not named Teresina Panzi, Cardinali answers that he wouldn't be able to explain the contradiction, because it was entirely De Luca's affair.

The hilarity that Cardinali's testimony causes in court comes from his inventive but contorted and entirely unconvincing efforts to explain away the most damning evidence. Vassallo remarks,

> Cardinali has a volubility and facility of speech I hope his lawyers can equal. But because of the difficulty of his situation, he does nothing but tangle and pile up one circumstance on another, such that you can't keep track of it. He has an insinuating voice that he modulates with the skill of a perfect comic actor. He repeats *good, good* over and over, even when he intends the opposite; his discourse is punctuated, seeded with *not at all* and *you must realize.* He gestures like an algebra teacher or anatomy professor who is cross that he hasn't been able to make his students understand the clearest and simplest thing in the world.[48]

Upon their arrival in Rome, Cardinali and De Luca register under false names at the *Locanda del Sole*. Because this hotel charges 3 lire per night for a room, they will subsequently change to the *Albergo delle Marmorelle*, a few steps from Fadda's apartment, where they will share a room with two other men for only 75 cents per night. Here also they give false names to the elderly woman who runs the establishment. At the front desk, they register a long knife with a triangular blade. The next morning Cardinali goes to Fadda's apartment but finds only the captain's orderly, who explains that Fadda is away from the city and won't return for some days.[49]

To explain why he would visit Fadda, a man he claims never to have met or seen, Cardinali presents a complicated tale of having met on the train a certain gentleman from Chieti who wished to present the gift of a small chest to Fadda, and that Cardinali had offered to help. The story is preposterous from the outset and the details have altered considerably since the accused first introduced it under interrogation. His description of the size and shape of the man from Chieti, as well as that of the chest, have changed markedly since the first questioning by investigators. The judge's ironic comments on these contradictions again spark loud laughter from the assembled audience. Rather than systematically following the chronology of the murderer's movements, the judge begins to respond improvisationally to Cardinali's lies by asking him to explain other actions that appear clearly and outrageously culpable. Why did the defendant give false names at the two hotels he registered in? If he came to Rome to audition for the Guillaume Circus, why didn't he bring his acrobatic equipment with him? How can he explain his words, overheard by the third occupant in the cheap hotel room: "We have to do it early in the morning; otherwise we'll be seen," and "Damn these women! Look what they drive us to!"? In answer to each, the defendant offers a tangled rationalization that draws rebuke from the judge and laughter from the audience.

Having learned from the orderly that the captain was away, Cardinali proceeded to the regimental headquarters for more information, only to discover that the captain had taken a short leave to go to Castrovillari, where his brother lived, an hour away from his wife's family's residence in Cassano. Thus victim and killer have crossed paths in opposite directions, Fadda carrying a box containing Raffaella's jewelry, Cardinali bearing a revolver and the knife with which he intends to kill the captain. Having come all the way to Rome to slay Fadda, Cardinali has found out to his surprise that captain has returned in the direction of Raffaella, possibly in hopes of a rapprochement.

Police examination of the crime scene has revealed that Fadda had removed a photograph of Raffaella from its position on the wall of the Roman apartment he had rented for the two of them. After their rupture in January, he had moved to smaller rooms, but rather than throwing the photo away, he had preserved it, enfolding it in a book.[50] In a similar way, the captain's last trip to Calabria to give back his wife's jewels may have been a definitive act of closure, the end of a process that began when he sent back her prized piano in January. But Fadda's trip may have had an opposite valence: perhaps he traveled 90 percent of the way back to his wife in the hope that she might learn of his presence nearby and take the initiative to come see him in a last-minute gesture of reconciliation. He had received official permission to stay in the South at least until the seventh, but when it became clear that Raffaella would not see him, Fadda cut short his leave and returned to Rome, where his orderly and military brethren remarked that he seemed despondent. A fellow captain of the Thirty-second remembered that he looked "as though existence were wearing him down (*gli logorava l'esistenza*)."

Upon his return to Rome, Fadda's orderly, a young soldier named Angelo Mattea, tells the captain that a man with an elaborate moustache, Calabrian cloak, and high riding boots had come to the door asking for him. Over the next several days, Fadda notices a man fitting that description who seems to be following him and even loitering for hours with another sinister figure at the inn on the piazza. On Saturday, the day before the murder, as the forlorn captain stands gazing out his second floor window onto the piazza, he notices the same man standing in the street across from his house. Fadda calls his orderly to the window, indicates the man, and asks whether that's the one who had come to his door. When the young soldier answers yes, the captain wonders aloud, "If he's looking for me, why doesn't he come to my house when he knows I'm home?"[51]

According to the prosecutor's reconstruction of the sequence of events leading to the murder, when he learns on Thursday that Fadda has gone to Calabria, Cardinali sends Carrozza the first of several coded telegrams. His urgent concern is to find out when Fadda will return to Rome, and whether, with Fadda nearby in Castrovillari, Raffaella might decide to see her husband, speak with him, and change her mind. On the evening of October 3, Cardinali sends a telegram to Carrozza using a circus jargon term, *vasca*:

> Facci conoscere vasca che lui trovasi Castrovillari presso suo fratello, vorrebbe sapere se è andato trovare essa se ha cambiato idea verso me rispondami.

This might be rendered in English as,

> Tell Vasca that he's in Castrovillari at his brother's, need to know if he went to see her, if (she) has changed her mind about me, answer me.

"Vasca," the court will learn, is a word with a wide range of possible meanings. If it is used here to refer to Raffaella, the telegram would constitute proof of a plot between Cardinali and Saraceni. On October 4, Carrozza sends a reply to Cardinali in Rome containing a much denser usage of circus jargon:

> Mamma latte detto tutto vasco non è andato vasca, vasca istessa, marco mamma andrà Castrovillari vedere vasco quando sbignerà.

A compound of Italian, condensed telegraphic syntax, and slang, this is virtually impossible to translate but might be rendered as:

> Mamma latte told everything, Vasco did not go Vasca, Vasca the same, Mamma's Marco will go to Castrovillari to see when Vasco will leave.

With the assistance of witnesses familiar with circus language, investigators have interpreted this telegram to mean:

> Mamma latte (literally, "Mother Milk", a reference to Raffaella's aged wetnurse, Maria Ferraro, suspected of complicity but not charged) has been told everything. Vasco (Fadda) did not go to see Vasca (Raffaella). Vasca (Raffaella) has not changed her feelings toward you. Marco Mamma (the husband of the wetnurse) will go to Castrovillari to find out when Vasco (Fadda) will depart for Rome.

Presented with this evidence, first by the investigating magistrate and now by the presiding magistrate during public deliberations, Cardinali objects to the court's translation of his words—saying for example that the jargon word for "captain" is not *vasco* but *capociano*—and concocts a story that the telegram refers instead to the clown named Carluccio who had abandoned the company, about whose whereabouts Cardinali claims to have received word from acquaintances met in Rome. Vassallo attempts to render Cardinali's explanation of the telegram for readers of the *Messaggero*, but appends an apology: "Readers will have understood nothing of this explanation, because it is incomprehensible even to he who made it up; however I have referred it as exactly as possible. Cardinali does nothing but pile words on words."[52] Coboevich instead inserts a parenthetical statement that "(at this point the accused wraps himself in a labyrinth of contradictions, countersense, and nonsense, repeatedly drawing hilarity from the audience)."[53]

Together with the open discussion of adultery and impotence, and the material presence of the bloody knife and letter, the role in the trial of the scabrous dialect of circus performers contributes to its scandalous fascination. Something hidden, a gruesome, menacing underside of human society was being exposed to public view. Mixing the overlapping concepts of language, dialect, and slang, Cesare Lombroso dedicates significant attention to the phenomenon of secret codes of criminal communication in the 1878 edition of his *Criminal Man*. Although a special lexicon is typical of many social groups, a private language is one of the identifying characteristics of the inveterate criminal, its invention motivated by the necessity of avoiding police observation.[54] Its very transmission is curious, suggesting invisible, subterranean connections: Why is it, Lombroso wonders, that Italy's known dialects tend to be regionally isolated, but Calabrian thieves share the same lexicon with those in distant Lombardy? The tendency to formulate a private jargon increases among individuals who practice the same trade, "especially if it is a dubious one, most of all among those compelled to a nomadic way of life and temporary stays, especially if they are subject to intimidation in the face of the public."[55] But the most basic explanation for the phenomenon of private languages among criminals resides in Lombroso's key concept of atavism: "They speak differently, because they feel differently; they speak like savages, because they are living savages in the midst of flourishing European civilization."[56] While the captain accountant was consulting his handy standard dictionary to write correspondence in Rome, clowns and acrobats in the hinterlands were scheming in the tongue of savages.

In court before judge and jury, it now remains for Cardinali to account for his actions on the morning of the captain's murder. As he awaited Fadda's return to Rome, he arranged to audition on Saturday, October 5, with the Guillaume Circus, then performing at the Politeama. The circus director, Emilio Guillaume, will be summoned to testify early in the trial and will confirm what he has already deposed: that he granted Cardinali an audition and found him to be quite a good acrobat, one capable of earning 400 lire a month. This figure might be compared with Captain Fadda's monthly salary, which, he mentions in a letter to his wife, was less than 200 lire. Guillaume did not hire the Calabrian performer, however, because of the man's furtive conduct; for example, Cardinali had come to the audition without his own costume and shoes, considered essential in the trade. Another Guillaume company performer, Giuseppe Pinta, known for his trained mule and dog acts (and whose face, Vassallo jibes, "takes on oenological nuances"), confirms his boss' words, remembering that Cardinali "was a good acrobat but refused to have a drink with me, and arrived without equipment."[57] Both circus people are asked what they know of the secret language of circus performers. Guillaume, with a ringmaster's aristocratic air, claims to know of the slang's existence but to be unfamiliar with it. Pinta tells the court that *vasco* and *vasca* mean *signore* and *signora* and that *marco* can mean either "boss" or "husband." Both men bow upon their exits and receive applause from the spectators in the courtroom.

Cardinali's alibi for his actions on the morning of Fadda's murder involves the gentleman from Chieti he claims to have met on the train to Rome. Cardinali says that he knocked at the captain's door early on the morning of Sunday, October 6, to inform him that the cabinetmaker from Chieti, who had a shop in Piazza Montecitorio, wished to consign a chest to Fadda before leaving the city. Cardinali asked that Fadda's orderly accompany him to Piazza Montecitorio to receive the box. Receiving Fadda's approval, Cardinali and Mattea proceeded to Montecitorio, only to find that the shop indicated by Cardinali as belonging to the cabinetmaker was closed. The equestrian then told the orderly that the man from Chieti must be in Piazza Venezia, saying, "Wait for me here, I'll go get him."

With this maneuver, Cardinali has drawn protection away from the man he is intent on killing. Fadda is now alone in his apartment, reading the newspaper in his underclothes. Cardinali's alibi continues: Failing to find the man from Chieti in Piazza Venezia, he returned to Piazza Montecitorio in search of the orderly, but not seeing him, he headed back toward his hotel. In the street he encountered De Luca looking pale and agitated, who asked him for 50 lire. Cardinali claims he gave money to De Luca and, disturbed by his appearance, he asked whether the horse groomer had fought with someone. Telling him no, De Luca took the money and disappeared in the direction of the Forum of Trajan. Cardinali's story here is transparently intended to shift guilt for the murder onto De Luca, who, having died in prison of tuberculosis in January, cannot defend himself. Proceeding on his way, Cardinali continues, he found himself in a street near the captain's house, where he suddenly heard cries and was shocked to be seized and accused by police officers.

The prosecutors offer a different interpretation: having stranded the orderly in Piazza Montecitorio, Cardinali returned, running, to recover his knife where he had left it, and then to Fadda's apartment, where he gained entry with the excuse of the false letter. When Fadda looked down to read the letter, Cardinali pulled out the blade and fatally stabbed the captain.

In the courtroom, the presentation of the knife creates a sensation. The judge astutely times its display so as to overwhelm a rising wave of increasingly intricate details in Cardinali's alibi; the brutal materiality of the knife cuts the tangled persuasion of the murderer's rhetoric. This critical moment of intense courtroom spectacle is precisely what the Fadda trial provides for the new nation, a moment when everyone, as individuals and as representatives of the state, pays attention to the same thing. Vassallo's description is particularly dramatic: "Commotion in the audience: the bailiffs are displaying a package; we realize that the knife is about to come out; as the strings and seals are broken, they give off a sinister snap. Widow Fadda hides her face in her handkerchief. From the galleries, people crane their necks and squint their eyes. A long dagger appears, its black horn handle streaked with yellow. The wide blade, as long as a man's hand, is horribly stained with blood."[58]

The notable divergence in the two reporters' descriptions of this sequence in the trial may be due to the fact that so much was going on, so much drama concentrated into one moment, that they were distracted from following the exact testimony. Coboevich describes Cardinali as turning his gaze away from the knife, as though to flee from looking at it. Vassallo tells us that Raffaella Saraceni weeps uncontrollably.[59] Several minutes later, the prosecution introduces the bloodstained false letter, signed "Teresina Panzi," which the murderer used to distract the captain before stabbing him. Found on the floor at the scene of the crime, the letter carries bootprints matching Cardinali's riding boots. The letter and boots are then passed around together, first among the jury, then on to the defense table for observation by the lawyers, and lastly, hand to hand among the seated and standing gentlemen of the press.[60]

The prosecutors argue that, mortally wounded, Fadda collapsed, at which Cardinali dropped the knife and fled, leaving bloody bootprints on the counterfeit letter. The coroner has reported that a sudden concentration of blood in the victim's crural artery must have blocked the outflow and momentarily returned enough circulation to Fadda's brain that he was able to rise again and stumble downstairs into the street, where he pointed after his killer. The victim's cry and those of passersby summoned the policemen from the barbershop, and Cardinali was arrested at the scene. In the trial archives, a court-hired architect's watercolor map rendering the respective locations of Fadda's apartment, the barbershop, and the point of arrest demonstrates that of four alternatives Cardinali chose the escape route that led him directly into the hands of the police. He could not have been more unlucky.

If the state's version of the events is true, it would appear that Cardinali's conduct since his arrival in Rome so patently trumpets his guilt as to make listeners marvel at the degree of the man's foolishness. Cardinali committed the classic blunder of yokels in the big city: imagining himself to be anonymous in the swarming crowd, he instead stuck out like a sore thumb. The government will produce numerous witnesses who describe with almost comic glee the acrobat's huge equestrian boots, his Calabrian cape, and the goatee he had shaved off at a barbershop the day before the murder. Apparently wishing to alter his appearance, Cardinali went to a barber and asked him to remove the goatee, except that, by using the Calabrian dialect word for goatee, *pizzo*, rather than the Roman one, *pappafico*, he sparked a conversation that the barber and his clients remember well. The false names he gives at hotels, the gun permit he brandishes proudly, the Northern accent he adopts, the explanation he gives that his long knife is for cutting horse tackle, all serve rather to draw attention to him than shift it away. In his testimony in open court, Cardinali employs the same incongruent mixture of superficial frankness and clumsy deviousness he applied to his conduct in Rome, with the result that he becomes a sort of clown version of the most negative stereotype of the Calabrian.

The audience leans forward as he speaks, anticipating with open mouth the next convoluted lie to trigger their delight. The president of the court responds to the defendant's testimony with witty, ironic remarks to spark spectators to laughter: "They don't call you *Francone* for nothing!"; "First he's an ox, now he's an ant!" (responding to Cardinali's changing description of the gentleman from Chieti); "It seems impossible: there's never been a case where the prosecutor agrees with the defendant!"[61] Not only is the trial a dramatic ritual, not only is it filled with salacious and gruesome detail. It is also *entertaining*.

Having dedicated most of the first day's inquiry to exposing the holes in Cardinali's testimony and displaying the material evidence against him, the judge's questioning late in the afternoon turns to his relations with women. There are at least four women with whom the acrobat appears to be having intimate relations to one degree or another at the time of the murder. Two are his codefendants in the trial. Cardinali explains that Antonietta Carrozza, the acrobatic equestrienne, "grew up in the company," meaning that she was adopted into the circus as a child and trained in the trade. Up to now, throughout his interrogations Cardinali has referred to Carrozza as his sister, but now in public he admits for the first time that she bore two children with him. Subsequent to his relations with Carrozza, Cardinali associated with another woman, Carolina Misuracca, who follows the company but is not a performer, and who has had three children from the acrobat.[62] She never appears at the trial and there is no record of an interrogation of her in the trial archives. Preceding and continuous with his apparently common-law marriage and his relations with Antonietta Carrozza, Cardinali has also been maintaining an intense epistolary relationship with a fan named Amalia (a woman in her forties from Molise, the wife of a prison contractor) who sends Cardinali gifts and puerile romantic letters on lacey, perfumed stationery. Forty such letters are included in the trial archive.

Then there is Raffaella. By the beginning of the second day of the trial, on October 1, the court and public's attention is beginning to shift to widow Saraceni. The later questioning of Cardinali dwells on his acquaintance with the woman accused of being his lover. The *cavallerizzo* denies having had more than a cordial acquaintance with her. As the defendant speaks, the audience's gaze continuously moves over to the alleged instigator of the crime, seated slightly behind him, who appears too engulfed in grief even to watch the proceedings. As Coboevich describes it: "On Raffaella Saraceni's face, always the same expression of pain; she appears distant from everything happening around her; perhaps she doesn't hear what's being said. She certainly can't see what's going on, because she never raises her eyes. The public watches her with interest, one would say even with a certain sympathy. Carrozza too has composed the same look of grief onto her visage. But what a difference between Raffaella Saraceni and Antonietta Carrozza!"[63]

The first press descriptions of Saraceni after the crime concluded that her character was not such as to achieve the stature of the great adulterous heroines, but with her appearance at the trial, public opinion begins to alter. "Saraceni is weeping for real," reports Vassallo. Coboevich notes the shift in sentiment toward her in the courtroom; the difference in style and class between the widow and her fellow defendants grants her a contrastive dignity. Rumors begin to circulate of her exemplary conduct in the Buon Pastore women's prison, where it is said she has bought meals for the less fortunate detainees and offers them lessons.

Against the testimony of numerous inhabitants of Cassano all'Ionio, Cardinali insists that he and Saraceni were mere acquaintances. The acrobat claims to have been a good friend of Raffaella's brother, Giuseppe, while Antonietta Carrozza was close to Raffaella, the four having met 12 years ago during an earlier tour through the Calabrian provinces. Cardinali uses this four-cornered friendship to explain why he dined so often in the Saraceni household, why he stayed and slept there for some days even after the company moved their tents to Corigliano, and why the four exchanged letters and gifts, with Cardinali sometimes serving as messenger of notes between the two women. The acrobat further insists that the 500 lire found on his person at the moment of his arrest came not from Raffaella, but were the income from a benefit performance in his honor held several nights before he left the company for Rome.

The prosecution completes its questioning of Cardinali. Now Raffaella Saraceni rises to answer the court. The judge addresses her: "Defendant Saraceni, stand: You are accused of having facilitated the murder of your husband. How do you reply? *Saraceni*: What can I say? I am an unfortunate wretch (Sono una disgraziata); I invoke justice for the crime that has taken place. I can say no more."[64]

In her study of the Fadda trial, "The Theatre of Justice: Guilty Women and Public Opinion in Liberal Italy," Angela Groppi concentrates especially on Raffaella Saraceni's performance during the trial and its effects on public sentiment.[65] In response to the prosecution's characterization of her as a debased, depraved creature of lust, Groppi observes, Saraceni's defense adopts three tactics to fully exploit to her advantage the opposite reigning stereotypes of bourgeois femininity: first, "dressed in black and with modest manner, she presents herself as a poor, afflicted widow deserving compassion."[66] Cloaked in mourning dress, veiled eyes ever downcast, fingers clutching a white handkerchief, her continuous, quiet weeping is broken only by an occasional loud sob. As the trial enters its third week, Vassallo reports, "Saraceni's eyes are red, her nose violet, and for a half hour she cries hot tears, just as she did at the first sessions."[67]

The second tactic is stressed especially by her lead attorney, Enrico Pessina, the illustrious penal expert and theorist, admired as much for his deep compassion and integrity as for his patriotism (he had been incarcerated under the Bourbons in Naples). Despite his defendant's denials, Pessina implicitly acknowledges Raffaella's adultery, but without appearing to excuse it, he explains it as a biologically determined outcome of her inability to bear a child due to her husband's impotence. According to this strategy, Raffaella Saraceni is a victim, not a perpetrator. Not lust, but frustrated maternity may have driven her into the clutches of a scheming assassin, but she could never have wished her husband dead. Groppi cites Pessina's plaintive appeal, "What is a house without children? Is it not a spring without flowers?"[68] "Although I profess myself a spiritualist," Pessina adds, "You cannot deny, ladies and gentlemen, that the flesh is sometimes an emanation of the spirit," an ambiguous statement that evokes the era's growing fascination with spiritualism, but serves here to legitimate sexual desire as a manifestation of spiritual longing.[69] Despite his opposition to the determinism of Cesare Lombroso's criminal anthropology, the great penalist draws on the Veronese scientist's thesis that frustrated maternity leads women inevitably toward crime because their natural destiny has been thwarted.[70] Lombroso's follower, Scipio Sighele, will write in a treatise on women titled *Eva moderna* that "woman is an enigma whose solution is called maternity."[71]

As a third tactic, employed particularly during the appeal after the initial verdict is handed down, the defense team brings attention to Raffaella's actions as a "guardian angel" of the other detainees in Buon Pastore. In performance of this strategy, Saraceni has invited her codefendant Carrozza to dine with her in prison. When they learn of it, the prosecution lawyers of the *parte civile* rise in court to object to this practice; there must be no fraternization among the defendants, as it contaminates testimony and increases the likelihood of a mistrial. Prosecutors complain particularly that information about Saraceni's conduct has circulated in the press, distorting public opinion in her favor. The court summons the chief guardian of the prison to respond to the charge that she has allowed the two women to dine together. The uncowed head guardian, an elderly nun who makes the court wait several days before she arrives to testify and is inclined to brook no nonsense from secular judges or attorneys, confirms the rumor, justifying her permissiveness by explaining that "once they were released from isolation, they dined together. Saraceni has a good heart, and also gave the other detainees the food that was prepared for her."[72] The defense seizes on the opportunity to demand a mistrial on procedural grounds, but after consultation, the chief judge insists on carrying forward with the trial. The prosecution's objection has backfired on them, tilting the audience further in Raffaella's favor.

The irregularities at Buon Pastore are a result of the still-incomplete transition from papal to secular rule in Rome. Run by a female conventual order modeled on the Jesuits, Buon Pastore had been established in 1615 as a charitable, penitential institution for women of all kinds who had fallen outside the strict confines of social order, including those abandoned by their husbands or families, prostitutes, syphilitics, and the insane. After 1871, the new government transformed Buon Pastore from a Casa della Penitenza (literally, a house of penitence) to a Carcere Giudiziario, a prison for female offenders. But the nuns remained in charge and carried on the institution's multiple functions as convent, insane asylum, reformatory, and school for wayward women, as well as a piecework factory for the textile industry.[73] By allowing the two female defendants to dine together, therefore, the chief nun is simultaneously obeying the pope's dictum of *non expedit*, the refusal of Catholics to collaborate with the secular government; reclaiming the traditional charitable and therapeutic function of her house and order over the new state's carceral, punitive regime; and resisting, in the name of female solidarity, an intrusive, presumptuous male power structure. The court is forced to bend to her authority, and Raffaella Saraceni emerges from the procedural contretemps looking like a victim.

The Roman daily *La Capitale* describes Saraceni as "the sad heroine of the Fadda trial."[74] A Genoese paper will report that shortly after sentences are handed down, an unbalanced priest arrived at the gate of Saraceni's prison, offering to serve her sentence in exchange for Raffaella's freedom.[75] In 1881, Alfonso Zara will publish a play, *The Murder of Captain Fadda*, portraying Raffaella as a helpless victim of her father's social ambitions, a diabolical Cardinali, and an unqualified jury.[76] "In the face of the accusation of having broken the law," Groppi explains, "Women immediately return, or demonstrate having returned, to the role that society imposes on them, and make use of the codes of feminine weakness and male domination to justify their infractions and negotiate their destiny."[77] The portrait of Raffaella in the Bracco publication of the trial confirms Groppi's assertion: her relentless crying, we might say, "brands" her sympathetically in public sentiment as "the weeping widow."

The first question posed to Saraceni by the court concerns not her material guilt, but her failure to enact her proper role: the judge asks why, when she first received word of her husband's death, "You didn't cry, you didn't abandon yourself to that act, which another woman in your situation would have abandoned herself to?"[78] The defendant replies that she responded first with shock, but cried later in her room, adding, "And I have

Figure 4.3 The Weeping Widow

Source: Illustration from *Processo Fadda illustrato*

been crying ever since." In contrast to the acrobat's disastrous performance, Saraceni's immediately garners the audience's sympathy. Vassallo observes, "She is more firm than we expected. Her voice is quite sweet. She speaks clearly and with good pronunciation." Coboevich notes that her answers are "frank and explicit, given without a shadow of cunning," and that her state provokes compassion in her listeners.[79]

In substance, Saraceni denies. She denies knowing that her husband was impotent, insists that their disagreements and separations were no different from those of any other married couple. The rumors circulating thickly about her conduct with various men in Cassano are strictly mean-spirited, small-town gossip. She admits that when they lived together in Chieti her husband one day surprised her as she wrote a letter that began with the greeting, "Dear Edoardo," but she explains that the letter was to her uncle Edoardo, and she only tore it up as soon as her husband saw it because it contained complaints against him; they had been arguing that day about something foolish and small. She dismisses as calumny the testimony of Fadda's orderly that one day in Chieti she had sent him away in order to entertain a male friend. In response to a reading by the court of a poem found in Fadda's rooms, transcribed and slightly adapted from a Neapolitan newspaper, in which a man accuses the woman he loves of having betrayed him, Saraceni answers simply, "I never received that poem, and my husband was no poet."[80] She denies having known Cardinali or Carrozza more than casually. When the judge brings her initial questioning to an end after less than half a day, Raffaella Saraceni appears to have begun to bend the sentiments of the spectators in her direction. The public sympathizes with her even as it recognizes that she is almost certainly lying when she claims to know nothing about her husband's supposed impotence and about her relations with Cardinali. The jury may ultimately judge her differently, but they have a much narrower responsibility than does public opinion. In any case, the jury is composed entirely of men selected through a process designed to weed out those likely to vote on the basis of extralegal considerations.

Raffaella testifies on October 1, the second day of the trial. On the trial's penultimate day, October 30 (before the verdicts and sentences are rendered on the 31), in the final speech given, Enrico Pessina presents his stirring appeal for the acquittal of his client, in which he offers his version of how Captain Fadda came to be murdered. According to Pessina, Raffaella Saraceni is, indeed, a fallen woman; her frustrated maternal cravings compelled her to betray her husband. However, the plot to murder him was entirely an invention of her deluded lover. All the testimony pointing to Raffaella's direct participation in the scheme can be easily impugned, argues Pessina, because it comes from unreliable sources: from the dead

De Luca, from Cardinali's cellmate in Rome, and from a circus clown. The 500 lire found on Cardinali at the time of his arrest must have come from the performer's own savings, Pessina insists, rather than from the wealthy Saracenis, and the incriminating coded telegrams between Cardinali and Antonietta Carrozza cannot be proven ever to have been communicated to Raffaella. Pessina is even willing to suggest that it is more likely that Raffaella's mother knew of the murder plot than Raffaella herself.

Pessina's defense is a rhetorical masterpiece; reporters tell how both fellow attorneys on the Saraceni side and those against him rush to embrace and congratulate him when he concludes, to a ringing ovation and cheers from the assembled audience. But it implicitly asks the jury to accept that Raffaella has perjured herself from the outset by continuing to deny that she and Cardinali were lovers or even that she knew anything of her husband's impotence. In effect, the lawyer is asking the court and jury to grant his defendant her weakness for having submitting to the wiles of a scheming intriguer, and at the same time to recognize her obligation, in the name of honor, to publicly deny her sins. Pessina's strategy appears to work on public sentiment both inside and outside the courtroom. But he will not convince the jury, which on October 31 finds Saraceni guilty together with Cardinali. The esteemed lawyer will become Minister of Justice in November 1884, serving until May 8 of the following year. Later that month, Raffaella Saraceni's life sentence will be commuted to time served, freeing her to return to her family.[81]

5

In Corte d'Assise

In fancy hats, they lean out from the oval gallery, the better to see the woman in the cage and hear every word of testimony. Some open fans against their lips, as though to hold in their own breath. Others peer through binoculars, purchased for the opera but perfect for this new purpose. Ruffled hats sport flowers. Lace sprouts from satin sleeves. Fur lines collars, fur capes rest on the backs of chairs, fur muffs sit in laps. Listening and anticipation are intense, but one lady whispers into her giggling neighbor's ear; the woman on her other side, finger to lips, hushes them. Others have ordered coffee, now being poured by a waiter and his boy. Female customers and their male servers try to reduce the rattle of china and clink of coins as they perform the transaction without removing their eyes from the court below; one of the ladies is so distracted that she's about to spill her coffee over the balustrade onto the packed crowd.

Figure 5.1 Francesco Netti, *In Corte d'Assise*

Source: By kind permission of the Pinactoteca Provinciale di Bari

In the background, on the opposite balcony, they are all men, but their angle of view is poor compared to that of the women's gallery.[1] Because of the way the courtroom has been set up within Borromini's chamber, the men have to stand dangerously up against the edge of the balcony and lean out to get a clear view of the accused in her hat and veil, as she covers her mouth and chin with a handkerchief. From our point of view behind the ladies, we can just see the bars of the *gabbione*, the waist-high railing used in Italian courtrooms to contain incarcerated defendants. The term *gabbione* suggests a large cage, but a journalist has facetiously remarked that the courtroom is so crowded that rather than prohibiting escape, the *gabbione* serves to reserve the accused their seats. On both sides of the defendant dressed in mourning black, the red plumes of the carabinieri guards stand erect. In the painting's perspective, the bayonet point of one guard almost seems to touch her chin. On the curving wall of the balcony just beneath the spectators in the opposite gallery, we cannot fully make out the final words of an inscription in Italian: "-UALE PER TUTTI" (that is, "-QUAL FOR ALL").[2] The marble plaques on the walls of the gallery carry epigraphs in Latin. In the painting's dissolving perspective, they are only partly readable: DIALECTICA (unreadable) RATIONIS, AEQUITAS (unreadable) ARBITRA, ETICA MORUM EMENDATRIX, ELOQUENTIA ANIMORUM DOMINATRIX. How many in the gallery crowd have the education to be able to decipher the messages in the venerated, ancient language of religion and law?[3]

At the far right edge of the painting, one woman grabs our attention more than any other because we see her in profile rather than from behind. She has retired from the balcony edge to sit back fully in her chair, resting her hands in her muff, as though taking a moment to reflect on the scene before her. Although exposed to view, her expression is inward, fixed, and difficult to read. Is it avidity, scorn, or bitter regret? Only in the lips can we read something, but we can't make out whether she is reacting to the tearful witness' testimony or rather to a thought those words have provoked within herself. In the version of this image published as an engraving in the Milanese illustrated weekly, *L'Illustrazione italiana*, her expression is radically simplified, translated for readers at home into a stereotypical look of malicious glee.[4]

The painting, *In Corte d'Assise*, dated 1882, records a moment of Raffaella Saraceni's testimony in the early days of the Fadda trial. The image doesn't represent the trial itself so much as the phenomenon of the trial, the fact that crowds of well-dressed, attractive young women flocked to the daily hearings, finagled tickets, and breathlessly followed every word of testimony, every twist and turn in the case. The painter, Francesco Netti, was from a landowning Southern family.[5] Since coming to Rome after several years in Paris, he had turned away from rendering mythical and historical scenes to dramatic moments of modern life, such as this trial, or another showing the aftermath of a suicide in Venice, with passersby gazing down at the body of a woman who has thrown herself out a window onto the narrow street below. Netti was more recognized as a critic than as a painter. In a review of the great 1883 National Exposition of Modern Art in Rome, where he displayed his own *In Corte d'Assise*, he criticized an artist who still relied on mythological, historical subjects (in this case, the legend of Virginia), saying, "The murder yesterday of an unknown person, reported in the local crime news, interests me far more than this famous parricide described by Livy."[6] The statement sounds like a phrase from a manifesto, and in fact, the painter-critic is here identifying himself as a fellow traveler, if not an adept, of verismo, the Italian realist school opposed to reliance on academic, historical, or pastoral/arcadian subject matter. Netti was fascinated with the new generation of women: one of his works, *Reading*, shows a young woman, probably the artist's sister, in a modest bourgeois interior, midmorning light, drinking coffee as she reads an illustrated newspaper, perhaps *L'Illustrazione italiana*.[7] The scene suggests not the leisure of the propertied class but rather a pause between chores. In another Netti work, *The Post-prandial Cigarette*, a plump woman in black reclines on a red velvet couch, smoking a cigarette with a great air of pleasure and self-enjoyment.[8] Large-featured, appearing somewhat packed into her dress, the woman looks like a person who runs a household; her moment of enjoyment comes either from having completed her tasks for the day or because this evening, for once, someone else has done the work.

Netti has been to Paris and his work combines specifically Italian interests with progressive developments happening in France. Certainly from Courbet, and perhaps from Manet, he may have drawn the objective factuality of the scene in tension with the way the paint adheres on the surface. The tilted, partial point of view in *Corte d'Assise* recalls Degas, an ellipse tense within the rectangular confines of the frame, and like many of the French artist's racetrack scenes, we watch more audience than action. We observe observers. The women in the gallery look down through opera glasses toward another woman, much like themselves, whose handkerchief, dabbing her eyes, partly conceals her expression. From our position behind the spectators, we see more ears than noses, while the focus of the watchers' attention is farther down, away from us. Our eyes begin to sweep around the balustrade, but we are interrupted, distracted by the gloved hand of the spectator closest to us, its silk fabric orange like cherrywood, not without a certain erotic charge. The curve of the arm and hand in the foreground create a visual path to the tiny figure of the defendant at the center of the painting. The glove's raised thumb forms a straight line with the carabinieri's bayonet, pointing at the accused woman's head. Each enclosed finger distinct, the excited hand presses tentatively against the cold marble balustrade as though ready to draw back in surprise and scandal at some new monstrosity rising up from below. Why are all these well-dressed women so absorbed by what they see down there? Why the intense push and pull of their attention?

The figure is unrecognizable at this distance, but it could be no one but Raffaella Saraceni, the grieving young wife, now widow, at the center of the trial. Although not visible in the painting, the man she is accused of loving adulterously and inciting to kill her husband is sitting only inches away from her. She pleads innocence, she denies everything. The primary action in the painting consists of the three bands of color: the dark white marble of the curving balustrade; the flaming rose of the women's excited faces, their flowers and fans; and above that, the blacks of their hats, connecting around with the dark suits in the men's gallery on the other side. The arc of the marble balcony begins lower left foreground and carries low toward the middle right edge, then slants away in perspective around the men's gallery, circling back across the painting's upper surface, finally disappearing off left. The arrangement of spectators around an ellipse (evocative of Jean-Léon Gérome's *Phryne before the Areopagus*, 1861, another painting of a woman alone before a court) has a multiple function. An apparently eyewitness representation of the trial and thus a statement of verismo, it also links the oval amphitheater of the courtroom to two forms of circular performance: the contemporary equestrian circus and the ancient games in the Roman Coliseum. In his painting, Netti evokes the modern circus to remind viewers that the accused murderer in this sensational trial was a *cavallerizzo*, a bareback equestrian who performed his stunts around the circus ring. Netti's elliptical composition also pointedly evokes the arena of the Coliseum. Thus the painting declares a double inspiration: the trial itself, certainly, but even more specifically, the denunciatory poem by Giosue Carducci, "On the Fadda Trial," which appeared in the top left column of the sophisticated weekly, *Fanfulla della Domenica*, while the trial was under way, on October 19, 1879. In it, Italy's bard of the Risorgimento harshly compares the excited modern women who attend the Fadda trial to Roman matrons exalting at bloody scenes of combat and death in the Coliseum (as pictured in Gerome's *Pollice Verso*, 1872). Before *In Corte d'Assise*, Netti had painted a classical scene representing the aftermath of gladiatorial combat, with the helmeted victor dragging the corpse of the vanquished loser along a narrow city street in Pompeii past a banquet, where intoxicated revelers look on with jaded mien as young women crowd excitedly around the winner. This painting was reproduced for mass dissemination in *Illustrazione italiana*, where it was interpreted as an admonitory commentary on cultural decline:

> (The painting) is a page from the customs of the epoch of the decadence of Imperial Rome and reflects the bloody practices, the tiredness of the pleasures, the luxury, the lust, and the ferocity of a world about to collapse.[9]

Netti's Pompeii scene, that is, uses a classical theme to comment on contemporary moral decadence. The subsequent *In Corte d'Assise* portrays a modern scene, but the circular composition and the spectatorial view from above allude explicitly to the Coliseum and to Carducci's apostrophic epode evoking the fall of Roman Empire. Where Carducci's poem (echoing the invective characteristic of its model, the Horatian epodes) is harsh and lacerating, however, Netti's painting is festive and its satire is allusive; we are drawn to the image by the gaiety and color of female movement swirling around the foreground edges, all bright murmuring and rustling silk. Only as our gaze settles do we notice the hushed, tragic scene unfolding in the central background, slightly beyond focus: the weeping woman in mourning flanked by the carabinieri. Carducci instead names the trial in his title, then describes a scene of ancient brutality, only to contrast imperial Roman spectacle with its modern counterpart, which the poet charges with being equally if not more morally repugnant, because the stately, leonine women of classical Rome have been replaced by chattering, snack-munching adulteresses:

A Proposito del Processo Fadda

I.

Da i gradi alti del circo ammantellati
di porpora, esse ritte
ne i lunghi bissi, gli occhi dilatati,
le pupille in giù fitte,
abbassavano il pollice nervoso
de la mano gentile.
Ardea fra bianche nuvole estuoso
il sol primaverile
su le superbe, e ne la nera chioma
mettea lampeggiamenti.
Fremea la lupa nudrice di Roma
da i lor piccoli denti,
bianchi, affilati fra le labbra rosse

A loose translation:

I.

Seated on high in the circus, mantled
in purple, the women, erect
In their long togas, eyes dilated,
pupils fixed on the scene below
Turn down nervous thumbs
in their delicate hands.
In estrus among white clouds,
the spring sun blazed
over the proud women, flashed like lightning
in their ebony locks.
As the nursing mother-wolf of Rome seethed,
their fine white teeth
sharp between red lips

contratte in fiero ghigno.	contracted in a fierce grimace.
Un selvatico odor su da le fosse	A savage odor rose from the pit
vaporava maligno.	on waves of malignant vapor.
Era il sangue del mondo che fervea	The blood of the world was steaming
con lievito mortale,	with its mortal yeast,
su cui provava già Nemesi dea	over which Goddess Nemesis tested the wind,
al vol prossimo l'ale.	ready to take wing,
E le nipoti di Camilla, pria	And the nephews of Camilla, before
di cedere le mani	offering their hands
ai ferri, assaporavan l'agonia	to the irons, savoured the agony
de' cerulei Germani.	of the blue-eyed Huns.
II.	II.
Voi sgretolate, o belle, i pasticcini	You bite down, lovely ladies, on your snacks
fra il palco e la galera;	between the stage and cell.
ed intente a fornir di cittadini	Intent on furnishing citizens
la nuova italica era,	for the new era of Italy,
studiate (o professor Giovanni Rizzi,	You study (oh professor Giovanni Rizzi,
anche questo è ideale)	this too is the Ideal)
gli abbracciamenti dei cavalerizzi	The embraces of circus horsemen
fra i colpi di pugnale;	with slashing knives
e palpate con gli occhi abbracciatori	and stroke with clinging eyes
le schiene ed i toraci,	their backs and torsos,
mentre rei gerghi fra sucidi odori	As criminal tongues confess kisses
testimonian su i baci.	in the stink of sweat.
Poi, se un puttin di marmo avvien che mostri	Then, if a marble *putto* happens to show
qualcosellina al sole,	some little something in the light of day,
protesterete con furor d'inchiostri,	you will protest with storms of ink,
con fulmin di parole;	with thunderbolts of words;
e pur ieri cullaste il figliuoletto	But just yesterday you rocked your baby
tra i notturni fantasmi	amid nocturnal fantasies
co'l piè male proteso fuor dal letto	With naked foot sticking out of the bed
ne gli adulteri spasmi.	in your adulterous spasms.
Ma voi siete cristiane, o Maddalene!	But you are Christians, O Magdalenes!
foste da' preti a scuola.	Schoolgirls under priests no more
Siete moderne! avete ne le vene	You are modern! In your veins
l'Aretino e il Loiola.[10]	run Aretino and Loyola.

In the first stanza, patrician Roman matrons, monumental despite their arousal and hunger for blood, turn down quivering thumbs to condemn to death a wounded gladiator in the Coliseum below. The women are described as the she-wolf mother of Rome who suckled Romulus and Remus, white teeth sharp behind red lips contracted in a savage grimace. From the massacred bodies in the pit arise waves of heat, thick with the odor of blood and death, upon which the goddess of vengeance prepares to take flight, an allusion to the providential and just collapse of the Roman Empire, spurred by barbarian invasions, slave revolts, and the advent of Christianity. The very women who now take pleasure in watching the agony of the Huns will soon become their slaves.[11]

The second section harshly compares modern society ladies to the imperial matrons of the first. The new generation loudly chews snacks while vicariously swooning to the gross, bloody passions recounted by criminals speaking in low dialects. The Coliseum has become a modern courtroom, the dilated pupils of the Roman matrons become the eyes of fashionable young wives and mothers, greedy to cling and clutch the brawny trunk of a knife-wielding, treacherous circus horseman, whose malevolent violence stands against the victimized, blue-eyed Hun of the first stanza. Carducci's condemnation of the women at the Fadda trial attacks their hypocrisy with ironic reference to two current topics presumably familiar to readers of the *Fanfulla*. His mocking allusion to professor Giovanni Rizzi's principle of the *ideal* strikes a blow in the battle waged in the journals between those poets, like Carducci, who insisted that poetry deal with the reality of modern life, against those, such as Rizzi, for whom poetry's duty was to incarnate an ideal unsullied by vulgar actuality.[12] These lines will disappear from later editions of the poem; Carducci's polemic with Rizzi softened over time as the bard abandoned his youthful "satanic" poetics (lines 29 and 30 become, "Studiate, e gli occhi mobili dan guizzi/Di feroce ideale,").[13] Line 13 of the second stanza condemns the women spectators for their hypocrisy by making reference to the sort of public brouhaha that might accompany the unveiling of a marble statue portraying a putto urinating. Carducci is suggesting that the women who attend the trial, avid for salacious testimony about adultery and impotence, are the same as the types of ladies who write high-minded letters to newspapers to object to artistic nudity in public places.[14] In fact, line two in Carducci's first version of this stanza referring to the putto, "Un po' di pipi al sole" (A little peepee in the sunshine), was censored and altered by Ferdinando Martini, editor of the *Fanfulla*, to the euphemistic "qualcosellina al sole," (a little something in the sunshine) apparently to avoid offending the same hypocritical propriety that Carducci wishes to condemn.[15] In his commentaries in the *Fanfulla* Martini often targets the excesses of the Italian *veristi*, whom he accuses of being too eager to record in detail the trivial indecencies of modern life.[16] Carducci's evocation of a spray of urine sparkling in the sun—although the poet is speaking of a marble fountain—apparently struck the editor as too vivid. This is only one of many episodes of censorship of Carducci imposed by editors, more often for reasons of propriety than politics.[17]

The poet's irony becomes harshest in the penultimate stanza, with a portrayal of a mother fantasizing (or having) adulterous sex who reaches a naked leg out from her bed to rock her baby's cradle, even while in the throes of orgasm. So extreme is the poet's imagery here that one critic has spoken of "the ambiguous fascination exercised on the author by the sado-erotic components of the crime," which is to say that, in the heatedness of his denunciation, the poet betrays his arousal, provoked by the image hovering irresistibly over the trial of the rough acrobat and young wife having illicit sex, and by the impassioned spectatorship of the act by hordes of fashionable young women.[18]

Many readers objected to Carducci's decision to write on the Fadda trial and to the blunt language he adopted to evoke its most salacious aspects. Shortly after the poem's publication, the poet wrote to Martini, asking, "What do you and my friends say about 'On the Fadda Trial?' Have you too joined in the general excommunication?"[19] The *Osservatore romano*, already hostile to the "satanic" poet, described"On the Fadda Trial," as "one of the most abominable poems ever to have come from his pen."[20] The Catholic paper's objection was not to the parallelism the poet draws between the decadent matrons of pagan Rome and their modern, secular counterparts—a charge with which they most strongly concurred, finding themselves strangely in concord with a man they regarded as a demon incarnate—but rather they took vehement exception to his graphic depiction of feminine ecstasy and to the blame he assigned to religious hypocrisy.

The poem's last stanza directs an apostrophe to the women watching the trial. He reproaches them as Magdalenes (opposed inevitably to Madonnas), whose vaunted modernity means that rather than being educated in modesty by decent, humble clerics, they have been trained in corruption by such as the Renaissance priest Pietro Aretino (recalled for his pornographic writings) and by the founder of the Jesuit Order and the Inquisition, Ignatius of Loyola, whom the staunch secularist Carducci regards as the embodiment of ecclesiastical venality.

At this point in his career, the poet is in a moment of transition; his republican fervor is waning, discouraged by the sprawling vulgarity of the emerging Italian citizenry that has trampled underfoot the poet's idea of patriotic democracy. In 1876 Carducci was elected to Parliament as an antimonarchist Republican, but by the next year had already allowed his term to run out and did not care to renew it. In July 1878, he still refused to swear fealty to the crown to receive a literary prize, but in November of that year, one month after the Fadda murder, he met the new queen, Margaret, and within two weeks had written his ode, "Alla Regina d'Italia" (To the Queen of Italy), exalting her as the divine incarnation of the feminine spirit of his nation, despite her foreign origins. His brutal invective against the modern women of Rome in "A proposito del processo Fadda" of 1879 is thus a reverse image of his apotheosis of the queen. In 1882 Carducci will publish in a Roman periodical, the *Cronaca Bizantina*, an account of his meeting with the queen titled "Eterno femminino regale," in which he identifies Margaret as the "eternal feminine" and justifies his special devotion to her, mixing the rhetoric of political tactics with that of the *dolce stil novo*, speaking as a troubadour dazzled by the more than human poise and perfection of his beloved.[21]

In "A proposito del processo Fadda," Carducci accuses the female spectators of being guilty of the same crime, perpetrated against Italy itself, that Raffaella Saraceni was alleged to have committed against her soldier husband.[22] Politics aside, the highly visible presence of mothers, wives, and unmarried young women at the trial seemed to betoken the collapse of the Italian family. Those who attended the trial in person represented only the tip of an iceberg consisting of the millions of women throughout the peninsula reading about the trial and heatedly discussing its most minute details with their friends and neighbors. Why weren't these women at home instead, looking after their babies, their households, their husbands, and nurturing the next generation of secular leaders? The disgrace of women's interest in the Fadda scandal bothered the Risorgimento conscience because the conduct of the ladies seemed the realization of the Church's threats about what female literacy would lead to.

The poem appears in the October 19 *Fanfulla*. When the trial reopens at 11 a.m. the next morning, news of the poet's condemnation of the female spectators has already been so widely disseminated that one of the defense attorneys begins his remarks with a response to Carducci's diatribe. Before he moves to defend his client, Antonietta Carrozza, advocate Carlo Palomba first offers to the court and nation a defense of the women of the public. Contrary to what the poet has charged, the mothers of Rome are not munching pastries up there in the galleries, Palomba avers, nor are they followers of Aretino and Loyola. Rather they have come as compassionate witnesses to the tragedy of a valorous son of the nation whose medal of honor was unable, by fatal chance, to protect his breast from an assassin's stiletto.[23] The lawyer's remarks acknowledge that passive spectators had become active protagonists in the trial's symbolic drama, that the media are playing a crucial role in the determination of guilt and innocence, and that it was not only the defendants who were on trial in this case. Palomba also implies that Fadda had been stabbed in the heart, when in fact the fatal blow had been to the area of his groin. The poet ascribed women's attraction to the trial to the vicarious, decadent desire to experience the embrace of a rough equestrian, while the lawyer objected that they were drawn, rather, out of patriotic devotion to a martyred soldier, hero of the Risorgimento. Vassallo the journalist offered a third view, *contra* both Carducci and Palomba: "The ladies have gone to the trial not to see Cardinali, but to see the lady, the image of themselves."[24] Three contemporary commentators make an effort to draw conclusions about the troubling phenomenon of women's fascination with the Fadda trial. The poet's, the writer's, and the journalist's views are not mutually exclusive and each may have its partial validity. Most significant however is the common trait among the authors: none of them thought to actually ask the women who attended the trial why they did so.

"A proposito del processo Fadda" is the climactic application of poetry to the Fadda case, but it is by no means the only one. A street singer's tale of the Fadda case, which must have been composed and performed around the time the sentences were handed down, narrates the facts of the crime and recapitulates Carducci's view of the trial in Roman dialect, but with great concision and appealing humor. In telling the story, the singer claims to have been present in the Piazza of the Golden Keys on the morning of the murder, to have heard Fadda's cries for help and witnessed the commotion. Composed in the traditional meter of Italian epic poetry, in octaves (ABABABCC) of hendecasyllables, the account of the trial begins about midway through the poem with this stanza (approximate translation, without respect for line or meter, on the right):

Intanto le tribune so aripiene	Meanwhile all the galleries are packed
De tutte ste regazze e ste signore	With these girls and these ladies
Che se vanno a gustà tutte le scene,	Who go to enjoy the whole scene
E senza sta a guardà tanto ar pudore	And with few scruples as to modesty
Se mettono a sinti le cose uscene	Sit there and listen to the obscenities
Che Carluccio riconta co' calore.	That Carluccio describes salaciously
E tutte po' rideveno in presenza,	And they all laughed openly
Quanno che se parlava d'impotenza.[25]	When the subject turned to impotency.

From before the crime to after sentencing, parties high and low adopt poetry as a tool to shift the events into a more exalted rhetorical key, first to bespeak a particular viewpoint in the most eloquent, convincing form possible, and second, to exploit poetry's purported capacity to lift experience onto a higher plain of meaning in contrast to the essential transience and linguistic contamination characteristic of journalistic prose.

The first to make use of poetry is Captain Fadda himself. In May 1878, during the most angry phase of relations with his distant wife, he discovered a poem titled "Disprezzo" (Scorn) in a Neapolitan newspaper and transcribed it, slightly altered, perhaps with the intention of mailing it to Raffaella. In the poem, a furious, deeply hurt man condemns his beloved's perfidious infidelity, referencing her "infernal smile" and "tumid lips," and closing with the contemptuous, exclamation-pointed gesture of rejection indicated in the title. Fadda's handwritten draft, found among his letters, was released to journalists during the investigative phase of the trial and widely published. It was first attributed to the captain himself and only to its proper author after it appeared in the papers, when the uncredited poet wrote in to complain of the misattribution. During interrogations and again in open court, Raffaella Saraceni is asked to answer whether her husband ever sent her a copy of "Disprezzo," and why he might have done so. She insists that she never received the poem, adding, "And my husband was no poet," a dry remark that suggests that her accountant husband would never have thought, in happier times, of performing the opposite gesture of sending her a poem expressing his affection and esteem.

Next, during the second week of the trial, Vassallo comes across a poem titled "Pietro il saltimbanco" by a Calabrian author, Nicola Misasi, published in Cosenza earlier in the year. The reporter reprints excerpts of this heavy-handed, melodramatic composition in *Il Messaggero*, alternating selections of verse with his own sarcastic remarks on them.[26] Vassallo finds it appalling and telltale that the poem would have been printed in Cosenza, the provincial capital nearest to Saraceni's home town of Cassano all'Ionio because it presents a decidedly sympathetic portrait of the Southern lovers, in stark contrast to the way they are being represented in the Roman and national press. For Vassallo, the poem expresses a point of view that is mawkish, out of touch with the times, and in the worst possible taste. That it is bad poetry somehow suits and makes still more appalling its empathy toward the murderous adulterers.

"Pietro il saltimbanco" presents a sequence of three dramatic vignettes in varying meter and rhyme.[27] Neither Cardinali nor Saraceni are named but the identification is unmistakable. First a glittering circus scene unfolds: a heroic rider, proud as a "rebel angel," dominates his charging steed, setting hearts aflutter. As the horseman takes his applause, a rose lands at his feet; he picks it up and kisses it, then kisses it again, and disappears into the wings. Stanza two takes place in the candle-lit bedroom of the wife, who trembles with passion and distress. The *cavallerizo* enters in the darkness, unthreads his cape, and the lovers proceed to alternate burning kisses with confessions of love and guilt. The section's central sequence consists of a long, highly dramatic soliloquy beginning and ending with words of bloody foreshadowing, "Don't name that man!" in which the acrobat grips a knife as he describes his harsh upbringing as a circus orphan now redeemed by the impossible love he's found. In a shorter final sequence, we see the acrobat chained in a sunless dungeon. Published in July 1879, after the May release of the state's official charges against the accused but before the beginning of the trial, "Pietro il saltimbanco" anticipates in surprising detail both the predominant public sentiment toward Saraceni and her legal team's defense strategy by portraying her as a pitiable victim of passion, incapable of playing any role in a murder plot. Rather, the lyric implies, her husband shared responsibility for his fate by leaving his young wife alone too often. Given the evidence available in the press, the Calabrian poet's prophecy of Cardinali's life sentence is unsurprising, but the sympathetic, "psychological" rendering of the orphaned circus boy's deep rage at society is unprecedented, not to be found in any other treatment of the case.

More poetry follows Carducci's. Immediately after the trial, *Il Bersagliere* publishes an acrostic poem by Antonietta Carrozza's lawyer, Carlo Palomba, written in homage to Saraceni's defense attorney, Senator Enrico Pessina. Palomba was the same who had replied to Carducci's denunciatory epode in open court. Seven hendecasyllables, each line beginning with a letter of Pessina's name, heap praise on the deeply admired attorney from Naples for his brilliant final summation at the trial, saying, "You appeared Michelangelo reborn/You were painter, sculptor, and poet/You seemed the very genius of your native land!" The final line credits Pessina with having "seized the mystery of human fallibility!"[28]

In a different key, ten days after the verdicts were handed down, the Monday, November 10, *Messaggero* published Vassallo's final comment on the trial in the form of a poem, titled "Alla Contessa Nana" (To Countess Nana), 52 hendecasyllables, rhyming ABAB, CDCD, EFEF, and so on.[29] In its first lines, the poet addresses a countess with whom he had a brief love affair, expressing surprise at having heard that she too had attended the trial of Saraceni, perched high in the galleries. Had the same eyes ("stars") he had seen at mass intent on a prayer book, "religious and pious," also affixed the guilty adulteress in the criminal court? The poet then reminisces about their summer dalliance when, her husband away, she had "invited him to Citherea" and driven him nearly mad by whispering, "Oh, if it weren't for my husband!" as they embraced. The next time he saw her, the poet remembers, she already had a new favorite at her arm, but if not for that, he declares, he too might have ended up at a defendants' table accused of murder. "Be careful," the poet admonishes the countess, "You convert your many lovers into beasts!" and warns her never to mention her husband's name to her lovers because "the man you're kissing is demented!" Vassallo's poem is urbane and facetious where the Calabrian poet's is provincial and maudlin, the former epistolary and autobiographical, the latter theatrically dramatic. But in both, men are aroused to violence by an unsatisfied wife's uncontained desire.[30]

Unlike Vassallo, Carducci certainly did not attend the Fadda trial in person, for such a famous visitor would have been mentioned in the papers. Thus his indignation against the women was aroused not by direct experience but as a reader, following the minute daily coverage and the accompanying commentary on it by editors of dailies throughout the nation who reacted to the trial's developments and formulated its meaning for their audiences. *Fanfulla* editor and publisher of Carducci's poem, Martini attended the trial on at least two occasions and produced an extended satirical reflection on it for his column, "Chiacchiere della Domenica" (Sunday Chat), in his cultural weekly *Fanfulla della Domenica*. Martini's journal branded and advertised itself specifically for its virtue of covering every aspect of cultural life but rigorously excluding politics.[31] Published one week before Carducci's epode, Martini's humorous article focuses especially on the attendance of women at the trial, and what their appetite for such salacious diversion bodes for Italian men and the Italian state.

His October 12 commentary introduces itself as a review of a controversial new play by Emile Zola that has just opened at the Cluny Theater in Paris. In the first paragraphs, speaking as a critic, Martini offers a summary of the plot of the drama, but beneath the mask of reviewing a shocking realist play by Zola, he actually recounts—transposed to a French setting—the sensational story of Captain Fadda's murder. In Martini's rendering of the imaginary drama, Leonzia is a girl from a wealthy provincial family who meets and falls in love with a wounded soldier returned from the colonial campaigns in Algeria. The soldier notifies her parents that his wound might have negative effects on his ability to perform as a husband, but glad of the match, they neglect his warning and quickly contract the wedding. Martini explains he will spare readers the play's crude dialogues, instead putting it more delicately that "harsh military life and the wound had so compromised the husband's health as to render rare and weak the expansions the bride hoped for and wished vigorous and frequent." In consequence, the young wife abandons herself ("Here," warns Martin, "I run the lubricious path") to a series of loveless affairs, finally falling into the hands of a saltimbanco who, scheming to escape his wretched condition by marrying into wealth, ensnares her husband in a web of deceit and at last murders him.

"Next . . ." Martini continues, with a suspenseful ellipsis. But then he suddenly stops his summary of the plot: "I interrupt myself to hear the cries, screams of protest and hoots of anger rising all around me." He now imagines a dialogue with a respectable reader:

> "What? Someone is writing this trash?"
> "Eh, my friend, the new school . . . Delights of the veristi . . ."
> "And you want to bet they'll dare bring this to Italy too?"
> "Sure they will! When they can speculate on scandal, those theater managers will touch heaven with a finger."
> "But I say, where's it all leading to?"
> "Oh certainly it can't go much farther than this."
> "But a gentleman will no longer be able to take his family to the theater. These writers might remember there are wives in this world . . ."
> "And daughters . . ."
> "And granddaughters, for God's sake! Granddaughters!"

Now, saying "Peace, modest spirits," Martini removes yet another mask of his satirical conceit to reveal that this "foul, vulgar drama" was not invented by Zola at all; rather, it is real, unfolding day by day at the Criminal Court in Rome, where "wives, daughters, and granddaughters, whose modesty and innocence is so dear to you, go with keen curiosity, serene in spirit, and, unruffled, listen to rough men narrate obscene facts in language so filthy it would embarrass a crew of coachmen." Still more unsettling for Martini is that these women turn the squalid trial into a sort of gala, dressed as if for theater or the mass, "Chattering, smiling, pompously waving their *marabouts*, their sparkling bracelets, showing off the whiteness of their *fraises*, the boyish charm of their hats *alla bersagliera*. But if the day's session hasn't been very interesting, they exit the chamber (I've heard them myself) saying to their companions, 'Today there was no *juice*!'" This unattributed citation, "Today there was no *juice*!" constitutes the only occasion in the entire process that any journalist directly refers the words of a female spectator at the trial.

Martini is particularly attentive to the moral implications of the onslaught of French fashion spreading into urban Italy along with Zola's realism; the *marabouts* are ostentatious stork plumes worn in hats, the *fraises* a retro seventeenth-century collar. The *cappelli alla bersagliera*, instead, are Italian, a feminine take-off on the ceremonial hats with cockade and plume worn by the elite military order that seized Rome from papal forces in 1870. The ladies wear their hats perched at a jaunty, provocative angle; do they mean by this to mock the dignity and heroism of the army, or rather to honor it by citing it in a festive, playful key? A contemporary engraving in *Illustrazione italiana* portrays a young woman wearing just this kind of hat as she smokes a cigarette in a café, looking up from an article titled "Emancipazione" to gaze unapologetically out at the viewer. Her expression is unnerving, as though she were sizing the viewer up.[32] Consistent with Martini's observations, daily newspaper reports of the trial devote intense attention to the fashions worn by spectators. For the male reporters, these modern styles suggest (or promise) promiscuity in thought and behavior, as though the transgressive sex of the adulterous defendants were permeating the court and public through the flamboyant dress of the female spectators.

The hubbub, crowds, and gala atmosphere in a solemn judicial setting; the chatter and smiles amid a lurid penal trial; the heated thrall of the women's attention: Martini, a successful playwright as a young man, now reveals why all this so intimidates him: "From now on, if I had to write a drama, I'd feel hopelessly lost. I'd think: after the palpitations they've had at the Fadda trial, how will I be able to move them anymore?" Beneath his bemused tone, the editor is expressing two worries: as a playwright, how can his fictional inventions hope to match the real dramas played out in the nation's courtrooms? More intimately, as a husband, how can he hope any longer to thrill a wife who has been exposed to the visceral, violent passion of an acrobatic horseman? The reporter for the *Libertà* had expressed the same fear in reaction to the tumultuous presence of women at the first day of the trial: "This morbid curiosity, this fierce desire of powerful emotions is certainly no fine tribute to the gentle sex, which should be seeking the sweet joys, the pleasing sensations of affection, to conserve intact the gentle fragrance of their sensitive, delicate spirit... What are the ladies looking for in the febrile exploration of the feelings, of the sensations of the accused, in this moral vivisection? The science of good or that of evil?"[33] Through the Fadda trial, the menacing specter of female desire emerged to haunt Italy.

On the strictly juridical level, Raffaella Saraceni was being tried on the charge of murdering her husband. In the larger national imaginary, as reflected in the rhetoric of lawyers and journalists, poets and editors, she was on trial for the threat her sexuality represented against the liberal order. In her study of this case, Angela Groppi convincingly argues that women attended the Fadda trial and trials like it because courtroom galleries were the one public place where women could participate as citizens in the new democracy. Waving the banner of common sense, male journalists, intimidated by women's presence, reacted to their participation by portraying them as shallow, snack-munching seekers of sensation.[34] What most disturbed the paladins of bourgeois Italy in this particular case was the public exposure of male impotence and the threat of female identification with Raffaella's dilemma.

Martini closes his editorial by imagining the accused murderer's reflections as he sits in the *gabbione* watching the scene unfurl around him: "I am here because they accuse me of having offended society; but really, those women offer quite an idea of society's genteel customs and refined civility." For Martini, as in Carducci's apostrophe, the savagery of a people reveals itself under its gayest mask, among the very women who are both symbols and guardians of rectitude.

In the spring of 1881, a year after the appeals court rejected the Saraceni defense's argument for a retrial on procedural grounds, an author otherwise unremarked in bibliographies named Alfonso Zara published a five-act play, "The Murder of Captain Fadda," which dramatizes the famous events of the Fadda affair from the point of view of that majority of public opinion that sustained Raffaella's innocence.[35] The author avers in his preface that the work is to be judged on its dramatic effectiveness, but absence of evidence would suggest that the play may never have been staged. Alfonso Zara appears to have been a learned dilettante motivated to resort to the genre of theater to manifest his sense of injustice at the verdict against Fadda's widow. Like Carducci, the playwright seems never to have attended the trial in person, but had achieved a high degree of expertise on every detail of the affair by devouring the media's intensive coverage of it. One after another, the play reenacts the most notorious "true-life" moments of the Fadda narrative, allowing its audience to relive as witnesses, for example, the captain's jealous discovery of Raffaella as she writes the "Dear Edoardo" letter, a scheming Cardinali at Fadda's doorstep wheedling his orderly away from the apartment, the murder itself (the stabbing takes place just off stage), and Fadda's death on the street as he points at his assailant. Key moments of the trial are also represented, such as the pathetic episode of Fadda's father, too grief-stricken to testify when summoned in an early session, and the public hubbub at the arrival of Carluccio, who functions as comic relief. Even the little people of Rome are given their say in a lengthy scene outside the courtroom as they await the verdict and heatedly comment back and forth on contradictions in the clown's testimony. The play's dialogue includes several direct quotations drawn from published versions of the trial, placing into Raffaella's mouth, for example, lines drawn verbatim from her letters to her husband. The play thus mixes together a certain appearance of documentary authenticity with the playwright's interpretation of the events.

Weaving the events etched in the public mind into the conventional dramatic form of dialogues, monologues, asides, and act-ending *sentenze* (rousing speeches intended to bring the audience to its feet), Zara recasts the story so as to portray Raffaella as a devoted wife and daughter who becomes the innocent victim of her father's social ambitions, her husband's jealousy, and the demonic acrobat. This operation necessarily requires a certain degree of invention with regard to the evidence presented to the jury at the actual trial, but "The Murder of Captain Fadda" must represent to some degree the widespread public sympathy for Raffaella that gradually increased over the course of her trial, generated by her clearly-spoken, unwavering testimony, her continuous, apparently sincere weeping, her conduct in prison, and the oratorical genius of her lawyers.

In the prologue set on the couple's wedding day in Naples, Raffaella's father, Domenico, insists on the socially advantageous marriage over the objections of his wife. With maternal foreboding, the bride's mother, Carolina Nola, reminds her husband of the rumors about the captain's war wound and the hardship for a young girl in leaving her family to follow a soldier's military peregrinations. The mother's special clairvoyance, which the playwright may have considered a particularly Southern trait, is reiterated with her sudden arrival on scene at moments of her daughter's greatest need, such as at the end of Act Two, at the height of an argument between the young couple over the "Dear Edoardo" letter, and at the end of Act Four, during Raffaella's "mad scene" in prison, when she momentarily loses her mind, hallucinating the evil Cardinali hovering before her. At moments of crisis throughout the play, mother and daughter drop to their knees to pray, appealing to a power beyond humankind's limited ken. Zara resorts to this device to reconcile his dissatisfaction at the jury's eventual decision with his durable belief in the new Italian state. In effect, the play applies to the Fadda affair the contradictory ideology of the vast swath of the public that considered itself both Catholic and Italian, opposing the moral decay of modernity while believing in progress and the new state.

In Act One, shortly after her marriage, Raffaella prays for God's assistance in her "sacrifice" of herself to her "duty as a woman and daughter," to expiate her "father's guilt." Although couched entirely in euphemism, sympathetic audiences would have understood this episode as referencing Fadda's impotence: her father was guilty, that is, of having imposed the soldier on the girl despite his inadequacy, while her "sacrifice" and "duty" were to bear this misfortune with the patience of a saint. Following the Saraceni defense strategy, the playwright presents his heroine as utterly virtuous even as subsidiary characters explain that her sin should be excused by circumstances. Raffaella is deeply religious, highly principled, and devoted to her husband. She is granted ringing, climactic speeches on the ultimate triumph of divine justice, whether in mercy or punishment, over the flawed justice of man.

Although honored in the play for his uniform and sense of duty, the character of Fadda is portrayed as rigid and unfairly jealous of his wife in the scene of the "Dear Edoardo" letter. The dialogue in this scene recapitulates the cross-examination of Saraceni in court: Fadda accuses his wife of writing to a lover, but Raffaella answers that she is writing to her uncle

Edoardo. Rather than handing over the letter to prove her innocence, she tears it up, as though to say that even responding to such an accusation would be an intolerable indignity. Late in the play, as all await the jury's verdict, the playwright assigns to Fadda's own father the opinion that the captain was wrong to have married in the first place, considering his injury. He further erred, the father adds, by leaving Raffaella alone too often.

Cardinali, by contrast, is purely malevolent, in a manner perhaps best characterized by the stage directions the author provides for the actor, such as, "(. . . the actor is requested to execute this scene with true naturalness of gesture, and the convulsive agitations of a maniac)," and "(with a demonic cackle)." In the central scene in Act Two of the nocturnal meeting between Cardinali and Raffaella, the acrobat corners her to confess his uncontrollable passion, swearing, "I would even lick the dirt you tread beneath your feet!" But in contrast to the weak-willed wife of the Calabrian versifier mocked by Vassallo in the pages of the *Messaggero*, here an appalled Raffaella responds with dignified scorn at the man's audacity.

In effect, the dilettante dramatist's real play responds by negation to the anxious issues raised by the one merely imagined by the real playwright, Ferdinando Martini. Martini's parody dwelt on sex, female spectatorship, and corrupting language. Zara's heroine, instead, aspires to the high goal of renouncing her desire. Pursuing his greater theme of the ineffability of justice, Zara finds no role in his drama for the female spectators who so excited Carducci, but Raffaella's thundering final speech of sacrifice and submission is clearly intended to overwhelm and cancel out their morbid curiosity. In contrast to the "language so filthy it would embarrass a crew of coachmen" that so enlivened the actual trial, Zara's characters all speak the same stilted stage Italian of the era, devoid of regional, class, or dialectal flavor.

Simultaneous to the widespread poetic and artistic reiterations of the Fadda affair, several anecdotes suggest subtle ways in which the trial penetrated the imagination of Italians by becoming a subject of another form of figuration: popular jokes and metaphors. In its humor section, the *Libertà* carries a conversation overheard at a barbershop: A father brings his son in for a haircut and asks the barber to cut the boy's hair short on top but leave it long in the back. "I get it," the barber answers with a knowing smirk, "You mean, Cardinali style?" The joke that suggests that the accused acrobat's distinctive hairstyle had become familiar, even fashionable, at least in certain circles.[36] Several weeks after the trial, *Don Pirloncino* runs its regular riddle feature, "Sciarada-Ritratto" (Portrait Charade), where readers are invited to deduce the person described, but not named, in an enigmatic piece of verse. The answer—the paper mentions that many readers have guessed correctly—is Antonietta Carrozza, the third of the accused parties in the Fadda trial.[37] In December, the *Capitale* prints a short notice on a case of adultery and murder that has come over the wires from Russia, describing the wife as "the Saraceni of Imolski."[38] A joke, a rebus, and a metaphor all presuppose a shared culture, all demand a flash of mutual recognition, a momentary bond, between speaker and listener. In these examples, we witness the fulfillment of the prophecy embodied in Ferdinando Martini's definition of man as an animal who reads the newspaper. The Fadda affair has become a synapse in the shared cultural nerve system of the new Italian, a species that includes fallen nobility with pens and illiterate listeners in piazzas, enfranchised men, and disenfranchised women, Romans in the capital and readers in the most hidden corners of the peninsula.

In 1883, concurrent with the National Exposition in Rome, a commission was appointed to determine which works from the exhibition should be purchased by the state to establish the founding collection of a National Gallery of Modern Art. One member of the commission was none other than Martini, who, as we have seen, exploited the notoriety of the Fadda trial by condemning the salacious ladies who attended it so passionately.[39] Like the dailies, his cultural weekly too built sales by covering the trial, except that the *Fanfulla della Domenica* staked out the position of assailing the competing media, which it accused of trafficking in scandal and immorality.[40] Martini's moderate, reformist verismo may explain why Francesco Netti's *In Corte d'Assise* was not among the works chosen by his commission to be added to the national painting collection.[41] Instead Michele Cammarano's immense *June 24th at San Martino* was chosen, an epic representation of the battle at which Captain Fadda, then a young quartermaster, received his fateful wound and lost his testicle. A different work by Netti, an anodyne classical scene, is now included in the national modern art collection in Rome, while his *In Corte d'Assise* today hangs in the Pinacoteca Provinciale in Bari, a neglected museum on the fourth floor of a city administration building, one of the few remaining art galleries in Italy where a visitor can still wander undisturbed for hours. The next chapter will explore how, through works such as Cammarano's painting, the Battle of San Martino came to be enshrined as a crystalline moment of national unity, starkly opposed to the decadent feminine democracy of Netti's *In Corte d'Assise*.

6

King and Quartermaster

The Battles of San Martino

The final day of the trial is especially crowded with dignitaries who have come specifically to hear their parliamentary and ministerial colleague, Enrico Pessina, deliver the closing statement in defense of Raffaella Saraceni. Nicolò Coboevich lists the presence in the hemicycle behind the judge's bench of a deputy, a senator, the ambassador to Spain (a count), two "honorables," a baron, the Secretary General of Public Works, and many high officials in the Justice Ministry. The illustrious attorney, who had been named senator by the king in spring of the same year, addresses the court for several hours, so moving his listeners to repeated applause and shouts of admiration that the president is compelled to clear the regular public from the hall. When the calls of "bene" and "bravo" rise yet again, the judge threatens to clear the galleries as well, where the first class ticket holders are seated. In the climactic moment of his summation, Pessina evokes the memory of King Vittorio Emanuele II and Giovanni Fadda, linking the heroic king and valiant soldier who shared the field at Italy's most glorious battle. Turning back the praise of an opposing lawyer who earlier had compared him to Napoleon, Pessina says, "When I rise to defend innocence and rights infringed, I would like rather to be compared to Vittorio Emanuele, who rushed to wherever the battle was fiercest on the fields of Palestro and San Martino. And since I have mentioned those glorious fields of battle, allow me to bow and shed a tear over the tomb of Giovanni Fadda, that valiant soldier, whose noble existence was extinguished by a killer."[1]

By a highly effective rhetorical turn, the lawyer unifies and moves his audience, summoning his listeners' patriotic solidarity by joining the names of two dead heroes of the Battle of San Martino, one a king and the other a mere soldier who, until his murder, had been virtually anonymous. When describing Fadda, the newspapers tend to append the word "poor" before his name, and "poor Giovanni Fadda" is evoked regularly in court by lawyers on both sides. The single adjective seems to refer to three facts: that he was wounded in battle, that he was murdered, and that he was cuckolded by his wife. Over time, this last attribute inevitably imposes on the expression "poor Giovanni Fadda" an undercurrent of mockery. The newspaper biographies of the soldier concentrate on the two particulars of his glory: his wound, and where it happened:

> Giovanni Fadda was truly the ideal type of the brave and loyal soldier. On 24 June 1859, at the Battle of San Martino, Major Giovanni Fadda, quartermaster of the 14th Company of the Seventh Regiment, fought with ancient valor. He was twice wounded, in the groin and thigh. From one of the two wounds, surgeons removed a projectile; the other left him with a physical imperfection, rendering him monorchid.[2]

To understand why Fadda's murder aroused so much attention, it is important to explore the circumstances of his wound in the context of national mythography. Both before and after his murder, Fadda's destiny as man and symbol was wrapped up with that of his king. Two bodies, the mythical and the material, indissolubly confounded.

Fought on June 24, 1859, the Battle of Solferino and San Martino was the most costly in human life and one of the most decisive battles of the Second War of Independence that resulted in the establishment of the nation of Italy, finally achieved, although still geographically incomplete, in 1861. This battle, in fact, is generally known by European historians as the Battle of Solferino, because that is where they judge the decisive strategic action to have taken place. Only the Italians prefer to name it the Battle of San Martino, because that is where Italian troops fought and achieved victory; one fascist historian went so far as to insist that Solferino and San Martino were in fact two entirely separate battles, although occurring at the same time and place.[3] At this point in the war, Italian troops under Vittorio Emmanuele II, King of Piedmont and Sardinia, combined with the much larger French Army of Napoleon III to drive the Austrians from Lombardy. Solferino and San Martino are just south of Lake Garda, on the confines between the provinces of Lombardy and Veneto, an hour west, depending on traffic, of Verona. Having withdrawn from most of Lombardy, here the Austrians had established the western edge of a quadrilateral they considered their stronghold. It was to be the bloodiest single battle of the Italian Risorgimento.[4]

The battlefront stretched roughly 20 kilometers north to south from the shores of Lake Garda to the plains around Campo di Medole.[5] The combined attacking forces of the French and Piedmont numbered as many as 150,000 (of which Piedmont troops constituted approximately 50,000), while the defending Austrians numbered 170,000, with 500 cannon on both sides.[6] The French divisions under Napoleon III advanced in a wide formation on the southern front, centering their effort to break through the Austrian lines between the hill of Solferino (200 meters altitude) and Campo di Medole. The Piedmontese (the Armata Sarda) commanded the left, or northern, front, proceeding especially along the railway line south of the lake, then turning southeast to ascend the heights controlled by the Austrians. The terrain of the southern half of the long battlefront was a plain, across which the French advanced or retreated, largely exposed in open fields. Against the French to the west, the Austrians had the advantage of placing their cannon on higher ground in and around Solferino; against the Italians to the North, the Austrian artillery was on the hilltops of Madonna della Scoperta and San Martino (approximately 150 meters altitude). To control the field, the Italians would have to fight uphill to take control of those positions. When imagining the battle, it should be kept in mind that a percentage of the forces here described as Austrian would have been soldiers native to the regions of today's Veneto, Friuli, and Alto Adige, many of whom spoke dialects more closely related to Italian than to German.[7]

An encounter had not been anticipated by either side, a fact that accounts in part for the pattern of the dispersive, tentative back-and-forth actions throughout the day on the part of the Armata Sarda, leading to a final, desperate assault. The engagement began at around 7 a.m. in the morning under oppressive heat and humidity. While Napoleon's forces were attempting to punch through decisively below Solferino before the Austrians could encircle them with a flanking motion, the Armata Sarda was throwing individual regiments and battalions of various sizes and components up the low slopes to the North in a disordered sequence that military historians have decried for its poor coordination.[8] The hilltop church of San Martino itself was seized and then abandoned as many as five times between noon and 8:30 p.m., when it was finally, definitively overrun. Because of the extension of the front, King Vittorio Emanuele II spent part of the day galloping from place to place, then directed the troops from Castel Venzago, approximately five kilometers west of the decisive action.[9]

When news reached the king at around 3 p.m. that the French forces had gained the upper hand at Solferino, he immediately sent word to his commanders in the field that a supreme effort must be made for the conquest of San Martino, because a victory for Piedmont any less grand than that of the French would doom the Italian campaign to derision and infamy. A fascist historian under Mussolini reported how the king had to be restrained by his generals from galloping to lead the charge. In this version, General

Durand was reported to have cried, "Hold back, sire, the Sovereign is not a soldier!" to which the king answered, "You are mistaken, General, I am the first soldier of national independence!"[10] This phrase identifying the king as the first soldier of national independence will be firmly and unfailingly welded to his name in patriotic mythography. An English historian of the battle has conjectured of Vittorio Emanuele in this moment that "Cavour's words were ringing in his ears: 'Woe to us if we end up owing our independence to the French.'"[11] As a memoir written by a participant put it some months after the battle, "While the French had achieved immortal honor for themselves at Magenta and Solferino, the campaign would have ended for us without one of those grand episodes that inscribe eternal Glory in the history of armies and nations. It would have been deplorable that, in the war for Italian independence, the Italians had not fought at least one great battle."[12]

Nationalists such as Edmondo De Amicis will later render Vittorio Emanuele's order as an exhortation that galvanized the exhausted troops toward a final assault on the heights. In a description of San Martino written ten years later as part of a campaign to establish a monument to the dead, De Amicis asserts that once the order had come from the king, "hunger, thirst, scorching heat, exhaustion, it all vanishes; the soldiers feel newly fresh and vigorous, as in the morning when they break camp; a new dawn rises, more splendid; every gaze turns toward the heights; the enemy is many, thick with artillery, defenses strong; but he will be taken; he must be taken; it's impossible that he not be taken; it's the king's order."[13]

Before the assault can mobilize, however, at approximately 4 p.m. the day's unbearable humidity finally develops into a sudden furious tempest of rain and hail of a kind typical of the region, localized and violent. Now the soldiers must trudge and drag their cannon uphill through mud. Italian tradition has it, nevertheless, that the lashing storm "seems to incite the combatants to fiercer and bloodier struggle."[14] As it ascends the hill, the advancing attack front narrows, from the 15 kilometer breadth that began the day into a battle line no more than 1,500 meters wide, the soldiers ranked in dense echelons pushing upward, bayonets drawn, tripping on one another's heels, and easy prey to dense artillery and rifle fire. Military historian Piero Pieri describes this part of the battle as encompassing, "The crucial moment when the material and spiritual forces of a given historical period converge toward a culminating point and a decisive moment."[15] The onslaught is a mistake, a culmination of poor communication and indecision throughout the day on the part of army command, but the sheer density of the mass pushing up the hill overcomes the Austrian forces and secures the summit for the king. A German historian insists that by the time the Italian forces made their final assault, the Austrian commander at San Martino, Benedek, had already reluctantly begun the retreat ordered by his superiors in response to the decisive French victory at Solferino.[16] The Italians had already suffered significant casualties; generals shot, replaced by colonels, shot in turn, replaced by majors;[17] but the heaps of dead and wounded on the hillside of San Martino are predominantly regular soldiers. Approximately one of every nine soldiers was killed or wounded.[18] According to an English biographer of Vittorio Emmanuele, "The mountainsides were so bestrewed with wounded that the king's messenger had to lead his horse to avoid tramping on them."[19]

Giovanni Fadda, although a young quartermaster and not at that time a major, as erroneously reported by newspapers during the murder trial, was put in provisional command of the Second *Pelottone* (platoon) of the Fourteenth Company of the Seventh Regiment of the Third Division, under General Mollard.[20] Army reports record that the Seventh Regiment fought with particular valor and ferocity in close combat, having been ordered by the general to attack with bayonets drawn and without firing a shot, to gain control of a white house on a small elevation of little strategic value except that it was occupied by the enemy.[21] Over 14 hours of close combat, control of the summit changed hands repeatedly.[22] Struggling through mud toward the promontory, quartermaster Giovanni Fadda received a bullet that passed through his groin and fixed in his thigh, but the height was achieved, the little white house secured.

The victory at San Martino was crucial rather for moral than strategic reasons, but pyrrhic, costly in lost officers, infantry, and destroyed cannon.[23] As was typical before Joseph Lister introduced the use of carbolic acid to treat battle injuries in 1865, more soldiers died slowly that day due to untreated wounds than at the moment of being shot or bayoneted. The sight of thousands of dying men writhing in agony at Solferino provoked Henry Dunant, a Swiss businessman who found himself at the battlefield almost by chance, to found the International Red Cross. At Solferino and San Martino there were three possible modes of treatment for the wounded: a very limited number of mobile ambulances; makeshift hospitals set up behind the lines, especially at Castiglione delle Stiviere but also in many of the area's churches (wounded officers were customarily removed to private homes); and, for those whose conditions required the most intensive treatment, a hospital in Brescia. There were not enough medical personnel to meet the need in any case, but the most immediate problem as the battle wore on through the day was that of transporting wounded soldiers away from the field. There was an extreme shortage of carts, and the mud-rutted roads were hopelessly blocked with traffic of every sort. Thousands died where they lay. In the days after the battle, peasants were forced to dig trenches into which they heaped the bodies of the dead. Bones and skulls continued to resurface for years afterward until a national campaign finally resulted in the establishment of an ossuary ten years later.[24]

Fadda must have been among the wounded crying out for treatment. For those who did make it to a field hospital, conditions were hellish, with amputation often the only treatment for wounds in septic conditions in which, "suppurations, gangrene, septicemia, Saint Anthony's Fire (erysipelas, an acute bacterial infection of the skin), and tetanus raged among the traumatized soldiers before and after operation."[25] As people say in such occasions, Giovanni Fadda was lucky: using no anesthesia, a surgeon somewhere along the line must have worked an unsterile pair of forceps into his thigh to draw out the bullet, patching up the rest as best as possible. His left testicle would remain atrophied for the rest of his life, but the man survived, a victor. At the trial of his killers twenty years later, Tommaso Lopez, lawyer for the Fadda family, will begin his summation with the words: "Poor Captain Fadda! If only he had died on the glorious field of San Martino, he would not have had to end his life under the dagger of a *saltimbanco*."[26]

But Fadda did not die that day; he survived the battle, the wound, the waiting, and the surgery. Equally exceptional from a statistical viewpoint, he did not die during his convalescence either. For his sacrifice, quartermaster Giovanni Saturnino Fadda is listed among the soldiers of the Seventh Infantry who received an "honorable mention" for service at San Martino.[27] As Fadda's coffin proceeds through Rome toward Campo Verano Cemetery twenty years later, three medals will decorate his coffin: a French medal for military valor, a medal commemorating the war for Italian independence, and a French medal for the campaign of 1859. Among the array of medals awarded to soldiers and officers, these were impressive, but not among the highest distinctions.[28]

Two weeks after the battle, the opposing French and Austrian rulers excluded Piedmont from treaty negotiations that brought the war to an end considered ignominious by Italian patriots, reducing them to pawns in a continental strategy. Taking the Veneto off the table, the Austrians ceded Lombardy not to the Italians but to the French, then the French in turn granted the region to Vittorio Emanuele's Piedmont, which shortly thereafter handed to France the contested border regions of Nice and Savoy. With the humiliating Italian defeats at Custoza and Lissa during the Third War of Independence in 1866, the Battle of San Martino came to be enshrined in nationalist consciousness as the peak of Italian military glory in the entire Risorgimento, perhaps the single shining moment when ruler and subject became one, in a heroic sacrifice unsullied by the diplomatic scheming that played such a decisive role in achieving nationhood.

In Milan's Piazza del Duomo, the equestrian statue of Vittorio Emanuele (commissioned in 1880 but finally unveiled only on the anniversary of the battle in 1896) portrays the king's horse reining back in surprise at the explosion of a grenade at the Battle of San Martino.[29] The battle became an indispensable reference for speakers during annual celebrations of the Festa dello Statuto and was ubiquitously used in scholastic texts or popular books extolling patriotic virtue, such as Ernesto Mezzabotta's 15-cent *La Vivandiera di San Martino* published by editor Perino in 1886. In this sixty-page paperback novel, a young woman whose entire family has been slaughtered by the Austrians takes revenge by sleeping with an enemy officer so as to steal from him the Austrian battle plans, which she hands over to the Piedmont army just in time to turn the tide of battle.[30] A stunning reversal of the ancient legend of Lucrezia, whose honorable suicide after rape by Tarquin provoked the Romans to overthrow their kings and found the republic, here instead a maiden sacrifices her honor to the glorious cause of establishing Italy, and is redeemed rather than killed at the end. Aimed strictly at the popular reader, the pamphlet fiercely rebukes the Catholic cult of virginity. The Battle of San Martino, that is, was appropriated also by patriotic socialists in their rhetorical war against the Church's hold on the consciousness of Italians.

The distinguishing feature of the Battle of San Martino in the developing national mythography was that it crystallized a moment of classless brotherhood and mutual sacrifice between king and people. The Society of Solferino and San Martino, established in 1880 to "conserve and honor the memory of the fallen," dedicated itself to the erection of an immense tower at the battle site featuring the iconographical innovation, heretofore unprecedented, of commemorative plaques "bearing the names of *all* the combatants in *all* the campaigns for the independence and unity of Italy." In a request for funding support, the president of the society wrote to the Minister of Public Instruction Ferdinando Martini that the plaques would represent "an act of justice toward those citizens who had risked their lives for the cause of all."[31]

Still in the aftermath of the battle, in 1860 a young Giosuè Carducci joined the mythologizing process with a patriotic sonnet to the victors of San Martino:

San Martino	In rough translation:
Chi del German di doppia oste maggiore Là il barbarico nembo urta e sostiene?	Who against a German host twice as great withstands and beats back the barbarian storm?

Chi sovra mucchi di morenti muore Sorriso in volto di letizia e speme?	Who atop mounds of the dying, dies A smile on his face of joy and hope?
Qual d'ira e di virtù divin furore Su quel colle a le prove ultime viene? Chi ricaccia il gagliardo assalitore, E terribil lo folgora a le schiene?	What divine fury of rage and virtue comes to the ultimate test on that hill? Who throws back the fierce attacker and merciless, blasts his fleeing back?
Sei tu, sei tu, latin sangue gentile, Che ne i pugnati campi su la doma Austria risorge in tua ragion civile,	It is you, it is you, noble Latin blood whose national right rises again over defeated Austria on the field of battle.
Ed a l'Europa gridi—Oh, chi mi noma Servo mai più? Fine a l'oltraggio vile!	And to all Europe you cry—Oh, who dares ever call me slave again? No more coward submission!
Rendimi il serto di mia madre Roma.[32]	Give me back the crown of my mother Rome.

In Carducci's vision, the blood spilled at San Martino to drive out an invading enemy (whose proportions the poet has inflated) not only redeems the national aspirations of an enslaved people but also overturns the European perception of Italians as incapable of war. Evoking barbarian invasions and maternal Rome, the imagery is the same as that he will employ in his epode denouncing the female spectators at the Fadda trial, written almost twenty years later. At the battle, united Italy stood against Austria. Twenty years later, the Battle of San Martino was evoked to stand against the decadent thrall of women at the Fadda trial. The heroism in battle of 1859 becomes, in 1879, martyrdom for the cause of Italian rectitude.

As time passed, the symbolic value of the battle escalated, overwhelming its tactical significance. But compensation remained frugal at best for the simple foot soldiers who could prove they had served, taking the form of a sort of lottery awarding a cash prize of 100 lire to the lucky winner.[33] When the warrior king Vittorio Emanuele II died, removing thereby the living symbol of Risorgimento heroism from the national stage, it became still more imperative for the Battle of San Martino to be abstracted and idealized into a unifying myth applied against the deep fissures in the national edifice. The sword presented to the king as symbol of his victory at San Martino was carried in the funeral procession immediately before the hearse transporting his mortal remains, borne by his aide-de-camp, General Medici del Vascello, on horseback.[34]

Vittorio Emanuele died suddenly after a short illness on January 9, 1878, apparently due to complications from having contracted malaria while visiting the farmlands outside Rome. The king never liked the capital and had moved there only reluctantly. Although malaria—the word derives from *mal aria*, "evil air"—was endemic to parts of the North as well, for the vigorous king to have been undercut in this way seemed blunt proof of the hidden malevolence lurking in the disease-ridden South, and of the difficulty of the Northern temperament to adapt to it. His death sent shock waves through the nation, affecting lives both large and small in incalculable ways, sowing consternation especially among elder leaders who feared the passing of the king might trigger the collapse of the young state.[35] Besides the impact on the nation of the death of the larger-than-life figure who publicly embodied Italian military heroism while being privately legendary for his rampant sexual vigor, for Fadda and his wife the death of the sovereign came at a crisis point in their marriage. For the couple, a misunderstanding over details of state protocol triggered irreversible calamity.

Transferred to the capital in September 1877, from his posting in Chieti, a regional center in the Abruzzi, Fadda moved to Rome on his own to set up a household while his wife returned to her family in Calabria to assist in the complicated arrangements for her brother's wedding to the daughter of a prominent local clan. Once settled in the metropolis the captain sent for his wife, but she began to stall with the excuse that dowry negotiations required her presence as a calming influence on her vituperative mother. The big day was postponed several times. As a military bureaucrat, Fadda found her provincial family's dithering irritating, because every time there was a postponement in the date, he had to withdraw a previous formal request for leave and submit a new one, disturbing his relations with superior officers and making him appear vacillating and foolish.

By Christmas she still had not come, so the captain obtained leave to spend the holidays in Cassano, hoping to bring her back to the city with him. But he found Raffaella recalcitrant, even hostile. She refused to sleep with him and mocked him at the family table, saying he should use his uniform and ceremonial weaponry to resolve her family's disagreement with the rival clan. After New Year's, Fadda returned to Rome empty handed and depressed. On January 8 his king died. Bereft of the wife who disdained him, Fadda now lost the king who led him to glory at San Martino, for whose cause he sacrificed his manhood. The situation now rapidly precipitated.

The king's funeral on January 17 was a massive affair bringing hundreds of thousands of secular pilgrims into the city to grieve for their monarch, the gruff, beloved king who, legend held, captained the nation to its great battlefield victories and whose passing seemed definitively to seal the end of the heroic period of the Risorgimento. In De Amicis's patriotic *Cuore*, set in 1882, a middle school student stands before his classmates to present an oration remembering the grand and solemn event. In this "vision of national apotheosis," the Italian people are forged into one through shared grief over the death of their monarch.[36] Through the device of a memorial speech to his classmates, De Amicis makes the youth into a historian whose task is to establish the truth and cast it into the future. Although incredible in the mouth of a child, the long speech is cumulatively stirring because we hear it in a bright boy's high, piping voice over the grave drumbeat of a military cortège, as he seeks to impress listeners with his relentless mastery of numerical detail:

> Four years ago, on this day, at this hour, in Rome, the hearse carrying the corpse of Vittorio Emanuele II arrived at the Pantheon. The first king of Italy, who died after reigning twenty-nine years, during which the great Italian fatherland, broken into seven states and oppressed by foreigners and tyrants, was reborn into a single state, independent and free; after reigning twenty-nine illustrious, beneficent years of virtue, of fidelity, bravery in peril, wisdom in triumph, constancy in misfortune. The hearse arrived covered with crowns after having traversed Rome under a storm of flowers, amongst the silence of an immense, grieving multitude arrived from every corner of Italy, preceded by a legion of generals and a mass of government ministers and noblemen, followed by a cortege of wounded veterans, by a forest of flags, by guests from three hundred cities, by everything that represents the power and glory of a people, it arrived before the august temple where his tomb awaited him. In that moment, an honor guard of twelve lifted the coffin from the hearse. In that moment Italy gave its last farewell to its dead king, its old king, who had loved it so much, the last farewell to its soldier, its father, to the twenty-nine most fortunate and blessed years of its history. A great and solemn moment. The gaze, the spirit of all trembled between the casket and the flags draped in black of the eighty regiments of Italy carried by eighty officers lined along the path; for all Italy was there, in those eighty symbols of the thousands of dead, the torrents of blood, our most sacred glories, our most holy sacrifices, our most fearsome suffering. The casket moved forward carried by the guard, and all the flags bowed down at the same moment in gesture of salute, the banners of the new regiments, the old, torn banners of Goito, Pastrengo, Santa Lucia, Novara, Crimea, Palestro, San Martino, Castelfidardo; eighty black veils fell, a hundred medallions struck the coffin, and that sonorous noise moved the blood of all, like the sound of a thousand human voices speaking at once:—Farewell, good king, brave king, faithful king! You will live on in the hearts of your people as long as the sun shines over Italy.[37]

In his conjuration of the king's funeral, De Amicis artfully exploits the persuasive power of numbers, having his student recite quantity after quantity—4 years, the first king, 29 years, 7 states, 300 cities, an honor guard of 12, 80 regiments, officers, symbols and veils, 100 medallions, 1,000 voices—so as to coerce the contradictory sociopolitical tensions at play into an imaginary edifice that appears indubitable, statistically proven, and ultimately monolithic. *E pluribus unum*. In the mouth of the child, the obsessive repetition of numbers evokes and unintentionally parodies the new generation of social scientists who were crisscrossing Italy in every direction to collect massive amounts of quantitative data in service to positivist science and the unitary state. However factual the numbers may have been in isolation, De Amicis applies them here not for scientific but for mythographic purposes.

Through trivial and unmanageable circumstance, unlucky Captain Fadda is tragically forced to bear the contradiction between the myth of Italian unity and the raucous disunity of its people. In a bitter letter from Rome to his estranged wife, he complains of how the brouhaha surrounding the funeral has upset his measured existence. Although a matter of the greatest solemnity, the atmosphere in the capital city resembles *Carnevale*. Not only is he unable to find a seat in a restaurant, Fadda also happens to bump into the man from Chieti named Edoardo whom he suspects of having had an affair with his wife. The captain's sarcastic description of meeting the man seethes with rancor. Raffaella replies to Fadda's letter, ignoring his aggrieved tone, and comments lightly on the death of Vittorio Emanuele. It turns out that yet another postponement in the wedding has become necessary, "because of the mourning period for the king." She explains that her brother's wedding will now be held "as soon as the mourning period is over."

The problem is that there are two mourning periods: there is the closure of government offices for one week after the funeral, but there is also the official national period of mourning of six months, during which business is conducted but certain protocols are observed, such as flying the flag at half-mast. Fadda interprets Raffaella's letter as referring to the latter, longer period, taking her to mean that she intends not to move to Rome for another six months at least. Fadda snaps. In an ugly gesture of rejection, he sends back her piano, now to him a symbol of her family's smug provincialism, that he sets against the heroic example of his king. Giovanni and Raffaella will exchange bitter letters but never see one another face-to-face again.

Two heroes of San Martino thus died in 1878: the adulterous king, in January, survived by the morganatic wife who had been his mistress; and his loyal foot soldier, in October, slain by his estranged wife's lover. The soldier's funeral cortège through the streets of Rome must have touchingly evoked the gaudy excess that marked his king's earlier in the year, according to Fadda's spartan rites a contrastive and virtuous dignity.

Twenty-four years after the Battle of San Martino, shortly after the end of the Fadda trial, Michele Cammarano began work on *June 24th at San Martino*, a gigantic painting, 8.2 meters wide and 4.2 meters high, that shows King Vittorio Emanuele II on horseback in the middle distance, exhorting a roiling mass of soldiers in left foreground up a muddy slope toward a hilltop, where the ruins of a white house emerge from smoke.[38] Hovering beyond the king is a leaden gray cloud, referencing the sudden lashing rainstorm that De Amicis says changed the course of battle in favor of the Italians (In Carducci's poem instead, this cloud becomes the "barbarico nembo," a "barbarian nimbus" that represents the attacking Austrian forces). This immense work, a keystone of the first National Exposition of Fine Arts held in Rome, became one of the first and principal acquisitions for the city's National Gallery of Modern Art, which had been planned in 1878 but established in 1883, just in time for the National Exposition.[39]

The unashamedly propagandistic goal of the National Exposition and the National Gallery was to present the history and culture of the new, modern, unified Italy as a worthy descendant of the greatness of the ancient republican, imperial, and holy city of Rome.[40] The creation of the National Museum had a very specific but multiple purpose. In a national perspective, establishing an art museum in Rome was an effort to reinforce the prestige of the city, which in fact had played a comparatively small role in the wars of independence, as a worthy site for a national capital, as well as a cultural center on par with other modern European metropolises. Within the municipal context of the Eternal City itself, the modern museum was to serve as a secular monument to rival the ancient visual hegemony of the Church.[41] Toward the end of the first decade after Rome had joined Italy and become its capital, subsequent to the sudden death of the nation's king, national leaders felt an urgent need for a cultural monument to shore up the fraying sense of patriotism, as the heroic tenor of the unification struggle under Vittorio Emanuele II ceded ground to the unglamorous rivalries and divisive economic and social crises that marked the reign of his uncharismatic son Umberto.

The ascension of the *Sinistra*, the Left parliamentary wing, to power in 1876 had seemed to mark less a change in policy than the passing from the scene of the generation of Cavourian Liberals who had achieved the Risorgimento. The new governments under Agostino Depretis shifted political balance toward the South, and by enlarging enfranchisement, began to admit less-educated voices to the democratic discussion.[42] The exclusive, genteel paternalism that marked the parliamentary rhetoric of the first generation was increasingly perceived as undermined by a new attitude of cynical expediency that came to be called *trasformismo*, where principle bowed to political jockeying. The publication of Pasquale Villari's *Lettere meridionali* (the "Southern Letters") in *L'Opinione* in 1875 and similar studies, made it impossible to ignore the profound ruptures between North and South, where vast masses of the population continued to live benighted lives, entirely untouched by the supposed benefits of freedom. Inhabitants of Rome in particular saw these people in increasing numbers in the city streets.[43] Public concern over the menace of violent crime, regarded as a moral emergency and cause for national shame as well as fear, sparked government studies and the new science of criminal anthropology; the first edition of Cesare Lombroso's *L'Uomo delinquente*, "Criminal Man," was published in 1876.

Historian Umberto Levra argues that the year 1878, begun with the king's death in January, continued with an accelerating sequence of crises, deaths, and growing republican agitation that seemed to spiral the nation toward apocalypse. Levra lists them in order: (1) January: death of the king (as well of august statesman and general Alfonso La Marmora) and tensions surrounding his son's accession to the throne; (2) February: death of Pope Pius IX; (3) March: imminent threat of collapse of governing coalition; (4) April–May: first issue of *Rivista repubblicana*, and first Rome Congress of republican organizations, which threatened the monarchy at the core of the state; (5) Summer: irredentist demonstrations, internationalist congress in Cesena with violent denunciations of the monarchy; (6) August: the bumbling killing of mystical cult leader Davide Lazzaretti by the forces of order; (7) Summer–Fall: resurgent *brigantaggio* in Sicily; and (8) November (and most shockingly of all): Giovanni Passanante's attempted assassination of King Umberto.[44] Levra might have further mentioned the acquittal by a citizen jury in August of the *banda del Matese*, the 26 internationalist anarchists who had attempted the year before to provoke a violent peasant revolution in the impoverished hill country beyond Naples by occupying towns and shooting *carabinieri*.[45] In a different cultural sector, the Italian contribution to the great Universal Exposition inaugurated in Paris in May 1878 had been judged a national embarrassment, exposing Italy as shamefully retarded in comparison to the rest of Europe.[46] The October murder of "poor Captain Fadda," its exploitation by a sensationalist press, and the morbid attraction of apparently respectable women to the trial of his murderers in October of the next year added to the distressing trend Levra identifies, wherein political breakdown and random misadventure mutually contributed to growing alarm that the tenuous social fabric of unified Italy was rapidly unraveling.

Begun in 1880 and still unfinished at the inauguration of the huge 1883 National Exposition of Fine Arts in Rome, Cammarano's massive painting represents an event of 1859, a key moment in the folklore of the Risorgimento, but its theme, placement, and sheer size are determined to counteract disconcerting and disheartening events of the immediate national past. Although the painting received criticism for its infelicitous formal results, competing focal points and disordered narrative,[47] the work's intention was to unify, in the most grandiose terms possible, the brave leadership of the much-mourned king and the transcendent sacrifice of anonymous soldiers into a single, heroic image of shared national identity. The experience of viewing the scene was described as an intensely moving patriotic experience: "Observing that painting, one trembles with emotion and our thoughts rush back to that memorable day. Those fearless, valiant soldiers seem to come alive."[48] When the same artist, now renowned for his patriotic military scenes, was commissioned six years later to paint another great Italian battle, he was enjoined by the nominating official with the words, "I am sure that your patriotic inspiration, joined with the virtue of your brush, will guarantee that the canvas will speak to the heart of our youth."[49] The official must have had in mind the kind of imaginary youth who described Vittorio Emanuele's funeral in De Amicis's *Cuore*, recently published. Cammarano himself considered his painting overgrown, unbalanced, compromised, and unfinished. On the right, a life-size figure of a soldier advances forcefully over an upturned cannon, but he has no legs below the knee. It is not that he is wounded; the legs were simply never painted in (making this section look rather like a work by Neo Rausch, the contemporary German artist who parodies historical painting). Another soldier directly in front of that one, rather than participating in the infantry charge, seems to be sitting in repose and gazing adoringly at the king, oblivious to the thousands advancing behind him. Despite its stylistic weaknesses *June 24th at San Martino*, won a prize of 3,000 lire for historical painting offered by the Order of Saints Maurizio and Lazzaro, which donated the painting to the national collection.[50] Too large to reproduce in small format on a mass scale, studies for the painting were rendered as engravings in *L'Illustrazione italiana* (two weeks after the periodical published its engraving of Francesco Netti's *In Corte d'Assize*) and disseminated widely. Among the studies selected for publication was a sketch of a scene, virtually unreadable in the completed painting, of two men carrying a third, which *L'Illustrazione italiana* describes as, "two peasants carry a wounded bourgeois," further stressing the work's aim to constitute an epic representation of sacrifice shared by all Italian society.[51]

With the acquisition of Cammarano's painting for the National Gallery, Captain Giovanni Fadda, so tragically and unfairly killed, became an unnamed martyr of the altarpiece in a national shrine, homage to the San Martino patriots devoted to their king who sacrificed their lives to create the nation of Italy. As mentioned previously, Netti's *In Corte d'Assise* was not chosen for the patriotic collection. Cammarano's epic work hangs today in the Gallery's Salone di Giordano Bruno, competing for attention with equally grandiose images of two Italian military catastrophes, the *Battle of Custoza*, by Giovanni Fattori, and the *Battle of Dogali*, also by Cammarano. An image of arduous victory, *June 24th at San Martino* denounces the fragmented patriotism and sense of deviating national purpose, prey to decadence, distraction, and crime that had befallen Italy almost as soon as nationhood was finally achieved. The mostly faceless soldiers follow the king's pointing finger toward destiny, sovereign and subjects joined in glory under a terrible, providential sky. The next chapter will further explore the state's effort to combine military force and mythography to overcome division and resistance among the populace.

7

"To Liberate Italy from the Italians"

One of the mysteries of the Fadda case is by what currents of culture and love an impaired Sardinian military clerk should have come to marry a privileged, protected eighteen-year-old from provincial Calabria. What could each have seen in the other and what could the young woman's parents have imagined they would obtain for themselves and their daughter by agreeing to the match? The couple met and married in 1871 in Naples, where the Saracenis kept a city house. The captain's younger brother, Cesare, remembers that the marriage took place rather precipitously, "as though there were something going on behind it." Giovanni, for example, found out that his bride's family was from Cassano only on the day of the wedding.[1] The sentiments between husband and wife, however, appear to have been genuine: a Roman friend to whom Fadda confessed his despair over his collapsing marriage testifies that only several days before he was killed, Fadda still insisted, despite her betrayals, that he was "extremely in love" (*innamoratissimo*) with Raffaella.[2] The matrimony between Northern soldier and Southern civilian must have been, at some level, an idealistic leap of faith, a gesture of belief that it was possible for two people of such different backgrounds, reborn as Italians in a new country, to reach across the chasm of diffidence and ignorance that separated them. As much as to each other, their wedding must have been an act of commitment to the nationalist rhetoric of the young state, a blind and blissful challenge to the history of suspicion and open violence that marked relations between the Italian army and the Southern population. Twenty years after liberation had been imposed on the South, Fadda's murder, apparently a crime of passion, was perceived also as a particularly intimate variant of Southern violence directed against the North. This chapter will examine Italy's efforts to use the army as an instrument to civilize its South, only to discover that the South was not a purely geographical entity.

The Italian army was officially born in May 1861, two months after the declaration of the establishment of the Kingdom of Italy in its first capital, Turin. The Veneto and the Papal States had still not been assimilated into the new nation. A nucleus of approximately 180,000 soldiers combined those of the Piedmont monarchy of Vittorio Emanuele di Savoia, King of Sardinia, with former enemy soldiers of the Bourbon Kingdom of Naples and veterans of Garibaldi's legendary *Mille* (The Thousand), the irregular troops who had landed in Sicily in 1860 and fought their way up the peninsula to free Southern Italy from Bourbon and papal domination. The victory of Garibaldi's army, which entered Naples in September 1860, led to the plebiscite that annexed Southern Italy to the kingdom of Vittorio Emanuele. But in composing the new national force, the king's generals far preferred their safely institutionalized former battlefield opponents from royal Naples, academy-trained career officers like themselves, over Garibaldi's undisciplined fighters, whom they regarded (correctly) as "a potential source of revolutionary contagion."[3] A campaign to purge the newly absorbed Southern forces of Bourbon influence had the effect of preserving the status of the higher officers while throwing those at the lower ranks out of work.[4]

In its origin, the Italian army might be said to have swallowed the war of unification. Where it had originally fought an ostensibly foreign enemy on the battlefield, with unification the army absorbed the populations of territories it had only recently intended to liberate militarily, thereby taking into itself the conflicted national identity it meant to resolve by force of arms. Few of the newly liberated peoples favored the Italian nationalist regime, and most initially suffered rather than benefited under the new government. In the South those who did benefit, a narrow slice of bourgeois landowners, were widely regarded as the most corrupt and craven elements of the old regime, devoid even of the old nobility's paternalist charity toward the poor. The Risorgimento had very little popular support. It cannot be called a revolution as the term is usually applied, for it was orchestrated by Northern elites and achieved more in the courts of Europe than on the battlefield or in the streets of Italy. It was the defeat, rather than victory, of the Italian forces at Custoza and Lissa that resulted in the Austrian cession of the Veneto to the Savoy monarchy. The armed forces of the Piedmont kingdom were led by generals who, like their civilian counterparts, were far more comfortable in Paris or Vienna than Rome or Naples.

From the beginning, in John Gooch's words, "The national army's relationship with the Italian people was founded on suspicion."[5] The Northern army distrusted the populace of the Southern lands they now occupied, whose customs appeared strange and primitive; the people's feeling toward the occupiers was mutual. As historian Fulvio Cammarano describes it, "The army itself became the first serious problem for the Italian ruling class, a problem that emblematized various unresolved knots of the Risorgimento: completing the unification, homogenizing politics and administration in the South, and the role of democracy and Garibaldi's forces within the new State."[6] Thus the army was now compelled to fight a domestic war on two fronts, internal and external. Its internal task was to homogenize its newly conscripted troops into Italian citizens, although few of them identified themselves as Italian or spoke the national language. On the contrary, most regarded the new state administrators and military chiefs from distant Turin, if they thought of them at all, as merely the most recent in a long line of foreign oppressors.

The army's second task, far more costly and bloody than expelling Austria from the Veneto or deposing the pope in Rome, was to suppress revolt and put down insurrection among the populace. The longest, cruelest campaign in the succession of civil wars that constitute the Risorgimento was not against Austria, France, or the Bourbons, but against the Southern population.[7] Beginning from the national plebiscite, this war was ostensibly directed against the problem of *brigantaggio* (banditry, brigandage), and focused on wiping out the ragged assemblages of disaffected peasants, draft dodgers, outlaws, and leftover remnants of Bourbon forces who organized and dissolved periodically to fight against what they regarded as the new barbarian invaders from the North.[8] The very term *brigante* was selected and employed to rob the liberal regime's Southern opposition of any political, social, or moral legitimacy, not unlike the way the word *terrorist* is used today.[9] Encouraged to various degrees by unrepentant Bourbons and elements in the Church, groups of peasants joined under local chieftains (often seasonally, in obedience to the agricultural calendar) to carry out guerrilla attacks on isolated Italian garrisons and vendettas against perceived collaborators. Since the brigands widely enjoyed the support of local populations from which they arose, the army was compelled to a policy of violence against the very citizens it meant to have liberated and who it now claimed to protect and represent. The military occupation and martial law imposed on the South transformed citizenship into subjection. Peasant demonstrations calling for land redistribution were determined to be acts of brigand terrorism and were attacked militarily.[10] Peasants found in possession of arms were shot on sight; carrying a suspiciously large amount of food was enough to condemn a farmer to the firing squad. At its peak, almost half the entire Italian Army was engaged in this civil war, and the severity of their treatment of the population was matched only by the savagery of the brigands' response. Records of 1863 count 1,038 men found in possession of arms and summarily shot, 2,413 enemy combatants killed in combat, and 2,768 prisoners taken.[11] The presence of statistics may give an idea that the conduct of the invading troops toward the inhabitants was ordered and systematic. It was not, however, restrained. Here is how one official, Angiolo De Witt, described the army's reprisal against Pontelandolfo, a hill village east of Naples where brigands had seized and killed forty government soldiers. Two days after the uprising, five-hundred special troops, the *bersaglieri*, drove out any resisting brigands, then entered the defenseless town:

> Handfuls of *bersaglieri* flushed yesterday's reactionaries out of their homes, terrified, and drove clumps of yokels into the street at bayonet point, where half-squads of soldiers immediately shot them down. Many ate dirt, some were unhurt, the wounded were left scattered where they fell. The survivors were forced to gather up sticks and straw and set fire to their own shacks.[12]

In the context of practices such as these, we might remember Finance Minister Quintino Sella's description of King Vittorio Emanuele, shortly after the monarch's death in 1878, as "the last of the *conquistadores*."[13] Even when it was not a matter of open warfare, relations between occupying soldiers and native peasantry were incendiary. Ligurian Edmondo De Amicis, later author of *Cuore*, was trained at the military academy in Modena. After fighting in the humiliating Italian defeat at Custoza near Verona in 1866, his regiment was sent to Sicily with the official purpose of assisting the populace during a devastating cholera outbreak. This assistance consisted primarily of repressing sedition and keeping down an outraged populace. During this period De Amicis began writing the accounts of military life that established his reputation. Here he describes an episode of his service in Sicily:

> The hardest assignments were those imposed by sudden, unexpected popular uprisings, in the middle of the night, sometimes occurring simultaneously at different points around a town. A handful of soldiers had to face an armed multitude a hundred times greater, beating furiously on the barrack doors, throwing rocks at the windows, and threatening to set fire to the place, screaming, "Death to the poisoners, death to the assassins of the people," and every other possible kind of abuse.[14]

De Amicis explains that the Sicilians believed that cholera had been spread intentionally by the new government, through the very soldiers sent to assist relief efforts. In another passage, he describes how the native population fought soldiers who were sent to remove decaying cholera-infected cadavers from homes.

In the footsteps of the occupying troops came the intellectuals, with their literature, science, and technology. Among innumerable lasting side effects, the war on banditry also provided a boost to the nascent technology of photography.[15] Thousands of Italian soldiers paid to have themselves photographed in uniform, either in large format to send home, or in the popular, smaller, visiting card format, to be distributed to friends, girlfriends, and potential girlfriends. For many of these soldiers, the portrait in uniform would have been the only photograph taken of them in their entire lives.[16] The Fadda trial archive contains two small-format photos of soldiers: one is of Fadda and was found bundled among his letters together with a similar small-format photo of his wife, which Fadda was apparently unable to bring himself to destroy or send back to her. The other photographic visiting card shows a smiling, handsome young soldier. It was found in Pietro Cardinali's room among the forty-odd love letters written to him by female fans. Perhaps Cardinali and this unknown young soldier had exchanged photos.

Brigands too, men and women, posed for photographs, enough to establish an iconography of outlaw representation: a heroic solo pose with rifle ready, and small or larger group compositions, either in the field or in the studio, and before and after capture. Brigand photographs, often turned into less-expensive engravings and reproduced, enjoyed an active market in Northern cities, where images of live brigands were only slightly less popular than images of their dead bodies or decapitated heads. A significant number of brigand images, live and dead, find their way into Cesare Lombroso's Museum of Criminal Anthropology in Turin, and form the basis of many of his observations about innate criminality as evinced by facial, cranial, and body types.[17]

More soldiers died in this civil war than in all the wars of the Risorgimento combined. Most fatalities among the royal troops came not from combat but from diseases endemic to the South, such as malaria and cholera. In 1863, a government commission sent to study the South returned to Turin to report to a secret parliamentary session that banditry decreased wherever the peasants had greater control over the means of agricultural production. In addition to a series of punitive measures, the commission proposed aiding the army with social initiatives designed to reduce violence, including establishment or expansion of public education; land redemption; equitable distribution of state lands; road construction; agricultural development; and public works.[18] The government's immediate response to these proposals was to pass the Pica Law, which instituted martial law throughout the rebellious provinces, authorized summary shootings, and offered rewards to informers and traitors.[19] A parallel law, not ultimately passed, proposed that once an individual's name had appeared on the official list of brigands, that person could be killed "not only by the forces of public order, but by anyone."[20] Summary military justice was to be exercised against any social elements not overtly subservient to the regime, including "loiterers, vagabonds, suspicious types, criminals, and collaborators."[21] Military executions were orchestrated for maximal exemplary impact. It was common practice for the national troops to execute their condemned prisoners by shooting them in the back rather than allowing them to face the firing squad, as an ultimate gesture of contempt.[22] Heads on pikes, bodies heaped or strung up in crossroads were spectacles produced and performed to make the most vivid possible impression of state power on the local populace. The officers and troops who carried out such actions regarded the natives as savages incapable of understanding anything but brutality.[23] Despite the effectiveness of the Pica Law (some historians give 1866 as the date of the end of the war against *brigantaggio*), the nascent phenomenon of emigration—to regional capitals, then beyond the borders, and finally to the industrial cities of Northern Italy—may have done more to end the violence than any other measure except, perhaps, for conscription.[24] Instead of fighting hundreds of thousands of hungry peasants, the army conscripted them.

The most effective and direct means of transforming recalcitrant peasants and Southerners into Italians was to draft them into the armed forces. Other than the task of suppressing revolt among the people, the new army's most important task was the one sometimes assigned to Fadda, that of homogenization, of creating citizens out of draftees. Among the handful of scared soldiers facing the enraged Sicilians described by De Amicis, there would have been a young officer whose academy training would have prepared him very poorly for a riot. Most of the regular soldiers facing the bloody minded townspeople would have been draftees at the lowest ranks little different from the people trying to set fire to them. Cases were not unheard of in which National Guard troops allowed themselves to be disarmed, taking the side of the peasants.[25]

The earliest national conscription regulations were extremely onerous, requiring the first generation of draftees to choose between eight years of active service or five active and six in the reserve; these limits were continuously modified and reduced in response to public resistance.[26] Those with sufficient resources could buy their way out, a regulation whose effect helped to guarantee that the foot soldiers would consist predominantly of boys whose families had the most meager resources. Readers of Giovanni Verga's 1881 novel, *I Malavoglia*, will remember the effect on a Sicilian fisherman's family when their most able son is called away to military service in a land that seems impossibly distant for a period so long as to doom the family's hopes. By contrast, there is no evidence that Raffaella's brother Giuseppe (Peppino) ever had to serve; presumably, his well-to-do family purchased his exemption or paid a "volunteer" to serve in his place. Draft dodging, desertion, self-mutilation, and hostile actions against superior officers were common phenomena among Southern recruits. Especially during the era of the Pica Law, and especially in Sicily, fleeing the draft became such a massive phenomenon that it effectively blurred with the problem of *brigantaggio* and the government evoked the same states of emergency and martial law to combat both problems.[27] Civilians accused of assisting recruits to evade the draft or to desert were tried by military tribunals.[28] Faced with the choice, it was only natural for many young men to join the brigands rather than the army.

A short article in the local crime news in the April 27, 1879, *Messaggero* embodies the two-front war taking place along the external and internal borders of the Italian state:

> A sad event has taken place at the San Calisto Artillery Barracks. A soldier named Albano from the southern provinces was taking sentry duty, and it seems that instead of performing his duty he was joking with passersby. The corporal of the guard recalled him to order, saying that otherwise the soldier would be relieved of his post. Albano took no notice of this warning, so the corporal was constrained to have him relieved by another soldier. Albano became angry, and abandoning his post he aimed his rifle at the corporal and fired a shot. Fortunately, the bullet failed to hit its mark, thanks to another soldier who struck Albano's gun with his fist, deviating the shot. Albano was arrested and disarmed by his companions and guards, against whom he opposed active resistance.

Almost twenty years after the nation's official unification, this notice manages to insert the "sad event" into a familiar stereotype of the carefree, lethal, childlike and traitorous Southerner unable to conform to the discipline established for the protection of his best interests. In its brevity, the article's writer betrays a sentiment that he and his readers have seen this all before and are likely to see it again. In fact this "sad event" chillingly foreshadows the similar but far more tragic case of Salvatore Misdea, a Calabrian recruit in the Pizzofalcone barracks in Naples in 1884, who snapped and went on a bloody rampage, killing five soldiers and wounding seven.[29] He ranged through the dorms, the quartermaster's office at the end of the hall, and the latrine, unsystematically targeting Piedmont and Lombard soldiers, low-ranking officers, and anyone he didn't like.[30] Among the characters in the Fadda trial, two have been incarcerated for crimes similar to Albano's: Cardinali's accused accomplice, stableboy Giuseppe De Luca, who died in prison before the trial, had earlier been incarcerated for striking a superior officer during his military service; Rosario Morrone, a barber in Corigliano, testifies during the trial that he had met De Luca while in prison in Gaeta for desertion.[31] The trivial episode at San Calisto and the massacre at Pizzofalcone demonstrate how the war against *brigantaggio* and draft dodging was not merely a matter of fighting armed opponents, deporting suspects, or prosecuting collaborators. It was a problem within the army itself, within each barracks unit, and within each recruit.

In 1876, Cesare Lombroso published the first edition of his *Criminal Man*, which discovered atavistic traits in the skull structure of an alleged Calabrian brigand named Villella (there was no actual record of brigandage; he was a 60-year-old peasant from Catanzaro incarcerated for theft).[32] Like De Amicis, as a young surgeon Lombroso had been sent to the South to serve in the war against the brigands, the campaign, as he described it facetiously in a letter "to liberate Italy from the Italians."[33] There he began cataloguing massive amounts of data drawn from examinations of draftees. At the same time he studied the native population of Calabria. Largely from these two sources Lombroso formulated his theory of atavism, according to which criminal behavior and social degeneration can be explained by the presence in certain subjects of anatomical characteristics inherited from earlier, more primitive forms of life. Lombroso conjectured that the reason Calabrian recruits fell prey to disease at a higher rate than conscripts from other regions was because they were deprived of their traditional postprandial siesta between 12 and 3 p.m.[34] The Veronese inventor of criminal anthropology regarded the Southern population through a diagnostic microscope, as specimens.

The liberal government of the new Italian state quickly put the army to use as a school, mandating for all recruits a basic level of skill in reading, writing, and numbers, while instilling principles of patriotism and national uniformity.[35] The first regimental schools were established for royal troops in 1849 and later confirmed under the national government, with regulations stipulating that all recruits learn to read, write, and do basic mathematics. From 1872 onward, soldiers were not permitted leave until they could demonstrate satisfactory basic literacy. In 1881, the Minister of Public Education declared to parliament that the army was "the university of the people."[36] The success of the regimental schools is difficult to measure, but in an 1886 study, 334,617 citizens newly qualified for voting privileges by having studied in regimental schools during their military service, a number constituting 14 percent of the total electorate.[37]

In a study of the widely mandated practice of systematically transferring abandoned children from orphanages into military training, Simonetta Polenghi has observed that subsequent to the French Revolution "The phenomenon of military training of abandoned children took on a new form: not only was it a factor advancing social mobility, it now also became a secular model of behavior."[38] Not only does the military actually teach literacy skills to hundreds of thousands of recruits and substitute the missing parents of abandoned and orphaned children but it also establishes for civil society an intensive, secular model of virtuous behavior, decorum, and discipline to replace the religious construction of social life imposed and maintained by the Church throughout the previous millennium. In an 1862 school reader titled *Book of the Italian Soldier. Duties and Affections of the Italian Soldier*, author Giovanni De Castro presents soldiers as "the good priests of our civil religion."[39] Polenghi explains, "The pathway established by military instruction, directed as much toward adults as toward children, demonstrates its progressive secularization, which would be fully achieved over the course of the nineteenth century, corresponding to the secularization of the State."[40] In his career of nomadic peregrination as a military bureaucrat from one army base to another throughout the southern provinces, Giovanni Fadda's duty was to present to the local inhabitants a living model of how civilized people conduct themselves. With every step he took, however, he carried invisible baggage of the violent subjection of the very people he was sworn to protect.

The conflicted status of the army in Italian national life might best be captured by contrasting the career of one soldier writer, De Amicis, with that of another, Igino Ugo Tarchetti. Edmondo De Amicis's earliest tales of military life were published in readers for the regimental schools to reinforce a mythos of the Risorgimento as a heroic struggle of the united Italian people and the army as a beneficent, moralizing institution. The magazine *L'Italia militare*, was founded in Florence in 1867 specifically to combat "the difficulty the army encountered integrating itself into Italian society of the era."[41] Hostility to the institution of a permanent army was widespread, from Garibaldi himself, whose early proposal for a people's army modeled on his *Mille* had been quickly vetoed, to the *Messaggero*, which campaigned against the army as a huge waste of tax revenue, to the earliest Italian feminists such as Anna Maria Mozzoni, who identified the army as the source of the problem of prostitution and resultant disease and moral decay.[42]

De Amicis's sketches were disseminated through military channels both to conscripts and the civilian population in response to the impact of antimilitary, antidraft writings such as those by Tarchetti, another young enlistee from the North, who, like De Amicis and Lombroso, had been stationed in the South in the campaign against banditry. Born in 1839 in the Piedmont town of San Salvatore Monferrato to a family he described as "wealthy and terribly unlucky," Tarchetti enlisted after secondary school and was sent in 1861 to Foggia, Lecce, Taranto, and Salerno. Six years older than De Amicis, Tarchetti also discovered his literary vocation while serving in the war against the brigands, but Tarchetti's response was the opposite of that of his counterpart. In the preface to the second edition of his antimilitarist novel, *A Noble Madness: Dramas of Military Life*, Tarchetti reacts to De Amicis's recently published *Army Life: Sketches*:

> One single book appeared in the past year with a contrary thesis. The young author of those pages, recently graduated from a military academy, speaks about the army the way a boarding school student might speak about men and a society he still hasn't known. It is deplorable to waste his talent defending a universally condemned cause. He might as well have written an apotheosis of prison . . . Did a young man really write those pages? I can't make sense of it. Youth is more generous to those who suffer.[43]

The two men's military careers differ markedly, but Tarchetti erred to think De Amicis had not seen action, as the latter's account of the Sicilian uprisings demonstrates. After his first sketches were published in 1867, De Amicis took advantage of the influence of his brother-in-law, a colonel, to transfer to Florence to write full time for *L'Italia militare*. Away from the field, the directness of the early pieces, suggesting affinity with the principles of verismo, gives way increasingly to the tone of paternalistic exhortation that will come to make the episodes described into rhetorical artifices suited to the author's predetermined themes. The reporter loses out to the propagandist but not before providing many convincing images of camp life, for example, the role a young *furiere* such as Giovanni Fadda played among the soldiers. In De Amicis's sketches, the *furiere* or quartermaster is a distinct type, and may illuminate for us the character of Fadda, who served as quartermaster in the Seventh Regiment at the fateful Battle of San Martino. In "The Camp," he is the reliable, overworked soldier whose arrival with the mail always provokes commotion, momentarily becoming an angel for the lucky and an object of curses for the bereft. "What confusion!" writes De Amicis, "What clamor! Letters!"[44] In "The Italian Army during the Cholera Epidemic of 1867," the *furiere* reads roll call at the morning assembly and announces each soldier's task for the day, serving as intermediary between the officer class and the conscripted soldiers. In De Amicis's sketches, it is the quartermaster's task to justify the often mysterious decisions of superiors to the lower orders while reciprocally informing his superiors of the tenor of the troops.[45] In the camp, the quartermaster is an essential go-between, a letter-carrying messenger who plies the zone between superiors and recruits and between recruits and their families. After being promoted to major, we know from his letters to his wife that Fadda traveled continuously, sent for example to Parma, in place of a captain, to drill fresh troops and train them in the use of a new kind of rifle. When he marries Raffaella Saraceni in Naples in 1871, former *furiere*

Fadda steps body and soul into a still more liminal zone: a career soldier, he marries into a civilian family with no military tradition; a mature man from the Northern army, he marries a Southern girl in her teens; son of a notary, he becomes son-in-law to a Calabrian landowner. A strict observer of military regulations, Fadda joins the sort of family that casually invites traveling circus acrobats to dinner in their home.

The propagandist function, aiming at once to give heart to soldiers and honor them to the public at large, accompanies the realist elements in De Amicis's sketches from the beginning. In this universe the reigning metaphor is the nation as family: "Love of *patria* is no more than love for one's family extended beyond the walls of our paternal home as far as the borders of the State in which we are citizens."[46] In the sketch titled, "Child of the Regiment" (Il figlio del reggimento), love of soldiery becomes the first expression of a child's budding awareness of the world: "After the members of our family and household, our first affection, our first heartbeats of passion are for the soldier. Soldiers are the first stick figures we draw on the walls at school and on the covers of our schoolbooks . . . Oh! Our first sword is such happiness!"[47] In a society in which the permanent army was widely opposed, De Amicis invents an image that deposits soldiering deep within the family and proposes a collective vision of the conscript as a sort of lovable puppet, a child's stick figure come to life. In his treatise on Calabria, Cesare Lombroso will evoke this same image of boyhood, contrasting the healthy habits of Northern boys who grow up playing soldier with the unhealthy habits of Southern boys who grow up playing priest.[48] From the Southern perspective, on the contrary, the war against the secular North was a struggle against infidels and atheists. Brigands wore protective amulets bearing images of the Madonna into battle. Members of a "Religious Association" formed to organize resistance against the Northern invaders took an oath to wage holy war in defense of the Church and against "il Lucifero infernale Vittorio Emanuele."[49]

In the Italian family that is the army, the conscripts are children and the officers a mixture of father and teacher. De Amicis devotes an affectionate sketch to his Sardinian orderly, presented as a sort of mascot, who proudly learns to read and write in six months of assiduous effort in the military school but whose very personal take on grammar and orthography results in an incomprehensible Italian. In a passage from "Il campo," the teacher-officer offers a blessing to a young draftee-catechumen:

> —Who are you writing to? asks an officer, pausing behind a prone soldier writing a letter.
>
> —A letter home?
>
> —Yessir, answers the soldier, rising to his knees.

—No, no, stay there, carry on. Have you just learned?
—Four months ago.
—Let's see. Not bad. Bravo.[50]

In this telling moment, the role of the priest has been taken by an officer, the cassock and chasuble changed for a uniform.

In his later military writings, De Amicis's hortatory tone becomes still more pronounced. By the mid-1880s the war against banditry is mostly resolved and the permanent army is about to discover a new national purpose as colonialist invaders in Africa. Once unification is complete with the addition of Rome as capital, De Amicis's campaign for moral betterment, first waged against Southern primitivism, now opens a new front against urban decadence. In a piece published in 1884 in the form of an open address to draftees, "To The Conscripts," De Amicis argues a new line: that the draft and the discipline it teaches represent a solution for a nation now become physically soft and morally lax. Those who complain about a permanent army, he says, "don't see the great moral work done there, the flabby characters tempered anew, the good principles reinforced, the generous aspirations brought forth." In his first published sketches, the army saved young men from the ignorance and illiteracy of their rural origins; now the draft saves them from the moral decay of modern society: "Man is not honest except when and as long as it serves his aims. Recognizing no other motive or norm to guide his actions than what contributes directly to his own well-being, when this stops counseling honesty, brute instinct comes to the fore and subverts the moral order."[51]

The solution to this new threat is the same as it was in 1867: that of the great school of military service. He exhorts the young recruits,

> Learn to read to advance your knowledge of your duties as soldier by reading your regulations and instructions, and to have a useful, enjoyable pastime in your leisure hours. The soldier—said a French writer—is a handsome sight principally in these two cases: when he launches himself against the enemy with bayonet lowered, and when seated at the foot of his bed with a schoolbook in his hands.[52]

The regime's ideal of the army as a lay priesthood exercising a morally corrective influence on bourgeois society comes forth in a popular comedy set in 1880 and published in 1883, "A Young Official, or The Comic and Dramatic of Life," by Paolo Ferrari.[53] In the play (performed successfully in Bologna, Milan, Reggio, Parma, Piacenza, Venice, Trieste, Treviso, Turin, Genoa, and Rome), the young official of the title, an artillery lieutenant, intervenes beneficently to straighten out the adulterous entanglements of a marquis, a count, and a young gentleman, while heroically suppressing his passion for the marquis' wife into chaste devotion. At the end of Act One, the lieutenant and the wife discover a bond in their mutual enthusiasm for De Amicis's *Military Sketches*. When the lady lauds the poetry "in the fibre, the heart, and the fantasy of the novelist," the officer insists that the true poet is the soldier himself, "this other poet, modest, anonymous," who gives the nation, "his discipline, his fidelity, his life!" In a stirring speech that aroused ringing applause and scattered antimilitarist whistles, the officer protests the fetid, collapsing barracks soldiers are forced to live in while the government spends millions on "sumptuous architectonic edifices to house reasoning madness or the irresistible force of our interesting assassins!" The derogatory reference is to the new scientific theories of penal science and criminology, which proposed more humane forms of incarceration to contain the atavistic criminals discovered by Lombroso and others.[54] On one side of the moral divide, the playwright places the chaste wife and the soldier; on the other, the adulterous class and the social progressives who coddle criminals. Within this dialectic, the forced chastity of Fadda's disability becomes in the mind of official Italy a virtuous attribute, a marker of the discipline and high moral character required of the soldier.

The contrast between De Amicis and Tarchetti is so striking as to suggest a sort of Jekyll and Hyde: two men from good families in Northern Italy who discover their vocation while serving in the war against banditry. Igino Tarchetti (he adopted the middle name Ugo in tribute to patriot Ugo Foscolo) did not attend military academy, but enlisted after secondary school and was sent in 1861 as an attaché to the military commissariat in Foggia. His service was plagued by the early onset of tuberculosis and a series of disciplinary actions, further complicated by a succession of socially and psychically damaging love affairs. The last of these, with the epileptic niece of his superior officer, led to his discharge in 1865 (and ultimately to his most famous work, the unfinished novel *Fosca*). After returning to Milan, he wrote for journals and joined the literary circle called the "Scapigliati," modeled on the Parisian *bohémiennes*. His 1867 novel, *A Noble Madness*, sets an extended denunciation of the draft, the military, and war in the frame of a tragic love story that pushes at the boundaries of generic convention. Tarchetti died of typhus in March 1869 after writing the preface to the second edition, but before completing the final chapters, of his most lasting novel, *Fosca*, a harrowing study of suicidal love between a young officer and the neurotic daughter of his superior. In *Fosca*, as in the Fadda case and the Ferrari play just described, the Italian army's war to establish order, once resolved on the field of combat, shifts onto the field of domestic intimacy, unfolding not against an external enemy but within, between a male soldier and a female civilian.

Tarchetti is particularly interested in the damage military regimentation does to the psyche of vulnerable youth. In the preface to *A Noble Madness*, Tarchetti explains that his novel was intended as the first in a series of works intended to reveal "the intimate and secret life of the barracks" to the public at large, but that his efforts had been thwarted by military authorities, including uniformed officials who tore up his pages as he wrote them in Milan cafés. He claims success for his first edition, citing the encouragement of an illustrious writer and editor, Francesco Dall'Ongaro: "Four or six of these dramas of military life, disseminated in the barracks and among the people, would be enough to reawaken the conscience of the multitudes and Italy would be quickly cured of this cancer that devours our life, our wealth, and something still more precious, our liberty."[55]

Like De Amicis, Tarchetti dwells less on the battlefield than on daily life in camp, but to opposite effect. His attack focuses on the hallucinatory banality of martial training and the cruelty of imposing mindless, arbitrary discipline on unprepared young draftees: "It is impossible to apply any firm principle to make sense of what unfolds in the mind of a conscript during his first days of military service . . . He comes to see everything through a cloud; nothing has form or nature that doesn't appear strange and shifting: he cannot distinguish between facts and ideas; something stands between the two that is neither one nor the other—one conscript told me, 'I have these green ideas that pass continuously before my eyes.'"[56]

After describing cases he witnessed in which a young shepherd or fisherman lost his mind in response to boot camp, Tarchetti dissects the way each barracks becomes a miniscule universe whose only ethic is the relentless invasion of individual integrity:

> To be transformed, to be turned into a brute, this is the curse of the draftee, the ideal of the soldier. Once he has put on his uniform, rarely will he remove it without hesitation. A few oppose a painful, useless resistance. Then follow ridicule, isolation, persecution; he will be subjected to every torture one man can inflict on another; even the slightest infraction becomes an enormous violation of discipline; then begin the punishments, incarceration, isolation, the diet of bread and water, the irons, the shackles on the feet and hands; gradually the will is overpowered, perseverance yields, the heart grows hard and breaks. Now he is defeated, he joins the flow. His comrades say, "Lie," and he lies; "Become a brute," and he becomes a brute; "Renounce your will," and he renounces.[57]

In both De Amicis and Tarchetti, doing battle is a negligible element of military life. A foreign enemy is rarely seen, a distraction from the army's true and daily function, the huge social task of nation-building focused inward, by disciplining the recruits themselves, and outward, by modeling conduct for the surrounding population. For De Amicis, the barracks is a school that forges integrity and citizenship; for Tarchetti, the same location is a torture chamber from which the only possible escape is utter submission and abandonment of individual will. For both writers, military success is measured not by battlefield conquest or the successful defense of territory but by the transformation of soldiers.

Until he met Raffaella Saraceni, Captain Giovanni Fadda's career would seem more to confirm De Amicis's vision than Tarchetti's. However modestly, the man had established an honored place for himself in the national apparatus. Like De Amicis, Tarchetti, and Lombroso, Fadda too had been sent to participate in the North's military occupation of the South and had become an instrumental part of it. The regimental bases among which he continued to be transferred between his marriage and his death—Cosenza, Caltanissetta, Chieti—had all been established as military outposts during the war on *brigantaggio*, and continued to exist as such, isolated islands of authority, even now that the populace had been mostly pacified. The career soldier's attraction to the spirited, artistic young woman is perhaps easy to understand, but of the eligible men on display in Naples, what would incline Raffaella and her parents toward Giovanni Fadda in particular? When they met him, perhaps the Saraceni family saw more uniform than man; recognizing his appearance of rectitude and benevolent devotion, the parents decided that his clerkish attention to protocol and detail would balance their daughter's impulsiveness and love of spectacle. The Fadda *parte civile* maintains in court that the soldier informed his wife's family of his war injury before the matrimony was agreed upon, while the Saracenis insist they knew nothing about it. Whoever is telling the truth, the wound must have represented a badge of honor and a symbol of sacrifice rather than a practical problem. Against the hostility and resistance that defined relations between army and populace in the South, the Fadda-Saraceni marriage in 1871 must have represented an optimistic spring, a hopeful new beginning, a belief that the nation could indeed be one. When the marriage falls apart, leading finally to murder, all express dismay, but no one expresses surprise. The next chapter will explore the tragic gap between the ideal soldier Raffaella married and the lived circumstances of Giovanni Fadda's nomadic career as revealed through their private correspondence.

8

Poor Giovanni Fadda

Almost 20 years after the Fadda trial, in 1898, Scipio Sighele, a lawyer and first-generation sociologist of the Lombroso school, describes the average Italian:

> The average type has a fortunate and knowing dose of resignation, such that he contents himself with the place that nature has given him. He has neither great ambitions nor unachievable desires; perhaps he complains, verbally, about the numerous injustices that weigh down upon him, as on everybody, but doesn't find in himself the energy to attempt to rebel in one way or another against these injustices, and thus he resigns himself to living the less bad life possible, in the place and condition that his birth, his family, and his economic status have assigned him.[1]

No statement could more clearly demonstrate that the heroic period of the Risorgimento has by century's end receded into distant memory. The sacrifice of generations paves the way for the complacency of those who follow. When he took a bullet in the groin on the bloody hill of San Martino, did Giovanni Fadda imagine that he was offering up his own well-being for the birth of this new Italian man?

Once he was murdered, Fadda's afterlife in national mythography depended on the tributes of his military brethren, the arguments of lawyers, and on the rhetorical use made of him by journalists, commentators, and illustrators who unfailingly represented Fadda as a flesh and blood embodiment of ideal soldierly virtue. An essential part of the media circus phenomenon is that the living or dead individuals at the center of the tempest get lost in the rising storm. Their figures become abstracted—Pirandello style—into immaterial entities far more real in effectual terms as social actors than their human counterparts. But who was Giovanni Fadda really? Despite his heroism in battle, Captain Fadda's letters suggest that he may have held no greater ambition than to fit comfortably into Sighele's description. In the absence of other evidence, all we have to go on when seeking to understand Fadda's relationship to Raffaella Saraceni are his letters. Those letters, the subject of this chapter, describe a life and character at odds with the use made of the man in the national imaginary. Documenting a slide into catastrophe, the letters witness the failure of the young state's liberal model to engineer social transformation. Uniquely in the Fadda correspondence, that macroscopic failure is witnessed within the mechanics of an intimate relationship. The irony is that it was not the marriage, but the murder of Fadda that ultimately contributed, as judicial procedure and media spectacle, to the achievement of a shared Italian cultural identity.

Lieutenant Fadda married Raffaella Saraceni on May 2, 1871, in Naples, where he was stationed and the bride's family maintained a home. Her dowry amounted to 19,500 lire, mostly in cash, but including precious objects such as beds, bedclothes, fine clothing, and jewelry, with a combined value of 5,500 lire. These figures suggest that the family was what might be called "comfortable," rather than "rich." During the trial, Raffaella's defense makes repeated efforts to break down the media-created preconception of her wealth in the minds of the jury. The bride could have been no more than eighteen; the soldier's age is uncertain, but it was probably around twice hers at the time of the marriage.[2] Apparently, the courtship and wedding took place over an unusually short span of time. When Cesare Fadda takes the stand, he remembers that "the wedding was agreed upon precipitously, so much so as to make you wonder whether something was going on . . . as though there were some intrigue behind it, pressing for the marriage. Giovanni didn't even find out until the ceremony that the Saracenis were from Cassano all'Ionio."[3] Having met them in Naples, Fadda, it would seem, imagined that the Saracenis were comfortably cosmopolitan inhabitants of the nation's largest city, when in fact they were small-town Calabrians who only spent a few months a year in their city house. For some reason, the Saracenis chose not to disabuse their prospective son-in-law of his misconception until the marriage was under way. The fact that Fadda was unable to distinguish—linguistically, behaviorally, culturally—between Neapolitans and Calabrians would suggest that he knew and understood little of the South despite having served there for some time. Although the army lived in and among the southern population, it remained a world apart. Fadda, meanwhile, had a secret of his own; the degree to which he explained his physical condition to his bride's family remains in dispute.

Fadda was a quartermaster (paymaster and accountant), promoted to the rank of lieutenant after his wounding in 1859, and then to captain (*Capitano di contabilità*) some time after his marriage in 1871. Between then and his murder in 1878, the newlyweds were transferred from Naples (in Campania) to Cosenza (Calabria) to Caltanisetta (Sicily) to Chieti (Abruzzi) and finally to Rome, but even within these new stations the captain was continuously on the move, traveling for stays of a few weeks at a time, from as far south as Catania to as far north as Parma. Among Fadda's responsibilities was the training of new recruits, including draftees who were subjected to a 40-day boot camp before being remanded to their homes to await further orders or assigned to regimental schools for basic literacy education. His military career and its meager salary condemned him to an irregular nomadism, staying for shorter terms in barracks housing and longer ones in rented rooms, followed by solitary transfer to a new location with the hope of bringing his wife along later once things were stabilized. Although the national role of the soldier was exalted by writers such as Edmondo De Amicis through a series of government-sponsored publications, the actual circumstances of Fadda's way of life share similarities with other trades that require their practitioners constantly to move from place to place, always strangers in a settled milieu. The soldier's life in this sense is not unlike that of traveling circus performers or the kinds of marginal, suspect groups Lombroso identifies in his treatises on criminality, who wear uniforms to identify their trade and use a protective jargon exclusive to their profession. Common both to his early letters, when he seems mostly cheerful, and his later ones, troubled and angry, Fadda's viewpoint is always that of an outsider having to adapt to an alien environment.

For respectable families in the nineteenth century, the writing of letters was an important and defining ritual, a way of performing family.[4] As modern technologies and economies permeated southern Italy, literacy increased side by side with mobility, such that families relied on written communication to compensate for increasing separation of the nuclear group imposed by unification and facilitated by railroads. Giovanni Fadda is an example of a family man who spends very little time in the vicinity of his family. When individuals related by bonds of blood or marriage are separated for long periods of time, letters themselves "become" the family in that they provide a virtual, rhetorical surrogate for the missing physical intimacy.[5] The aspects of written correspondence that might be called performative—the purchase of materials; the establishment of the household location where writing is to take place; the sitting down to write; the preparation of draft and clean copies; the formulaic occasions and subject matter that call for writing; and the posting—negotiate with the ostensible privacy of the content. The content itself often consists of a form of display whose function is to reinforce bonds threatened by distance. By marrying Raffaella, Giovanni Fadda became a member of the Saraceni family; but because he was almost always absent, his belonging was virtual, expressed and maintained overwhelmingly in formulaic language sent by mail.

No matter where he was stationed, Fadda wrote letters: to his elderly father in Cagliari; to his brother, whose position as property inspector for state lands compelled him to constant travel as well; to his in-laws, whether at their city home in Naples or their country home in Cassano all'Ionio; and to his wife. The wife who Fadda affectionately addressed as "Raffeluccia" followed her husband's army-mandated peregrinations as far as Chieti (Abruzzi), where they lived from 1875 to 1877, but always spent a great deal of time with her family in Cassano in the house she regarded as her real home. We only have two notes from Fadda to his own father and brother, but there are numerous letters to his wife and mother-in-law (whom he addresses as "Dear Mother") in the form of drafts, which he wrote up and preserved among his papers, sending the corrected, clean copies to their addressees. These drafts were found in his apartment in Rome at the time of his murder, bundled together with the replies he received, and are now in the trial archive.[6] The fact that he kept his drafts and the letters he received testifies both to his affection for Raffaella and to his character, so well suited to his duties as accountant. Raffaella and the Saracenis, on the other hand, kept neither Fadda's letters nor drafts of their own to him. Raffaella will be asked to justify this difference in court; the prosecutor's implication is that affection would compel a proper wife to lovingly preserve her husband's letters, and their absence from a safe place among her private things would suggest either secret hostility toward him or a culpable wish to destroy evidence.

Certain letters play crucial roles in the trial for what they reveal of the breakdown of the captain's relations with Raffaella and her family and are prominently featured in media coverage, cited verbatim and at length. The fact that intimate, anguished communications between husband and wife were exposed to public view constituted another of the sensational aspects of the Fadda trial and must have increased, for newspaper readers, its novelistic appeal. Letters between Fadda, his wife, and his mother-in-law are read aloud in court and later excerpted in the Bracco publication of Nicolò Coboevich's coverage for the *Messaggero*'s competitor, *Il Bersagliere*.[7] The dramatic domestic situation revealed in the letters, combined with the fatal outcome, served polemicists as a proof of the need to legalize divorce.[8]

As revealed in his correspondence in the first years of his marriage, the newly promoted captain seems happy, proud, and well suited to the role of a lower official occupied with recruits, accounts, and protocol. Career military man, part-time husband, Fadda lives in the institution most actively committed to the national task at hand: that of creating Italians and embodying, in its daily conduct, the values of the new state. As a man with a shameful but invisible disability, Fadda has still more reason to prefer living inside the idealized image of the new Italian citizen. Son of a notary in the Kingdom of Sardinia and brother of a state lands inspector, Fadda is a soldier no longer dedicated to combat but to civilizing Italian society according to the liberal vision that holds sway between the Risorgimento and the close of the century.

Captain Fadda is not a philosopher, but in his letters he embodies a positivist man of his time and place, convinced of the perfectibility of his race, certain that the truth can be apprehended, and faithful that clear orders and reasoned dialogue can resolve both large and small problems. His is a peculiarly Italian positivism, a kind detached from its northern European founders. As it penetrated Italian social consciousness, positivism seized on its founder Auguste Comte's precept that "the great object" was "the endeavor to become more perfect" and applied that principal to the immediate task of nation building. Comte's axiom, "all our varied observations of phenomena can be brought into one consistent whole," became in Italy the campaign to bring all the varied and contradictory social phenomena of the peninsula into the one consistent whole of the unified nation.[9] As one historian states, "The ideology of the nation was born from positivist culture and never freed itself from it."[10] Northern liberals interpreted the conquest of papal Rome as a great victory for positivism, scientific proof that reason must inevitably vanquish superstition.[11] When Lieutenant Fadda is training his thickheaded recruits to march in step, he is enacting a positivist crusade for the betterment of the Italian people, a movement that in Alberto Asor Rosa's words, "moved from the north in conquest of the south."[12]

Even in his drafts Fadda's script is clear, but when upset or angry the hand becomes sharp so that the tops of letters are serrated and strikethroughs are common. His handwriting is quite legible, distinguished by the curling flourish of his *d*s and the way he finishes words that end with *e* or *a* with a tail of ink that loops back over the preceding word to cross *t*s. Only in one document does the captain's hand seem to change style radically. The two narrow, black-bordered pages headed "Scorn" (*Disprezzo*), the transcription of the poem Fadda found in a Neapolitan newspaper in March 1878, seem ragged and agitated, almost as if written by a different hand entirely.

Fadda's drafts are not always dated, nor are several from Raffaella and her mother, especially when the disputes reach a peak, making it hard to retrace their sequence. In an era when most Italians were illiterate and no more than 10 percent regularly spoke the national language, the exchange of pleasantries and conventional salutations in written Italian, a language most people encountered only in bureaucratic, journalistic, or literary contexts, was itself a performance of gentility and of a national, rather than local, consciousness. Fadda's job would have required him to be versed in both spoken and written Italian; thus, his is quite comfortable, as though it were his native tongue. He appears to enjoy writing; his letters become a realm where abstract values of character come to the fore, while physical limitations recede to secondary status. Raffaella also writes in a comfortable, effective Italian that bespeaks mature feminine poise. Her use of language would rather belie the image of her as small minded and provincial, except that when not disputing with Fadda in the later letters, she speaks only of family affairs and clothing. She is able to express warmth or anger more directly than her husband. Her handwriting is generally clearer than his, but its graphic appearance varies notably from letter to letter, sometimes delicate, sometimes more flattened and forceful, but always characterized by a decisive forward inclination.

The mother-in-law's letters to Giovanni are far longer than anything written by Raffaella herself, demonstrating Carolina Nola Saraceni's dominance over her daughter and central position in the family, as well as impressive rhetorical skills. Her Italian is vivid but less formally correct, marked by broken syntax and reliance on formulaic expressions, suggesting that her daily spoken language may not have been Italian. She is prolix and her hand is heavy, with individual letters crowded on the page and words often difficult to separate one from another on each line. The sometimes drippy ink suggests that she may not have bothered to compose a clean copy after writing her first draft. Of the three writers, however, the mother-in-law has the greatest command of language, with a special virtuosity in reproach of her son-in-law: "I feel sorry for you, because it isn't you acting, but rather the goal you've set for yourself that you press forward to accomplish no matter what, for no reason, abusing everything and everyone around you." Carolina Nola also writes bitterly to Giovanni about her new daughter-in-law, Teresa Samengo, who, she tells him, was presented to the family as an "angel" but has turned out to be a "poisonous snake" (*vipera velenosa*).

Despite the presence of her letters in the investigative records, and though local police in Cassano assert that she should be arrested as "the prime cause" of Raffaella's discord with her husband and her relations with Cardinali, Carolina Nola is never deposed by investigators and is not summoned to testify during the trial, protected by her right not to incriminate her daughter.[13] Although she is never charged, the investigative records include an extremely harsh evaluation of her and the Saraceni family, given on October 12 by the commander of *carabinieri* in Cassano: "Given the character of those towns, the obstinacy of Raffaella's mother, named Carolina Nola, whose previous record recommends her not at all, being a woman who has always coupled with various persons and in whose footsteps her daughter seems to have followed."[14]

The commander adds about Carolina Nola's husband, Domenico Saraceni (whom the records variously describe as a landowner, architect, and engineer for the state railway system), that he is "extraneous, because he submits to all his wife's caprices" and about Raffaella's brother Giuseppe that he is "a young bachelor who only thinks about enjoying himself."[15] The carabiniere's statement is so strongly worded and yet so devoid of evidence as to reveal less about the character of the Saraceni family than it does about the abyss of hostile alienation separating Italy's national law enforcement personnel from the populace they were sworn to protect. Nevertheless, the mother-in-law's role in the events leading to Captain Fadda's murder remains most ambiguous.

For his part, Fadda has a special fondness for certain words, which he uses with particular pride, such as *sistema* (i.e., "system," a technical word probably drawn from military parlance); *giacchè* (an elegant-sounding conjunction for "as," "since," "seeing that"); and *qualche* (a partitive meaning "some"), which he applies to lessen the brute impact of any expression that might be too blunt or too crude, rather the way the stereotypical Englishman uses "a bit of."

Immediately after the salutation, epistolary convention called for the writer to ask after his or her interlocutor's health and to expand on his or her own. For the Faddas, her concern for his compromised health appears to be the primary motif through which the young wife manifests her affection for her older husband. Raffaella worries and Giovanni reassures, as in a letter from Parma dated June 15, 1873: "I am putting into practice your command not to overwork myself, because I know your orders are dictated out of love, so I obey scrupulously as though they were prescribed by an angel. But I cannot avoid doing what duty demands. Despite that, be assured that I'm in perfect health." As here, duty versus love might be called the fundamental topos of Fadda's correspondence with his wife and her family. His early, serene reassurances to his wife of his good health appear to be his way of demonstrating his tenderness to her. The game is that although he is much older, she babies him, fretting like a mother hen; the rigid soldier softens at the coddling but insists that duty calls.

In the later context of the trial, Giovanni's injury and just how much Raffaella knew about it becomes a matter of great import, such that the early letters between the couple become subject to analysis and interpretation by investigators and lawyers as well as a topic of discussion in cafés and dinner tables throughout the nation. Thus is torn away in death the discretion that characterized the captain in life. His face is hawked on street corners, his shame and secrets trumpeted to the four winds. Raffaella insists before the court that she knew nothing of any impairment, but several witnesses from Cassano swear that she complained openly, aggrieved that her husband was a useless tool. Fadda's brother Cesare and his army comrades insist that he informed the Saraceni family of his injury before the wedding and even underwent a medical exam that proved his ability to perform satisfactorily as a husband. However, the only medical document of such a nature in the investigation records is dated a year after his wedding and corresponds to a letter from Fadda in Sicily to his mother-in-law, where he describes having undergone a doctor's exam with the intention of obtaining a permanent medical leave.

In their exaltation of the captain's character, at no time do his family, their lawyers, or his military colleagues entertain the possibility that in the precipitous rush to the wedding, Fadda may not have notified his wife's family that his war injury had resulted in any disability. It's also possible, presumably, that he didn't learn of it himself until he was married. Summing up the facts prior to the first court session, Vassallo puts it that "his physical imperfection was not kept from the family of the bride. Fadda's honesty abhorred keeping silent about a matter that might later appear to involve trickery. But the imperfection was not an impediment to the marriage." Demonstrating his research, Vassallo continues with a brief discourse concluding that both history and science show that "monorchids do not lack the generative faculty," concluding that "the wedding thus took place under the most auspicious signs."[16] Fadda's letters, on the other hand, demonstrate that his compromised health, if not overtly his impotence, was a principal theme in his relations with his wife and her family.

Fadda's correspondence begins most optimistically, but as it proceeds, it dramatically chronicles the collapse of his marriage and his descent into despair. The letters reveal a man who believes that following regulations will lead justly and naturally to achievement and progress but whose situation gradually becomes too complicated for his resources—rhetorical, psychological, and institutional—to resolve. At first he responds as a gentleman, trusting that the model conduct assimilated in years of military discipline will resolve misunderstanding between people who care for one another. When this turns out not to achieve the desired results, he snaps: bitter sarcasm and self-pity break through the poise of his letters, and he takes the rash, irreversible action of sending Raffaella back her piano. Once he definitively recognizes that he has lost all sway with her, and worse, that she no longer loves him, he has only a few days left to live.

In a letter dated April 26, 1873, from Caltanissetta (central Sicily) to Cassano all'Ionio, Fadda greets his wife with the affectionate diminutive, "Cara Raffeluccia," and opens by answering her concerns about his health: "You can rest assured about my health. I only wish it was always so good. I eat and drink like a Turk, and sleep when time permits." He then describes the frustration and pride of whipping young troops into shape: "I assure you that they drive me to desperation. In the midst of them are some young men with education, and intelligent, but for the most part they are peasants with hard heads; but it matters little, for at 'Present Arms' I see to it that they line up and march magnificently."

Apparently, the young officer is reliable and does his job well, for he has been assigned a duty above his rank. He must go to Parma for two months to train recruits in the use of a new kind of rifle. The task would normally be carried out by a captain rather than a lieutenant, so the fact that it has been given to Fadda promises well for future promotion. He informs his wife of the new responsibility but takes care not to express enthusiasm about it, anticipating that another trip away might displease her. Duty to the state calls him away from duty at home. When he must make excuses for not being with her, Fadda asserts his helplessness as a low-ranking individual soldier in the face of the arbitrary mystery of military decision making. In weak compensation for the anticipated disappointment of his young wife, he promises to visit her before he departs for the north: "In mid-May I'll be in Cassano very briefly, just time enough for a hug." In retrospect, this last sentence reads as an evasive way of warning Raffaella to expect no more than a warm hug.

The letters between Fadda and his wife unconsciously document the complex relations between military and civilian ideologies as they condition individual lives. In a letter to his wife on June 15, 1873, he abandons himself to a monologue that reveals how perfectly he has internalized his role and status. After the canonical comments on his state of health, he expands breezily on his favorite leisure activity:

> My walks are always outside town; that way I aim to avoid any possible unpleasant encounters, since there are so many generals around in civilian clothes, and they scrutinize the officials to see that we're in perfect dress. As you can imagine, I'm so accustomed to wearing my dress gloves, whether in school or at the shooting range or in the office I'm always in gloves, but once in a while I get a little distracted and neglect my gloves, and well, in that little time that I'm without gloves, as chance could have it, I might run into some annoying examination. So therefore when I don't have a real need to go to a large center, I take walks outside town. Truly, I can assure you that there are some very beautiful places to stroll, extremely clean, shadowed by tall trees, so when you return to the city you needn't worry about finding yourself covered with dust or sweaty from the sun. I feel much better doing this than stretching out in a café like all the others, since in addition to being constantly in view, the superiors get the idea that you don't want to do anything.

Here is an ideal lower-ranking officer, surely, one who would fear no shame even to allow his superiors to examine his private letters to his bride. His nervous concern for his gloves even recalls Tarchetti's statement about the brainwashed soldier that "once he has put on his uniform, rarely will he remove it without hesitation."[17] While we could never gainsay Fadda's sincerity, the letter reads as an enactment of ideal sentiments for his own benefit and that of his wife. It also describes a fundamentally solitary man. Fadda did not attend the military academy and was not born into the officer class, thus his dress gloves may have particular symbolic value for him. His diction and syntax embody just how thoroughly he has absorbed and personalized the function the army has assigned him. He uses *qualche* repeatedly here as an adjective to euphemize "unpleasant encounters" and "annoying examination," specifically to eliminate any possibility that his story might be read to suggest that he resents his superior officers. He will begin to rely on the same term as a rhetorical crutch as his relations with his wife and her family break down.

Military-imposed separation increasingly strains the tenuous relationship. In a letter to his mother-in-law written almost a year later (May 10, 1874) from Cosenza, Fadda reveals quarrels with his wife during her recent visit to him. As a defense against rumor, Fadda describes the measures he takes, similar to those in the letter from Parma, to shore up the bulwarks of his reputation against the threat of calumny.

Dear Mother-in-Law,

> I was very happy to have Raffeluccia visit and I repeat to you what I said to her, that I'm the same person as three years ago, and if there was a moment or two with a bit of misunderstanding, that doesn't take anything at all away from the esteem in which I hold her. You tell me you've forgotten any little disagreement between us, I assure you that I forgot even before you did, and if on my part there was a bit of obstinacy, it was against my system of holding a grudge because of some little word that slipped out without thinking, but that my dignity and self-regard dwelt on. Another thing I advise is that you never believe anything people say; those who want to do evil seek any means and that's what happened to Raffaella. Since they couldn't wound me any other way they sought to insinuate in her the idea that I was going to the hotel while she was here visiting me; others might have laughed at this malicious insinuation, but it bothered me a great deal that she was so quick to believe it, and so, reflecting on these problems, I sought during the time she was away to be seen at the hotel for meals, for coffee, before going to bed, always together with respectable people of a higher position than mine, so that someone wanting to throw me in the mud would be forced to silence. Often I would have preferred to eat in my room, but thinking

> that my absence might lead to calumny, I tried never to alter the system I'd adopted since Raffaella's departure . . .
>
> Accept this embrace to be extended to all,
> Your most affectionate Giovannino

In contrast to the more serene tone of the letter from Parma, this one shows there has been a quarrel between Raffaella and Giovanni. Here, the husband's reparative actions appear misplaced and excessive. Apparently Raffaella has accused Giovanni of "going to the hotel" during her visit, which may be a euphemism for visiting prostitutes. In any case it appears that she believed he was carousing like a soldier instead of spending time with her. During her rare visit he had neglected to demonstrate the warmth she expected, and she guessed or chose to guess that he was directing his passions elsewhere. The accusation of libertine behavior is decidedly in contradiction to the rumor in Cassano that Raffaella despised her husband precisely because she found him a useless tool. What Fadda cannot say at this point, without rupturing a fragile pretense of civility, is that he suspects the "they" who insinuate malicious rumors against him to be Raffaella's mother. He directs his remarks here to the matriarch in acknowledgment that his relations with his wife ultimately pass through her mother. The letter suggests that Giovanni and Carolina Nola have traded barbs at some point, but both have made gracious gestures of having "forgotten" any injurious words. The problem therefore is not merely a personal one between husband and wife, but between his military role and the southern family he has married into. His perception of his wife's family begins to parallel that of the Italian military toward the inhabitants of the south in general. A year before his murder, Fadda will confess to a friend in Rome that he suspects the Saracenis want to kill him.

We know from this letter from Cosenza that Giovanni and Raffaella had quarrels and that their relationship triangulated through her mother. Between their marriage in 1871 and 1875, Fadda is stationed in Naples, Cosenza, Caltanissetta, and finally Chieti, a small metropolis beyond the Appennines from Rome, not far from the Adriatic. Although her doctor advises that the malarial air in Chieti is bad for her, Raffaella visits him there often enough that they establish a household, and she maintains friendships with local inhabitants who are old acquaintances of the Nola and Saraceni clans. One day, in an episode featured in high relief in the accounts of the trial, Giovanni surprises Raffaella as she writes a letter beginning with the greeting, *Mio caro Edoardo* ("My Dear Edoardo"). He asks to read it, but she tears it up, saying it is to her uncle of that name. Seeking to prove her adultery, the prosecution in the trial asserts that "My Dear

Edoardo," is far too intimate and informal a salutation for a young southern woman to use toward an older uncle, who should never be addressed with his given name. Raffaella answers in court that the letter was just a draft, that "Edoardo" would have been replaced by *Zio* ("Uncle") in the clean copy, that her uncle is comparatively young (35), and that she tore up the note only because she was describing to him an argument she was having with Giovanni. This destroyed letter, reported to investigators by Giovanni's brother Cesare during the inquest, is the only material evidence (if it can properly be called material) to support the widespread, detailed rumors of Raffaella's adultery that follow her from Chieti to Cassano, at least until Pietro Cardinali begins visiting the Saraceni house in 1878.

The extant Fadda-Saraceni letters tell a tale of the unraveling of their marriage beginning in the summer of 1877. The captain has received orders of a transfer to Rome. At the same time an agreement has been reached in Cassano between the Saraceni and Samengo clans for the marriage of Raffaella's brother Peppino to Teresa Samengo. Giovanni sends a note to his father-in-law that because of service obligations he cannot guarantee his attendance at the wedding. There is no aspect of Fadda's relations with his wife's family that does not entail some degree of conflict with his duties as a soldier.

On August 9, Fadda sends a postal card from Chieti to his mother-in-law, stating that his own mother is very ill and he must depart for Cagliari (his mother indeed dies in August). When he comes back from Sardinia, rather than returning to her husband Raffaella remains with her family to assist in wedding preparations for her brother. Fadda must organize the move on his own. He goes to Rome and writes his wife from the capital about the difficulty of finding an apartment:

September 10, 1877
from Rome

Carissima Raffeluccia,

> Yesterday I sent a telegram to find out whether you'd arrived, I await an answer impatiently. It has been raining continuously for three days, making me very irritated, because they gave me a place to stay far from headquarters, so I have to spend on a cab and get drenched just the same. I assure you our house is very nice, leaving out that they were shameless enough to ask 200 Lire for the rooms. I answered that if I had to pay 200 Lire for housing alone—that is, more than my salary—I would demand a discharge. They informed me that's what senators and congressmen pay. So I'll be content to pay 90 Lire and be comfortable. Dear Raffaella, I beg you to write me often, otherwise you make me worry, and as you see despite everything I have to do, I write you just the same, and I swear both my head and my legs are out

> of whack. *Addio*, I embrace you tightly to my heart, and give an embrace to mamma and everyone at home.

Slightly overwhelmed but excited to have set up house in the metropolis, Fadda longs for his wife's comfort, asking for sympathy for his nagging debilities. A month later he writes again in a more stabilized state of mind as he balances necessary frugality with the wish to satisfy her desires:
October 17, 1877

Cara Mia Raffeluccia,

> The house is all in order and I hope you'll like it, it's a little small but as you well know, in Rome, 200 or 300 lire for a room is nothing; all in all I'd say I've been lucky to spend only 90 Lire. Plus you have to consider the location, we're on one of the principal streets, the building and the stairway have gaslight, the other tenants all civil people. As always I await news of you. *Addio* cara Raffeluccia I hug you tight to my heart, your most affectionate husband.
>
> P.S. To explain what I mean by small, the house has three rooms and a kitchen, two of them full rooms with carpets and the other for general use or as a dining room.

In response to Giovanni's notes from this period, there is a single, undated response from Raffaella:

Carissimo Giovannino,

> I want to hope you are well for my consolation, thank the Lord I am well. I hope you're persuaded to let me stay for Peppino's wedding, because what are fifteen days more, there's no point you insisting anymore because you understand the need for me to stay and it's not a caprice. If it were months I would have said no too, but since it's only a matter of days I agreed, it's for my brother, I've only got one, we're already here and the wedding is soon, so let it go. You are so reasonable, that's what you'll say, won't you? Coming to you and leaving him before he's married, I just can't do that to him, that's all there is to it. Reply immediately and tell me everything.
>
> A thousand embraces.

Raffaella's tactics here reveal several key dynamics of the couple's relations. The wife has been tagged by her husband as capricious, while he is acknowledged as the reasonable one. Meanwhile, her appeal, "You are so reasonable, that's what you'll say, won't you?" is rich with intimate nuance;

she anticipates his objection but trumps it by praising his magnanimity, knowing that he can deny her no demand.

By the end of November the wedding still has not taken place. Fadda receives a letter from the would-be groom, Peppino, asking Giovanni to allow Raffaella to stay in Cassano through the wedding, especially to assist in the delicate task of keeping her mother calm. Using a tactic later employed by his mother, Peppino tells Giovanni that he is writing confidentially, unbeknownst to the rest of his family, but the pushy tone of speaking in confidence undermines his credibility.[18] By now Fadda suspects that there is a conspiracy among the Saracenis never to send Raffaella to Rome. In any case the Saraceni dithering about the wedding is irksome, as he has repeatedly told them how complicated it is to obtain leave from his superiors. He writes crossly to his wife immediately after receiving the letter from her brother:

November 27, 1877

Cara Raffeluccia,

> Since everyone wanted me to postpone my departure and to show that I make every sacrifice not to cause problems for your family, I put off my departure until the 4 or 5 of December. But understand that I absolutely cannot postpone until after that date, I will have 15 days of leave, so I hope Peppino will be able to finish all his business, if not I don't know anything else I can do. I also think you will agree with me that I have been understanding enough and so you will do what you can to persuade your family that it would be discourteous to ask anything more from me. Every day, the Colonel asks me, "when are you taking leave?" and since he is sly enough to see that something is holding me up, he repeats it every day to show that he isn't as mean as everyone believes, but rather that we're the ones who are so scattered as to ask for something and then forget about it.

The captain's exasperation grows to the degree that he refers to his brother-in-law's wedding as mere business, casting the marriage negotiations in a light both mercantile and shallow. All he wants from the family, which is embarrassing him in front of his superiors, is a firm date. Fadda is living on an intimate scale the failure of De Amicis' dream that the army shall civilize the south. Beneath his frustration is a growing anger that the Saracenis are lying to him with his own wife's connivance.

In December, with Peppino's marriage still up in the air, Giovanni Fadda travels to Cassano for the Christmas holidays with the intention of bringing Raffaella back to Rome. He returns empty handed. At the trial, his Roman friend Filomena Coller testifies that Giovanni had been very happy before his departure, but when she met him afterward, the captain tearfully told her how Raffaella had received him glacially: "He told me that when he arrived, his wife was standing there with a plate in her hand, not looking at him and acting coldly. He took her arm and asked what was wrong and she said, 'I have nothing against you; you're here to take me to Rome, and I don't want to go.'"

At dinner, conversation dwelt on the heated dowry negotiations with the family of Peppino's fiancé. Raffaella provoked him, saying, "You're a soldier, you should take a gun and go to their house and defend my brother." When the captain refused, saying he would do no such thing, Raffaella began to pout and later refused to go to bed with him, saying, "I can't sleep anyway; I'm anxious, I'm afraid something happened to my brother. I'll wait at the window." Coller testifies, "The captain told me she stayed there all night, looking out."[19] At his departure from Cassano, Carolina Nola presented the captain with a package of foods to eat during the return trip, saying that she would bring Raffaella to Rome "in eight days." Thinking the food might be poisoned, Fadda had thrown it out. Nevertheless, Coller stresses, until the end Giovanni was still "madly in love" with his petulant young wife.

As reported by the newspapers, Coller quotes Fadda as saying, "Don't you know that if I'd stayed there, they wouldn't have let me live eight days?" His fear of being murdered treacherously by his in-laws resonates with a widespread conception that southern Italians and Calabrians in particular had a deep inclination toward murderous violence, that killing one another was a far more casual affair than it was in the north. In his 1863 study of Calabria, Lombroso observed that among the Calabrians, "Shooting someone to death, where elsewhere a knife is used, is a simple prank" ("Uccidere qualcuno a fucilate, come altrove a coltello, è uno scherzo assai poco inconveniente."), adding, "I saw two mayors and two elected officials and, alas! A police chief, who had been convicted of murder!"[20] In Calabria, he adds, "The slang language of thieves (*amasca*) is used by educated people." Even the south's genteel classes, that is, carry the telltale stigma of atavism.

Shortly after the New Year, Vittorio Emanuele dies suddenly in Rome. Present in the capital for the state funeral, lonely Captain Fadda writes his wife. Among the throngs of citizens crowding the city for the funeral, he has happened to encounter the one person he would most have preferred to forget:

January 23, 1878,
Cara Raffaella,

> Finally one can breathe and Rome seems normal again. If it had gone on like that much longer it would have been intolerable. You couldn't eat because in the restaurants they took your plate away while you were still chewing,

> people were eating and sleeping in the cafés, and anyone with a place to sit down wouldn't give it up for any amount. In sum, you could say that in these days Rome is all Italy, you find people from everywhere, Cosenza, Milan, even Chieti. As a matter of fact I received greetings from a Mr. Edoardo Dongelli which he extends to you as well and even to Maria (Raffaella's maid—ed.); he's clearly a man of distinction because even though I've never had the honor of meeting him, he remembers me just the same, a pity I don't know him better and hope we can meet again. This individual even spoke to me about Mrs. Lombardi, who carries on with her jealous fits toward her husband, who rises early every morning to chase servant girls in marketplace; these jealous fits are so out of fashion. Mr. Edoardo tells me that he is vanquishing all Chieti (meaning of course all the women who seek to be vanquished), it seems impossible, him so ugly but so lucky with the ladies; I'm sure he'll come to regret it, because he'll end up with the numbers of all those open for business and all Chieti will take note.
>
> I had a fever for two days. Today I'm a little better; must be because of all the emotion. Give my best to mamma and papà, with embraces, your most affectionate Giovanni

The captain is offended at Italy's failure to conduct itself in a fashion appropriate to the solemnity of the state funeral. At the same time, he believes this Edoardo Dongelli to be the "Dear Edoardo" to whom Raffaella was writing on that day in Chieti. The tone of containment that so marked Giovanni's earlier letters now rapidly breaks down. But rather than charging his wife directly, he uses vicious irony to express the state of his sentiments. His heavy sarcasm anticipates that of Carducci's epode condemning the women at the Fadda trial, in that it conflates adultery with the raucous spectatorship of the Italian populace.

An undated reply, which must have been written in early February, arrives from Raffaella that refuses to respond to her husband's sarcasm:

Carissimo Giovannino,

> I was so sorry about the death of the king, but what can you do, we are all bound for death, some sooner some later, we all have to go someday. I bet you must be very busy now, no? Peppino's wedding should have happened Sunday the 3rd but because of the mourning period for the king it was postponed; we hope to have it as soon as the mourning period is over.

An already bitter Fadda must have been appalled by Raffaella's supremely shallow and blithely offensive dismissal of the death of Vittorio Emanuele, the first soldier of national independence. The king, the Risorgimento, Italy itself means little to her. In his ire, he misunderstands

Raffaella's use of the expression "mourning period" (*lutto del re* and *lutto*). As his mother-in-law will later explain, by "mourning period," Raffaella intended to mean that her brother's wedding was to be postponed until the new king was sworn in (as he was on January 19, two days after the funeral) and public officials (such as local clerks occupied with putting the state seal on marriage and dowry agreements) would return to their offices—that is, within a week. But Giovanni, versed in ceremonial protocol, takes her to mean that her brother's wedding—and thus her subsequent, long-awaited transfer to Rome—will be postponed until the end of the official national mourning period subsequent to the death of a king; a period of six months.[21] He had been deeply wounded by his wife's mockery of his military prowess over the family dinner table at Christmastime. Her challenge to use his weapon to right matters with the rival clan ridiculed him implicitly for the gap between the soldier he dressed as and the accountant he was in reality. Her conduct cruelly declared what everyone knew: that his real performance did not match the promise of his uniform. Then in January, by sheer chance he had encountered the man he suspected of cuckolding him, who ridiculed him in a veiled way, presenting himself as a friend and speaking in a chummy way about affairs with married women. As a last degrading offense on his dignity, the Saraceni family was now cheapening the king's death by using it as an excuse to further their own mean schemes against him. The sarcasm in his previous letter warned his wife that he was nearing a breaking point, but she had chosen to ignore it. At the end of his rope, Fadda reacts rashly: he orders her beloved piano sent back to Cassano.

Descriptions published after her arrest report that Raffaella was vain about her skills as a pianist. The couple had met in Naples, in fact, around the piano: as a newcomer in the same building, the captain had been a regular invitee to the family's evening soirees centered around Raffaella's musical demonstrations.[22] It is easy to imagine the loving indulgence with which her much older husband arranged to have her piano laboriously borne across the Appennines from Chieti to the capital. In the small apartment he prepared for her in Rome, the piano must have taken up a good deal of space, but perhaps cheerfully bespoke for the lonely captain his wife's imminent arrival, and the pleasure she would take in playing melodies in their new home. The effort and expense of transporting the piano now from Rome to Cassano must have been considerable, and its surprise arrival at the Saraceni home, probably by donkey cart up from the nearest train station at Buffaloria, must have represented a harsh public slap in the face of the family; the trip would undoubtedly have damaged the delicate instrument. At the same time, Fadda punishes himself: he terminates his lease with his current landlords and moves into a two-room apartment in a sketchy neighborhood.

Peppino's wedding finally takes place in early February, proving Fadda's error in his reading of Raffaella's note. Letters from his mother-in-law and wife admonish him for his irrational reaction. Carolina Nola reproaches him harshly, saying, "One could pardon a boy such conduct, but never a man," and describes her daughter as being in such a state of emotional prostration that she fears for Raffaella's very life, "for the shame you throw in the face of a family that has always loved you and treated you like its dearest son, in the face of your wife, the woman I entrusted to you, sure of your affection, trusting that you would be everything for her, a child with no experience of men or of love." She disingenuously claims to be writing Fadda secretly, going so far as to use two kinds of ink, presumably so Raffaella won't notice that ink is disappearing from the inkwell.

When Raffaella learns from her mother that Giovanni's strange reaction was provoked by her vague words about the mourning period, she writes him an angry letter, saying, "I am so irritated that I can't say anything but that everything you do is pure calculation, shameful calculation, but in time and when I am calmer we can talk about it, and I assure you that I'm not afraid of your sarcasm because I have nothing to be reproached for." Fadda replies with his most desperate, accusatory letter. The draft is filled with strikethroughs and interlinear insertions, suggesting he labored over it intensely, his hurt feelings struggling against his desire to state his case in the clearest possible terms. Vivid and wrenching, the letter's appearance in newspapers broadcast Captain Fadda's humiliation across the country, accusation vying with self-laceration:

> The state that you say has arisen diabolically in me is not that, but a situation you and your relatives have intentionally provoked for over seven years now, and if things have arrived at the present after all my suffering, tolerating all this, it's because I wanted to avoid publicity, always hoping for a better future. Instead it goes from bad to worse, and your neglect of me reached a peak I would call disgust, extremely pernicious in a wife, that makes a husband appear ridiculous. I had no one to defend me at your house, and you took advantage of this to make all those ugly remarks, snide comments and false insinuations against me—the true diabolical art—that wore away in you the affection there must be between husband and wife. If instead someone, moved by simple human charity, had not claimed for me merits I do not have, but at least made you reflect on those qualities of kindness and decency that I positively know myself to have, declaring the unfairness of your conduct, perhaps your behavior toward me would have been much better, and you would better have recognized your duties. But what can you expect, when I'm not capable of keeping a lady such as you, as you yourself threw in my face, it's the same as telling me I'm a scoundrel (*mascalzone*), and with all this I'm pointing out only the cause, for now I leave the effects to the side . . .

> Certainly I have never thrown around the expression separation, but surely, angry at such unjustifiable treatment, and above all seeing how unhappy you are to be with me, always playing the victim and showing it off to relatives and strangers. I struggled to hide my shame for a certain time [a word is crossed out here –ed.] since it clearly showed that you had been forced to marry me; this you cannot say because it's absolutely false, but in the meantime you made it clear to everyone with your behavior. In this state of things I believe I conducted myself as a gentlemen, accepting everything that you and your relatives wished; you yourself in Cassano threw this word in my face, your mother spoke to me about it in numerous letters. I believed that was how you felt, thus if I then in my letters showed myself to be gravely offended, you must place your hand on your conscience and judge me.

This draft ends at midpage. The next page among Fadda's papers contains a short draft that shows an effort to lessen the harsh tone of what has come before and proposes a path to a solution: "For now if we can suspend this tension that has been going on, I would certainly not oppose such a beneficent gesture, but without getting into a lot of gossip, something I have always been an enemy of, but rather facing problems that truly deserve attention, I wish to explain these things at a family meeting, including your father, my brother, and your uncle. This is necessary to explain my actions, to avoid the same things happening all over again."

Fadda's only hope rests in an appeal to the sense of honor of the men in the family. Giovanni proposes a meeting including himself, his brother Cesare, and the men of the Saraceni clan to take place in Taranto, in Puglia, a sort of middle ground by train. Fadda judges Raffaella's brother Peppino unreliable and to be excluded. In such a setting, he trusts, one may speak of duty, his own and that of his wife, and expect to be heard.

As a counterproposal, the women insist that the meeting take place in Cassano and that it include them as well. For readers sympathetic to her defense, Raffaella's reply to Fadda appears eminently reasonable. She refuses to respond to the harsh accusations leveled and the deeper ones implied in her husband's embarrassing diatribe, offering a compromise agreement. One finds here the clear, unpretentious voice that reporters later describe in court, with its winning effect on public opinion:

March 30, 1878

Caro Giovannino,

> In your most recent, you accuse me of having insulted you when I said you were calculating, I didn't know how to describe your conduct and I expressed it that way—but it isn't the first time I said that and it shouldn't have shocked you so, nor take it as an insult. You say you're unhappy, well I'm certainly not

> elated myself, but you're the one who created this situation, because it's not true that I didn't want to come. I just wanted to be present at my brother's wedding, and then I'd rush to you right away, when you decided to interpret that the wedding was postponed for 6 months and you broke up the house, sent the piano, some of my things, and you wanted my parents to come to Taranto for a meeting and there you'd give them the valuables. Now you tell me about your unhappy state and you wish to die, I repeat that you insist on creating this situation, while without this strange behavior of yours I would be by your side and there are lots of other things I want to say to you but you can't put everything on paper!!! So come here and by talking we'll each explain our reasoning. They won't refuse you a short leave and anyway you already planned to go to Taranto, they won't refuse you the one more day it takes to get here and it's your duty to do that much and if after the reciprocal justifications you demand and insist that we separate we can do it in peace.
>
> Raffaella[23]

The proposed meeting will never take place. Giovanni and Raffaella are never to see one another again.

Between the end of May and the first days of June, the Cardinali Equestrian Circus comes to Cassano. Pietro Cardinali had met Raffaella Saraceni 12 years before, she 13 and he 22, when the Saracenis had invited the company's stars for a dinner in their home. The two had rekindled their acquaintance earlier in the spring at a performance in Taranto, but now the company has returned to northern Calabria, where they hope to find enough engagements to stay through the summer.

Negotiations between Giovanni, Raffaella, and Carolina stall over the issue of where to hold the proposed meeting. In the meantime, wife and husband exchange dry notes, veined with Fadda's sarcasm, about Raffaella's possessions and interest payments on her dowry. Raffaella writes the last of the dated letters found in her husband's apartment on July 23, 1878, acknowledging the receipt of two trunks filled with her possessions. She signs with the salutation, "Your affectionate wife."

At the end of August, a man knocks on Giovanni Fadda's door just off the Piazza of the Golden Keys in Rome, claiming to be a cabinetmaker from Cassano, the husband of Raffaella Saraceni's hairdresser. Fadda tells his orderly to admit the man, who sits down and reports unsolicited gossip about Raffaella Saraceni's social life. Fadda listens patiently, tells his orderly to give the man a glass of good Sardinian wine for his trouble, and sends him on his way. That man, it will later be discovered, is not a cabinetmaker at all, but Pietro Cardinali, who has come to the city on a reconnaissance mission, scouting out the captain's habitation by adopting one of the guises he puts on and takes off at will. Did he act on his own initiative or spurred by Raffaella?

At the end of September, Fadda obtains leave to travel to Castrovillari, an hour on horseback from Cassano over Calabria's notoriously poor roads, where his brother keeps an office as state lands inspector. Fadda carries a box containing Raffaella's most valuable jewelry, which he intends to return to her. The fact, however, that he has requested a leave considerably longer than required for the task may betray his hope that Raffaella will make the peace overture of traveling that last bit of road to see him.[24] She does not. He will return to Rome sooner than planned, departing on the second. His orderly will testify that upon his return Fadda appeared, "darker and more melancholy than usual." A fellow officer will remember the captain as saying he repented of having gone, adding that judging from Fadda's appearance "existence was wearing him down."[25]

Only one letter from Fadda is found in the Saraceni house during the search subsequent to Raffaella's arrest. When police investigators asked Raffaella why there were no letters or documents from her husband in the house, she had answered, "You're too late." This last letter must have accompanied Raffaella's jewelry, which Fadda's brother had handed over for delivery to a registry official, who consigned them to Raffaella:

Raffaella,

> Through my brother you will receive all the valuables you left with me, as listed in the note below. As for the files, as for me I would be very willing, but military regulations charge that dowry records must absolutely be kept personally by the officer himself throughout his period of service, and that all deductions from them must be made personally by the officer. In any case you can be sure that I will see to it that you punctually receive the total amount of all interest payments, which will be sent by postal money order to your address, thus you can even save yourself the trouble of having to withdraw them from the provincial Treasury. With this, I believe I have fulfilled your wishes.[26]

With this final note, the captain notifies his wife that he has emptied his apartment of any last object that might remind him of her, but citing military duty he has stubbornly refused to hand over the most substantial and definitive matter remaining of the marriage: authority over her dowry. Military regulation prevails even over the end of love. As a despondent Fadda returns to Rome, Pietro Cardinali and an accomplice await him at the bar on the piazza. The captain's heroic, solitary campaign to conform his private life to the ideal held up by the state has failed, but he will be redeemed in martyrdom.

9

A New War Experiment

> Forse l'impero, pensò Kublai, non è altro che uno zodiaco di fantasmi della mente.
>
> —Italo Calvino, *Le città invisibili*

Having looked at the conflicted role of the army in united Italy's early decades, we now turn to the circus, equally expressive of the acute psychosocial tensions shaping the emergence of bourgeois Italy. Although existing at opposite ends of the social spectrum, the circus and the army turn out to be intimately related. The equestrian circus emerged in the nineteenth century as a spectacular reflection of the military and its conquests. Even as the rhetorical organs of the victorious regime exalted the soldier while shaming the saltimbanco, the two institutions, army and circus, shared a promiscuous intimacy in the national imagination.

The Fadda trial is not only a circus trial; it is also a trial of the circus. Of the four originally arrested for the crime (Cardinali, Saraceni, Carrozza, and De Luca, who dies in prison), two are equestrian acrobats and another tends the Cardinali Company's horses. Two witnesses in the trial's first week are circus celebrities: one is Emilio Guillaume, whose renowned company performs regularly at Rome's Politeama; the other is one of Guillaume's most popular acts, the bibulous Giuseppe Pinta, who answers the call of justice to make a rare appearance without his partner, Marco the talking donkey, but whose repartee brings down the house just the same. The Calabrian entrepreneur who contracted the Cardinali Company's performances in and around Raffaella Saraceni's hometown also testifies. And last but not least comes the sensational surprise witness: the long-lost clown named Carluccio, or Tony (Carlo Bertone in life) who appears with his even more ragged sidekick Bergamuccio, another provincial circus hanger-on.

In the rhetoric of the lawyers and the handling by the press, in both its play and execution, the Fadda trial poses the circus, personified by the accused killer, Pietro Cardinali, against the army, represented by the ghost of Captain Fadda. The men could hardly be more different but they had much in common. Both lived largely nomadic lives in service to ancient ways of life with great symbolic presence in the new nation and in professions that largely depend on displays of mastery and power that tend to transform all those outside into spectators. While one institution was planted by the modern state at the core of national identity, the other was doomed increasingly to a paradoxical, romanticized, highly visible marginalization, its practitioners at once celebrated as stars and ostracized as Turks and gypsies, acclaimed in the nation's fantasy life but shunned in the flesh. What follows in this chapter attempts to retrace how this came to be.

Sgt. Maj. Philip Astley of Eliott's English Cavalry, of the 15 King's Royal Regiment of Light Dragoons, hero of the Battle of Emsdorff, invented the circus in 1770 in London. First in Lambeth, then in a vacant lot at the Surrey end of Westminster Bridge, Astley laid out a circle of rope fixed to the ground by stakes he pounded into the soft earth by the riverside. Within that circle, at a regular hour every day, Astley demonstrated the skills he had developed as a breaker of horses and trainer of riders in the king's service during the Seven Years War. He passed the hat after performances.[1] In the morning he offered lessons in equitation and rented out as a horse breaker. Curious onlookers were astonished alternately at the heedless but precisely controlled savagery of the man brandishing his broadsword at full gallop and the mansuetude of the beast, blazing speed against total obedience to its master. Although retired from service, Astley wore his dragoon uniform and plumed hat within the ring, making no effort to deny rumors that he had obtained his fortunate position for having saved King William III's life when the sovereign's horse bolted during a great review of troops at nearby Westminster.[2] In truth, that king had died before Astley was born, the son of a Newcastle cabinetmaker, in 1742.

Passed by his wife, the hat filled with coin. She was an equestrian as well, the daughter of a voltige artist (the term *voltige*, for one who executes gymnastic exercises while on horseback, derives from *voltigeur*, a skirmisher in a French light infantry regiment). Income from their promotional demonstrations began to predominate over that of Astley's work as trainer and teacher. Onlookers expanded into crowds, which transformed into paying audiences, fascinated and thrilled by the combination of science, war, and the dashing figure of Astley, over six feet tall, with a deep, theatrical baritone. During breaks between routines, Astley allowed comic performers to entertain the crowd; some on horseback, some on foot. The exhibition of "cuts and guards made use of by Eliott's, the Prussian, and the Hessian Hussars," and ". . . the manner of Eliott's charging the French troops in

Germany, in the year 1760," began to evolve, in response to the enthusiastic reception, into enactments of heroic British military achievements.[3]

Facing growing competition, Sergeant Major Astley also discovered the attractive power of publicity, pasting flyers throughout the city to promote his performers and their numbers. Handbills promised demonstrations of "horsemanship by Mr. Astley, Mr. Taylor, Signor Markutchy, Miss Vangable, and other transcendent performers," featuring a minuet by two horses, a comic musical interlude called "The Awkward Recruit," and "an amazing exhibition of dancing dogs." Another "hippo-dramatic spectacle" featured "Surprising Equestrian Exercises—in the intervals, A New War Experiment, in which will be introduced a single combat with the broadsword between young Astley, as a British sailor, and Mr. J. Taylor, as a savage chief"; still another promised "the amazing little Military Horse, which fires a pistol at the word of command." From its beginning, advertising served not only to spur interest and point to his exhibitions; in its hyperbolic language and shouting graphics, Astley's advertising anticipated the performances themselves, salting his spectators with promises of the thrills to come. The advertising and its promises, that is, were an extension of the spectacle itself to every city wall they were posted on. Such was Astley's success that he was able to build and open Astley's Amphitheatre Riding School in 1780, a covered seating area facing a dirt ring. Eventually a proscenium stage was attached along the circumference.[4]

Joining two animals, horses and men, Astley's presentations joined two arts and two audiences. The equestrian arts of the refined classes (the *haute école*), with its military antecedents, ceremonial dress, powdered wigs, parade music, and heraldry, combined with the jugglers, vaulters, comics and freaks who had been following trade fairs and pilgrimage routes at least since the Middle Ages.[5] In a Foucauldian sense, the time was ripe for such a development: with the nascent Industrial Revolution, the ancient fairs tended to become industrial and commercial expositions. The festive element of the fairs moved indoors, subject to closer control. Voluntary contributions were replaced by tickets, which now authorized access, separating haves from have-nots. In displays of the equestrian arts, horses and their masters enacted a ritual of domination and power disbursed by the upper classes and military.[6] War became pageantry, pleasurable, safe and suitable for ladies and children. Astley was also an author of pamphlets, alternating guides such as *The Modern Riding-Master* and *Astley's System of Equestrian Education* with treatises on military subjects, such as *Remarks on the Profession and Duty of a Soldier*, sold by hawkers at his shows.[7]

In 1774, Major Astley and his son John brought their manege to Paris for the first time; six years later they returned to build the Amphitheatre Anglais, modeled on their London establishment, and thus became a regular part of Parisian spectacle. Adding to their expanding personnel, they hired the trained pigeon act of a wandering performer, entrepreneur, and *arriviste* named Antonio Franconi. Unlike Astley, Antonio Franconi came neither from a military background nor from one traceable through public records, but rather from self-created legend. Born in Udine in either 1737 or 1746, Franconi claimed, like Casanova, to be Venetian and to have fled from Italy after killing a rival in love in a duel. He traveled the French provinces with his wife, Elisabetta Massuccati of a horse-training family, working variously with his birds, as a tightrope walker, acrobat, and horseman. He tried and failed to introduce bullfighting in Rouen in 1776; his first manege was destroyed by fire in Lyons. He was working steadily for Astley as trainer and performer when the Revolution came. At first the Amphitheater carried on unperturbed, but with the declaration of war against England in 1793, Astley judged it prudent to flee to London disguised in the uniform of a French officer. He leased his Paris theater to Antonio Franconi.[8] That name will soon become synonymous with the future of circus on the continent. Astley had been every bit the soldier and patriot. Franconi, instead, was an essentially stateless opportunist with a genius for manipulating symbols.

Blind in one eye and notoriously mean, Franconi trained his two sons, Laurent and Henri, with the same whip he used on his horses. Through them he established the corporate-family dynasty that constituted the model for equestrian spectacle throughout the century, from Russia to Mexico. In this system, family and corporation meld into a single entity. Laurent and Henri both marry voltige artists, and when horseman Sébastien Gillet marries Henri's daughter Heloise in 1822, he rather than his wife is the one who changes his name (at least as his stage, or public, persona), becoming Bastien Franconi. Against the growing anagraphic precision of the state, circus identity both within and without the ring remained labile. Until the nationwide police investigation revealed his probable bastardy, Pietro Cardinali apparently truly believed himself to have been born into the Cardinali family corporation. But like Antonietta Carrozza, the woman he described alternately as his sister and wife, he was probably sold or given to the Cardinali Company as a young child. During the course of events leading to Fadda's murder, he shifted among at least three aliases besides his regular nickname. In an advancing realm of citizenship based on birth records, circus identity remained elusive and came increasingly to be classed as criminal.

Suiting their spectacle to the times, the Franconis choreograph Astley's demonstrations of bravura into "equestrian pantomimes," "pantomime militaire," "tableau militaire," and "mimodrames héroiques" presenting the great events of the day transformed into the spectacular language of circus—on horseback. The pieces were composed in collaboration between the performers and a writer, Jean-Guillaume-Antoine Cuvelier de Trye, an aged cavalry officer of the type who continues to wear his military dress long after retirement.[9] Especially popular were the "gloires militaires" inspired by Napoleon's victories. Functioning as a sort of *biblia populorum* of the new historical epoch, Franconi's apotheoses of Napoleon are credited by contemporaries with paving the way for the Second Empire.[10] Following the format established by Astley, the Franconis' epic representations are introduced, developed, and achieve sensational climax all within 12 minutes. Some representative titles from three generations of such pieces:

- The Dog of the Regiment (ou l'exécution militaire)
- The Flag
- Marechal de Villers, or the Battle of Denain
- Fra Diavolo, Bandit Chieftain of the Alps
- The Soldier Laborer
- The Bridge at Logrono, or the Little Drummer Boy
- The Seizure of the Trocadero
- Poniatowski or Crossing the Elster
- The Crossing at Lodi
- The Death of Captain Cook
- The Storming of the Bastille
- The Victory at Monte San Bernardo
- Filippo, or the Barracks—a Comedy
- The Emperor
- The Three Eagles (France, Poland, Russia)
- The Republic, the Empire, and the Hundred Days
- The Battle of Trafalgar
- The Great Naval Combat of 12 Vessels
- The Death of General Marlborough
- The Hussar's Daughter
- Man of the Century[11]

Franconi's formula was to channel fear of military power into *frisson*, leaden martial movement into acrobacy lighter than air, violence and danger into delight. At the circus, the stick-figure soldier described by De Amicis came to heroic life.

For example, in a *mimodrame* titled "Life of a Soldier," Bastien Franconi changes costume eight times: he appears as a clumsy draftee, who is given a heavy rifle whose loud *bang!* at first scares him, but he gradually learns to manage it with skill. Then he's an officer, grabbing hat and sword on the fly, whence he goes into battle and wins a medal. He kneels—always riding, the horse circling the ring at a steady pace—to kiss a portrait of his mother. Next comes a drumbeat announcing defeat. The soldier is old and wounded, broken arm bound in a sling. He returns to civilian life and becomes a laborer with a shovel. Then suddenly, a louder explosion, and the soldier is apotheosized, wearing a crown of laurels and purple cape, carrying a golden trumpet.[12]

Paul Bouissac has observed that "a circus performance tends to represent the totality of our popular system of the world; it actualizes in one way or another all the fundamental categories through which we perceive our universe as a meaningful system."[13] Semiotically, that is, a circus performance provides a little model of the world, a sort of allegory. Its every prop, gesture, and stunt manipulates symbols in the minds of its audience. Bouissac's remarks correspond to the Franconi method of representation, a hallucinatory propaganda that exploits as it serves the political forces, and the military force, to which it bows.

The Franconi circus contributes to the burgeoning industry in patriotic imagery, from the elaborate public spectacles of the revolutionary regime to the *tableaux historiques*, lithographic series for bourgeois collectors produced by such artists as Jacques-Louis David and Jean-Louis Prieure, which iconically enshrine key moments of the Revolution and the achievements of Napoleon.[14] Sensationally popular, the Franconis were engaged to orchestrate part of Napoleon's marriage festivities, and the royal couple attended the circus in person in 1813.[15] J-L David prepared five versions of his equestrian apotheosis of Napoleon, "Napoleon at the Saint Bernard Pass" (1801), almost as though it were a circus poster in multiple copies. The image represents the general in a pose drawn rather from contemporary equestrian spectacle than from the battlefield (the Franconi spectacle based on the same moment appears to have come after the painting).[16] Napoleon had neither time nor interest to pose for the painting; rather, he told the artist he wanted to be shown "calm on a spirited horse."[17] The ideal of the soldier upon which the legitimacy of military action depends was realized in the flesh for European audiences rather within the enclosure of the ring than in any lived experience. At the circus, the purchase of a ticket allowed the imaginary entity of military glory to approach reality for the duration of the spectacle.

Blending cavalry and circus motifs to please the tastes of his middle-class buyers, the leading military and equestrian artist of the day, Carle Vernet, portrayed Mlle. Eloise "Minette" Franconi in her role as La Fille de l'Air. Poised weightlessly *en pointe* on the back of a galloping horse, she mimics the pose of Fame familiar to sophisticated viewers from classic iconography (the same theme and pose will be taken up near the end of the century in Georges Seurat's *The Circus*, 1890–1891, Musée d'Orsay, Paris).

The print's companion piece shows her husband in a variation of her pose, embodying the masculine counterpart of the idealized values La Fille de l'air represents. Both images, series lithographs produced for affluent buyers, take the poetic license of transposing their scenes from the circus ring to the open air. The acrobats look like landed gentry, he a cavalry official in a parade ground exercise, while his wife floats weightlessly above her steed, a single toe reaching down to touch its back as though she were carrying out a domestic task with the verve and flair of a perfect wife. With no enclosing tent or swarming crowds, the equestrians appear to be fashionably slim, carefree young people performing for one another and a few friends, in touch with nature at a sort of genteel country festival.[18]

Success allowed Franconi to build his own theater in Paris, which opened in 1807 with the name Cirque Olympique. Later Franconis insist that this was the first time the name "circus" was applied to equestrian spectacle. As they tell it, in response to protests from what has since come to be called "legitimate theater," Napoleonic authorities prohibited shows such as Franconi's from calling themselves theater.[19] Thus arose the need for a new word to describe this new form of popular entertainment. The antagonism between circus and the institutions of legitimate theater, which felt threatened by the new phenomenon, will continue with laws seeking to limit the encroachment of circus on theater. In 1865, a French law determined that circuses must no longer present pieces with more than two speaking roles. This regulation, imposing wordlessness and solo performance, is said to have been instrumental in shaping the mute figure of the mime.[20] The silence of this arcane clown evolved, that is, in relation and response to the great noise made in the burgeoning public marketplace, in the theaters, in the forums of democracy, and on the marching grounds. Like the circus itself, such scintillas of cultural display as the silent clown (a subaltern trope in the symbolic order of the equestrian circus,) darkly illuminate the strange interdependence of that which the unstable regimes held up as admirable and desirable and that which, by contrast, was to be shunned.

Antonio Franconi's claim to have invented the term "circus" for this form of performance has been contested; he was professionally given to regard himself in legendary terms, and also claimed to have invented the traveling circus' traditional mode of transport and habitation, the caravan. Whoever may have been first to use it, the term circus most specifically denominates the circle, always and exactly 13 meters in diameter, at the center of the show. The diameter is scientific, following a law of physics, because as the horse gallops around the circumference at a sustained, unvarying pace, a "light centrifugal force" is set up that permits the equestrian acrobat securely to perform her or his leaps and tricks. The *chambrière* stands at the center of the circle with a long, single-strand whip with which he or she can cue the horses through the changes in their routines (advances in training pioneered by Laurent Franconi eventually render this role superfluous, but the whip remains in use for its dramatic effect).

The miraculous law of physics that obtains within the ring entails alterations to behavioral laws as well. After the Fadda trial, the next circus sensation in Rome was a tribe of Nubians that came to perform for the Shür Company. Newspapers report that upon their arrival in the city, the people of Rome hooted and derided the Africans as they walked through the streets toward the circus. Once they started dancing in the ring, however, the derision turned to wild adulation.[21] The Nubians were acclaimed as a spectacle in the capital's fantasy life but remained unacceptable in the reality beyond the ring.

For the traveling companies, the circus ring functioned like the castrum of Roman Army camps. That is, just as the army applied the same quadrilateral grid system wherever it established a city, always with the forum placed where the two cardinal lines crossed, just so a traveling circus anywhere in the world first marked out its 13-meter *pista*, then erected its tent, and around its tent, always in the same pattern, laid out its necessary spaces for human and animal use.[22] Like a Roman legionnaire, no matter where he or she may have traveled, a circus employee always knew where to find the mess and where the latrine. Besides its practical value, this form of standardization provided a greater sense of familiarity and continuity for both traveling circus people and the communities that received them.

The Franconi model rapidly spread throughout the world, the name becoming a metonym for a form of performance, the circus mode of family, and a style that exploited military pageantry. Napoleon's king of Naples, Gioacchino Murat, was nicknamed King Franconi by his subjects because he looked to them like a circus equestrian's gaudy take on military regalia and posture.[23] That an imperial king appointed by Napoleon would be nicknamed after a Parisian circus master testifies not only to the political acuity of the Neapolitan street but also to the breadth and power of the Franconi legend. When people speak of circus in this era, they mean the Franconi circus, the circus derived from that model in which war was transformed into spectacle.

The most successful companies were able to establish permanent amphitheaters in the major cities, with shows that grew to include hundreds of performers. The Biblioteca Nazionale in Naples holds in its collection a program souvenir of the Circo Olimpico delle Due Sicilie, with illustrations and text of the main feature of their 1838 season, the "spettacolosa pantomima" titled "Napoleon I in Egypt at the Battle of the Pyramids, or, The Death of General Kleber," which enacts the ruthless vendetta of a fanatic Muslim insurgent against the ultimately victorious French infidels.

Laid out in four acts, the show alternates intensely dramatic dialogues in the style of Vittorio Alfieri with huge ceremonies and battle scenes calling for magnificent costumes and dozens of horses. The conclusion of the second act conveys the grandiose scale of the show:

> Mourad Bey oversees the fortifications and spurs his men to determined resistance, making them swear to give no quarter to the enemy. The French troops approach. The Turks retire into their fort. Arrival of the French Troops. Battle lines drawn. Cavalry combat. General combat. A breach is opened. The French columns rush to the assault. Desperate resistance by the Turks, but the French banner is unfurled on the main tower. The Turkish troops are in full retreat; the French are masters of the city.[24]

Act three consists of a harem scene (difficult to imagine as an equestrian performance) and the drama concludes, after Kleber's assassination, with a grand finale including the total victory of the French, the execution of the unrepentant rebels, and fireworks.

At the very moment two circus equestrians are on trial in Rome for the murder of an army captain, progressive painters in Paris were exploring the circus as a social and visual subject leading to formal discoveries that revolutionize perception, or that specularly embody perceptual changes under way.[25] At the fourth impressionist exhibition in 1879, Edgar Degas exhibited *Miss La La at the Cirque Fernando* (1879, National Gallery, London), a painting with a remarkable, inside-out correspondence to Francesco Netti's representation of the Fadda trial, In *Corte d'Assise*. In Netti's courtroom scene, women spectators are arrayed around the edges of the painting, their gazes pouring down into the hole at the center, seeking the guilty woman at the bottom of the pit. The Degas shows just the reverse: a woman performer has been yanked up out of the center to hover in the space above us; as spectators, our necks crane back and up as she flies past us into the void. We gaze up out of our darkness at the protagonist lit from below, her satin and gold shimmering, and wonder both at her freedom and at the fearsome force it must require to keep her teeth clamped on the bit hooked to the rope that draws her up into the cavernous space. Raffaella Saraceni, a provincial bourgeois, was a fallen woman; Miss La La was a minute African who rocketed to the top of the Parisian *beau monde*. Her other famous number was to be shot from a cannon. In this classic routine, still popular today as a show closer, a fearful *boom!* and plume of smoke at one end of the tent result not in terrible death but the performer alive, smiling and waving high on a trapeze way at the other end of the tent. The audience laughs in relief and cheers the bravura of the illusion, happy to have been fooled. This was the same number with which

Pietro Cardinali climaxed his shows in deep Southern Italy, with necessary accommodations, we must presume, with regard to throw and the amount of gunpowder consumed. "Spettacolose pantomime" were unfolding in the great cities of Europe. It was for work, of course, but also for spectacular experiences that masses flocked to the urban centers. With a ticket to the circus, the modern citizen fleetingly acquired the right to take part in the grandeur of man's mastery over nature, to witness European sagacity and power at its most glittering and triumphant. In a momentary rush of freedom, the spectator could join Miss La La in space.

In the course of the nineteenth century, circuses increasingly became the cultural medium through which colonial conquests were represented to the European citizenry. Ever in search of novelty, entrepreneurs risked huge sums to bring to the cities the most exotic wild animal species and human races from Africa, Asia, Australia, and the Americas. The arrival of Buffalo Bill's American Circus, with its bison and bareback-riding Indians, was the peak of an economy of spectacle in constant, headlong inflation where every year each promoter sought to outdo all the others. Arab riders and Chinese acrobats had already thrilled crowds and then left them jaded, craving the next sensation. Throughout this evolution, the metaphor at the base of equestrian circus remained constant but multivalent as ever. Unmistakable was man's heroic domination of nature: whether horse, tiger, or elephant, sooner or later in the show they were always forced to kneel before their master. But at the same time, circus always realized an exhilarating sense of freedom and play beyond strictures, bourgeois man revealed as after all still a child, still in and of nature. To cite Bouissac again, "The circus freely manipulates a cultural system to such an extent that it leaves the audience contemplating a demonstration of humanity freed from the constraints of the culture within which the performance takes place."[26] Thus it must have been for Raffaella Saraceni as she watched Pietro Cardinali overcome gravity in the summer of 1878.

Even as we trace the rise of the equestrian circus as it glorified military conquest and the righteousness of the national state, we must simultaneously consider the systematic marginalization of the performers themselves. As the myths they actualized in their performances took root in European consciousness, the flesh and blood actors and their way of life were pushed increasingly to the far periphery of the demographic map. After unification, the liberal state unleashed an onslaught that took the form especially of counting, of compiling masses of statistical information by the military, state administration, and scientific researchers.[27] The flaunting of statistics, often of dubious reliability, became a characteristic fetish of Italian scientific positivism, especially in its treatment of the Southern population. An 1881 study reported in the *Annali di statistica* describes, for example, "the figures derived from 2,333,288 observations made by Prof. Sorman in his magisterial *Nosological Geography of Italy* on draftees rejected on account of insufficient stature."[28] In the expanded, French edition of his groundbreaking study, *L'Uomo delinquente* (published as *L'Homme Criminel*), entrepreneur-scientist Cesare Lombroso asserted the scientific value of the number of times assassins stab their victims during crimes of passion, citing as evidence Cardinali's blows against captain Fadda (not uncharacteristically, Lombroso gets his numbers wrong, claiming that the acrobat stabbed his victim only once).[29]

Under the regime of statistics, any entity that eluded counting necessarily verged toward invisibility. Having successfully repressed banditry but without yet having enfranchised the peasantry, the new state, with its authorities, scientists and press, now became terribly concerned with the problem of vagrancy. With the great waves of migration soon to come, Italy's ministers and social scientists brought to the forefront of national attention a word drawn from the penal codes of the first half of the century, targeting the *oziosi*, roughly translated as "loiterers." Derived from the Latin *otium*, a word with a long history in poetic discourse from Petrarch to Leopardi to describe the freedom from encumbrance that permits for poetic meditation, penal experts now applied it to the shiftless, underemployed thousands not yet integrated into the new national economy.[30] Although these persons were not necessarily engaged in criminal activity, they were believed likely to do so, the men as thieves and the woman as prostitutes.[31] The criminalization of potential criminality was a particularly rich theoretical field for the nascent school of criminal anthropology, the most vocal of whom was Lombroso. Even as geographical mobility increased along rail lines laid in Southern regions heretofore lacking any roads at all, nomadism and migration became increasingly subject to sanction. One might say that on the new national map, linear movement was regarded as rational and productive, while cyclical movement was suspect, evoking both ancient Catholic pilgrimage and the nomadic tribes beyond the Mediterranean to the South. Those whose professions traditionally carried them in circular routes, such as traveling circus performers, became increasingly identified as among the rootless *oziosi* in part because it was difficult for the state to find, categorize, and register them statistically.

Against all that is measurable in modernity, the circus, constantly in movement, appeared to float in a promiscuity prosecuting attorneys alternately characterize as "gypsy" or "Turkish," by which they mean especially to allude to polygamy and nomadism. In the specific case of the Cardinali Equestrian Company, no one knows precisely how many they are, what their names are, how they are related to one another, what each member's role is, whose children are whose, where they have been, or where they are going. When asked in court to estimate the size of the company he had contracted to perform in a small circuit of towns in north central Calabria, the hapless local promoter includes in a single number both its human and equine members, as though of equal legal status. This condition itself appears not only culpable, but simultaneously repulsive and enthralling. Carolina Misuracca, who never testifies, is repeatedly named as the wife who Cardinali preferred over Antonietta Carrozza, by whom he had two children. Misuracca is said variously to have had between three and six children by him, but her spousal status and frequency of maternity are verified nowhere in the investigative records. The love letters, gifts, and sometimes money sent to Cardinali by female fans are often addressed either to Misuracca or Carrozza. His "wife" and "lover," that is, appear to have set aside their social identifiers when necessary to participate in Cardinali's scheme to bilk these lonely hearts of their possessions. These sorts of facts were precisely the "juice" that Ferdinando Martini cited the Fadda trial's female spectators as seeking so immodestly. In the emerging piazza of national consciousness, the circus began to appear as a primeval miasma, a menacing but magnetic vestige of social atavism, but at the same time its gay mask remained in place as it transformed cavalry, gunpowder, and military aggression into festivity.

In the provinces, the periodic return of the traveling circuses provided a landmark in the revolving year, a time when new fashions and exotic influences suddenly penetrated the claustral atmosphere of isolated towns. Raffaella Saraceni testified that she first met Pietro Cardinali as a girl of 12, when his company came to Cassano and the dashing equestrian was invited to dine at the family table. By the time Cardinali returned to Cassano in 1878, he had adopted the stage name "Francone" or "Girolamo Franconi."[32] In the Italian of that era, the term "franco" pronounced his frank bravura, but could not also fail to suggest his direct descendance, spiritual if not genealogical, from the greatest of the great circus families. Although moving only within a perennial cycle of small southern cities and towns, Pietro Cardinali arrived in each new piazza carrying a whiff of Paris. Florid love letters to him from lonely women he met along the way address him with damp adoration as "Light of My Eyes," and "Idol of My Heart." In the next chapter, we will explore how three members of the Cardinali Company suddenly became receptacles of desire of the entire nation.

10

Characters

From the report of the interrogation of Pietro Cardinali, November 13, 1878: "In the company, I'd always been told I was born in Verona, but since Your Honors assure me that in Verona it was impossible to find my birth certificate, I have to guess that I was adopted into the company as a child and that the Cardinali brothers took me as their brother, and since then always called me by that name."[1]

We have seen in Chapters 2 and 3, on journalism, and in Chapter 5, on forms of art derived from the events, diverse but concordant ways in which the Fadda affair came to be plotted into a symbolic drama that temporarily enchanted newly unified Italy. The protagonists of this drama were not ultimately the captain, his wife, and his murderer but the media and its audience, who abstracted the wretched trio's tragic misfortune into a national spectacle. This chapter will begin with an examination of the dynamics of how that abstraction was carried out on the accused man in the courtroom, as Pietro Cardinali came to be marked as guilty of a crime greater and more ramified than simple murder. We will then proceed in a new direction to explore the real circumstances of the lives of two supporting characters, Carluccio the clown, a crucial witness, and accomplice Antonietta Carrozza, the equestrian acrobat identified as Cardinali's sister and wife. Performers by trade, neither Carluccio nor Antonietta triggered the murder plot nor its ensuing spectacle but both were caught up in its workings, becoming intensely famous for as long as public attention held, then quickly faded back into obscurity, prototypes of the phenomenon so famously prophesied by Andy Warhol. Their interest to us is virtually archeological, for they have vanished from memory even more utterly than the murderers and their victim. By exploring their respective comic and pathetic insignificance, we may contrastively understand what was demanded for an entity to fascinate the larval Italian consensus as it composed its symbolic order. Crucial to any nationalist consciousness is the capacity to forget. These two supporting characters, Carluccio the clown and Antonietta the acrobat, are for us emblems of that which is picked up, then left forgotten by the wayside in a media environment fixed on dreams of progress and national advancement.

Both prosecution and defense argue, against her constant denials, that Raffaella Saraceni grew sick of her real soldier and turned instead to an ideal one. Townspeople say that she attended the circus night after night in Cassano, always sitting in the same place near the performers' entrance, sharing enthralled glances with Pietro Cardinali as he demonstrated his mastery over the galloping horses. Just when most troubled by her husband's attack on her honor, she encountered a man she had first met many summers earlier, as a girl of twelve. Inspired by his frank bravura, the prosecution holds, Raffaella came to believe that the charismatic performer could vindicate her shame as well as he satisfied her desire, which frustrated maternity had perverted into naked lust. The Saraceni defense, on the other hand, holds that the botched murder plot was entirely the invention of Cardinali, a delusional, violent fool incapable of distinguishing make-believe from reality, who never shared his scheme with the woman who was the object and goal of his desire. Adultery shames all involved, a taboo that attracts and repels, but adultery leading to murder was here taken to represent an eruption of atavistic rage, a savage congress of male brutality and female lust tearing away the fragile civility so tentatively established under the new state order. More than just another squalid, stupidly executed killing for love or money, the murder of Giovanni Fadda by a Calabrian acrobat was inflated into an assault on the virtues that sustained the state, identified in turn with modern civilization itself.

Both prosecuting and defense attorneys portray Saraceni's serial adultery as a fall from the highest form of man to the lowest, from her soldier-hero husband, rendered even more symbolic and ideal by his battle injury, to the wandering saltimbanco. She passes in reverse evolutionary order from one to another of the various men with whom she is rumored to have had affairs. In Chieti, there had been Edoardo, the bank official. In Cassano, there were stories of a tryst with a local engineer, a veterinarian who serenaded her outside her window, and a blacksmith. Lowest of all was her affair with Pietro Cardinali. As diagrammed by prosecutor Rutigliano, "Her adulterous affairs represent a descending scale: first, it seems, she loved a certain Edoardo, held to be of high standing, then an engineer, next a veterinarian, and finally Cardinali, who represents the last and lowest social level."[2] The *Messaggero* reporter renders Rutigliano's words here in more detail as, "Last of all, the man of the circus, the gymnast, without a country (*patria*), without a roof over his head, without education, without conscience."[3] Cardinali is guilty not only of having killed a man. His moral debasement rather lies in the fact that he cannot produce identity papers, that he lives a nomadic existence. The very movement of his body as a gymnast is rhetorically construed as evidence of an absence of conscience, of an identity trained and fixed in place.

One after the other, the prosecuting attorneys hammer away at this evolutionary motif. The second lawyer for the Fadda family, Antonio Ponsiglioni, a parliamentary deputy from Cagliari, introduces himself as a friend of Giovanni Fadda and his family, then contrasts the murdered captain and the accused acrobat. First he offers up an elegiac apotheosis of his dead friend:

> Fadda grew up in Cagliari, in his honored family, amid examples of severe virtue. He could have had a splendid career in the civil service, because his family had distinguished connections; but inspired by love of country (*patria*), he preferred to volunteer to serve and defend his nation (*paese*). His character was as faithful, as full of integrity, as can be imagined. There was in him that desire for the vital, intimate joys of domestic life that only takes root in the most select hearts.[4]

Spare but dense with powerful words, brief but packed with loaded images, the evocation concentrates its listeners on patriotic selflessness and domestic devotion, ideals realized in fact. There must have been a pause in the lawyer's speech here, followed by a new breath launching a longer discourse inevitably describing the evil opposite:

> Now we come to the figure of Cardinali. He is a child of the circus, of this gypsy tribe that exists in the midst of civil society. He claims, without knowing, that he was born in Verona. His idea of the family is considerably worse than a Turk's. But we must consider that along with his consummate cunning, he has committed blunders that not even a mediocre intelligence would be capable of. But there is a fact, psychological, that explains everything perfectly. His natural shrewdness has been entirely acquired and exercised within the circus; he has no experience of what constitutes life, of civil society. Accustomed to commanding his *saltimbanchi*; accustomed to leaping through paper hoops, puncturing them; accustomed to his *lazzi*, to the tricks of pantomime, the quickness of equestrian stunts, he supposes that his circus skills will help get him out of a jam in the other circumstances of life; he believes that even facing prison, even before the investigating magistrate, he can pull it off by jumping through paper hoops, performing somersaults, and reciting low-grade witticisms. Removed from his element, outside the circus, he is nothing but in imprudent ignoramus committing blunder after blunder.[5]

Despite its martial origins and history of dramatizing military glory, here the contrast between circus and army could not be more stark: honor, family, social standing, patriotism, service, integrity, fidelity, domesticity, a "select heart," versus circus, gypsies, tribes, Turks, cunning, deception, ignorance, and stupidity. Cardinali here becomes a scheming other crouching hidden in our very midst, paradoxically stupid but cunning; the irreconcilable opposites make the figure freakish. The lawyer's ostentatious flaunting of the sophisticated term, "psychological," suggests these circus Turks are something to be isolated and examined scientifically, a social disease, an infection within civil society. The circus survives atavistically in the midst of civil society like the festering vestige of some more brutal, primitive form of life now surpassed by urban man. Lawyer Ponsiglioni's performance here, his rhetorical leaps and stunts, provoke frequent applause and cries of "bravo!" in the halls of the Filippini during the summation phase of the Fadda trial. Cardinali has become a prop brilliantly manipulated by a still more ingenious rhetorical acrobat.

Guilty of statelessness, Pietro Cardinali does indeed appear as the trial wears on to be increasingly confused, especially about masks and roles. The first lawyer to summarize the case against him is young, ambitious Tommaso Lopez, noted for the high, sharp timbre of his voice. Before being hired by the Fadda family, Lopez had initially been assigned by the chief magistrate, Pietro Giordano, to serve as Cardinali's defense lawyer and had visited the accused man in prison to prepare his case. But shortly before sessions began, the Fadda family's principal attorney suddenly died. To replace him at the last minute, the chief magistrate urged upon the Faddas the choice of Lopez, the same he had previously assigned to defend Cardinali. The irregularity of this maneuver, which entailed also the indignant resignation of the second lawyer initially hired by the Faddas, did not pass without notice in the press.[6] With questioning of witnesses complete, on October 14, Lopez addressed the court to present the Fadda family's version of events, full of harsh accusations against the acrobat. When court is called to session the next morning, Cardinali rises to his feet and says to the presiding judge:

> "Mister president, please allow me a word: When I was being held in the Carceri Nuove, Advocate Lopez offered to defend me, saying that he had several good points in my defense . . . about the captain . . . and so forth . . ."
>
> "But this matter," observes the president, shrugging his shoulders, "is entirely extraneous to the trial!"
>
> "No, I mean to say," continues Cardinal, undaunted, "what I don't understand is that yesterday, he acted so adverse . . . and spoke so badly of me."

"If he had been your defending attorney," responds the judge, "naturally, he wouldn't have mauled you like that, but given that he isn't . . ."

"Yes, but he was chosen by you, Judge, to defend me . . ."[7]

Here Cardinali reveals such a complete lack of understanding of public trial procedure—which, after all, was still quite new—that he appears neither as a dark, dashing *cavallerizzo* nor as a murderous Calabrian, but as a figure of derision, a yokel hopelessly lost in the city. The "child of the circus" is bewildered by the hidden machinations through which his defense attorney has become his prosecutor. Cardinali hasn't understood that a lawyer's job is to advocate as best he can the position of whoever is paying him; that is, that Lopez' previous sympathetic conduct and encouraging words toward him had been sheer masking, a performance. The attorneys for the prosecution will continually seize on Cardinali's cultural unpreparedness—of this too, he is guilty—to contrast his false world of circus with the civilized society the rest of us live in, but in this moment it is Cardinali who feels he has been tricked.[8] Only now does he glimpse that the realm of law is one of shifting appearances, in comparison to which the illusions of circus are the stuff of childhood.

The Fadda trial contains in prototypical form all the nightmarish elements that have since become canonical to the media circus phenomenon. One of the most universal of these elements is the gap between the desperate individual psychic or material lives of the actors in the drama and the reconstituted, symbol-infested representation of those lives constructed by a society endlessly avid for spectacular illusions. The people demand monsters. Pursuing the circumstances leading to the murder of Captain Fadda, the investigating magistrates are forced to explore and bring to light the tenuous, nomadic existence of the Compagnia Cardinali, turning up many individuals virtually without legal identity, of no fixed abode, who possess scattered, inconsistent papers if any at all, orphans, deserters and recidivists for whom return to prison means a steady meal. The Cardinali Circus is composed of undocumented people for whom the myths of family and fraternity, upon which the new national regime depends, have no experiential reference, people who do not know whether those they call mother, father, and brother are biologically or legally so. One of the constants of the fascination of circus, much exploited in the era of verismo in painting, theater, opera, and verse, was its flimsy grandiosity, the stark contrast between its sequined sparkle and the tawdry misery of its practitioners' actual lives, between public display and private abjection.[9] We now turn to the lives of two circus performers devoid of legal identity who suddenly found themselves splashed across newspapers all across Italy, were saluted and vilified, and then just as rapidly disappeared from view.

Carluccio

After addressing the court for several hours in defense of his client, Raffaella Saraceni, Pietro Rosano asks the court for a brief recess to restore himself. Newspapers commented humorously on the multicolored bottles of medicine, syrups, and elixirs for the voice cluttering the lawyers' tables. During the pause, a messenger hands a note to the chief magistrate, who reacts with a gasp, then immediately summons the court back into session to make a stunning announcement: Carluccio has been found! The next day's *Corriere della sera* reports breathlessly but mockingly on the impact of the rediscovery of the "famous, long-lost, untraceable" Carluccio:

> How can it be, the *clown*, the pagliaccio, the jester Carluccio, that pure spirit who refused with horror the hundred piastres offered him by Raffaella as the price for the murder of Giovanni Fadda, that Arabian phoenix who has remained invisible, nowhere to be found for an entire year despite the *maréchaussée* throughout all Italy, sprouts mushroom-like from the earth and arrives like the *Deus ex machina* of ancient theater, late perhaps but still in time to take part in the debate, and change, possibly, the face of things!

Carlo Bertone, Carluccio the clown, was being described in newspapers as "famous" from early on in the investigation, subsequent to the leaking to the press of the deposition of a woman of Castrovillari named Rosina Garramone, alternately identified as a *stiratrice* (a laundress specialized in ironing), a *pettinatrice* (a hairdresser, summoned to ladies' homes to prepare their coiffure before social events), and a prostitute. Although Garramone is now married and living in Castrovillari, the defense, in an effort to impugn her testimony, introduces as evidence police reports from Naples in 1871 confirming that Garramone had been a prostitute. Vassallo's remark is that "she had been one of those we refer to as a lost woman, although they can be found everywhere."[10] In addition to describing how she carried letters between Saraceni and Carrozza, Garramone testified that in midsummer she had come across Carluccio the clown looking glum. At first he refused to explain his mood, but she prodded him until he finally told her that Raffaella Saraceni had offered him 100 piastres to go to Rome to kill Captain Fadda. Carluccio was worried that if he refused, Cardinali would beat him again. At Rosina's urging, Carluccio soon fled the company together with a stableboy named Federico Trebisondo, or Bergamuccio.

Despite intensive searches, neither national nor local police had been able to track him down. He gained further notoriety in the media for an incriminating joke he made before his flight in the presence of the director of the Cassano municipal band, whose ensemble had been hired by Lorenzo Cardinali to provide musical accompaniment for the company's shows in Castrovillari. The musicians arrived for their debut performance only to learn from Lorenzo that the show had to be cancelled because Pietro, the star, had not turned up. When the musical director asked why not, Lorenzo explained that his brother had remained in Cassano to spend the evening with Raffaela Saraceni, with whom he enjoyed a great friendship. Overhearing Lorenzo's explanation, Carluccio had burst out laughing, saying, "Some friendship! He eats, he drinks, and he fucks!" (the Italian in this case would be *fottere*, although in all texts it appears as "f . . . !").[11] For the prosecution lawyers, the clown's joke reveals the degree to which the adulterous lovers' affair was common knowledge, and they repeat it throughout the trial, pointedly refraining from pronouncing the final word, as though to titillate their scandalized audience. In a pattern characteristic of circus trials, law and media engage continuously in a play of repetition of the most salacious elements in the story, even as they pose as disassociated from, and dispassionately or scientifically above, the morally compromising effects of the scabrous facts they place at the forefront of the public's attention.

The hairdresser's assertion to investigators triggers a nationwide search for the missing clown, whose continued absence in the flesh serves only to increase his looming presence in spirit as the trial date finally approaches. Despite the efforts of police forces throughout the peninsula, he is nowhere to be found. Halfway through the trial, in their initial summaries before the jury, both Tommaso Lopez and Ippolito Rutigliano, the chief prosecutor, speculate in court that the only reason the law had not been able to find Carluccio is that he must have been done away with. In his distinctive, wheedling voice, Lopez conjectures,

> in a country as eminently civilized as ours, furrowed in every direction by rail, telegraph, and roads of every kind, how can it happen that an individual known in Italy and beyond be eclipsed, that he vanish like the vision of a dream, that the entire police force not only cannot find him, but cannot locate even the slightest trace, cannot pick up even the slightest whiff of him? How can it happen? Despite everything the defense might object, the explanation is very simple. Carluccio? If this witness were found, the entire skein, the entire plot would untangle, would be undone. It was thus convenient for Carluccio to disappear, necessary that Carluccio not appear before this court. It was an urgent, absolute necessity that his mouth be shut! Therefore, despite rummaging through the most hidden corners of this peninsula, and minute exploration abroad, the pagliaccio so feared by the accused has probably already been a cadaver for some time.[12]

The charge is sheer invention, but Lopez's speech demonstrates the degree of dramatic and poetic latitude permitted to lawyers by the chief magistrate and, we might say, demanded of them by their listeners. It thus causes a sensation when Carluccio, by now presumed dead, turns up after all, working under his regular stage name in a third-class circus in Giovinazzo, a coastal town in the province of Bari. Carlo Bertone's disappearance had less to do with murderous conspiracies imagined by lawyers and more with the fact that the nomadic subject of the search continued to live as he always had, off the demographic map. Investigators had been assiduous in sending inquiries throughout the peninsula and local police officials had been exemplary in fulfilling the task of seeking the subject and reporting their fruitless results back to Rome. Following all established procedure, for 12 months they failed to find him. Finally, almost by chance, regional carabinieri happen to come across him working in the Santo Nava equestrian circus. Santo and Nava, brothers, evaded the charge of harboring a fugitive by deposing that Carluccio had given his name as Antonio Bartolo (His clown name, in fact, was Tony). Both sign their police statement with the traditional X that denotes illiteracy. Before the official investigating magistrates arrive to take his statement and without swearing a legal oath, Carluccio has already provided a statement to a carabiniere in Puglia: "I am Carlo Bertone, called Carluccio, son of Felicia Bertone and unknown father, aged 20. When I was six, the gymnastic company of Francesco Sgritti came to my town (Contursi, in the borderlands between Puglia and Basilicata—ed). I followed that company as an apprentice for about twelve years, then went with the company of Lorenzo Cardinali, with whom I traveled through the Abruzzi, Basilicata, then to Taranto, and from there to Cassano all'Ionio, where we stayed for a month and a half."[13]

Since the age of six, it would seem, a stay as long as a month and a half in a single location would be something of note to remember for Carlo Bertone. The sudden announcement of the discovery of Carluccio provokes from the defense team an immediate demand for a mistrial, due especially to significant procedural irregularities in the handling of his interrogation, which should have been conducted by investigating magistrates rather than by the local police or carabinieri in Puglia. Furthermore, to justify transporting him to Rome, the police have arrested him on dubious charges based on hearsay. Persevering, and against the strong complaint of Enrico Pessina, one of the nation's greatest authorities on judicial procedure, Chief Magistrate Giordano cites his special *poteri discrezionali* (which might be translated as "authority to use his discretion") and rules that the trial will continue. When Carluccio arrives by train at the central station on the morning of October 22, the crowd awaiting him, estimated at a thousand people, is even greater than the one that received Raffaella

Saraceni. Public interest is overwhelming, frenzied.[14] Vassallo, present for his last day of reporting the Fadda case before transfer to the Lazzaretti trial in Tuscany, remarks, "All the puritans, all the moralists, all those who flee such spectacles as these, put both their hands together like Jesus to obtain a place."[15] Before Carluccio enters the courtroom, Cardinali's defense lawyer, Ercole Ranzi, insists that Garramone and the municipal concertmaster be removed from the hall so as to avoid possible contamination of their testimony. Later the judge will also have Cardinali and Carrozza removed, then summon them back to test whether they confirm or contradict details of Carluccio's account. When Carluccio is finally called to the stand, the *Pungolo* reports, "it was as though an enormous electric battery had unleashed its fluid, impregnating every spectator."[16] The *Messaggero* describes Carluccio as an extremely vulgar figure in dress and physiognomy, with the appearance of a peasant (*contadino*, used here with derogatory intent). Both journalists and lawyers note that the witness delivers his testimony strangely, declaiming pedantically and without pause, as though having memorized a part.

His testimony is detailed and damning to all the defendants, especially his accounts of watching Pietro Cardinali ascend by rope into Raffaella Saraceni's bedroom; of Cardinali's threat, while waving a revolver in a dressing room, to blow Carluccio's brains out if he should tell anyone what he had seen; and most crucial of all, of being summoned to the Saraceni household, where in the presence of Antonietta, Raffaella offered him 100 piastres, 50 now and 50 after the act, to go to Rome to kill her husband. In Carluccio's version, Antonietta explained that they would provide a disguise for him and Raffaella said that after the murder he would have to "disappear from that part of the world forever." Temporizing, Carluccio explains, he asked Raffaella for a loan to pay certain debts, and she immediately provided him with six silver piastres, a currency rare but still in circulation from the preunification era of Ferdinando II. When Carluccio speaks of coinage, he alternates between "ducats" and "piastres," at times using specific terminology to refer to the obsolete silver currency used under the Bourbons, at other times alternating ducats and piastres as a generic term for any form of money. After speaking with a fat laundress from Cassano about his dilemma, he decided to flee the company. Joining up with a stableboy in the company named Federico Trebisondo, nicknamed Bergamuccio, he left Castrovillari on foot in the direction of Naples, first stealing a circus costume that he sold along the way. Trebisondo is summoned to confirm Carluccio's testimony and arrives the next day. When he stands before the court, this new arrival provokes great comic reaction because his appearance is still more pathetically ragged than that of Carluccio. The crowd at court had thought that Carluccio represented rather the limit in the way of clodhopping, so they delight to the entrance of another character so bedraggled and patched that he makes the clown look almost respectable by comparison. Just as the Roman newspapers had misreported and confused the names of the Southern towns from which the crime had originated, they seem unable to settle on the correct spelling of the rootless stableboy's surname. The Bracco edition's illustration of Bergamuccio's testimony conveys the crowd's delighted view of him: the boy, hair all uncombed cowlicks, leans toward the bench with legs splayed, tattered pants too short, a ragged plaid under his arm, as the judge leans forward to admonish him, shaking a finger. The comic scene anticipates Chaplin's Tramp.

In their escape, when possible the boys hitch rides on carts, paying their passage by grooming carthorses, and nourish themselves on blackberries picked along the road. At Lagonegro they split up; Bergamuccio returns to his native Campobasso, while Carluccio finds a position with his old gymnastic company, under Francesco Sgritti, passing through Naples. After three months he joins yet another company, one that features trained chimpanzees, and travels to Campobasso, Terni, Foggia, Giovinazzo, Bari, Contursi, Palo, and several other towns. Next he joins the Santo Nava Company, which passes through several villages and the larger center of Altamura, before arriving in Giovinazzo, at which point he is discovered by carabinieri.

As Carluccio's story unrolls, however, small discrepancies begin to emerge as to who had summoned him to the Saraceni household, whether a maid or Cardinali himself, how many times he had visited the house, who exactly said what and when. Although he describes having discussed his plight with a fat laundress in Cassano, he denies having ever spoken about it to Rosina Garramone, who, being very thin, does not fit the clown's description of the woman he confessed to. The defense attorneys rise to point out contradictions; Carluccio's subsequent responses serve rather to confuse than clarify, and as he drifts from his prepared remarks, his tone of voice grows ever more uncertain and plaintive, provoking suspicion among those sympathetic to Saraceni that the clown has been coached by the officials who arrested him and conducted him to the capital. Resorting to the same conspiracy theorizing earlier used by Lopez to explain why Carluccio could not be found, a defense lawyer now suggests that the sudden discovery of Carluccio had been orchestrated by the state once it recognized that public sentiment heavily favored the absolution of Raffaella. Such a crescendo of hubbub and disgruntlement rises in the crowd that the judge is compelled to clear the courtroom several times.

One by one, each of the defendants is given an opportunity directly to challenge Carluccio's testimony. Saraceni denies having ever seen him, much less having spoken with him in her home. As she cross-examines the clown, her apparent conviction and serenity impress journalists and audience. The judge summons Antonietta Carrozza back to the courtroom; she too denies ever having had compromising conversations with Carluccio, but in rebuttal the twenty-year-old clown describes how she had forced him to pose in public as the husband of Carolina Misuracca, Cardinali's common-law wife, and absurdly, as the father of Misuracca's three children, so that the acrobat would be free to pursue Raffaella. Carluccio explains to the crowd:

> People said: "What? A clown so young has a wife with three children?" So I answered, "She was a widow when I married her."—"It's all lies!" cries Antonietta.[17]

The atmosphere in the courtroom slides toward farce as the judge permits defendants to cross-examine hostile witnesses and they break out into bickering. Now the judge summons Cardinali. Asked to explain whether Carluccio might have motive to cast him or the Saraceni family in such a harsh light, the acrobat regales the court with the background story of his relationship with the young clown. The tale provides a crystalline but surreal glimpse into a way of life for which there exist no categories in the statistical profiles of the positivist regime:

> In Acerra, I found this youngster sleeping side by side with a bear in the stable. We took him with us to look after the horses. We gave him a costume, he had never performed as a clown. He ran away. My brother and I went after him; 23 or 24 miles away we found him in a caravan with his old master. He never paid for anything; debts on all sides. Around our caravan, all you could see were Carluccio's debtors.
>
> —You mean creditors?
>
> Yes, sir. In Altamura I had a trained goat who worked with the horses. I told Carluccio to keep the goat away from the horses in the stable. He didn't obey. One night a horse kicked the goat and killed it. I said to the stableboy: *You wretch! You dare bring me the goat like this, a goat I respect more than myself?* Carluccio was afraid and ran away; it took me two days to find him. He was afraid I'd beat him. But I swore I'd never touch him again. I needed him, because he was the one who tossed me the iron balls when I did the human cannonball number.[18]

Behind the foreground where facts are being delineated and ordered, a looming background image takes shape in the minds of jury and public composed of circus, provincial geography, Southern society, and promiscuous criminality. The conflicting testimony, the rapidly degenerating content of the discourse, and loud, open, overlapping disagreement among Carluccio, Bergamuccio, the ex-prostitute Garramone, Cardinali, and Carrozza, with loud protests from the defense and rising public outcry, threaten to undermine the dignity of the court and throw the entire procedure into utter, comic disarray. Finally, the president of the court re-establishes a semblance of order.

Figure 10.1 Bergamuccio testifies before the court

Source: Illustration from *Processo Fadda illustrato*

Carluccio and Bergamuccio released, the defense attorneys take up again their interrupted summations. Impugning his testimony, Pietro Rosano often refers to Carluccio as "the bastard from Contursi."[19] Many of his tribe, in fact, are bastards because they cannot demonstrate their provenance in the state's registries: Cardinali, his children by Carolina Misuracca, Carrozza, her two abandoned infants, Carluccio, and his companion in flight Bergamuccio. Traveling companies cyclically crisscross the provinces, marking the seasons and carrying fresh stimulation into static hinterlands, incarnating in their performances strength, patriotism, bravery, and grace. But their exoticism is also dangerous and increasingly out of place in the new order, their habits those of "gypsies" and "Turks." When they finally find him in Giovinazzo, police charge Carluccio with the previously nonexistent crime of "having no fixed address."[20] Commenting on Carluccio's great popularity in the media and social talk, marveling that his notoriety has already lasted more than a week, *Illustrazione italiana* facetiously announces that "ours is the epoch of *saltimbanchi*."[21] At the same moment that the prosecution consigns the equestrian acrobat to the bottom of the evolutionary scale, a fashionable journal satirically declares the dawning of the age of the saltimbanco. The contending assertions stand side by side in the nation's collective imagination. In the media's discovery and declaration of the fashion of the saltimbanco, we witness the extinction of the saltimbanco and the recreation of its figure as modern myth. What is being born for Italy in the Fadda trial is the epoch of massive, mediatic production and consumption of transient monsters. The ritual sacrifice of these monsters on a national stage marks the new society's calvary of progress.

Antonietta

The court is fascinated by Antonietta Carrozza's role as go-between in the affair and murderous plotting of Cardinali and Saraceni. The motives of the adulterous couple appear to the public to be vile and outrageous, but comprehensible: Cardinali driven to escape the miserable life of a traveling saltimbanco into one of bourgeois comfort; Saraceni by weakness of character, lust for the acrobat and anger at her impotent husband. After all, everyone has experienced envy and lust and teased at the idea of transgressing the bounds of propriety. But what could motivate Carrozza to serve as mask and alibi, posing as Raffaela's dear friend so as to facilitate meetings between the lovers, and as their agent, rushing between town and telegraph office to send and receive messages coded in the jargon of traveling players? While posing as Cardinali's sister, she had in fact at 17 and 18 borne two children by him, which she abandoned to foundling hospitals, former religious institutions now placed under state purview. At some point Cardinali had taken up with another woman, Carolina Misuracca, whom he called his wife. With her he fathered three more children who remained with the company as he continued to exploit Antonietta. Beginning in the summer of 1878, Cardinali needed her to cover his affair with Raffaella by pretending that she, rather than he, was on intimately friendly terms with the well-to-do young wife from Cassano. Once he departed for Rome to kill Fadda, he and Raffaella used Antonietta as an intermediary to communicate coded messages by telegram. The court and the ladies in the galleries crave to understand her voluntary submission to abuse. In answer to the investigator's question, "But how could you imagine that Pietro would ever marry you?" Carrozza replies, "At first I believed his words of love were true, then he gained sway over me and I no longer had the strength to resist his desires, since I felt sure that his mother and brothers would have forced him to marry me. I also have to add that he beat me often, so that I couldn't resist his impure desires."[22]

Antonietta's helplessness is brilliantly construed by her lawyer, Carlo Palomba, into an early version of the insanity defense, portraying his client as so psychologically damaged by the sadist she regarded as an older brother as to be incapable of resisting his will. The term Palomba invents for the purpose is *forza irrestibile*, an irresistible force that compelled Antonietta to submit to Cardinali's demands, thereby rendering her not culpable for her complicity in the crime. Summarizing the verdict, *Illustrazione italiana* will describe Carrozza as a *strumento idiota*, that is, an "idiot instrument," with "idiot" intending "devoid of will."[23] The idea that Carrozza, cast off, was so conditioned by the circus as to accept any demand from her master, no matter how degrading it might appear to society at large, met great receptivity in the minds of the jury and public. Palomba will dramatically plumb the mystery of how a woman could become so subject to the sway of an evil man as to bear and abandon two of his children, then pose as his sister and assist him in a scheme to replace herself in his embrace with a rich lover.[24] When at trial's end she is found guilty of the charges against her but absolved by reason of irresistible force, Naples' *Pungolo* frames it as a paradox: "The poor gymnast (*saltatrice*) found her anchor of salvation in the same brutal force that made her a victim. It seems a paradox, but isn't. Irresistible force has triumphed. Lombroso must be overjoyed."[25]

Most striking in the lawyers' rhetorical handling of Antonietta's role throughout the trial is the irreconcilable gap between the normative conception of feminine conduct entertained in public court (and as represented, for example, in the representation of Raffaella in Alfonso Zara's play, discussed in Chapter 5) and the actual, lived circumstances of Antonietta Carrozza's life. Her investigator's question cited above, which supposes that Antonietta might have expected Pietro ever to marry her, is indicative of this gap. In their summations, lawyers on both sides tap into a rich network of cultural reference to characterize the motivations and behavior of the three defendants, projecting their actions against an imaginary backdrop dense with poetic and religious allusion. In contrast to this inflated contextualization and culturization of the events on trial, the facts of Antonietta Carrozza's experience appear so mean as to be practically inadmissible.

Figure 10.2 Antonietta Carrozza, *cavallerizza*

Source: Illustration from *Processo Fadda illustrato*

From the days of Philip Astley, women performers were crucial to the success of circus in the nineteenth century, especially to its ability to draw audiences from the upper as well as lower classes. Equestriennes were generally displayed according to two models, likely codified by the first Franconi. The first model was as an ethereal representation of some idealized value, as in the Vernet engraving of Eloise Franconi raised *en pointe* on the back of a galloping horse. Female acrobats borrowed the maillot and tutu of romantic ballet to play angels and sylphs. The technical bravura of these performers allowed them to so overcome the rigor and sweat of their acrobatic act as to appear serene, platonic abstractions barely cloaked in flesh. Circus historian Alessandro Cervellati records an anecdote of a special performance given for the pope in the late nineteenth century in which the female acrobat was required to change her pink tutu for a blue one. Along with the color white to represent virginity, blue is the traditional color of the Madonna's cloak, representing virtue and humility. By contrast, the pope's handlers may have regarded a pink tutu as too exquisitely literal a reference to carnal secrets of the female body.[26] Altering the color of the performer's tutu changed her act from a brazen display of feminine power into an enactment of submission to divine will, reminiscent of the Madonna.

The second model for the female equestrian acrobat opposed that of the allegorical sylph: an agile, strong, dominating figure, sexually enticing and intimidating, a type named as the "amazon." The sylphs and nymphs rode side-saddle; the amazons rode "like a man," a position considered dangerous for childbirth, suggesting thus to popular imagination that these women scorned both motherhood and the cult of femininity.[27] Cervellati cites Parisian bohemian writer Romain Coolus (pseudonym of René Weill) speaking of the 1880's, "In that moment the supreme chic was to luck into the favors of a *cavallerizza*."[28] During her interrogations and testimony, Antonietta Carrozza never specifically describes her performances. As the only woman rider in the company, it is reasonable to guess that during shows she changed costumes several times, alternating between sylph, amazon and clown as the need arose, just as she alternated as Cardinali's wife or sister outside the performance circle. An abyss separates the dream images of sylph and amazon from the biography of Antonietta, idiot instrument of an irresistible force.

Lorenzo Cardinali, Pietro's elder brother and company manager, testifies to investigators that Antonietta was probably born in Catania in 1853 of a certain "Marianna," and taken into the company as an apprentice in 1860 in Palermo.[29] During her own interrogation, Antonietta describes her mother as an *interprete* working in Messina. The term *interprete* would mean actor or actress, but it is such a sophisticated usage for this context that it seems rather a euphemism to conceal a still more degrading profession.[30] At seven or eight, therefore, Antonietta leaves her mother and native town to begin her apprenticeship into the *arte* of circus.

In 1870, at the age of 17, Antonietta gave birth to a child. She told investigators, "About eight years ago, promising to marry me, Pietro Cardinali seduced me and took my honor, such that on March 28 of 1870 I brought to light a baby boy in Ascoli di Puglia, which was exposed as a 'projetto.'"[31]

Because of the shadow it casts over the Fadda case, it would be worthwhile here to open a parenthesis to discuss the massive phenomenon of infant abandonment in the period preceding the Fadda trial. "Exposed" (*esposto*) and *projetto* ("cast off") are terms used in the procedure for handing over unwanted children to religious or state entities. Abandoned children were an endemic problem throughout Europe and in Italy the phenomenon reached a peak in the years before national unification.[32] In most urban centers, foundling hospitals accepted unwanted illegitimate children, called *trovatelli* (close to the English word "foundling") or *gettatelli* (in this usage the root verb signifies "to throw" or "to throw away"), passing them to wetnurses who were employed both inside and outside the hospitals, and paid a small fee to provide milk for the waifs in their care. In most cases orphanages refused to accept legitimate children whose parents were unable to raise them, but this policy in practice drove parents to various forms of deception to unburden themselves of babies who were sure to starve if kept at home. The imperative to reduce infanticide and discourage parents from leaving their children at night along public roads, subject to chance, weather, and foraging pigs led to the curious institution of the "wheel" (*ruota, rota, torno, tornio, curlo, buca, presepio, pila, scaffa, scaffetta*).[33] Its form derived from the dumbwaiter apparatus by which provisions could be passed from the outside world to cloistered nuns inside a convent, the wheel was a round wooden box centered on a pivoting axel set inside the wall of a foundling hospital. A person standing outside the hospital would place her infant inside the box, then ring a bell or turn the box on its pivot so that it would revolve, the contents passing inside, where a person on the other side could recover it. The anonymity of the parents was guaranteed in Italy by legal statute as well as by the architectural arrangement of the wheel.[34] In practice, however, anonymity was relative, gradually undermined by institutional record keeping, but especially by the desire of mothers to register their exposed offspring in the hopes of one day being able to recover them. In the case of the first child of Antonietta Carrozza, for example, a formally irregular document details the circumstances of her placement of her infant in the wheel. Apparently written by a barely literate worker at the hospital whose handwriting is very difficult to decipher, the text reads:

> There appeared Antonia Sarocci, twenty six years, profession (unreadable) atrice, born and residing in Ascoli, daughter of Matteo and Saveria Reggiero, deceased, who declared to me that on the seventeenth day of March at ten o'clock in the evening, while alone in the place of the wheel of the projetti of the municipal administration . . . a male infant was exposed in the wheel, presented to me poorly swaddled. I consigned the infant to Maria Romano, wife of Aniollo Trebbiano, farmer.[35]

Virtually all the information given in this memo is incorrect or false, due to a combination of the marginal literacy of the scribe and the apparent wish of the mother to conceal the facts of her shame, even as she guarantees that essential services protect the life of her baby. While the misspelling of the mother's family name may be an error of the writer, Antonietta has apparently intentionally falsified her age, her place of birth, and the names of her parents. On the other hand, the record-keeper has been very attentive to compose the document in such a way as never directly to attest that the child found in the box is Antonietta's. She is present at the moment of discovery of the child, but it is never stated that it is her child. As though concerned for the feelings of the agonized child-mother, the writer never records literally that Antonietta abandoned her baby. Both the wheel and the record, that is, paradoxically conceal and announce a secret, they institutionalize shame while serving as a vehicle for its relief.

No further record here indicates the fate of her first child by Pietro Cardinali, whereas that of the second one is clear, as described in a note from the Prefecture of Foggia in response to the judicial inquiry: "13 April 1871, that a male infant was exposed, wearing around his neck a half-medallion of brass, to whom was given the name Errico Eristola, who was entrusted to the wetnurse Maria Luigia Persichella, under whose purview it died in November of the same year."[36]

Parents who were unable to raise their children consigned them to charitable hospitals either publicly or anonymously, often placing into the wheel together with the child an object intended to guarantee its identification in the eventuality that the parent be able to recoup the child at a later date. In this case Antonietta broke a brass medallion in two pieces, placed one half on a ribbon around her baby's neck, and kept the other half, thinking of a moment in the indeterminate future when her circumstances might allow her to reclaim her child. By matching her half of the medallion to that of the child, she would prove her motherhood and the two would be reunited. Putting letters, coins, medallions, sacred objects, benedictions, precious stones, buttons, ribbons and cloth into the wheel along with the infant were signs of the concern of the parent for the child, and were taken to suggest that the babies in question were legitimate rather than bastard offspring.[37] The institution of the wheel succeeded in reducing the number of children exposed in public places, but in the vast majority of cases the result was the same. In the foundling hospitals, to cite the words of Giovanna Da Molin, a principal historian of infant abandonment in modern Italy, "Dying was the norm."[38] Statistics suggest that seventy to eighty percent of *gettatelli* died within a year.

Despite the success of lawyer Palomba's tactic of "irresistible force" in winning over the courtroom, transforming his client into an object of pity in the popular mind, at no point during the inquest or trial will Antonietta betray either Cardinali or Saraceni; she will never admit that they were indeed lovers and that they exploited her passivity to embroil her in their murderous plot. Nor will she ever implicate Raffaela's wetnurse or mother, despite the insistence of police officials in Cassano and the conjectures of lawyers and journalists that both must have been more actively involved in the scheme than Antonietta herself. When the jury announces its verdicts on October 31 after less than an hour of deliberation, Antonietta will be found guilty of material complicity in the murder, but because her actions were compelled by a power beyond her control, she must not be held morally culpable and is therefore acquitted. The judge orders her immediate release. The public applauds.[39] According to one reporter, Antonietta, "doesn't wait to be asked twice, and rushes away from the defendants' table."[40]

Her story does not end there. It is Antonietta, in fact, who provides the last chapter by moving the Fadda trial out of the courtroom and back into the circus. No sooner are the verdicts announced than the Fadda trial cedes its primacy and column inches to others still in suspense. Even before the lawyers finished their summations, Vassallo had already been sent to cover the Lazzaretti trial in Florence, handing over his duties in Rome to another reporter. But Milanese readers still not surfeited with the case note the headline, "Echoes of the Fadda Trial" in an inside page of the November 3–4 edition:

> Antonietta Carrozza, who began to enjoy her contested liberty, was arrested by the police, who wished to constrain her to return to her home country. She refused. Her lawyer, Palomba, immediately appealed to the Ministry of Justice and obtained the release of his client. Mr. A. Shür, proprietor of the circus now playing at Rome's Politeama, offered Carrozza a contract to join his troupe, but she refused, seeking better terms.[41]

Thus begins the coda that keeps the Fadda case regularly in the news for three weeks in November, climaxing with her performances before cheering, sold-out crowds in Rome, not far from the courtroom. Shortly after verdicts were announced, local police received word that the Shür circus was seeking to hire Antonietta Carrozza. A police official who found it improper that she would exploit her criminal notoriety to advance her career issued an order that she be arrested and compelled to return to her *patria* (here translated as "home country"). But the official forgot what was made so clear in the trial: Antonietta had no home to return to; there was never one she came from. Her only home now is Italy. Having been acquitted, no limits can now be placed on her freedom to circulate and seek a livelihood anywhere she chooses in her new *patria*, the unitary state, that glorious achievement for which soldiers like Fadda gave their blood, their testicles, and their lives. Discharged from Buon Pastore and with nowhere to go, Antonietta took refuge in the office of her lawyer, who defended her from the police and began to act as her agent.[42] Soon she was entertaining offers from major circuses in Rome and Naples, as well as from Lorenzo Cardinali, who hoped to reconstitute his own ruined company around the newfound notoriety of his former supporting equestrienne. After several days of negotiations, she finally accepted an extremely handsome offer from the prestigious Shür company, which had taken over the slot previously filled by Guillaume's at the Politeama. Antonietta will be paid 3,000 lire for 15 performances.[43]

The press is horrified and thrilled at this crass commodification, which they call terribly American.[44] From Milan, the November 9–10 *Corriere della sera* denounces:

> It is to be severely reproached that no one has prohibited the ugly dragging-on of the Fadda trial, that is, the *debut* of equestrian Antonietta Carrozza at the Politeama. Respect for freedom should never exceed the limits of decency. Other favorable offers from other equestrian companies had come to Carrozza. She could have, she should have, accepted those. Instead, in Rome itself, at the Politeama, only a short distance from the Criminal Court, a disgusting merchandise and ugly promotion is made of her. And the authorities, guardians of order, morality, and decency, do nothing?[45]

At her debut performance, the Politeama with seating for 4,000, is filled to the gills. The proprietors cannot remember it ever having been so full, not even for the leading opera singers or the legendary tragedienne, Adelaide Ristori.[46] The piazza and streets are packed with frustrated ticketseekers, while senators, parliamentary deputies, and magistrates arrive in cabs with wives and children. Significant portions of the Roman patriciate have deigned to attend, spurred by free tickets given them by impresario Shür.[47] Even the assassin's brother is noted in the crowd, perhaps chagrined at not having been able to offer his former actress a deal to match the Roman one.[48] The *Bersagliere* remarks that it's impossible to distinguish whether the event is a judicial or an equestrian spectacle, adding that the trial should have continued rather in the Court of Appeals than in the ring at the Politeama.[49]

With the entire nation's eyes on her, Antonietta's performance is a letdown, but she is excused by the fact of having spent the past year shut up between prison and court; unable to train, her legs have grown thin, her balance shaky. Overwhelmed with emotion, she is barely able to stand alone on the back of the whirling horse and must be supported by a male equestrian at her side.[50] Despite her less than mediocre performance, the audience adores her. Not strong enough to perform an encore, she is nevertheless called out three times to take her bows.[51] With smug disgust at this secular orgy, the *Osservatore romano* records, "She was even saluted by hundreds and hundreds of white handkerchiefs waved by feminine hands! Such an ovation was never accorded to any true artistic celebrity, never to any great citizen honored by the fatherland, never to any monarch or conqueror."[52] The Catholic paper's implication here is that it is not the Vittorio Emanueles, the Garibaldis, the Carduccis who are the true heroes of free Italy, but the Antonietta Carrozzas, the Saracenis, the Carluccios and Bergamuccios.

Antonietta's debut at the Politeama also provokes a long editorial in the *Times* of London. "The scene of Monday," says the *Times*, "is itself only the culmination of an excitement with which Italy has been seething for a whole year."[53] Carrozza's performance, the editor notes, has followed ironically on the heels of a circular issued by the Italian Minister of Justice sharply criticizing his own magistracy for its handling of the Fadda trial, beginning with the decision to build seating and distribute tickets, as though the defendants were to be "stared at like wild beasts exhibited in a circus."[54] Seizing the occasion for an opportunity, not unfamiliar in the British press, to represent Italy as the lunatic flipside of English moderation, the *Times* expresses gratitude that home authorities limit such excessive displays of public passion, adding that the more measured themes of English popular literature, compared to that of Italy and France, have helped tranquilize the general public's dangerous appetite for violence and scandal.

The *Times* article stimulates a blowback of shame in Italy, stoking still higher the flames of impotent indignation.[55] *Illustrazione italiana* joins in the self-flagellation:

> By now we've come to this: a circus director is sure to get rich by presenting to his audience an "artist" who is not in prison only by a miracle. And the Roman public applauded her most warmly. We should blush reading news of this sort. What did they applaud her for? For having helped an assassin?

> For having assisted the lovemaking of her lover? Or for having been such a helpless idiot that she could only be acquitted? Is what has happened in the very center of the capital of the kingdom not the most filthy of all filth?[56]

Thanks to the media that made her a celebrity, Antonietta's moral disgrace is commodified into a stardom defined by hysterical transience. Even as hundreds of women wave handkerchiefs in a gesture of solidarity with her suffering, she becomes an international puppet that represents something deeply wrong about Italy and deeply characteristic of its people. Did Antonietta actively choose her new destiny, or rather, with the definitive incarceration of Pietro Cardinali, did the numb passivity that led her into such trouble simply transfer into new hands? It little matters, for once her run is up in Rome she vanishes back into the same mists of history that swallowed her children.

11

Conclusion

Upon hearing the guilty verdict announced against her, Raffaella Saraceni falls into a swoon (*deliquio*). Sobbing, she cries out to her mother. The youngest lawyer on her team, Saverio Tutino, leaps over the railing of the defendants' *gabbione* and rushes to comfort her. Her prime accuser, victorious prosecutor Rutigliano, mercifully orders that she be conducted from the hall. Once she is gone, the president of the court reads out the sentences: Pietro Cardinali is condemned to death, Saraceni to life imprisonment. Throughout the courtroom, the *Messaggero* reports, "Not a voice can be heard, not a breath."[1] The awful gravity of justice has stunned the crowd into silence. The public rises and exits the hall. Within days the seating in the Filippini will be disassembled.

Immediately upon adjournment Justice Minister Giovanni Battista Varé released a circular condemning the theatrical drift contaminating the solemn dignity of judicial procedure: no more gallery seating is to be constructed in courtrooms, no more tickets distributed; such practices, admonishes the minister, are repugnant. Defendants are not to be exhibited like beasts in a circus. Witnesses are to offer only testimony directly pertinent to the charges. State's prosecutors are never to resort to the sorts of oratorical excess practiced by defense attorneys; no ornamental redundancy and no playing on the emotions of public and jury, but severe and simple logic in the quest for truth.[2] The minister pointedly declined in his circular to mention the name of the trial that had prompted his reforms. His silence seemed to impose a standard that the Fadda trial, a shameful episode, was not to be mentioned again. Subsequent historians have mostly obeyed the minister's implicit decree.

Because of its apparent transience, we might regard the Fadda story as an example of microhistory, but it was rather something like the opposite in that it blew up and burst with a huge noise, then disappeared almost as suddenly from view. Historians in search of crucial moments of change, intent on locating ruptures or tracing evolutionary trends, have generally overlooked it. Perhaps they have dwelt so little on the case because it did not change Italy at all. On the contrary, it left Italy more the same than ever.

Why then did this story seize national attention? Why did women flock to the trial and why did their attendance so disturb men? How did the murder and trial influence national perceptions of crime, the army, the South, and social progress? Posed in the Introduction, these questions have determined the structure of this study but have not been definitively answered. The event produced more contention than consensus, leaving behind sharp disagreement about what had taken place and what it all boded for the present and future of Italy. Therein lies the value of the Fadda case as an object of study, for it manifested and prophesied at high volume the characteristic fractiousness of the Italian public sphere.

The one point of consensus regarding the Fadda case was that it was a disgrace, but there was little agreement as to where exactly the shame lay. For the government, the disgrace lay in the way the trial had been conducted. Orders for reform did not prevent citizens from flocking to trials to watch lawyers as though they were operatic tenors. The Corriere saw the disgrace in the proliferation of violent crime that threatened civil society at its core and against which the press functioned as a beacon of progress. The *L'Osservatore romano*, on the contrary, allied for once with anticlerical scientist Cesare Lombroso to argue that the free press provided a disgraceful spotlight for criminal egos seeking notoriety. In and around the trial, Giosué Carducci and Edmondo De Amicis each condemned the decadent urban classes for social habits that were undermining the young state. De Amicis posited the alternative of a Spartan ideal of military discipline, while Carducci carried a torch for Queen Margaret as the incarnation of feminine virtue against hordes of snack-gobbling pleasure-seekers.

The Fadda murder drew the nation's attention not only because violence, adultery, shame, and scandal fascinate irresistibly, but also because the crime took place in the heart of the capital in a moment when newspapers, driven by the need to survive on sales, experimented with ways to reach a new audience of readers hungry to reflect themselves in print. People demanded their daily dose of common sense mixed with senseless violence, their news mixed with fiction and advertising, acts of God with rebuses and riddles. Playing fortuitously on the magnetism of the Fadda case, the press expanded its reach demographically across the nation but psychologically as well, taking up permanent residence in the minds of Italians who began to recognize themselves in the normative definition of man as "an animal that reads newspapers."

The trial enchanted Italy because, with all eyes fixed on them and spurred by avid crowds, lawyers for the prosecution and defense, poets, and cultural commentators transformed a squalid murder into a national drama by abstracting the victim and accused into symbols of opposed forces threatening Italy's fragile cohesion. Giovanni Fadda was not merely a military bureaucrat but an immortal spirit of the Risorgimento, Pietro Cardinali not a sadistic bully but an atavistic savage emerged from mankind's underbelly. Raffaella Saraceni was either a pathetic victim of frustrated maternity or an avatar of feminine treachery, while Antonietta Carrozza represented abjection metamorphosed, in her performances after the trial, into a model of survival after abuse. Once the public sated itself with the manipulation of these symbols, their interest turned expectantly to the next sensation, the next scandalous bubble. The real individuals subjected to the transformation receded back into shadow, as thoroughly forgotten in flesh and blood as they had previously been abstracted into immaterial figures.

Roman women flocked to the trial because it was virtually the only function of public citizenship from which they were not excluded, and also undoubtedly for many other reasons as well.[3] From the high podium of poetry, Giosué Carducci accused the women spectators of being destroyers of nationhood, their venal appetites eternally in search of vicarious thrills, and aroused by talk of transgressive sex. Carlo Palomba demurred on the contrary that women attended out of maternal devotion to the *patria*, while Vassallo proposed that they mirrored themselves curiously in an adulterous widow accused of slaying her impotent husband. Each of these explanations tells us more about the motivations of the speakers, locked in their rhetoric and perceptual frames, than about those of the people they purport to analyze. In Francesco Netti's painting, *In Corte d'Assise*, among the women pictured we can make out expressions of pity, distraction, empathy, titillation, deep reflection, pure spectatorship, self-display, and warm concern; still others remain enigmatic. Like the other commentators, Netti too is a male observer of women spectators, but his viewpoint at least has the virtue of encompassing diverse individual possibilities. In the absence of their own words, it would be presumptuous to reductively generalize their motives or assume that all women who attended the trial had a motive in common, except to say perhaps that *everyone* wanted to get in to the Fadda trial. The ones who attended did so because they were smart or lucky or connected enough to obtain tickets. Men (and women too) were disturbed by their highly visible presence because men have always been disturbed by women's autonomy, because their colorful participation offended decorum, because the men felt threatened sexually, and because they feared that identification with Raffaella Saraceni undermined a key myth at the base of the state: that of female submission and sacrifice to the ideal values of the nation.

The third question, as to the influence of the Fadda case on the formation of national issues, is still more elusive. The Fadda phenomenon was less a cause of change than a public stage for a general exacerbation of social and psychic tension. Through the trial, editors trumpeted the progressive value of the press in exposing evil even as they fed their avid readers' appetite for shame and filth. In the name of freedom, the liberal state opened to public view the functions of justice formerly held by the Church, even as it created new categories of sanction and punishment, ostracizing the unregistered and nomadic. Dedicated to the painstaking collection of fact, positivism entered the courtroom to serve the objective determination of guilt or innocence, only to encounter seductive oratory, unreliable juries, and the caprice of public sentiment. Using statistical technologies and cutting-edge theory, scientists conjured up primeval specters. A circus model of entertainment, of the grand gesture and juggled symbol, permeated even the solemn reserves of state dignity. The shining ideal of civic fraternity was sullied in its democratic realization as women erupted into the public sphere with their fashions, their passions, their opinions, and desires. Opposed Catholics and republicans found themselves on the same side in decrying the moral landslide of feminine visibility. A murdering adulteress garnered widespread sympathy while fans cheered her accomplice, a mother who abandoned two infants. Soldiers were held up as a model of citizenship no one aspired to. The army was secretly impotent, while the circus revealed a savage face under its gay mask. No matter how intimate, no transaction occurred between North and South untainted with diffidence and the threat of violence. After the Risorgimento, Italian national identity formed in the process not of bridging these chasms but in enacting them. Through periodic staging of its radical divisions, resilient Italy advanced toward a vision of national unity ever beyond reach.

Notes

Introduction

1. *Corriere della sera*, November 9–10, 1879.
2. The trial archive is catalogued in the Archivio di Stato di Roma as Tribunale Civile e Penale di Roma—Corte d'Assize. AD 3659, fascicoli penali 18958–18959, and is housed in the Sede Succursale in Via Galla Placidia. The archive consists of a cardboard box approximately twelve inches high containing four folders, each with an annotated paper wrapper. The folders include in roughly chronological order the legal documentation of the investigation (such as the autopsy, the arrest reports, interrogation records, and photographs and letters recovered from the victim's habitation), the official charges (*Atto d'Accusa*), documentation of the constitution of the jury, the *verbale* of the trial proceedings, the verdict, the sentences, and a small amount of extraneous material. Each of the four folders is indexed. Although the indexing is assiduous, the great variety of page sizes, decay of page edges where numbers are marked, and the difficulty of deciphering the handwriting of several of the scribes reduce the utility of the indexes. Following the practice of other scholars, in this study footnotes will refer to the Fadda archive as ASR, Tribunale Civile e Penale di Roma, b.3659. More detailed indications have been provided whenever possibile.
3. The two published collections of trial coverage are those of Luigi Arnaldo Vassallo for the *Messaggero* and of Nicolò Coboevich for the *Bersagliere*, which will be noted respectively throughout this study as Vassallo, L.A., *Processo Cardinali e coimputati per l'assassinio del Capitano Fadda commesso in Roma il 6 ottobre 1878*. Rome: Perino, n.d. (but 1879) and as Coboevich, Nicolò, *Processo Fadda illustrato*, Rome: Bracco, 1879. It is important to note that one week before the end of the Fadda trial, reporter Vassallo was transferred to cover another trial (the famous Davide Lazzaretti trial in Tuscany) and handed over his duties at the Roman courtroom to another, unnamed reporter. For both the book published by Perino of the *Messaggero*'s coverage, and that published by Bracco of the *Bersagliere*'s coverage, the principal author is not named on the title page.
4. See Davis, "Introduction," *Italy in the Nineteenth Century*, 1–24.
5. Banti, *La storiografia sull'Italia contemporanea*, 183–208.

6. Cardoza, Anthony L., "Rethinking Modern Italy after the Cultural Turn," *Journal of Modern Italian Studies*, 541–49, see also Ascoli and von Henneberg, *Making and Remaking Italy*, 1–26.
7. Croce, *A History of Italy, 1871–1915*, 10.
8. Porciani, *La festa della nazione*, 99; see also Tobia, *Una patria per gli Italiani.*
9. "Biopolitics, as Foucault terms this other form of power, challenges the juridico-ideological operations of the state, though, despite its incursions, it does not entirely displace them," Stewart-Steinberg, *The Pinocchio Effect*, 10.
10. The first chapter, titled "Corte d'Assisie," of prosecutor Lino Ferriani's 1886 study of infanticides, *La infanticida nel codice penale e nella vita sociale. Considerazioni*, consists of an extended reflection on theatre, public trials and journalism, in which the author cites the Fadda trial, 7–37; see also the unsigned article, "Modificazioni al codice di procedura penale," in D'Addio, *Politica e magistratura*, 428–32.
11. A concise, helpful definition of performance in this sense (influenced by the thought of Judith Butler) is proposed by Duttlinger et al.: "something is performative when its representation and itself overlap; when the act of representing something *is that thing itself*," *Performance and Performativity in German Cultural Studies*, 12–13 (italics in the original). The sense of performance here is more literal but phenomenologically related to what Stewart-Steinberg calls "continuous stagings of a crisis identity," *The Pinocchio Effect*, 5.
12. The conception and treatment of this third level of spectacle throughout the present study owes a great deal to Debord's *The Society of the Spectacle*. The peculiar case of Italy in the late nineteenth-century may constitute a prototype version of the society Debord describes, especially in terms of the submission of "cyclical time" to "the irreversible time of the bourgeois," no. 141, 104. Given the retarded sociohistorical and economic conditions of Italy in comparison to England and France, however, the same period can equally be regarded as a particularly late and concentrated exemplar of Jürgen Habermas's description of the formation of the public sphere.
13. A sufficient example is Armati and Selvetella, *Roma criminale, il lato oscuro della Città Eterna, misteri, delitti, fattacci e criminalità dal rapimento di Aldo Moro all'assurda morte di Marta Russo, dal controverso assassinio di Pier Paolo Pasolini alla banda della Magliana*, 28–31.
14. The model for the concept of "national imaginary" used here is that of Benedict Anderson's *Imagined Communities.*
15. "At stake, then, is the *mode of attachment* of the postliberal subject to the state and to the ideological state apparatus," Stewart-Steinberg, *The Pinocchio Effect*, 156.

Chapter 1

1. Gnoli, *Topografia e toponomastica di Roma medioevale e moderna*; see also, D'Amelio, "Foro di Cesare," *Fori Imperiali.*
2. Kostof, *The Third Rome 1870–1950*, 19, 60.

3. Cuccia, *Urbanistica edilizia infrastrutture di Roma capitale 1870–1990, Una cronologia*, 156; see also Meneghini, "Lo scavo dei fori Imperiali e la scoperta del catasto imperiale romano."
4. Pesci, "I primi anni di Roma capitale (1870–1878)"; Talamo, *Il Messaggero e la sua città*, 4.
5. Serianni, *Storia della lingua italiana*, 24.
6. Cuccia, 9.
7. Vidotto, *Roma capitale*, 8; De Jaco, *Antistoria di Roma capitale*, 815–21.
8. Beltrami Scalia, *La riforma penitenziaria in Italia*, 107–13. Beltrami Scalia is identified as director general of prisons in Lombroso, "Il mio museo criminale," *Illustrazione italiana* 33, no. 13, April 1, 1906. The article is reprinted in Lombroso, *Delitto, genio, follia*, 326.
9. Vassallo, L. A., *Processo Cardinali e coimputati per l'assassinio del capitano Faddo*, 52.
10. ASR, Tribunale Civile e Penale di Roma, b.3659, Autopsy report. Number of wounds given at pp. 19–20.
11. Fadda's age estimated at 35 in the autopsy report at p. 17. The Neapolitan daily *Il Pungolo* cites the Roman newspaper *L'Opinione* as giving Captain Fadda's age as 45. *Il Pungolo*, October 7, 1878, no. 278.
12. *Corriere della sera*, October 7–8, 1878, no. 276, 1–2.
13. *Il Bersagliere*, October 7, 1878, 4, no. 274.
14. The report in *Il Diritto* is republished in Naples' *Il Pungolo*, October 7, 1878.
15. *Corriere della sera*, October 7–8, 1878, no. 276, 1–2.
16. *Corriere della sera*, October 8–9, 1878, no. 277, 1.
17. *La Capitale*, October 7, 1878, 1, no. 1048. Italics in the original.
18. *Il Bersagliere*, October 9, 1878, no. 276.
19. *Corriere della sera*, October 11–12, no. 279, 1.
20. "Signori, il 6 ottobre 1878 surse nefasto per Roma: surse nefasto per l'Italia." The words by Rosano (before practicing law he had founded and directed a theatrical journal in Naples) are recorded in *Il Bersagliere*, and published after the trial, by journalist (and lawyer) Coboevich, *Processo Fadda illustrato*, 140; see 143–44 for a brief biography of Rosano.
21. *Corriere della sera*, October 11–12, 1878, no. 279, 2.
22. Maria Paola Fiorensoli, *La città della dea Perenna*, 180–81.
23. *Il Diritto* is cited in *Il Pungolo*, October 11, 1878, no. 282.
24. *Corriere della sera*, October 12–13, 1878, 2.
25. *Il Bersagliere*, October 12, 1878, no. 279.
26. *Corriere della sera*, October 13–14, 2.
27. "Immense grief," *Il Bersagliere*, October 10, 1879, no. 277; "great consternation," *Il Diritto*, October 9, 1878, no. 282; "long roadway," *La Capitale*, October 9, 1878, no. 1050.
28. *L'Avvenire d'Italia*, October 9, 1878, no. 233.
29. *Il Bersagliere*, Thursday October 10, 1878, no. 277. Echoing this funerary oration, the motive of revenge ("vendetta") is exploited during the trial by

chief prosecuting attorney Ippolito Rutigliano during his closing remarks, as reported in *Il Messaggero*, October 17, 1878, no. 286.

30. *L'Opinione*, October 14, 1878, no. 282.
31. Pessina, Enrico, *Dei progressi del diritto penale in Italia nel secolo XIX*, 183.
32. In addition to the original document in ASR, Tribunale Civile e Penale di Roma, b. 3659, The *Atto* is reproduced in Coboevich, *Processo Fadda illustrato, 5–6.* All citations from the *Atto* are from these sources.
33. *In momenti di ebbrezza amorosa* (in moments of amorous intoxication) is the expression by Antonio Ponsiglioni, lawyer for the Fadda family, reported the hearing of October 20 in *L'Opinione*, October 21, no. 288.
34. *Corriere della sera*, Wednesday–Thursday September 24–25, 1879, no. 263, p. 1. The reporter here counts three women as defendants, but when the trial opened, there were only two. The third would have been Maria Ferraro, known also as "Necco" or "Mamma latte," widow Saraceni's wet nurse, who had been implicated for her role as courier of messages and telegrams between the three accused defendants. Although not ultimately charged of complicity in the murder, she will be cited and incarcerated for contempt of court when her public testimony contradicts that she had given under interrogation.
35. Fiorensoli, *La città della dea Perenna*, 205.
36. *Il Bersagliere*, September 27, 1879, no. 264. The description of "first and second class tickets" comes from the circular released by the minister of justice commenting on the trial, dated November 3, 1879 (Gabinetto N. 243–340), titled "Giudizi innanzi alle Corti d'Assise," in *Raccolta delle circolari emanate dal Ministero di Grazia e Giustizia e dei Culti.*
37. *Don Pirloncino*, October 5, 1879, 8, no. 120.
38. *Corriere della sera*, October 12–13, 1878, 2.

Chapter 2

1. Castronovo, *La stampa italiana dall'unità al fascismo*, 29–34; see also, Malgeri, *La stampa cattolica a Roma dal 1870 al 1915.*
2. Castronovo, *La stampa italiana nell'età liberale*, 11–12.
3. Lodi, *Giornalisti*, 20.
4. Cammarano, "La Costruzione dello stato e la classe dirigente," 3–112. Cammarano cites Arrangio-Ruiz, *Storia costituzionale del Regno d'Italia (1898).*
5. Castronovo, *La stampa italiana nell'età liberale*, 30–31; see Magnanti, *Catalogo dei quotidiani romani dell'Emeroteca dell'Archivio Storico Capitolino*,10, for the number of newspapers in Rome; see also Nasi, *Il peso della carta. Giornali, sindaci e qualche altra cosa di Milano dall'unità al fascismo*, 24–25.
6. Castronovo, *La stampa italiana nell'età liberale*, 13.
7. Martini, "I Nuovi Ricchi: commedia in quattro atti," act 3, scene 4, 75.
8. Serianni, *Storia della lingua italiana*, 27.
9. Talamo, *Il "Messaggero" e la sua città: cento anni di storia*, 4–6 and 41–42.
10. Cordova, "Giornali e giornalisti a Roma nell'Italia umbertina," *Dall'erudizione alla politica*, 239–58; see 241 where Cordova provides an extended description

of newspaper publishing costs from Bernardini, *Guida della stampa periodica italiana, compilata dall'avv*, 111–12.

11. Castronovo, *La stampa italiana nell'età liberale*, 32.
12. Lodi, *Giornalisti*, 26–32.
13. Martini, "Confessioni e ricordi" in *Memorialisti dell'Ottocento*, 1126; Talamo, *Il "Messaggero" e la sua città: cento anni di storia*, 32.
14. Fonterossi, Giuseppe, "L'assassinio del Capitano Fadda,"*Roma fine Ottocento*, 124.
15. Martini, *Confessioni e ricordi*, 205–6, 317, 334.
16. Martini, "nota biografica," *Confessioni e ricordi*, 303.
17. Serianni, *Storia della lingua italiana*, 27.
18. Nasi, *Il peso della carta*, 62–66. Oblieght is the subject of a brief item written by Vassallo, *Illustrazione italiana*, January 22, 1882, 9, no. 4, 67; see also Sommaruga, *Crónica bizantina (1881–1885)*, 91; further on Oblieght, Lodi, *Giornalisti*, 147.
19. Majolo Molinari, *La stampa periodica romana dell'Ottocento*, 115–118 (on the *Bersagliere*), 302–304 (on *L'Opinione*).
20. *La Capitale*, October 24, 1879, no. 3309.
21. *Il Messaggero*, October 24, 1879, no. 293.
22. Licata, *Notabili della terza Italia*, 78–79, note 7.
23. Martini, *Confessioni e ricordi*, 213–15; Talamo, *Il "Messaggero" e la sua città: cento anni di storia*, 34–35. Murialdi, *Storia del giornalismo italiano*, 73–75; on E. E. Oblieght: Luigi F. Bona, "Appunti sulle origini e sulla storia del fumetto italiano," nuovo testo, aumentato, dal volume *Il fumetto italiano* Fondazione dell'Associazione Franco Fossati, Milano, http://www.lfb.it/fff/fumetto/storia/st_it/st_it_010.htm (accessed August 24, 2010) ; see also Lega, *Cinquant'anni di giornalismo*, 176; Bruno Tobia names Oblieght as the financier behind a lottery held to raise funds for the Turin World Exposition in 1884, *Una patria*, 71.
24. Telegraphy came to Italy in 1853, but daily telegraphic news reports from Rome to Milan began only in 1877. Franco Nasi, *Il peso della carta*, 76.
25. Serianni, *Storia della lingua italiana*, 29–30, and n5.
26. Talamo, *Il "Messaggero" e la sua città: cento anni di storia*, 30.
27. *Ibid.*, 35.
28. *Ibid.*, 37.
29. Montanelli, *Storia d'Italia: L'Italia dei notabili (1861–1900)*, 155–57.
30. *Il Messaggero*, March 8 1879, and Talamo, *Il "Messaggero" e la sua città: cento anni di storia*, 38.
31. Murialdi, *Storia del giornalismo italiano*, 77. Unfortunately, the author here provides the wrong date for the coverage of Jack the Ripper, giving 1860 when he should have given 1888.
32. Valera, *Milano sconosciuta e Milano moderna*, 341. The passage is carried over into Nasi, *Il peso della carta*, 23.
33. Talamo, *Il "Messaggero" e la sua città: cento anni di storia*, cites Chierici, *Il quarto potere a Roma: Storia dei giornali e dei giornalisti romani*, 103.
34. *Il Messaggero*, March 9, 1879.

35. Lodi, *Giornalisti*, 28–47.
36. Lodi, *Giornalisti*, 35–36; Lega, *Cinquant'anni di giornalismo*, 138–39.
37. Lodi, *Giornalisti*, 36.
38. Bartezzaghi, Stefano, "Combinazioni segrete e figure di parole: La 'Metametrica' di Caramuel e l'impossibile storia dell'enigmistica," *Engramma*, N. 54, http://www.engramma.it/engramma_revolution/55/055_saggi_bartezzaghi.html. Publication forthcoming. As for the proliferation of the rebus and similar games, they can be found, for example, in every issue of the weekly *Illustrazione italiana*.
39. Lodi, *Giornalisti*, 41.
40. Lega, *Cinquant'anni di giornalismo*, 133–208, particularly 147–48.
41. Lodi, *Giornalisti*, 30.
42. Caffiero and Monsagrati, *Dall'erudizione alla politica*, 240.
43. Lodi, *Giornalisti*, 30.
44. Majolo Molinari, Olga, *La stampa periodica italiana dell'Ottocento*, 594–95.
45. Perodi, Emma, *Roma italiana, 1870–1895*, 474. Perodi's *annals* were published originally in 1896.
46. Caffiero and Monsagrati, *Dall'erudizione alla politica*, 242; and biographical notes by Pisu, Associazone Franco Fossati—Museo del Fumetto e della Communicazione, 2006, http://www.lfb.it/fff/giorn/aut/g/gandolin.htm; Talamo, *Il "Messaggero" e la sua città: cento anni di storia*, 38–39.
47. Angeli, "Fondi e figure dell'Ottocento romano: giornali e giornalisti," in *Il Marzocco*, 3 April, 1931. This was cited in Talamo, *Il "Messaggero" e la sua città: cento anni di storia*, 21.
48. Donaver, *Rivista ligure di scienze, lettere ed arti*, March 31, 1911, 127. Cited in Caffiero and Monsagrati, *Dall'erudizione alla politica*, 242.
49. In a discussion of the social ramifications of publications of causes célèbres in eighteenth-century France, Aldo Mazzacane describes the, "daily repetition of a spectacle in which the spectators witness themselves in performance" (782). Mazzacane goes on to say, "The interaction between the juridical and literary dimensions produced the nucleus out of which developed the founding critical position of a new political subject" (786). Mazzacane, "Letterature, processo e opinione pubblica," *Rassegna forense*, 757–92.
50. Lega, *Cinquant'anni di giornalismo*, 135–140.
51. *Il Messaggero*, September 26, 1879; see also, Talamo, *Il "Messaggero" e la sua città: cento anni di storia*, 39.
52. Lega, *Cinquant'anni di giornalismo*, 170.
53. Talamo, *Il "Messaggero" e la sua città: cento anni di storia*, 22.
54. Perodi, *Roma italiana, 1870–1895*, 471–472.
55. ASR, Tribunale Civile e Penale di Roma—Corte d'Assize. b. 3659.
56. Kalifa, *L'Encre et le sang*, 34. The citation is from Babini, Valeria, *Il caso Murri: una storia italiana*, 48.
57. Serianni, Luca, *Storia della lingua italiana*, 72.
58. Kalifa, *L'Encre et le sang*, 34; see also "Faits divers et romans criminels au XIX siècle," *Crime et culture au XIX siècle*, chapter 6, 131–56 ; "Entre littèrature,

journalisme, et 'science criminelle' se noue progressivement une sorte de relation de validation rèciproque," *Crime et culture au XIX siècle*, 147.

59. Santi, Mara, "Commento al testo" to Serao's "Telegrafi dello Stato" in Santi, Mara, ed., *Racconti italiano dell'Ottocento*, 674.
60. Cesana, *Ricordi di un giornalista*, 363–83.
61. Ibid., 376–77.
62. Ibid., 377–78.
63. Ibid., 371–73.
64. Scarfoglio, "Il Capitan Fracassa" in *Le più belle pagine di Edoardo Scarfoglio*, 54–55.
65. In Nasi, *Il peso della carta*, 79, cites the advice given by *Corriere della sera* editor Eugenio Torelli Viollier to his Paris correspondent Paolo Bernasconi, explaining how to elaborate upon the dry notices supplied by the Stefani agency.
66. Vassallo, *Gli uomini che ho conosciuto, seguito dalle memorie d'uno smemorato*, xiv.
67. Mannori, "La crisi dell'ordine plurale," in *Ordo Iuris. Storia e forme dell'esperienza giuridica*, 137–80, 141.
68. Martini, Ferdinando, *Confessioni e ricordi*, 263.
69. Martini, *Il diario eritreo*, ix–xiv.
70. Jonathan White discusses a similar self-mirroring function for the new commercial arcades, the galleries, which were constructed as stages for bourgeois display in major Italian cities in the mid to late nineteenth century. White, *Italian Cultural Lineages*, 231–33.
71. *L'Italie. Journal politique quotidien*, October 8, 1878. (No issue number given. Some issues of the *Italie* can be found on microfilm in the Biblioteca Nazionale in Rome.)
72. *Il Bersagliere*, October 1, 1879, no. 268.
73. *La Libertà*, October 1, 1879, no. 273.
74. Restucci, "Il territorio," in *Italia moderna*, 457.
75. Vassallo, L. A., *Processo Cardinali e coimputati per l'assassinio del Capitano Fadda*, published without author's name (but L. A. Vassallo) (Rome: Edoardo Perino, undated, but 1879), in at least two editions. See the advertisement in *Il Messaggero*, October 28, 1879, no. 297.
76. *Il Messaggero*, November 7, 1879, no. 307.
77. See, for example, *La Libertà*, November 1, 1879, no. 304.
78. Coboevich, Nicolò, *Processo Fadda illustrato, dibattimento alla Corte d'Assise di Roma dal 30 settembre al 31 ottobre 1879*. The more neutral portrait is in the volume, lacking title page, in collection of the Archivio del Senato in Rome. The weeping widow portrait is in the collection of the Biblioteca Gambalunga, Rimini.
79. In 1885, Nicolò Coboevich will collaborate with Tommaso Lopez (who represents the Fadda family in the present trial) to defend notorious, bestselling polemicist Pietro Sbarbaro against charges of libel brought by Senator Pierantoni. Sbarbaro, Pietro, Lopez, Tommaso, and Coboevich, Nicolò, *Via crucis (Per la libertà della stampa)*, Rome: Angelo Sommaruga, 1884. Shortly

thereafter Lopez himself will stand trial, in disgrace, for having accepted hundreds of thousands of stolen lire from a client he was defending.

80. *Don Pirloncino*, December 31, 1879, anno VIII, no. 156. This newspaper was issued thrice weekly, on Wednesday, Friday, and Sunday.
81. *Corriere della sera*, December 16–17, no. 346.
82. See, for example, *Il Messaggero*, October 4, 1879, no. 273. This issue is available only in a microfiche in the archive of *Il Messaggero*.
83. *La Libertà*, October 23, 1879, no. 295.
84. *Don Pirloncino*, October 29, 1879, no. 130.
85. Antonio Ponsiglioni's speech is recorded in detail in *Il Diritto*, October 21, 1879, no. 294.
86. *Il Messaggero*, October 24, 1879, no. 293.
87. Excerpted in Groppi, "Il teatro della giustizia. Donne colpevoli e opinione pubblica nell'Italia liberale," *Quaderni storici*, no. 111, anno xxxvii, fascicolo 3, December 2002, 666–67.
88. *Il Messaggero*, April 5, 1879.
89. *Corriere della sera*, December 16–17, 1878, no. 346; see also Nasi, *Il peso della carta*, 61 on the founding of the *Corriere*.
90. Croce is quoted in Macry, Paolo and Romanelli, Raffaelle, "Premessa" to "Quaderni storici," 56/ anno XIX, no. 2, August 1984. See also Banti, *Storia della borghesia italiana*.
91. Mazzacane, *Rassegna forense*, 779.
92. Magistrali, *Il lettore e il suo doppio*, 76. The author cites Roland Barthes, *Essais Critiques*. Paris: Sevil, 1951.
93. Cavalli Pasini, "Scienza e letterature tra processo e commedia," *Intersezioni*, 563–86.
94. Santucci, "Positivismo e cultura positivistica: problemi vecchi e nuovi," in *L'Età del positivismo*, 23–73, esp. 26; Ferrari, Stefano, "Gli studi sull'ipnotismo e la suggestione tra scienza e misticismo," in *Immagini della scienza* (Rome: Riuniti, 1977), 130. Lombroso, *Delitto, genio, follia*, especially "Introduzione," 24.
95. Lodi, *Giornalisti*, 29.
96. Babini, Valeria, *Il caso Murri: una storia italiana*, 47–49.
97. Santi, Mara, ed., *Racconti italiano dell'Ottocento*, 623.
98. Papa, *Il giornalismo*, quoted in Serianni, Luca, *Storia della lingua italiana*, 30.
99. Letter of Pope Pius IX to Vittorio Emanuele II, August 21 1871 was printed in *La Civiltà Cattolica*, December 27, 1872; De Jaco, *Antistoria di Roma capitale*, 826–27.
100. *L'Osservatore romano*, October 1, 1879, anno XIX, no. 224.
101. "Emporio pittoresco: illustrazione universale," (Milan: Editore Edoardo Sonzogno), anno XVI, no. 793, November 9–15, 1879, 218; on the Emporio pittoresco, see Michele Giordano, *La stampa illustrata in Italia dalle origini alla Grande Guerra*, esp. 89–93.
102. *Corriere della sera*, November 1, 1879, 1, under the heading "Judicial Spectacles."

103. Lombroso, Cesare, *Delitto, genio, follia: scritti scelti*, 761–62.
104. *Il Pungolo*, October 16, 1879.
105. *Il Bersagliere*, October 9, 1879, no. 276.
106. *La Libertà*, October 24, 1879, no. 296.
107. *Don Pirloncino*, October 1, 1879, no. 118.
108. *Il Diritto*, October 27, 1879, no. 300.
109. *Il Bersagliere*, "Furor" October 3, 1879, no. 279; *L'Osservatore romano*, "thousand people,"October 24, 1879, no. 244 (citing *Il Bersagliere*, with adaptations); see also "on the steps of the Filippini church, clusters of people are reading and commenting of the numerous, various reports released by the press" in *Il Messaggero*, October 2, 1879, no. 271.

Chapter 4

1. This information on the Oratorio dei Filippini comes from a plaque in the building's courtyard. As part of a long-term restoration of the entire building, the Archivio Capitolino was indefinitely closed as of June 2009.
2. Cuccia, *Urbanistica Edilizia Infrastrutture di Roma Capitale*, 53; see also Fonterossi, *Roma fine Ottocento*, 51.
3. *Il Bersagliere*, September 27, 1879, no. 264; *Il Diritto*, September 26, 1879, n. 269; *Il Diritto*, September 28, 1879, no. 271.
4. *L'Osservatore romano*, October 1, 1879, no. 224: "Roma da più giorni è coperta dai vostri manifesti con cui promette mari e monti per questo processo"; "Le vie della nostra città sono tappezzate di cartelli di ogni dimensione e di ogni colore. Dovunque uno volge lo sguardo è certo di incontrare un nome che da qualche giorno fa le spese di tutte le conversazioni," in *La Capitale*, October 4, 1879, no. 3289.
5. *Il Bersagliere*, October 3, 1879, no. 279.
6. *Processo Cardinali e coimputati per l'assassinio del Capitano Fadda*, 1879, 7.
7. *Enciclopedia dello spettacolo* (Rome: Le Maschere, 1956), Vol. 3, 882–93, "Circo equestre."
8. *Processo Cardinali e coimputati per l'assassinio del Capitano Fadda*, 1879, 7.
9. Ibid., 6.
10. Ibid., 7.
11. The *Messaggero* reporter is cited in the *Corriere della sera*, October 1–2, 1879, n. 270.
12. Vassallo explains, "As I write, I have before my eyes the effigies of the three eternal actors of this human spectacle, which, depending on moods and circumstances, will turn out to be a farce, a comedy, or a drama; I have before me the wife, the husband, the lover," "Processo Fadda," quoted in Contorbia, *Giornalismo italiano*, 837. The anthologized selection from Vassallo's coverage of the Fadda Trial runs from pages 837 to 849.
13. In order to offset the charismatic sway of defending attorneys in the courtroom, prosecutors turned to leaking details of their investigations to the press prior to the opening of the public phase of the trial, a tactic invented "to create

in public opinion the conviction of the guilt of the accused," Mancini quoted in D'Addio, Mauro, *Politica e magistratura 1848–1876*, 1966, 100. To put a stop to this practice, the Minister of Justice in the last of the *Destra* governments, before the advent of the *Sinistra* to power, passed a reform to prohibit the public dissemination of information regarding a criminal trial before the sentence had been determined. On this reform (Articolo 49) prohibiting press coverage of investigations and trials still underway, see Fonterossi, *Rome fine Ottocento*, 52. Soon after the *Sinistra*'s victory in the election of 1876, the new minister of justice abrogated the law, which in any case had been widely circumvented in practice, Groppi, "Il teatro della giustizia," 653–54.

An alternative source for the photograph could be that the captain's brother, Cesare Fadda, may have had his own copy, which he made available to the press as part of his aggressive campaign to prove Raffaella's direct involvement in the plot to murder her husband.

14. ASR, Tribunale Civile e Penale di Roma, b. 3659, 10 in cartella blu.
15. In this same year at the Prefecture of Police in Paris, Alphonse Bertillon will begin to apply his invention of anthropometry to the identification of criminals. To fill in the inevitable gaps in his objective, quantitative system of measurement of the physical characteristics of criminal recidivists, Bertillon proposed that investigators include also a "spoken portrait," "the verbal, analytical description of the separate entities (nose, eyes, ears, etc.), the sum total of which should have restored the image of the individual—thereby permitting the process of identification," Ginzburg, *Clues, Myths, and the Historical Method*, 120.
16. Pessina, *Dei progressi del diritto penale in Italia nel secolo XIX*, 99, 183.
17. D'Addio, 97.
18. D'Addio, *Politica e magistratura (1848–1876)*, 431.
19. Ibid., 431.
20. Ibid., 442.
21. Gotti, *Alcuni processi celebri e ricordi di un vecchio avvocato*, 35.
22. Ibid., 130.
23. Ibid., 35.
24. *Il Diritto*, October 27, 1879, no. 300; on Lopez, see Gotti, *Alcuni processi celebri e ricordi di un vecchio avvocato*, 35–36; on Lopez's legendary elegance, see Perodi, *Roma italiana*, 553. A half-decade after the Fadda trial, Lopez found himself disgraced, in court not as lawyer but as defendant, accused of having financed his opulent lifestyle with proceeds from the famous robbery of 2 million lire from the Bank of Ancona. He had defended the accused thieves and then extorted their hidden booty from them. The story of Lopez and the theft from the Banca Nazionale d'Ancona is recounted in Fonterossi, *Roma fine Ottocento*, 109.
25. Rosano attempted suicide twice as a young man and finally ended his life in 1903. Deeply religious, he was said to have prayed before speaking in court and dedicated lifelong efforts to honoring the saints of Naples and his home town of Aversa, Archivio Bibliografico Italiano, 103. This source on

microfiche in the Biblioteca Nazionale di Roma, includes entries from Lauri, Achille, *Dizionario dei cittadini notevoli di Terra di Lavoro*, 160, and Sarti, Telesforo, *Il parlamento italiano nel cinquantenario dello Statuto*, 252.

26. *Il Bersagliere*, November 18, 1879, no. 300.
27. *Il Diritto*, October 27, 1879, no. 300.
28. Materi, *L'eloquenza forense*, ix; Babini, *Il caso Murri*, 150. As courts were becoming theatres, performing artists began attending public trials to study the human dramas unfolding there. See Groppi, Angela, "Il teatro della giustizia. Donne colpevoli e opinione pubblica nell'Italia liberale," 669. The era's leading playwright, Pietro Cossa, whose tragedies took a *verista* approach to stories of Roman classical history, was a frequent visitor to the Fadda trial. When the Milanese weekly *L'Illustrazione italiana* described Raffaella Saraceni as "the Messalina of Cassano allo Ionio," the allusion was to Cossa's recent hit play about Emperor Claudius's legendarily promiscuous wife, in which the queen couples with a gladiator. See *L'Illustrazione italiana*, 6, no. 41, October 12, 1879, 127.
29. Galantini, Novella, "L'educazione dei giudici popolari," 142.
30. D'Addio, *Politica e magistratura*, 84.
31. Chiaves, *Il giudice del fatto negli stati sardi*, 1853, 23, quoted in Galantini, "L'educazione dei giudici popolari," 144.
32. D'Addio, *Politica e magistratura*, 85.
33. Ibid., 92.
34. Pessina, *Dei progressi del diritto penale in Italia nel secolo XIX*, 183.
35. Amodio, "Giustizia popolare, garantismo e partecipazione," in *I giudici senza toga*, 19.
36. Macry, *Ottocento*, xix.
37. Galantini, "L'educazione," 156 and note. 49.
38. Macry, "Borghesie, città e Stato," *Quaderni storici*, 339–84; list is at 362–63.
39. D'Addio, *Politica e magistratura*, 91.
40. ASR, Tribunale Civile e Penale di Roma, b. 3659. Mattea deposition, vol. III, 67–68. I have not been able to find the file that lists the names of the fourteen who were chosen to serve.
41. ASR, Tribunale Civile e Penale di Roma, b. 3659. vol. 4, 247.
42. Vassallo, L. A., *Processo Cardinali e coimputati*, 7.
43. *Il Bersagliere*, October 1, 1879, no. 268.
44. On witnesses socializing, Vassallo, L. A., *Processo Cardinali e coimputati*, 49.
45. ASR, Tribunale Civile e Penale di Roma, b. 3659, vol. 4, 246–413.
46. Vassallo, L. A., *Processo Cardinali e coimputati*, 36.
47. Nicolò Coboevich, *Processo Fadda illustrato*, 15.
48. Vassallo, L. A., *Processo Cardinali e coimputati*, 10.
49. ASR, Tribunale Civile e Penale di Roma, b. 3659. Mattea deposition, cartella blu, 2–3.
50. ASR, Tribunale Civile e Penale di Roma, b. 3659. Mattea testimony, cartella blu, 41
51. ASR, Tribunale Civile e Penale di Roma, b. 3659. cartella blu, "Existence . . . ," 2, "How come . . . ," 12.

52. Vassallo, L. A., *Processo Cardinali e coimputati*, 18.
53. Coboevich, *Processo Fadda illustrato*, 21.
54. Lombroso, *Delitto, genio, follia: scritti scelti*, 430–37.
55. Ibid., 433.
56. Ibid., 436.
57. Vassallo, L. A., *Processo Cardinali e coimputati*, 26, 32; Coboevich, *Processo Fadda illustrato*, 30, 36–37; ASR, Tribunale Civile e Penale di Roma, b. 3659. 82–83.
58. Vassallo, L.A., *Processo Cardinali e coimputati*, 12–13.
59. Coboevich, *Processo Fadda illustrato*, 15; Vassallo, L. A., *Processo Cardinali e coimputati*, 13.
60. This is recorded in the Neapolitan newspaper *Il Pungolo* of October 2, 1879 and in Pio, Oscar, *Processi celebri contemporanei italiani e stranieri*, 53–54.
61. Coboevich, *Processo Fadda illustrato*, 13; Vassallo, L. A., *Processo Cardinali e coimputati*, 11; Coboevich, *Processo Fadda illustrato*, 14, respectively.
62. Cardinali claims to have three children by Misuracca in his October 8 interrogation: ASR, Archivio Civile e Penale di Roma, b. 3659. Interrogatorio di Pietro Cardinali nelle Carceri Nuove di Roma, 8 ottobre, 101. Giuseppe De Luca, during his interrogation, says that Cardinali and Misuracca have two children, 96.
63. Coboevich, *Processo Fadda illustrato*, 19.
64. Coboevich, *Processo Fadda illustrato*, 21.
65. Groppi, "Il teatro della giustizia," 649–80.
66. Ibid., 670.
67. Vassallo, L. A., *Processo Cardinali e coimputati*, 62.
68. Groppi, "Il teatro della giustizia," 671; Coboevich, *Processo Fadda illustrato*, 194.
69. Vassallo, L. A., *Processo Cardinali e coimputati*, 126.
70. On Pessina as a representative of the "classical" school, opposed to Lombroso, see Schiavone, *Stato e cultural giuridica in Italian dall'unità alla repubblica*, 160–64; see also Pessina, *Enciclopedia del diritto penale italiano*, 720–21; and Alessi, *Il processo penale*, 176.
71. Sighele, *Eva moderna*. The citation is made in the author's dedication of the volume to his sister.
72. Vassallo, L. A., *Processo Cardinali e coimputati*, 62.
73. Fiorensoli, *La città della dea Perenna*, 180–83. I am indebted to the archivist at the Centro Internazionale delle Donne, which has occupied the former site of Buon Pastore since the 1980s, for this information. See also Groppi, Angela, "'Un pezzo di mercanzia di cui il mercante fa quel che ne vuole'. Carriera di un'internata tra Buon Pastore e il manicomio," 189–224.
74. Groppi, "Il teatro della giustizia", 672, and note. 88, 679. *La Capitale*, November 18, 1880.
75. *La Capitale*, November 13, 1879, 3329.
76. Great thanks to the Biblioteca Labronica for having sent me digital copies of this play, which is bound into a larger volume.

77. Groppi, "Il teatro della giustizia", 672.
78. Coboevich, *Processo Fadda illustrato*, 21.
79. Vassallo, L.A., *Processo Cardinali e coimputati*, 18; Coboevich, *Processo Fadda illustrato*, 23.
80. Coboevich, *Processo Fadda illustrato*, 23.
81. In *Roma fine Ottocento*, 1960, Giuseppe Fonterossi reports that around 1906, newspapers stated that Saraceni was seeking to clear her record so as to be able to gain employment as a teacher. Fonterossi offers no source for this information and thus far I have been unable to find it. Fonterossi, Giuseppe, *Roma fine Ottocento*, 84. On Pessina's term as Minister of Justice: Sabbatucci and Vidotto, *Storia d'Italia. Vol. 2. Il nuovo stato e la società civile*, 564. On her pardon, *Un secolo di grazie, 1860–1960. Mostra documentaria dei decreti di grazia conservati negli archivi del Ministero della Giustizia*, Rome, March 8–31, 2006, n. 12. I am indebted to one of the curators of this exhibition, Cristina Ivaldi, for this information.

Chapter 5

1. These men are probably seated in the press gallery, but the painter has chosen to show them without the tools of their trade.
2. The slogan would be, "La legge è uguale per tutti," that is, "The Law is Equal for All."
3. These maxims would be dialectica fax rationis (logic is the torch of reason), aequitas negociorum arbitra ("fairness the arbiter of business"—in this case, of legal determinations or justice), etica morum emendatrix (ethics are the reformers of habits), eloquentia animorum dominatrix (eloquence is the ruler of minds). I thank Professor Katherine Bosher for assistance, although all errors are mine.
4. *L'Illustrazione italiana*, 10, no. 26, July 1, 1883. The engraving by Paolo Mancastropa is centered across two pages, 8–9. On *Illustrazione italiana*, see Moe, *The View from Vesuvius*, 187–223.
5. Willard, *The History of Modern Italian Art*, 379–85, 402.
6. Sperken, Christine Farnese, *Francesco Netti* (Naples: Electa Napoli, 1996); see also Farese Sperken, *Francesco Netti (1832–1894)*, 18.
7. On women readers in nineteenth-century Italian painting, see Re, "Passion and Sexual Difference," in *Making and Remaking Italy*, 155–202.
8. Both of these works are in the Pinacoteca Provinciale di Bari.
9. "Dopo un giuoco di gladiatori ad una cena a Pompei," reproduced "from the author's sketch" in *Illustrazione italiana*, 7, no. 49, December 5, 1880, 356. The painting, "Lotta dei gladiatori durante una cena a Pompeii, 1880" was purchased by the Queen and is in the Museo di Capodimonte, Naples; Magni, *Storia dell'arte italiana dalle origini al Secolo XX, Vol. III*, 802.
10. Carducci's poem appeared in the weekly insert to the daily *Il Fanfulla*, *Fanfulla della Domenica*, October 19, 1879, no. 13. The poem is collected, with alterations, in Carducci, *Giambi ed epodi*.

11. Giosué Carducci, *Tutte le poesie*, 495.
12. Martini, *Confessioni e ricordi*, 279.
13. On Giovanni Rizzi, see Cattaneo, *An Italian Reader Consisting of Choice Specimens from the Best Modern Italian Writers*, 162, note 14. Rizzi is mentioned also in Lodi, *Giornalisti*, 50.
14. Ferdinando Martini discusses the heated letters he received as editor of *Fanfulla della Domenica* from women readers in *Confessioni e ricordi, 1859–1892*, 284.
15. Sommargua, *Crónica bizantina (1881–1885)*, 80.
16. Martini, *Confessioni e ricordi*, 279. On Federico Martini, "il maestro," see Lodi, *Giornalisti*, 24.
17. Pavarini, *Carducci*, 123–24.
18. Ibid., 31.
19. Ibid.
20. *L'Osservatore romano*, October 22, 1879, no. 242.
21. See also discussion in Stewart-Steinberg, *The Pinocchio Effect*, 114–15.
22. On the "cult of domesticity" imposed on Italian women in this period, see Re, "Passion and Sexual Difference," 158
23. Vassallo, L.A., *Processo Cardinali e coimputati*, 87; Nicolò Coboevich, *Processo Fadda illustrato*, 131–32. Here, as throughout the two texts, the journalists purport to cite exact words of the speaker but they do not agree with one another. Only Vassallo cites the trope of the medals of honor unable to protect the "petto" (meaning "breast" or "chest," but implying "heart") from the assassin's blade. Groppi, "Il teatro della giustizia," 667. Palomba had already gained fame for his defense of Luigi Morelli during the 1875 trial for the murder of editor Raffaele Sonzogno and before that for having defended patriots Ajani and Luzzi when Rome was still under papal rule; Fonterossi, *Roma fine Ottocento*, 52.
24. *Il Messaggero*, November 6, 1879, no. 306: "Contro Carducci, le signore non sono andare [*sic*] per vedere Cardinali, ma per vedere la signora, la loro simile."
25. *Assassinio e Processo Fadda in versi romaneschi per L. A.*
26. *Il Messaggero*, October 12, 1879, no. 281. This issue is available only in a single microfiche copy in the archive of *Il Messaggero*; I am grateful to Silvio Biella for having made this available to me.
27. Misasi, *Leggende e liriche*. Section one is in octaves of *settenari*, rhyming ABABCDCD; section two consists of unrhymed hendecasyllables not divided into stanzas; section three consists of quartains of hendecasyllables, rhyming ABAB. After this publication, the author abandoned poetry for journalism and prose. From Cosenza he moved first to Naples and then Rome, where he soon joined the circle around Ferdinando Martini and became a regular and popular contributor to *Crónica bizantina* and other journals. Iannuzzi, Lina, ed., *Nicola Misasi. Pagine calabresi: antologia* (Bologna: Capelli Editore, 1969).
28. *Il Bersagliere*, November 18, 1879, no. 300.
29. *Il Messaggero*, November 10, 1879, no. 310.
30. It is not clear whether "Alla Contessa Nana" corresponds to actual events in Vassallo's life or whether, more likely, he was parodically evoking stock characters

and situations familiar from the imaginary of his social milieu. Poetess and novelist Contessa Lara, a pseudonym of Evelina Cattermole (1844 –1896), was by 1879 already making a name for herself in Roman and northern circles, both for her private life and her thematically, if not formally, transgressive but highly fashionable poetry featuring female desire. In 1890, a "Contessa Nanà" published in Milan, *Libro proibito: novelle infranciosate* (*Banned Book: French-style Stories*), whose title suggests that it was a comic parody of a certain style of book. Contessa Nanà, *Libro proibito.*

31. All citations that follow in this section are from Martini, "Chiacchiere della domenica," in *Fanfulla della Domenica*, October 12, 1879, no. 12, 1. For the branding of *Fanfulla della Domenica*, see the advertisement in *Il Diritto*, July 1, 1879, no. 182: "Fanfulla della Domenica, giornale settimanale non politico di letteratura, dei arte e critica diretto da F. Martini, e contenente novelle, versi, rassegne letterarie, musicali, drammatiche a artistiche, su lavori italiani e stranieri; curiosità letterarie e storiche, leggende, vbiaggi, rassegne bibliografiche e tutto ciò che può interessare **esclusa la politica**."
32. *L'Illustrazione italiana*, March 13, 1881, no. 11.
33. *La Libertà*, September 30, 1879, no. 272.
34. Groppi, "Il teatro della giustizia," 657, 665–66.
35. Zara, *L'Assassinio del capitano Fadda*. It should be mentioned that the Italian word *assassinio* can be translated either as "murder" or as "assassination."
36. *La Libertà*, October 26, 1879, no. 298.
37. *Don Pirloncino*, November 16, 1879, no. 138.
38. *La Capitale*, December 10, 1879, no. 3356.
39. Mimita Lamberti, "Roma 1883," in *Storia dell'arte italiana. Parte seconda: Dal medioevo al Novecento*, 42–46.
40. Squarciapino, *Roma bizantina*, 168–69.
41. Martini was summoned to testify in an August 1885 trial against Roman editor Angelo Sommaruga, who had been charged with trying to illegally influence the commission in favor of certain painter friends in exchange for payments. Between 1897 and 1907 Martini will serve the state as the imperial governor of the colony of Eritrea, see Gotti, *Alcuni processi celebri e Ricordi di un vecchio avvocato*, 92–93; see also Drake, *Byzantium for Rome*, 44, 79–80, 148, and 254, note 28.

Chapter 6

1. Nicolò Coboevich, *Processo Fadda illustrato*, 195.
2. Vassallo, L. A., *Processo Cardinali e coimputati*, para. 1. In the trial records, Fadda is described as having been the commander of the second platoon of the 14th Company.
3. Monti, *Vittorio Emanuele II, 1820–1878*, 237.
4. Pieri, *Storia militare del Risorgimento*, 619.
5. Francesco Ogliari, *Commenti al testo di Edmondo De Amicis, "La battaglia di Solferino e San Martino*. viii.

6. Martucci, *L'invenzione dell'Italia unita, 1855–1864*, 80. Ogliari, *Commenti al testo di Edmondo De Amicis*, viii, gives a lower number, which also contrasts with the number given by Nava, *L'Armata sarda nella giornata del 24 giugno 1859*, 135.
7. Mack Smith, *Vittorio Emanuele II*, 89–90.
8. Pieri, *Storia militare del Risorgimento*, 616–18; Luigi Nava, *L'Armata sarda nella giornata del 24 giugno 1859*, 123–25.
9. Martucci, *L'invenzione*, 84–88.
10. Delvecchio, *Il valore italiano*, 131. The quote here is attributed to the king himself, "First soldier of Italian independence." It was a familiar cliché first noted in numerous newspapers published in homage to the king immediately after his death; see Levra, *Fare gli italiani*, 68.
11. Turnbull, *Solferino*, 143–44.
12. Rovighi, *Storia della Terza Divisione dell'esercito sardo nella Guerra del 1859*, 116.
13. Ogliari, *Commenti al testo di Edmondo De Amicis*, 33.
14. Nava, *L'Armata sarda nella giornata del 24 giugno 1859*, 92.
15. Pieri, *Storia militare del Risorgimento*, 616.
16. Rüstow, *Guerra d'Italia del 1859*, 385; see also Mack Smith, *Vittorio Emanuele II*, 83–84, note 44.
17. Rovighi, *Storia della Terza Divisione*, 141.
18. Rüstow, *Guerra d'Italia del 1859*, 379.
19. Godkin, *Life of Victor Emmanuel II, First King of Italy*, 163.
20. Della Rocca, *Rapporto a S.M. il Re di Sardegna dal capo di Stato Maggiore*; Nava, *L'Armata sarda nella giornata del 24 giugno 1859*, 119.
21. Della Rocca, *Rapporto a S.M. il Re di Sardegna dal capo di Stato Maggiore.*
22. Ogliari, Francesco. *Commenti al testo di Edmondo De Amicis, "La battaglia di Solferino e San Martino*. Pavia: Edizioni Selecta, 2005, 4–70.
23. Pieri, *Storia militare del Risorgimento*, 619; see also the diagram of the battle, 627–28.
24. Quarenghi, *L'altra battaglia*, 93–136, 137–46,
25. Giacanelli, "Introduzione," *Delitto, genio, follia: scritti scelti*, 12. Pierluigi Baima Bollone says that antiseptic techniques and early forms of anesthesia were being introduced in some European field hospitals during this period; Baima Bollone, *Cesare Lombroso ovvero il principio dell'irresponsabilità*, 39–40.
26. Vassallo, L. A., *Processo Cardinali e coimputati*, 65.
27. Rovighi, *Storia della terza divisione dell'esercito sardo nella Guerra del 1859*, 285.
28. *Il Bersagliere*, October 10, 1878, no. 277; *La Libertà*, October 9, 1878, no. 281.
29. Tobia, *Una patria per gli Italiani*, 149.
30. Mezzabotta, *Vivandiera di San Martino*; see also Porciani, *La festa della nazione*, 67, on the usage of San Martino during speeches celebrating the Statuto.
31. Tobia, *Una patria per gli Italiani*, 189, 190, note 10, and 13, 233.
32. Carducci, *Tutte le poesie*. The poem appears in Libro VI of *Juvenilia*, 91, 238.

33. *La battaglia di San Martino ed I premi. Dialoghi fra un caporal furiere e due soldati.* This booklet was sold at a price of ten cents to raise funds for the erection of a monument to Vittorio Emanuele II at San Martino, subsequent to the death of the king; *Commemorazione dei benemeriti della Società di Solferino e San Martino morti dalla fondazione (1870) della società al 24 giugno 1884*, 18; Nina Quarenghi, *L'altra battaglia. Solferino e San Martino tra realtà e memoria*, 150.
34. Levra, *Fare gli italiani*, 19, 21.
35. Ibid., 41–80.
36. Ibid., 22–23.
37. De Amicis, *Opere scelte*, 175–76.
38. The *Storia dell'arte italiana* gives the painting's dimensions as still larger, 10 meters by 6, *Storia dell'arte italiana*, 46, note 22.
39. Cuccia, *Urbanistica Edilizia Infrastrutture*, 63, 71.
40. Di Majo, *Galleria Nazionale D'Arte Moderna*, 14–19. See also Frandini, "Nino Costa e l'ambiente artistico romano tra il 1870 e il 1890," in *Aspetti dell'arte a Roma dal 1870 al 1914*, xxvii–xxviii; on "a new image for Rome," see also Stewart-Steinberg, *The Pinocchio Effect*, esp. chapter 3, "The Queen and the Deputy: The Representative Politics of Matilde Serao's *La Conquista di Roma*," 97–138.
41. Tobia, Bruno. *Una patria per gli italiani. Spazi, itinerari, monumenti nell'Italia unita. 1870–1900*, 21–24.
42. Capone, *Destra e sinistra da Cavour a Crispi*, 274–315.
43. Villari, *Le lettere meridionali ed altri scritti sulla questione sociale in Italia*; see also Moe, *The View from Vesuvius*, 224–49, on Villari and other studies of the South.
44. Umberto Levra, *Fare gli italiani. Memoria e celebrazione del Risorgimento*, 48, 50.
45. Di Corato, "Magistratura, anarchici e governo," in *Rivista di storia contemporanea* 13, no. 3 (1984: July), 321–72.
46. Frandini, "Nino Costa e l'ambiente artistico romano tra il 1870 e il 1890," in *Aspetti dell'arte a Roma dal 1870 al 1914.*
47. See Gabriele D'Annunzio's remarks, in Contorbia, "Arte e artisti. Inseguimento," in *Giornalismo italiano*, 947; see also, De Majo, *Galleria Nazionale D'Arte Moderna*, 231; and Netti, "Esposizione di Roma.—Note di un visitatore," in *Francesco Netti, Scritti critici*, 213–71, esp. 214, 263–64.
48. De Gubernatis, *Dizionario degli artisti italiani viventi*, 90.
49. Biancale, *Michele Cammarano*, 84.
50. On the work's prize and purchase, see *Storia dell'arte italiana. Il Novecento.* (1982 ed.), 46, note 22; see Biancale, *Michele Cammarano*, 75, 77–78, on Cammarano's dissatisfaction with it.
51. The sketch is described as, "Due contadini portano innanzi un borghese ferito" in *Illustrazione italiana*, 39.

Chapter 7

1. Vassallo, L. A. *Processo Cardinali e coimputati*, 23; Nicolò Coboevich, *Processo Fadda illustrato*, 27.
2. Coboevich, *Ibid.*, 78.
3. Fulvio Cammarano, "La costruzione dello stato e la classe dirigente," in *Storia d'Italia 2. Il nuovo stato e la società civile*, edited by Giovanni Sabbatucci and Vittorio Vidotto, 3–112. Citation 44. See also Dennis Mack Smith, *Storia d'Italia, 1861–1969*, 90. Also, Piero Pieri, *Storia militare del Risorgimento: Guerre e insurrezioni*, 631, 690, 727.
4. Roberto Martucci, *Emergenza e tutela dell'ordine pubblico nell'Italia liberale*, 9–24.
5. John Gooch, *Army, State and Society in Italy, 1870–1915*, 17.
6. Fulvio Cammarano, "La Costruzione dello stato e la classe dirigente," in *Storia d'Italia. Vol. 2: Il nuovo stato e la società civile, 1961–1887*, edited by Giovanni Sabbatucci and Vittorio Vidotto, 42.
7. Dennis Mack Smith, *Storia d'Italia: 1861–1969*, 119.
8. Molfese, Franco, *Storia del brigantaggio dopo l'Unità.*
9. Dickie, John, "Una parola in Guerra: l'esercito italiano e il 'brigantaggio' (1860–1870)," *Passato e presente* 10 (1991): 53–74, 75.
10. Martucci, Roberto. *Emergenza e tutela dell'ordine pubblico nell'Italia liberale*, 82.
11. Dennis Mack Smith, *Storia d'Italia: 1861–1969*, 116.
12. The passage from De Witt's memoirs is cited in Salvatore Scarpino, *La Guerra 'cafona': il brigantaggio meridionale contro lo stato unitario*, 40. De Witt was not present at Pontelandolfo but based his account on stories by participants in the reprisal.
13. Ferdinando Martini, *Confessioni e ricordi*, 237.
14. Edmondo De Amicis, *Opere scelte*, edited by Folco Portinari and Giusi Baldissone (Milan: Mondadori, 1996). The selection, found in the editors' introduction at XCVII, is from "Nuova Antologia," March, 1869, later published as "L'esercito italiano durante il colera del 1867," in *La vita militare*, definitive edition 1880. "L'esercito italiano . . ." is in Bovio, Oreste, ed., *Edmondo De Amicis: pagine militari*, 93–133, selection at 99.
15. Carlo Bertelli and Giulio Bollati, *Storia d'Italia: Annali 2, L'immagine fotografica 1845–1945. Tomo I*, 70–76. See also the comments by Suzanne Stewart-Steinberg, *The Pinocchio Effect: On Making Italians. 1860–1920*, 109 (photo on following page).
16. Ilaria Porciani, *La festa della nazione. Rappresentazione dello Stato e spazi sociali nell'Italia unita*, 82.
17. Among many other sources, see Silvana Turzio, ed., *Lombroso e la fotografia*; Umberto Levra, ed., *La scienza e la colpa. Crimini criminali criminologi: un volto dell'Ottocento;* Cesare Lombroso, *Delitto, genio follia: scritti scelti*, edited by Delia Frigessi, Ferruccio Giacanelli, and Luis Mangoni. Also see Giorgia Alessi, *Il processo penale. Profilo storico*, 179–83.

18. Romano Canosa, *Storia della criminalità in Italia, 1845–1945*, 63–64.
19. Scarpino, Salvatore, *La Guerra 'cafona': il brigantaggio meridionale contro lo stato unitario*, 63, and 154–56; Franco Molfese, *Storia del brigantaggio dopo l'Unità*, 260–300. Also see Alessi, *Il processo penale*, 173–74.
20. Molfese, *Storia del brigantaggio dopo l'Unità*, 267.
21. *Storia d'Italia. Annali 12: La Criminalità*, 127.
22. John Dickie, *Darkest Italy: The Nation and Stereotypes of the Mezzogiorno, 1860–1900*, 76–77. Both Dickie and Mario Isnenghi speak of what Isnenghi terms the "spettacolarizzazione del confronto fra lo stato e la sovversione," which is to say the way in which punishments, summary judgements, and executions of Southerners by Northern forces were carried out more for their exemplary, performative impact than for their strategic efficacy. Mario Isnenghi, *L'Italia in piazza. I luoghi della vita pubblica dal 1848 ai giorni nostri*, 75.
23. See the selection from the diary of a soldier from Udine, Ermenegildo Novelli, in Aldo De Jaco, ed., *Il brigantaggio meridionale. Cronaca inedita dell'Unità d'Italia*, 52–53.
24. Fortunata Piselli, *Parentela ed emigrazione. Mutamenti e continuità in una comunità calabrese*, see the Introduzione, 3–18, and Appendice 1, 313–15. See also, Gianfausto Rosoli, ed., *Un secolo di emigrazione italiana (1876–1976)*. On the effect of the Pica Law in ending brigandage, Pier Paolo Balbo et. al., eds., *Per un atlante della Calabria*, 557.
25. Molfese, *Storia del brigantaggio dopo l'Unità*, 51; cited in Martucci, *Emergenza*, 85.
26. John Gooch, *Army, State and Society*, 6.
27. Molfese, *Ibid.*, 280.
28. Martucci, *Emergenza e tutela dell'ordine pubblico nell'Italia liberale*, 79 sgg.
29. Christopher Duggan, *The Force of Destiny. A History of Italy since 1796*, 287. Manola Fausti, citing a contemporary newspaper, reports that four rather than five soldiers were killed, with seven wounded. See the "Premessa" to Edoardo Scarfoglio, *Il romanzo di Misdea*, edited by Manola Fausti, 8, note 3. In the same volume's Appendix, a report in the "Gazzetta piemontese," a. XVIII, n. 106, 16 aprile 1884, [p.1], reports five killed and seven wounded, 181.
30. "Il Corriere del mattino di Napoli," May 20, 1884, in Giada Patarini, "Il processo Misdea". One witness testifies, "He said he was angry at everyone except the Calabrians . . ."
31. Vassallo, L. A. *Processo Cardinali e coimputati*, 34 (the barber's name is Vincenzo Marino).
32. Lombroso, "Il caso Villella," in *Delitto, genio, follia*, 235–39; see also, Umberto Levra, ed., *La scienza e la colpa*, 248.
33. Pierluigi Baima Bollone, Cesare Lombroso *ovvero il principio dell'irresponsabilità*, 43. "To liberate Italy . . ." Gina Lombroso-Ferrero, *Cesare Lombroso. Storia della vita e delle opere*, 91, note 10.
34. Lombroso, "Dell'igiene" in *Delitto, genio, follia*, 105.
35. "Sovereign and people, people and sovereign, labor and nation, nation and labor, school and army, army and school . . . The circle closes." Silvio Lanaro,

"Il Plutarco italiano: L'istruzione del 'popolo' dopo l'Unità," in *Storia d'Italia, Annali*, vol. 4, *Intellettuali e potere*, 570. Cited in Umberto Levra, *Fare gli italiani. Memoria e celebrazione del Risorgimento*, 52–53. See also Duggan, *The Force of Destiny*, the section "Military Service," 283–90.

36. Bruno Tobia, "Una cultura per la nuova Italia." In *Storia d'Italia. Vol. 2. Il Nuovo Stato e la Società Civile, 1861–1887*, 427–529. Minister Bacelli is quoted at 489.
37. Fulvio Cammarano, "La Costruzione dello stato e la classe dirigente," in *Storia d'Italia. Vol. 2: Il nuovo stato e la società civile, 1861–1887*[0], 96.
38. Simonetta Polenghi, *Fanciulli soldati. La militarizzazione dell'infanzia abbandonata nell'Europa moderna*, 14.
39. Giovanni De Castro, *Il libro del soldato italiano. Doveri e affetti del soldato italiano*, 124. Cited in Rigotti Colin, Mariella, "Il soldato e l'eroe nella letteratura scolastica dell'Italia liberale," *Rivista di storia contemporanea* 14, no. 3 (July 1985): 330, and in Ilaria Porciani, *La festa della nazione*, 86.
40. Polenghi, *Fanciulli soldati*, 19.
41. Edmondo De Amicis, *Pagine militari*, 9–15.
42. Franca Pieroni Bortolotti, *Alle origini del movimento femminile in Italia, 1848–1892*, 97–100. See also Mary Gibson, *Prostitution and the State in Italy, 1860–1915.*
43. Igino Ugo Tarchetti, *Tutte le opere*, vol. 1, 384.
44. De Amicis, *Pagine militari*, 87.
45. *Ibid.*, 87, 103.
46. *Ibid.*, 164.
47. *Ibid.*, 49–50. See also Ilaria Porciani, *La festa della nazione*, 88–90.
48. Lombroso, *Delitto, genio, follia*, 106. The motif contrasting boys who play soldier against boys who play priest turns up in the memoirs of Giuseppe Ricciardi, a political exile from Bourbon Naples, whose brother grew up to become a collaborator in the regime: Angela Russo, *"Nel desiderio delle tue care nuove", Scritture private e relazioni di genere nell'Ottocento risorgimentale*, 67.
49. Adolfo Perrone, *Il brigantaggio e l'unità d'Italia*, 230–32, 53–55.
50. De Amicis, *Pagine militari*, 87.
51. De Amicis, *Pagine militari*, 161.
52. De Amicis, *Pagine militari*, 170.
53. Paolo Ferrari, "Un Giovane Ufficiale, Commedia in un prologo e tre atti".
54. Paolo Ferrari, "Un Giovane Ufficiale," Atto Primo, Scena III, 57. See also the author's preface, 5–12.
55. Tarchetti, *Tutte le opere*, 382.
56. Tarchetti, *Tutte le opere*, 450.
57. Tarchetti, *Tutte le opere*, 454.

Chapter 8

1. Sighele, *La mala vita a Roma*, 15.
2. ASR, Tribunale Civile e Penale di Roma, b. 3659. The autopsy (Quaderno n. 4455) guesses Fadda's age as 35 at the time of his death, but if this were so, he would have been only 14 years old when he served as *furiere* in the Battle of San Martino. The ages of 41–45 mentioned in early newspaper reports of the murder would thus seem more likely.
3. ASR, Tribunale Civile e Penale di Roma, b. 3659, Quaderno n. 4455, 136, first interrogation of Cesare Fadda.
4. Maria Luisa Betri, and Daniela Maldini Chiarito, eds., *"Dolce dono graditissimo": La lettere privata dal Settecento al Novecento*, 13.
5. Russo, *'Nel desiderio delle tue care nuove,'* 60 and note 6.
6. ASR, Tribunale Civile e Penale di Roma, b. 3659. These letters are gathered as pages 157–91 in vol. 4. Because the letters vary in size and shape and due to damage, the page number is not always legible on every letter.
7. Nicolò Coboevich, *Processo Fadda illustrato*,180.
8. *Il Bersagliere*, Monday October 6, 1879, n. 273; The controversy over divorce and the rhetorical use made of the Fadda crime and trial in public discussion of the issue of divorce is discussed in Seymour, *Debating Divorce in Italy*.
9. Observations on the particular character of Italian positivism are discussed in Cavalli Pasini, "Scienza e letteratura tra processo e commedia," in *Intersezioni*, 566, note 6; 576, note 17; Auguste Comte, *A General View of Positivism*, 1–7.
10. Antonio Santucci, "Positivismo e cultura positivistica: problemi vecchi e nuovi," in *L'Età del positivismo*, edited by Paolo Rossi, 65.
11. Carlo A. Madrigani, "Scienza, filosofia, storia e arte nella cultura del positivismo," in *Il Secondo Ottocento: Lo stato unitario e l'età del positivismo*, 83.
12. Alberto Asor Rosa, "Il positivismo," in *Storia d'Italia. Vol. 4: Dall'unità a oggi, Tomo II*, 878–99.
13. ASR, Tribunale Civile e Penale di Roma, b. 3659, October 9 1878 arrest report, p. 113 of Quaderno n. 4455.
14. ASR, Tribunale Civile e Penale di Roma, b. 3659, 12 October 12 1879 statement by Cesare Torresani, brigadiere dei Carabinieri, comandante. The syntax is thus in the original language.
15. Ibid.
16. Vassallo, L.A., *Processo Cardinali e coimputati*, 3.
17. Tarchetti, *Tutte le opere*, 454
18. 25 November 1877
    Carissimo Giovannino,

    You'll call me importunate, impertinent and everything you want, but just the same I have to turn to you to help me again, to implore your aid and understanding to allow Raff to stay here until after my wedding that will certainly take place in the month of December. You know how fussy my mother is and how my father allows himself to be pulled by the nose by her. Therefore it would be painful if because of her caprice the whole thing went by the wayside. You also know how influential your wife is with them, and I'm sure that with her present everything will work out for the best. So if you care for my peace and tranquility, don't deny me this one thing I ask of you and that I need from you as a special favor. It's just a delay of fifteen days or so, do me this favor and I will be eternally grateful, and take it as another demonstration of your affection for all of us and especially for me. I beg you not to mention this letter, not even to Raff, especially not of any little expression of resentment of mine, I have vented my state of mind into yours as though to another myself. I await affectionately your favorable response, as always, your most affectionate, G Saraceni"

19. October 11, Coboevich, *Processo Fadda illustrato*, 76–78; Vassallo, L. A., *Processo Cardinali e coimputati* 57–58.
20. Lombroso, *Delitto, genio, follia*, 102; see also Renzo Villa, *Il deviante e i suoi segni: Lombroso e la nascita dell'antropologia criminale*; Fortunata Piselli and Giovanni Arrighi, "Parentela ed emigrazione," in *Storia d'Italia. Le regioni dall'Unità a oggi. La Calabria*, edited by Piero Bevilacqua and Augusto Placanica, 384–85; Alfredo Niceforo, *Italiani del nord e italiani del sud.*
21. For the length of the official mourning period after the death of King Vittorrio Emanuele II, I am indebted to Dr. Massimo Sgrelli and his staff at the Dipartimento del Cerimoniale di Stato, Ufficio del Cerimoniale. See Massimo Sgrelli, *Il cerimoniale*, 224.
22. *Il Bersagliere*, September 30, 1879, no. 267.
23. The original letter in the trial files is not dated, but this date is given in parentheses in the letters printed in Coboevich, *Processo Fadda illustrato*, 7.
24. Cesare Fadda's title is "Ispettore del Registro e Bollo." ASR, Tribunale Civile e Penale di Roma, b. 3659 cartella blu, 10.
25. ASR, Tribunale Civile e Penale di Roma, b. 3659, Cartella blu, 12.
26. ASR, Tribunale Civile e Penale di Roma, b. 3659, 116.

Chapter 9

1. Thomas Frost, *Circus Life and Circus Celebrities*, 16.
2. Earl Chapin May, *The Circus from Rome to Ringling* 7–14. See also Samuel McKechnie, *Popular Entertainment Through the Ages*, 1955, 195–206.
3. May, Ibid., 9.
4. Frost, *Circus Life and Circus Celebrities*, 18, 20, 30.
5. Sylvestre Barré-Meinzer, *Le cirque classique, un spectacle actuel*, 20.
6. Ibid., 19.
7. R. Toole-Stott, *Circus and Allied Arts: A World Bibliography, 1500–1957*, 139.
8. Accounts of Antonio Franconi's life vary in the specific dates given for events but agree on his influence on the development of the modern equestrian circus. Giancarlo Pretini, *Antonio Franconi e la nascita del circo;* Alessandro Cervellati, *Questa sera grande spettacolo: storia del circo italiano.*

9. Paul Adrian, *Histoire Illusstrée des Cirques Parisiens d'hier et d'aujourd'hui*, 23–24.
10. Alessandro Cervellati, *Storia del circo*, 26.
11. Pretini, *Antonio Franconi e la nascita del circo*; Adrian, *Histoire Illusstrée des Cirques Parisiens*, 19–20.
12. Cervellati, *Storia del circo*, 93–94.
13. Paul Bouissac, *Circus and Culture: A Semiotic Approach*, 7.
14. Warren Roberts, *Jacques-Louis David and Jean-Louis Prieure, Revolutionary Artists. The Public, the Populace, and Images of the French Revolution*, 60.
15. Adrian, *Histoire Illusstrée des Cirques Parisiens*, 24.
16. Given its origin as a promotional image of Napoleon produced in multiple copies, it is perhaps not surprising that by the second half of the twentieth century this image was widely disseminated as an advertisement for cognac.
17. Warren Roberts, *Jacques-Louis David, Revolutionary Artist: Art, Politics, and the French Revolution*, 144.
18. Paul Colin, *L'oeuvre de Carle Vernet*, 27. May, *The Circus from Rome to Ringling*, 13.
19. Pretini, *Antonio Franconi e la nascita del circo*. Cervellati traces the word "circus" to the road around London's Hyde Park. Cervellati, *Storia del circo*, 74.
20. Barré-Meinzer, *Le cirque classique*, 27. On the phases of regulation distinguishing the types of performance legally suitable for circus and theater, see Tristan Rémy, "Introduzione," *Entrate clownesche*, edited by Ceclia Cruciani, 13–29.
21. *Il Diritto*, November 13, 1879, n. 317.
22. Barré-Meinzer, *Le cirque classique*, 23.
23. Cervellati, *Storia del circo*, 93.
24. Circo Olimpico delle Due Sicilie, alle Fosse del Grano, *Programma della spettacolosa pantomima: Napoleone I in Egitto alla Battaglia delle Piramidi, ovvero la morte del Generale Kleber*.
25. Crary, Jonathan, *Suspensions of Perception: Attention, Spectacle, and Modern Culture*.
26. Bouissac, *Circus and Culture*, 8.
27. Virginio Oddone, "Descrivere, quantificare, classificare," in *La scienza e la colpa. Crimini criminali crimonologi: un volto dell'Ottocento*, edited by Umberto Levra, 147.
28. Alfredo Niceforo, *Italiani del nord e italiani del sud, 34*. The essential study of the use of statistics in this era is Silvana Patriarca, *Numbers and Nationhood: Writing Statistics in Nineteenth-Century Italy*, esp. the Introduction, 1–23.
29. Cesare Lombroso, *L'Homme Criminel: Etude Anthropologique et Psychiatrique*, vol. 2, 178.
30. John A. Davis, *Conflict and Control: Law and Order in Ninetheenth-Century Italy*, 67–90.
31. Steven C. Hughes, "The Theory and Practice of Ozio in Italian Policing: Bologna and beyond," *Criminal Justice History. An International Annual* 6 (1985): 89–103; and Silvana Patriarca, "Indolence and Regeneration: Tropes and

Tensions of Risorgimento Patriotism," *American Historical Review* 110, n. 2 (2005): 380–408.

32. Carluccio testifies that Cardinali demanded to be called "Girolamo Franconi," and a love letter in the trial archive is addressed to Cardinali by that name. Carluccio's testimony, *L'Opinione*, October 23, 1879, Num. 290.

Chapter 10

1. ASR, Tribunale Civile e Penale, Rome, b. 3659. Vol. E, 138
2. Nicolò Coboevich, *Processo Fadda illustrato*, 113.
3. Vassallo, L. A., *Processo Cardinali e coimputati*, 78. As English language readers of Italo Svevo's celebrated novel, *La coscienza di Zeno*, will know, the meaning of the Italian word "coscienza" can include both "conscience" and "consciousness." Thus the prosecutor is not only saying Cardinali is heartless; Cardinali is not really human at all.
4. Coboevich, *Processo Fadda illustrato*, 70.
5. Ibid.
6. *La Capitale*, September 18, 1879, n. 3278, and September 28, n. 3283. *L'Osservatore romano*, October 12, 1879, n. 234.
7. Coboevich, *Processo Fadda illustrato*, 69.
8. The Milanese illustrated weekly, *Illustrazione italiana*, lists Lopez' act of precipitously and opportunistically switching sides among the examples of questionable legal conduct that characterize the Fadda case. See the regular column, "Gli Eccetera della Settimana," in *Illustrazione italiana*, 6, n. 45–49 November 1879, 294–295.
9. Francis Haskell, "Il pagliaccio triste: note su un mito ottocentesco," in *Arte e linguaggio della politica e altri saggi*, 181–94. Haskell observes that the figure of the sad clown, beginning with Watteau, was analogized both to Christ and the Wandering Jew. Certainly the most noted example of the trope of the happy clown compelled to conceal his desperation would be Leoncavallo's "Pagliacci," 1892. Of note also is the 1863 painting by Guglielmo Stella in the Galleria Nazionale d'Arte Moderna, Rome, "Il saltimbanco al letto della moglie morente." See further, Jean Starobinski, *Portrait de l'artiste en saltimbanque*.
10. Vassallo, L. A., *Processo Cardinali e coimputati*, 87.
11. Vassallo, L.A., *Processo Cardinali e coimputati*, 29; Coboevich, *Processo Fadda illustrato*, 112.
12. "Corriere" 15–16 October 1879. Coboevich, *Processo Fadda illustrato*, 112. On Lopez' falsetto, *Illustrazione italiana*, Anno VI, N. 43–26 October, 1879, 259.
13. ASR, Tribunale Civile e Penale di Roma, b. 3659, vol. 4, 223 v.
14. *Il Pungolo*, October 22, 1879.
15. Vassallo, L. A., *Processo Cardinali e coimputati*, 101.
16. *Il Pungolo*, October 23, 1879.
17. Vassallo, L. A., *Processo Cardinali e coimputati*,106. In other moments Carolina Misuracca is said to be the mother of six children by Pietro Cardinali.
18. Vassallo, L. A., *Processo Cardinali e coimputati*,107.

19. Coboevich, *Processo Fadda illustrato*, 168.
20. Vassallo, L. A., *Processo Cardinali e coimputati*,117; the charge is "mancanza di recapiti."
21. *Illustrazione italiana*, 6, n. 44–2 November, 1879, 275.
22. ASR, Tribunale Civile e Penale di Roma, b. 3659, 131.
23. *Illustrazione italiana*, 6, n. 45–9 November 1879, 290.
24. Palomba had made a name for himself when Rome was still under the popes for his defense of two nationalist patriots, Ajani and Luzzi, and for his defense in 1875 of one of the accused killers of editor Raffaele Sonzogno. See Giuseppe Fonterossi, *Roma fine Ottocento*, 52.
25. *Il Pungolo*, November 1, 1879.
26. Alessandro Cervellati, *Storia del circo*,129.
27. An 1890 photograph of Annie Oakley in Rome shows her riding side-saddle. Vitali, Lamberto, *Un fotografo fin de siècle. Il conte Primoli*, 139 (photo n. 102). The 1932 monument to Anita Garibaldi, partly designed by Mussolini, shows her riding side-saddle (Fogu, Claudio, "'To Make History': Garibaldism and The Formation of a Fascist Historic Imaginary," 203-240 in *Making and Remaking Italy*, 211).
28. Cervellati, *Storia del circo*, 129.
29. ASR, Tribunale Civile e Penale di Roma, b. 3659, 131, 28.
30. Ibid., 131r.
31. Ibid.,159.
32. Angela Carbone, *Esposti e orfani nella Puglia dell'Ottocento*, 8–9.
33. Ibid., n13, 50; 9.
34. Volker Hunecke, *I trovatelli di Milano: bambini esposti e famiglie espositrici dal XVII al XIX secolo*, 50. Also of particular interest, Gabriele De Rosa, "L'emarginazione sociale in Calabria nel XVIII secolo: Il problema degli esposti," in *Ricerche di storia sociale e religiosa*, 13:5–29 (1978). At p. 26 an 1801 document describes in detail the form and purpose of the wheel.
35. ASR, Tribunale Civile e Penale di Roma, b. 3659, 162.
36. Ibid., 161.
37. Anna Maria Maccelli, "Bambini abandonati a Prato nel XIX secolo: il 'segnale' come testimonianza di un'identità da perdere o da ritornare," in *Enfance Abandonée e société en europe XIV–XX siècle. Acts du colloque international, Rome 30–31 janvier 1987*, 815–36.
38. Giovanna Dal Molin, "Illegitimi ed esposti in Italia dal Seicento all'Ottocento," in *La demografia storica delle città italiane*, Società italiana di demografia storica: Relazioni e comunicazioni presentate al Convegno tenuto ad Assisi nei giorni 27–29 ottobre, 1980, 543. Angela Carbone, *Esposti e orfani nella Puglia dell'Ottocento*, 10.
39. *Il Bersagliere*, November 1, 1879, n. 299.
40. Vassallo, L. A., *Processo Cardinali e coimputati*, 128.
41. *Corriere della sera*, November 3-4, 1878.
42. *Il Messaggero*, November 6, 1879, n. 306.
43. *Il Pungolo*, November 9, 1879; *L'Osservatore romano*, November 12, n. 259.

44. *La Capitale*, November 12, 1879, n. 3328.
45. *Corriere della sera*, 9–10 November 1879.
46. *Times of London*, November 13, 1879, 9.
47. *Il Diritto*, November 12, 1879, n. 316.
48. *L'Osservatore Romano*, November 12, 1879, n. 259.
49. *Il Bersagliere*, November 12, 1879, n. 309.
50. *Don Pirloncino*, November 12, 1879, n. 136. *Il Bersagliere*, November 12, 1879, n. 309.
51. *Il Diritto*, November 12, 1879, n. 316.
52. *L'Osservatore romano*, November 12, 1879, n. 259.
53. *Times of London*, November 13, 1879, 9.
54. The circular issued by Ministro di Grazia e Giustizia e Culti, Giovanni Battista Varé, who served in the second Cairoli government from July 14, 1879 to November 25, 1879, was issued on November 3 (Gabinetto N. 243–340). *Raccolta delle circolari emanate dal Ministero di Grazia e Giustizia e dei Culti: anni 1871–1880.*
55. *La Capitale*, November 19, 1879, n. 3335; La Libertà, November 17, 1879, n. 320.
56. *Illustrazione italiana*, Anno VI, N. 46, November 16, 1879, 307.

Chapter 11

1. Vassallo, L. A. *Processo Cardinali e coimputati*, 128.
2. *Raccolta delle circolari emanate dal Ministero di Grazia e Giustizia e dei Culti: anni 1871–1880.*
3. Groppi, "Il teatro della giustizia," 657.

Bibliography

Adrian, Paul. *Histoire Illusstrée des Cirques Parisiens d'hier et d'aujourd'hui*. Bourg-la-Reine (Seine): Adrian, 1957.

Ago, Renata. *Il lavoro delle donne*. Bari: Laterza, 1996.

Album-Ricordo della Esposizione di Belle Arti a Roma, 1883. Milan: Fratelli Treves, 1883.

Alessi, Giorgia. *Il processo penale. Profilo storico*. Bari: Laterza, 2001.

Amodio, Ennio, ed. *I giudici senza toga: esperienze e prospettive della partecipazione popolare ai giudizi penali*. Milan: Giuffrè, 1979.

Anderson, Benedict. *Imagined Communities: Reflections on the Origin and Spread of Nationalism*. Rev. ed. London: Verso, 2006.

Andreoli, Annamaria, ed. *Giosué Carducci e l'identità italiana*. Milan: Biblioteca di Via Senato Edizioni, 2007.

Ardini, G. *La donna delinquente e la legge penale: considerazioni medico-legali*. Catania: Galatola Editore, 1883.

Armati, Cristiano, and Yari Selvetella. *Roma criminale, il lato oscuro della Città Eterna, misteri, delitti, fattacci e criminalità dal rapimento di Aldo Moro all'assurda morte di Marta Russo, dal controverso assassinio di Pier Paolo Pasolini alla banda della Magliana*. Rome: Newton & Compton, 2007.

Arrangio-Ruiz, G. *Storia costituzionale del Regno d'Italia. 1898*. Naples: Jovene, 1985.

Arslan, Antonia, and Mariagrazia Raffele, eds. *Fanfulla della domenica*. Dosson/Treviso: Canova, 1981.

Ascoli, Albert Russell, and Krystyna von Henneberg, eds. *Making and Remaking Italy. The Cultivation of National Identity around the Risorgimento*. Oxford: Berg, 2001.

Archivio di Stato di Roma, Tribunale Civile e Penale di Roma, b. 3659. Circolo d'Assise. Procedimento Penale 18959.

Assassinio e processo Fadda in versi romaneschi per L. A. Rome: Tipografia Capaccini e Ripamonti, [date cut out of volume].

Asor Rosa, Alberto. "Il positivismo," in *Storia d'Italia. Vol 4: Dall'unità a oggi*. Turin: Einaudi, 1975, 878–99.

Babini, Valeria. *Il caso Murri, una storia italiana*. Bologna: Il Mulino, 2004.

———. M. Cotti, F. Minuz, and A. Tagliavini. *Tra sapere e potere: la psichiatria italiana nella seconda metà dell'Ottocento*. Bologna: Il Mulino, 1982.

Baima Bollone, Pierluigi. *Cesare Lombroso, ovvero il principio dell'irresponsabilità*. Turin: Società Editrice Internazionale, 1992.

Balbo, Pier Paolo et al., eds. *Per un Atlante della Calabria*. Rome: Gangemi Editore, 1993.

Banti, Alberto. *L'onore della nazione, identità sessuali e violenza nel nazionalismo europeo*. Turin: Einaudi, 2005.

———. "La storia sociale: Un paradigma introvabile?" In *La storiografia sull'Italia contemporanea*, edited by Cristina Cassina. Pisa: Giardini Editori, 1991, 183–208.

———. *Storia della borghesia italiana*. Rome: Donzelli, 1996.

Barbiera, Raffaello. *Vite ardenti nel Teatro. 1700–1900. da Archivii e da Memorie*. Milan: Fratelli Treves, 1931.

Barré-Meinzer, Sylvestre. *Le cirque classique, un spectacle actuel*. Paris: L'Harmattan, 2004.

La battaglia di San Martino ed I premi, dialoghi fra un caporale furiere e due soldati. Rome: Tipografia del Senato, 1878.

Beales, Derek. *The Risorgimento and the Unification of Italy*. London: Allen & Unwin, 1971.

Belardelli, Giovanni, et al. *Miti e storia dell'Italia unita*. Bologna: Il Mulino, 1999.

Bell, Vikki, ed. *Performativity and Belonging*. London: Sage, 1999.

Beltrani Scalia, Martino. *La riforma penitenziaria in Italia: Studi e Proposte*. Rome: Tipografia Artero, 1879.

Benjamin, Walter. *Illuminations*. London: Pimlico, 1999.

Bentley, Michael, ed. *Companion to Historiography*. London: Routledge, 1997.

Berengo, Marino. *Cultura e istituzioni nell'Ottocento italiano*. Edited by Roberto Pertici. Bologna: Il Mulino, 2004.

Bernardini, N. ed. *Guida della stampa periodica italiana*. Lecce: Tipografia Editrice Salentina, 1890.

Bertelli, Carlo, and Giulio Bollati. *Storia d'Italia. Annali 2: L'immagine fotografica 1845–1945. Tomo I*. Turin: Einaudi, 1979.

Betri, Maria Luisa, and Daniela Maldini Chiarito, eds. *"Dolce dono graditissimo": La lettere privata dal Settecento al Novecento*. Milan: Franco Angeli, 2000.

Betri, Maria Luisa, and Ada Gigli Marchetti. *Salute e classi lavoratrici in Italia dall'unità al fascismo*. Milan: Franco Angeli, 1982.

Bevilacqua, Piero, and Augusto, Placanica, eds. *Storia d'Italia: le regioni dall'unità a oggi: La Calabria*. Turin: Einaudi, 1985.

Biagini, Mario. *Giosué Carducci*. Milan: Mursia, 1976.

Biancale, Michele. *Michele Cammarano*. Milan-Rome: Arti Grafiche Bertarelli, n.d.

Bianchi, A. G. *Cronache criminali italiane*. Milan: Treves, 1896.

Bianchi, A. G., G. Ferrero, and S. Sighele. *Il mondo criminale italiano*. Milan: Zorini, 1895.

Bianchi, A.G., *Cronache criminali italiane*. Milan: Treves, 1896.

Bietoletti, Silvestra, and Michele Dantini. *L'Ottocento italiano. La storia, gli artisti, le opere*. Florence: Giunti Gruppo Editoriale, 2002.

Blasi, Benedetto. *Stradario romano*. Milan: Edizioni del Borghese, 1971.

Bois, Yve-Alain, and Rosalind Krauss. *L'informe*. Milan: Mondadori, 2003.

Bolis, Giovanni. *La polizia e le classi pericolose delle società*. Bologna: Zanichelli, 1879.

Bona, Luigi F. "Appunti sulle origini e sulla storia del fumetto italiano," nuovo testo, aumentato, dal volume *Il fumetto italiano* Fondazione dell'Associazione Franco Fossati, Milano. http://www.lfb.it/fff/fumetto/storia/st_it/st_it_010.htm. Accessed August 24, 2010.

Bonanni, Francesca. *Teatro a Roma, studi e testi*. Rome: Lucarini, 1982.

Bonetta, Gaetano. *Corpo e nazione. L'educazione ginnastica, igienica e sessuale nell'Italia liberale*. Milan: Franco Angeli, 1990.

Bonetti, Mario, ed. *Storia dell'editoria italiana*. Rome: Gazzetta del Libro, 1960.

Bortolotti, Franca Pieroni. *Alle origini del movimento femminile in Italia, 1848–1892*. Turin: Einaudi, 1975.

Bovio, Oreste, ed. *Edmondo De Amicis: pagine militari*. Rome: Stato Maggiore dell'Esercito, Ufficio Storico, 1988.

Briganti, Alessandra. *Intellettuali e cultura tra Ottocento e Novecento. Nascita e storia della terza pagina*. Padua: Liviana Editrice in Padova, 1972.

Broca, Paul. *Mémoires d'anthropologie zoologique et biologique*. Paris: Reinwald, 1877.

Bouissac, Paul. *Circus and Culture: A Semiotic Approach*. Bloomington: Indiana University Press, 1976.

———. *Circo e cultura*. Palermo: Sellerio, 1986.

Bourke, Angela. *The Burning of Bridget Cleary*. New York: Viking, 2000.

Brizzi, Bruno, ed. *Emma Perodi: Roma italiana, 1870–1895*. Rome: Centro Romano Editoriale, 1980.

Bruni, Francesco, ed. *La maschera e il volto: Il teatro in Italia. Venice: Marsilio, 2002.*

Burrow, John W. *The Crisis of Reason in European Thought, 1848–1914*. New Haven: Yale University Press, 2000.

Caffiero, Marina, and Giuseppe Monsagrati, eds. *Dall'erudizione alla politica: Giornali, giornalisti ed editori a Roma tra XVII e XX secolo*. Milan: Franco Angeli, 1997.

Calhoun, Craig, ed. *Habermas and the Public Sphere*. Cambridge, MA: MIT Press, 1992.

Caligo, Silvio Antonio. *Processo Fadda, versi di Ausonio De Liberi. a Giosué Carducci*. Genoa: Tipografia del R. Istituto dei Sordo-Muti, 1879.

Cammarano, Fulvio. "La Costruzione dello stato e la classe dirigente." In *Storia d'Italia. Vol. 2: Il nuovo stato e la società civile, 1861–1887*, edited by Giovanni Sabbatucci and Vittorio Vidotto. Rome: Laterza, 1995, 3–113.

Candeloro, G. *Storia dell'Italia moderna. vol. 5: La costruzione dello stato unitario, 1860–71*. Milan: Feltrinelli, 1968. See esp. 176–212.

Canosa, Romano. *Storia della criminalità in Italia, 1845–1945*. Turin: Einaudi, 1991.

Capelleti, Mauro, John Henry Merryman, and Joseph M. Perillo. *The Italian Legal System: An Introduction*. Stanford: Stanford University Press, 1967.

Capelli, Anna. *La buona compagnia: utopia e realtà carceraria nell'Italia del Risorgimento*. Milan: Franco Angeli, 1988.

Capini, Anita Ginella. *Gandolin fotografa Genova. Immagini e frammenti sulle trace di Luigi Arnaldo Vassallo*. Genoa: De Ferrari Editore, 1999.

Capone, Alfredo. *Destra e Sinistra da Cavour a Crispi*. Turin: UTET, 1981.

Cappiello, Agata Alma et al., eds. *Donne e diritto: due secoli di legislazione 1796–1986*. Rome: Presidenza del Consiglio dei Ministri, 1988.

Cappuccio, Carmelo, ed. *Memorialisti dell'Ottocento*. Tomo 2, vol. 59. Milan: Riccardo Ricciardi Editore, 1958.

Caracciolo, Alberto. *Roma capitale: Dal Risorgimento alla crisi dello Stato liberale*. Rome: Editori Riuniti, 1984.

Caracciolo, Alberto, ed. *Subalterni in tempo di modernizzazione: Nove studi sulla società romana nell'Ottocento. Annali vol. VII. fondazione lelio e Lisli Basso–Issoco, Roma*. Milan: Franco Angeli, 1985.

Carbone, Angela. *Esposti e orfani nella Puglia dell'Ottocento*. Bari: Cacucci Editore, 2000.

Cardoza, Anthony L. "Rethinking Modern Italy After the Cultural Turn." *Journal of Modern Italian Studies* 13, no. 4 (December 2008): 541–49.

Carducci, Giosué. *Giambi ed epodi. 1867–1872. Nuovamente raccolti e corretti*. Bologna: Zanichelli, 1882.

———. *Giambi ed epodi*. Testimonianze, interpretazioni, commento di Enzo Palmieri. Bologna: Nicola Zanichelli Editore, 1959.

———. *Rime nuove*. Bologna: Zanichelli, 1887.

———. *Tutte le poesie*. edited by Carlo del Grande. Basiano: Bietti, 1967.

Carlson, Marvin. *The Italian Stage from Goldoni to D'Annunzio*. Jefferson, NC: McFarland, 1981.

Cassina, Cristina, ed. *La storiografia sull'Italia contemporanea*. Pisa: Giardini Editore, 1991.

Castronovo, Valerio. *La stampa italiana dall'unità al fascismo*. Bari: Laterza, 1976.

———. *La stampa italiana nell'età liberale*. Bari: Laterza, 1979.

———. *La stampa 1867–1925*. Milan: Franco Angeli, 1987.

Cattaneo, Giovanni. *An Italian Reader Consisting of Choice Specimens from the Best Modern Italian Writers*. Heidelberg: J. Groos, 1891.

Cavalli Pasini, Annamaria. "Scienza e letteratura tra processo e commedia." *Intersezioni: Rivista di storia delle idee* 3, no. 3 (1983): 563–86.

———. *Tra eversione e consenso: Pubblico, donne, critici nel positivismo letterario italiano*. Bologna: CLUEB, 1989.

———. *La scienza del romanzo*. Bologna: Patròn, 1982.

Cecchini, Luigi. *Dieci grandi processi d'amore e di morte*. Milan: G. De Vecchi, 1965.

Cederna, Antonio. *Mussolini urbanista. Lo sventramento di Roma negli anni del consenso*. Bari: Laterza, 1979.

Cervellati, Alessandro. *Storia del circo*. Bologna: Il Resto del Carlino, 1956.

Cesana, Giuseppe Augusto. *Ricordi di un giornalista. Parte II e ultima. 1851–1871*. Milan: Giuseppe Prato, 1892.

Ceva, Lucio. *Storia della società italiana dall'unità a oggi: le forze armate*. Turin: UTET, 1981.

Chelli, Gaetano Carlo. *L'eredità Ferramonti*. Turin: Einaudi, 1972.

Chiaves, Desiderato. *Il giudice del fatto negli stati sardi. Istituzioni all'ufficio di giurato e manuale teorico-pratico per esercitarne le funzioni*. Turin: Stabilimento Tipografico Fontana, 1853.

Chierici, Aldo. *Il quarto potere a Roma, storia dei giornali e dei giornalisti romani.* Rome: Enrico Voghera, 1905.

Circo Olimpico delle Due Sicilie, Compagnia Equestre Guillaume. *Programma della spettacolosa pantomima Napoleone I in Egitto alla battaglia delle primaidi, ovvero la morte del General Kleber.* Naples: Tipografia Strada San Giuseppe 37, 1838. Biblioteca Nazionale di Napoli.

Coboevich, Nicolò. *Processo Fadda illustrato. Dibattimento alla Corte D'Assise di Roma dal 30 settembre al 31 ottobre 1879.* Rome: Bracco Editore, 1879.

Colin, Paul. *L'Oeuvre de Carle Vernet.* Bruxelles: Editions de la Galerie Giroux, s.d.

Colla, Eugenio Monti. *The Magic World of Marionettes. Campagnia Marionettistica Carlo Colla e Figli.* Chicago: Istituto Italiano Di Cultura, 2003.

Collodi, Carlo. *Opere.* Edited by Daniela Marcheschi. Milan: Mondadori, 1995.

Colombo, Giorgio. *La scienza infelice. Il museo di antropologia criminale di Cesare Lombroso.* Turin: Bollati Boringhieri, 1975.

Comanducci, A. M. *Dizionario illustrato dei pittori e incisori italiani moderni. 1800–1900.* Vol. 1. Milan: S. A. Grafitalia, già Pizzi & Pizzo, 1945.

Commemorazione dei benemeriti della Società di Solferino e San Martino, morti dalla Fondazione (1870) della Società al 24 giugno 1884. Padua: Tipografia dei fratelli Salmin, 1884.

Comte, Auguste. *A General View of Positivism.* London: Routledge, 1907.

Congresso penitenziario internazionale. Catalogo della Esposizione Industriale Carceraria e della Esposizione dei tipi delle celle, ecc. Rome: Tipografia delle Mantellate, 1885.

Contessa Nanà. *Libro proibito: novelle infranciosate.* Milan: Fratelli Bietti e G. Minacca, 1890.

Contini, Gianfranco, ed. *Storia della letteratura italiana di Francesco De Sanctis.* Turin: UTET, 1968.

Contorbia, Franco. *Giornalismo italiano, vol. primo 1860–1901.* Milan: Mondadori, 2007.

Cordova, Ferdinando. "Giornali e giornalisti, a Roma, nell'Italia umbertina." In *Dall'erudizione alla politica: giornali, giornalisti, ed editori a Roma tra XVII e XX secolo,* edited by Marina Caffiero and Giuseppe Monsagrati, 239–58. Milan: Franco Angeli, 1997, 239–58.

Cortese, Nino. *Il mezzogiorno ed il Risorgimento italiano.* Naples: Libreria Scientifica, 1965.

Cossa, Pietro. *Messalina, commedia in 5 atti in versi, con prologo.* Turin: F. Casanova, 1877.

Costantini, Costanzo. *La storia del Messaggero.* Rome: GREMESE, 2008.

Covino, Luca. *I baroni del "buon governo": istruzioni della nobiltà feudale nel Mezzogiorno moderno.* Naples: Liguori, 2004.

Crary, Jonathan. *Suspensions of Perception: Attention, Spectacle and Modern Culture.* Cambridge, MA: MIT Press, 1999.

Croce, Benedetto. *A History of Italy. Storia d'Italia dal 1871 al 1915.* Translated by Cecelia M. Ady. New York: Russell & Russell, 1963.

Ceclia Cruciani, ed. *Entrate clownesche.* Rome: Editoria & Spettacolo, 2006.

Cuccia, Giuseppe. *Urbanistica Edilizia Infrastrutture di Roma Capitale 1870–1990. Una cronologia*. Bari: Laterza, 1991.

Cultura e società in Italia nell'età umbertina: problemi e ricerche. Centro di ricerca 'Letterature e cultura dell'Italia unita'. Atti del primo Convegno, Milano 11–15 settembre 1978. Milan: Vita e Pensiero, 1981.

D'Addio, Mauro. *Politica e magistratura. 1848–1876*. Milan: Giuffrè, 1966.

D'Amelio, Angela Maria. "Foro di Cesare." In *Fori Imperiali. Demolizioni e scavi. Fotografie 1924 / 1940*, edited by Rosella Leone and Anita Margiotta, 420–23. Rome: Electa, 2007.

Dal Molin, Giovanna. "Illegitimi ed esposti in Italia dal Seicento all'Ottocento," in *La demografia storica delle città italiane*. Società italiana di demografia storica: Relazioni e comunicazioni presentate al Convegno tenuto ad Assisi nei giorni 27–29 ottobre, 1980. Bologna: CLUEB, 1982, 497–564.

———. *Nati e abbandonati: aspetti demografici e sociali dell'infanzia abbandonata in Italia nell'età moderna*. Bari: Cacucci Editore, 1993.

———, ed. *La famiglia ieri e oggi: trasformazioni demografiche e sociali dal XV al XX secolo*. Bari: Cacucci Editore, 1992.

———, ed. *Trovatelli e balie in Italia: Secc. XVI–XIX. Atti del Convegno Infanzia Abbandata e Baliatico in Italia. Secc. XVI–XIX. Bari, 20–21 maggio 1993*. Bari: Cacucci Editore, 1994.

Dardano, M. *Il linguaggio dei giornali italiani*. Bari: Laterza, 1973.

Davis, John A., ed. *Gramsci and Italy's Passive Revolution*. London: Croom Helm, 1979.

———. *Conflict and Control: Law and Order in Nineteenth-Century Italy*. Atlantic Highlands, NJ: Humanities Press International, 1988.

———, ed. "Remapping Italy's path to the Twentieth Century." *Journal of Modern History* 66, no. 2 (June 1994): 291–320.

———, ed. *Italy in the Nineteenth Century, 1796–1900*. Oxford: Oxford University Press, 2000.

Davis, John A., and Paul Ginsborg, eds. *Society and Politics in the Age of the Risorgimento*. Cambridge: Cambridge University Press, 1991.

Dayot, Armand. *Les Vernet: Joseph–Carle–Horace*. Paris: Armando Magnier, 1898.

De Amicis, Edmondo. *De Amicis*. Edited by A. Baldini. Milan: Garzanti, 1945.

———. *Opere scelte*. Edited by Folco Portinari and Giusi Baldissone. Milan: Mondadori, 1996.

———. *Pagine militari*. Edited by Oreste Bovio. Rome: Stato Maggiore dell'Esercito, Ufficio Storico,1988.

Debord, Guy. *The Society of the Spectacle*. Translated by Donald Nicholson-Smith. New York: Zone Books, 1995.

DeCastro, J. *The Memoirs of J. DeCastro, Comedian*. London: Sherwood, Jones, 1824.

De Castro, Giovanni. *Il libro del soldato italiano. Doveri e affetti del soldato italiano*. Milan: Agnelli, 1862.

De Giorgio, Michela. *Le italiane dall'unità a oggi: Modelli culturali e comportamenti sociali*. Bari: Laterza, 1992.

De Gubernatis, Angelo, ed. *Dizionario degli artisti italiani viventi*. Florence: Le Monnier, 1889.

De Jaco, Aldo, ed. *Antistoria di Roma capitale*. Rome: Editori Riuniti, 1970.

De Jaco, Aldo, ed. *Il brigantaggio meridionale. Cronaca inedita dell'Unità d'Italia*. Rome: Editori Riuniti, 1969.

Della Rocca, L. G. *Rapporto a S. M. il Re di Sardegna dal Capo di Stato Maggiore; 28 giugno 1859* http://www.cronologia.it/storia/a1859.htm. Accessed August 24, 2010.

Del Grande, Carlo. *Tutte le poesie di Giosuè Carducci*. Basiano: Bietti, 1967.

Del Negro, Piero. *Esercito, Stato, Società: saggi di storia militare*. Bologna: Cappelli Editore, 1979.

De Longis, Rosanna, ed. *La stampa periodica delle donne in Italia. Catalogo 1861–1985*. Rome: Presidenza del Consiglio dei Ministri, 1986.

Delvecchio, Pietro. *Il valore italiano*. Rome: Casa editrice Pinerolo, 1934.

Demografia storica delle città italiane. Bologna: CLUEB, 1982.

De Rosa, Gabriele. "L'emarginazione sociale in Calabria nel XVIII secolo: il problema degli esposti." *Ricerche di storia sociale e religiosa*. Rome: Edizioni di Storia e Letteratura, 13 (1978): 5–29.

Dezza, Ettore. *Saggi di storia del diritto penale moderno*. Milan: LED, 1992.

Di Bazancourt, Barone. *La campagna d'Italia dell'anno 1859. Cronaca della Guerra*. Naples: Luigi Chiurazzi, 1862.

Di Bello, Giulia, and Patrizia Meringolo. *Il rifiuto della maternità: L'infanticidio in Italia dall'Ottocento ai giorni nostri*. Pisa: Edizioni ETS, 1997.

Di Bello, Giulia. *Senza nome né famiglia: I bambini abbandonati nell'Ottocento*. Florence: Luciano Manzuoli Editore, 1989.

Dickie, John. *Darkest Italy: The Nation and Stereotypes of the Mezzogiorno, 1860–1900*. New York: St. Martin's Press, 1999.

Di Corato, Susanna. "Magistratura, anarchici e governo. La vicenda della banda del Matese." *Rivista di storia contemporanea*, 13, no. 3 , July 1984. 321–72.

Dijkstra, Bram. *Idols of perversity: Fantasies of Feminine Evil in Fin-de-Siècle Culture*. New York: Oxford University Press, 1986.

Di Majo, Elena, and Matteo Lafranconi, eds. *Galleria Nazionale d'Arte Moderna: Le Collezioni, il XIX secolo*. Milan: Mondadori, 2006.

Dini, Piero. *La donna e la moda nella pittura italiana del secondo '800 nelle collezioni private* Montecatini Terme: Azienda autonoma di cura e soggiorno, 30 luglio–30 settembre, 1988.

———. *Movimenti pittorici italiani dell'Ottocento: I macchiaioli e la scuola napoletana*. Milan: Alfieri & Lacroix, 1965.

Di Salvo, Niccolò. "A G. C. in risposta alla poesia del processo Fadda." Caltanissetta, 27 ottobre, 1879. In the collection of Casa Carducci, Bologna, Cartone LXXVII, 1b XV–Scritti d'altri–1, p. 295.

Drake, Richard. *Byzantium for Rome: The Politics of Nostalgia in Umbertian Italy, 1878–1900*. Chapel Hill: University of North Carolina Press, 1980.

———. *The Aldo Moro Murder Case*. Cambridge, MA: Harvard University Press, 1995.

Duggan, Christopher. *The Force of Destiny. A History of Italy since 1796*. New York: Houghton Mifflin Company, 2008.

Dunant, Jean-Henri. *Un ricordo di Solferino. Con documenti, testimonianze e saggi aggiuntivi*. Edited by Giusti Renato. Florence: La Nuova Italia, 1961.

Dupuy, R. Ernest, and Trevor N. Dupuy. *Encyclopedia of Military History from 3500 BC to the Present*. New York: Harper & Row, 1986.

Durbè, Dario, ed. *Aspetti dell'arte a Roma dal 1870 al 1914*. Rome: De Luca Editore, 1972.

Duttlinger, Carolin, Lucia Ruprecht, and Andrew Webber, eds. *Performance and Performativity in German Cultural Studies*. Oxford: Peter Lang, 2003.

Enciclopedia dello Spettacolo. Rome: UNEDI, 1975.

Enciclopedia dello Spettacolo. Rome: Le Maschere, 1956.

Enfance Abandonée et Société en Europe, XIV–XX Siècle. Actes du Colloque International, Rome, 30–31 Janvier 1987. Rome: Ecole Française de Rome, Palais Farnèse, 1991.

Esposizione internazionale di Belle Arti in Roma, 1883. Catalogo delle opere esposte nella mostra retrospettiva d'Arte Italiana, edited by the Executive Committee. Rome: Fratelli Bencini, 1883.

Farese Sperken, Christine. *Francesco Netti*. Naples: Electa, 1996.

———. *Francesco Netti. 1832–1894: Un intellettuale del Sud. Catalogo della mostra, Bari, Pinacoteca Provinciale, marzo-maggio 1980*. Rome: De Luca Editore, 1980.

Farinelli, G., and E. Paccagnini, eds. *Storia del giornalismo italiano*. Turin: UTET, 1997.

Farolfi, Bernardino. *Le voci del tempo: Tradizione documentaria e storiografia economica nel novecento italiano*. Bologna: CLUEB, 1995.

Ferrari, Paolo. "Un Giovane Ufficiale, ossia Il Comico e Il Drammatico nella Vita," Teatro Italiano Contemporaneo, Fascicolo 78. Milan: Libreria Editrice, 1883.

Ferrero, Ernesto, ed. *La mala Italia: storie nere di fine secolo*. Milan: Rizzoli, 1973.

Ferriani, Lino. *La infanticida nel codice penale e nella vita sociale. Considerazioni*. Milan: Fratelli Dumolard, 1886.

Fiorensoli, Maria Paola. *La città della dea Perenna*. Austin: Anomaly Press, 1999.

Florian, Eugenio, Alfredo Niceforo, and Nicola Pende, eds. *Dizionario di criminologia*. Milan: Vallardi, 1943.

Florian, Eugenio, and Guido Cavaglieri. *I vagabondi. Studio sociologico-giuridico*. Vol 1. Turin: Fratelli Bocca, 1897.

———. *I vagabondi. Studio sociologico-giuridico*. Vol. 2. Turin: Fratelli Bocca, 1900.

Fonterossi, Giuseppe. "L'assassinio del Capitano Fadda." In *Cronaca italiana*. December 1, 1956. Rome: 1956.

———. *Roma fine Ottocento*. Rome: Edizioni Moderne Canesi, 1960.

Foot, John. *Modern Italy*. New York: Palgrave Macmillan, 2003.

Fournier-Finocchiaro, Laura. *L'Italie menacee:Figures de l'ennemi du XVIe au Xxe siècle*. Paris: L'Harmattan, 2004.

Frandini, Paola. "Nino Costa e l'ambiente artistico romano tra il 1870 e il 1890." In *Aspetti dell'arte a Roma dal 1870 al 1914*, edited by Dario Durbè. Rome: De Luca Editore, 1972, XIX–XXXIII.

Franzo, Stefano. *Patron Découpé: mode maschili dall'unità d'Italia alla fine dell'età umbertina nei periodici italiani e francesi*. Padua: CLUEB, 2005.

Frost, Thomas. *Circus Life and Circus Celebrities*. London: Tinsley Brothers, 1875.

Galantini, Novella. "L'educazione dei giudici popolari. Esperienze della manualistica per i laici." In *I giudici senza toga: esperienze e prospettive della partecipazione popolare ai giudizi penali*, edited by Ennio Amodio. Milan: Giuffrè, 1979, 139–85.

Galasso, Giuseppe. *Il mezzogiorno nella storia d'Italia*. Florence: Le Monnier, 1977.

Ghisalberti, Alberto Maria. *Dizionario biografico degli italiani*. Rome: Istituto della Enciclopedia italiana, 1960–.

Giacanelli, Ferruccio. "Introduzione." In *Delitto, genio, follia: scritti scelti*, edited by Delia Frigessi, Ferruccio Giacanelli, and Luisa Mangoni. Turin: Bollati: Boringhieri, 2000, 5–43.

Giarelli, Francesco. *Vent'anni di giornalismo, 1868–1888*. Codogno: Tipografia Editrice A. G. Cairo, 1896.

Gibson, Mary. *Born to Crime: Cesare Lombroso and the Origins of Biological Criminality*. London: Praeger, 2002.

———. *Prostitution and the State in Italy, 1860–1915*. Columbus: Ohio State University Press, 1986.

Ginzburg, Carlo. *Clues, Myths, and the Historical Method*. Translated by John Tedeschi and Anne C. Tedeschi. Baltimore: Johns Hopkins University Press, 1989.

Giordano, Michele. *La stampa illustrata in Italia dalle origini alla Grande Guerra*. Milan: Guanda, 1983.

Giuntini, Andrea. *Il paese che si muove: le ferrovie in Italia fra '800 e '900*. Milan: Franco Angeli, 2001.

Gnoli, Umberto. *Topografia e toponomastica di Roma medioevale e moderna*. Rome: Grotta del Libro, 2004. First published 1939–XVII.

Godkin, G. S. *Life of Victor Emmanuel II, First King of Italy*. London: Macmillan, 1880.

Gooch, John. *Army, State and Society in Italy, 1870–1915*. New York: St. Martin's Press, 1989.

Gorni, Mariagraia, and Laura Pellegrini. *Un problema di storia sociale: L'infanzia abbandonata in Italian nel secolo XIX*. Florence: La Nuova Italia, 1974.

Gotti, Giulio. *Alcuni processi celebri e ricordi di un vecchio avvocato*. Milan: Società Editrice Dante Alighieri, 1926.

Groppi, Angela. "Il teatro della giustizia. Donne colpevoli e opinione pubblica." *Quaderni storici* 37, no. 111/3 (dicembre 2002): 649–80.

———. "'Un pezzo di mercanzia di cui il mercante fa quel che ne vuole'. Carriera di un'internata tra Buon Pastore e manicomio." *Annali della Fondazione Lelio e Lisli Basso–Issocco. Vol. VII, Subalterni in tempo di modernizzazione*. Milan: Franco Angeli, 1985.

Groppi, Angela, ed. *Il lavoro delle donne*. Bari: Laterza, 1996.

Groppi, Angela, and Margherita Pelaja. "Delitti e la loro narrazione: Le fonti criminali." *Percorsi del femminismo e storia delle donne*, Nuova DWF, supplemento al n. 22: atti del convegno di Modena (Aprile 1982), 108–118.

Grosso, Carlo Federico, Guido Neppi Modona, and Luciano Violante. *Giustizia penale e poteri dello stato*. Milan: Garzanti, 2002, 108–118.

Guida alla collocazione di bandi, manifesti e fogli volanti. Rome: Istituto Centrale per il Catalogo Unico della Biblioteche Italiane, 1999.

Gundle, Stephen, and Lucia Rinaldi, eds. *Assassinations and Murder in Modern Italy: Transformations in Society and Culture*. New York: Palgrave Macmillan, 2007.

Haskell, Francis. *Arte e linguaggio della politica e altri saggi*. Florence: SPES, 1978.

Headrick, Daniel R. *The Invisible Weapon, Telecommunications and International Politics 1851–1945*. New York: Oxford University Press, 1991.

Hobsbawm, Eric. *Il trionfo della borghesia*. Bari: Laterza, 1979.

Hughes, Steven. *Crime, Disorder and the Risorgimento: The Politics of Policing in Bologna*. Cambridge: Cambridge University Press, 1994.

Hughes, Steven C. "The Theory and practice of *Ozio* in Italian Policing: Bologna and Beyond." *Criminal Justice History. An International Annual* 6 (1985), 89–103.

Hunecke, Volker. *I trovatelli di Milano: bambini esposti e famiglie espositive dal XVII al XIX secolo*. Bologna: Il Mulino, 1989.

Iannuzzi, Lina, ed. *Nicola Misasi. Pagine calabresi: antologia*. Bologna: Cappelli Editore, 1969.

Indice biografica italiano. 3rd ed. Vol. 8. München: Saur, 2002.

Il giornalismo italiano dal 1861 al 1870. dagli atti del 5 Congresso dell'Istituto Nazionale per la Storia del giornalismo. Associazione Stampa Subalpino: Edizioni 45 Parallelo, 1966.

Illustrazione italiana: rivista settimanale. 5, no. 2. Milan: Treves, 1878.

Illustrazione italiana: rivista settimanale. 7, no. 49 (5 dicembre). Milan: Treves, 1880

Illustrazione italiana: rivista settimanale. 9, no. 4. (22 gennaio). Milan: Treves, 1882

Illustrazione italiana: rivista settimanale. 10, no. 26. (1 luglio). Milan: Treves, 1883.

Insolera, Italo. *Roma moderna: un secolo di storia urbanistica*. Turin: Einaudi, 1962.

Insolera, Italo and Alessandra Maria Sette. *Roma tra le due guerra. Cronache di una città che cambia*. Rome: Palombi Editore, 2003.

Isnenghi, Mario. *L'Italia in piazza. I luoghi della vita pubblica dal 1848 ai giorni nostri*. Milan: Mondadori, 1994.

———. ed. *I luoghi della memoria. Personaggi e date dell'Italia unita*. Bari: Laterza, 1997.

Istituto Nazionale per la Storia del Giornalismo. *Atti del II Congresso Nazionale di Storia del Giornalismo, Trieste, 18–20 ottobre 1963*. Trieste: Comitato Provinciale di Trieste, 1966.

Izzo, Luigi. *La popolazione calabrese nel secolo XIX. Demografie ed economia*. Naples: Edizioni Scientifiche Italiane, 1965.

Kalifa, Dominique. *Crime et culture au XIXe siècle*. Paris: Perrun, 2005.

———. *L'encre et le sang: récits de crimes et société à la Belle Epoque*. Paris: Fayard, 1995.

Körner, Axel. *The Politics of Culture in Liberal Italy. From Unification to Fascism*. London: Routledge, 2009.

Kosofsky Sedgwick, Eve, and Andrew Roberts, eds. *Performativity and Performance*. New York: Routledge, 1995.

Kostof, Spiro. *The Third Rome, 1870–1950, Traffic and Glory*. Berkeley, CA: University Art Museum, 1973.

Kritzer, Herbert M., ed. *Legal Systems of the World*. Santa Barnara, CA: ABC-CLIO, 2002.

Lanaro, Silvio. "Il Plutarco italiano: L'istruzione del 'popolo' dopo l'Unità." In *Storia d'Italia, Annali*, vol. 4, *Intellettuali e potere*, edited by C. Vivanti. Turin: Einaudi, 1981.

Lauri, Achille. *Dizionario dei cittadini notevoli di Terra di Lavoro antichi e moderni.* Sala Bolognese: A. Forni, 1915.

Lega, Gioacchino. *Cinquant'anni di giornalismo*. Rome: Casa della Stampa, 1930.

Leps, Marie-Christine. *Apprehending the Criminal: The Production of Deviance in 19th Century Discourse*. Durham: Duke University Press, 1992.

L'Esercito italiano dall'Unità alla Grande Guerra. 1861–1918. Rome: Stato Maggiore dell'Esercito Ufficio Storico SME, 1980.

Leone, Rossella, and Anita Margiotta, eds. *Fori Imperiali. Demolizioni e scavi. Fotografie 1924 / 1940*. Rome: Electa, 2007.

Levi, Fabio, Umberto Levra, and Nicola Tranfaglia, eds. *Storia d'Italia –3. Il mondo contemporaneo*. Florence: La Nuova Italia, 1978.

Levra, Umberto. *Fare gli italiani. Memoria e celebrazione del Risorgimento*. Turin: Comitato di Torino dell'Istituto per la Storia del Risorigmento Italiano, 1992.

Levra, Umberto, ed. *La scienza e la colpa. Crimini criminali crimonologi: Un volto dell'Ottocento*. Milan: Electa, 1985.

Leydi, Roberto. *Tanti fatti succedono nel mondo: Fogli volanti nell'Italia settentrionale*. Brescia: Grafo, 2001.

Licata, Glauco. *Notabili della terza Italia*. Rome: Edizioni Cinque Lune, 1968.

Lodi, Luigi. *Giornalisti*. Bari: Laterza, 1930.

Lombroso, Cesare. *Delitto, genio, follia: scritti scelti*. Edited by Delia Frigessai, Ferruccio Giacamelli, and Luisa Mangoni. Turin: Bollati Boringhieri, 2000.

———. *L'Homme criminel: Etude Anthropologique et Psychiatrique*. Paris: Felix Alcan, 1895.

———. *Mnemosine o fisiologia della memoria. Poesia nelle nozze dell'Ing. Alberto Olivetti*. Milan: Tipografia Bertolotti, 1878.

———. *Palimsesti del carcere. Storie, messaggi, iscrizioni, graffiti dei detenuti delle carceri alla fine dell'Ottocento*. Florence: Ponte alle Grazie, 1996.

———. *L'Uomo delinquente studiato in rapporto alla antropologia, alla medicina legale ad alle discipline carcerarie*. Milan: Hoepli, 1876.

Lombroso, Cesare, and Guglielmo Ferrero. *La donna delinquente, la prostituta e la donna normale*. 3rd. ed. Turin: Fratelli Bocca, 1915.

Lombroso-Ferrero, Gina. *Cesare Lombroso. Storia della vita e delle opere*. Turin, Fratelli Bocca, 1915.

Mack Smith, Denis. *Modern Italy: A Political History*. Ann Arbor: University of Michigan Press, 1997.

———. *Storia d'Italia, 1861–1969*. Bari: Laterza, 1982.

———. *Vittorio Emanuele II*. Bari: Laterza, 1972.

Macry, Paolo. "Borghesie, città e Stato. Appunti e impressioni su Napoli, 1860–1880." *Quaderni storici* 19, no. 2 (August 1984): 339–83.

———. *Ottocento. Famiglia, élites e patrimoni a Napoli*. Turin: Einaudi, 1988.

Macry, Paolo, and A. Palermo, eds. *Società e cultura dell'Italia unita*. Naples: Guida, 1978.

Madrignani, Carlo A. *Ideologia e narrativa dopo l'unificazione*. Rome: Savelli, 1974.

———. "Scienza, filosofia, storia e arte nella cultura del positivismo." *Il Secondo Ottocento: lo stato unitario e l'età del positivismo*. Franca Angelini, ed. Bari: Laterza, 1975, 465–507.

Maggi, Stefano. *Politica ed economia dei trasporti*. Bologna: Il Mulino, 2001.

Magistrali, Artemio. *Il lettore e il suo doppio. Analisi della cronaca minore nel quotidiano italiano*. Milan: I.S.U. Università Cattolica, 1990.

Magni, Basilio. *Storia dell'arte italiana dalle origini al Secolo XX. Vol. 3*. Rome: Officina Poligrafica Romana, 1902.

Majolo Molinari, Olga. *La stampa periodica italiana dell'Ottocento*. Rome: Istituto di Studi Romani, 1963.

Malgeri, Francesco. *La stampa cattolica a Roma dal 1870 al 1915*. Brescia: Morcelliana, 1965.

Mannori, Luca. "La crisi dell'ordine plurale: Nazione e costituzione in Italia tra Sette e Ottocento." In *Ordo Iuris. Storia e forme dell'esperienza giuridica*. Edited by Mario Sbriccoli. Milan: Giuffrè, 2003, 135–92.

Marino, Giuseppe Carlo. *La formazione dello spirito borghese in Italia*. Florence: La Nuova Italia, 1974.

Marselli, Nicola. *Gl'Italiani del Mezzogiorno*. Rome: Sommaruga, 1884.

Martini, Ferdinando. *Confessioni e ricordi*. Florence: Bemporad, 1922.

———. *Confessioni e ricordi. 1859–1892*. Milan: Treves, 1929.

———. *Confessioni e ricordi*. Edited by Mauro Vannini. Florence: Ponte alle Grazie, 1990.

———. "Confessioni e ricordi." In *Memorialisti dell'Ottocento*, vol. 59. Edited by Carmelo Capuccio Tomo II. Milan: Riccardo Ricciardi Editore, 1958.

———. *Il diario eritreo*. Vol. 1. Introduction by Riccardo Astuto di Lucchesi. Florence: Vallecchi, 1946

———. *Di palo in frasca: dal "Fanfulla della domenica" e da "La domenica letteraria."* Milan: Treves–Treccani–Tumminelli, 1931.

———. *Fra un sigaro e l'altro*. Treviso: Canova, 1981.

———. *Lettere. 1860–1920*. Milan: Mondadori, 1934.

———. *Nell'Affrica italiana*. Milan: Treves, 1935, prima edizione 1891.

———. *I Nuovi Ricchi*. Milan: Barbini, 1873.

———. *Pagine raccolte*. Florence: Sansoni, 1912.

———. *Simpatie: studi e ricordi*. Milan: Treves, 1926.

———. *Studi e ricordi*. Milan: Treves, 1926.

Martucci, Roberto. *Emergenza e tutela dell'ordine pubblico nell'Italia liberale*. Bologna: Il Mulino, 1980.

———. *L'invenzione dell'Italia unita, 1855–1864*. Milan: Sansoni, 1999.

Materi, Pasquale. *L'eloquenza forense*. Turin: Fratelli Bocca, 1902.

May, Earl Chapin. *The Circus from Rome to Ringling*. New York: Duffield & Green, 1932.

Mazzacane, Aldo. "Letteratura, processo e opinione pubblica: le raccolte di cause celebri tra bel mondo, avvocati e rivoluzione." *Rassegna forense* 36 (2003): 757–92.

McDonald, Terrence J., ed. *The Historic Turn in the Human Sciences*. Ann Arbor: University of Michigan Press, 1996.

McKechnie, Samuel. *Popular Entertainment Through the Ages*. London: Sampson Low, Marston, 1955.

Meneghini, Roberto. "Lo scavo dei fori Imperiali e la scoperta del catasto imperiale romano." Paper presented at the Field Museum conference, Chicago, November 1, 2007.

Mezzabotta, Ernesto. *Vivandiera di San Martino*. Rome: Editore Edoardo Perino, 1886. N. 15 in the series, "Biblioteca Patriotica."

Mimita Lamberti, Maria. "Roma 1883: l'esposizione internazionale di belle arti." *Storia dell'arte italiana. Parte seconda: Dal medioevo al Novecento. Volume terzo: Il Novecento*. Turin: Einaudi, 1982.

Misasi, Nicola. *Leggende e liriche*. Cosenza: Dalla Tipografia Municipale, 1879.

Modern Italy: Images and History of a National Identity. Vol. One: From Unification to the New Century. Milan: Electa, 1982.

Moe, Nelson. *The View From Vesuvius. Italian Culture and the Southern Question*. Berkeley: University of California Press, 2002. See esp. chapter 6.

Mola, Aldo A. *Giosué Carducci: Scrittore, politico, massone*. Milan: Bompiani, 2006.

Molfese, Franco. *Storia del brigantaggio dopo l'Unità*. Milan: Feltrinelli, 1966.

Molinari, Olga Majolo. *La stampa periodica italiana dell'Ottocento*. Rome: Istituto di Studi Romani, 1963.

Montanelli, Indro. *Storia d'Italia: L'Italia dei notabili. 1861–1900*. Milan: Rizzoli, 1999.

Monti, Antonio. *L'Italia nei cento anno del Secolo XIX. Vol. 5, 1871–1900*. Milan: Vallardi, 1942.

———. *Vittorio Emanuele II, 1820–1878*. Milan: Garzanti, 1941.

Mori, Maria Teresa. *Salotti: la sociabilità delle elite nell'Italia dell'Ottocento*. Rome: Carocci, 2000.

Morini, Enrica. *Storia della moda XVIII–XX secolo*. Milan: Skira, 2000.

Morro, Antonio. *I caratteri dei delinquenti. Studio antropologico-sociologico*. Turin: Fratelli Bocca, 1887.

Moscati, Amedeo. *I ministri del regno d'Italia. Vol. 4: La sinistra al potere*. Salerno: Edizioni del Comitato Napoletano, 1964.

Mozzini, Anna Maria. *La liberazione della donna*. Edited by Franca Pieroni Bortolotti. Milan: Gabriele Mazzotta editore, 1975.

Murialdi, Paolo. *Storia del giornalismo italiano*. Bologna: Il Mulino, 1996.

Murray, Marian. *Circus! From Rome to Ringling*. Westport, CT: Greenwood Press, 1956.

Musella, Luigi. *Individui, amici, clienti: Relazioni personali e circuiti politici in Italia meridionale tra Otto e Novecento*. Bologna: Il Mulino, 1994.

Nasi, Franco. *Il peso della carta. Giornali, sindaci e qualche altra cosa di Milano dall'unità al fascismo*. Bologna: ALFA Edizioni, 1966.

Nava, Luigi. *L'Armata sarda nella giornata del 24 giugno 1859*. Rome: Enrico Voghera, 1907.

Nava, Paola, ed. *Operaie, serve, maestre, impiegate: Atti del convegno internazionale di studi, il lavoro delle donne nell'Italia contemporanea: continuità e rotture. Carpi 6–7–8 aprile 1990*. Turin: Rosenberg & Sellier, 1992.

Netti, Francesco. "Esposizione di Roma—Note di un visitatore." In *Francesco Netti, Scritti critici*, edited by Lucio Galante. Rome: De Luca Editore, 1980, 213–71.

Niceforo, Alfredo. *Criminologia, veccchie e nuove dottrine*. Milan: Fratelli Bocca, 1949.

———. *Il gergo nei normali, nei degenerati e nei criminali*. Turin: Fratelli Bocca, 1897.

———. *Italiani del nord e italiani del sud*. Turin: Fratelli Bocca, 1901.

———. *Le Génie de l'Argot*. Paris: Mercure de France, 1912.

Ogliari, Francesco. *Commenti al testo di Edmondo De Amicis, "La battaglia di Solferino e San Martino*. Pavia: Edizioni Selecta, 2005.

Olivieri Sangiacomo, A. *San Martino. Novelle militari*. Catania: Niccolò Giannotta Editore, 1899.

Olson, Roberta J. M. *Ottocento: Romanticism and Revolution in 19th Century Italian Painting*. Philadelphia: University of Pennsylvania Press, 1992.

Padovani, Tullio. *Diritto penale*. 5th ed. Milan: Giuffrè, 1999.

Palladini, Luisa Amalia, ed. *Lettere di ottimi autori sopra cose familiari, ad uso specialmente delle giovinette italiane*. Florence: Le Monnier, 1861.

Patarini, Giada. "Il processo Misdea." *Modelli, giudizi, pregiudizi: materiali per una storia di fine secolo*. Dipartimento di Storia Moderna e Contemporanea. Facoltà di Lettere e Filosofia, Università degli Studi di Roma "La Sapienza" a.a. 1999–2000. http://w3.uniroma1.it/dsmc/old/ricerca/materiali_fine_secolo.htm. Accessed on August 24, 2010.

Patriarca, Silvana. *Numbers and Nationhood: Writing Statistics in Nineteenth-Century Italy*. Cambridge: Cambridge University Press, 1996.

———. "Indolence and Regeneration: Tropes and Tensions of Risorgimento Patriotism." *American Historical Review* 110, no. 2 (2005): 380–408.

Pavarini, Stefano. *Carducci*. Palermo: Palumbo, 2003.

Pelaja, Margherita. *Matrimonio e sessualità a Roma nell'Ottocento*. Bari: Laterza, 1994.

———. *Scandali, sessualità e violenza nella Roma dell'Ottocento*. Rome: Biblink Editori, 2001.

Perodi, Emma. *Roma italiana 1870–1895*. Edited by Bruno Brizzi. Rome: Centro Romano Editoriale, 1980. (Orig. published in 1896.)

Perrone, Aldo. *Il brigantaggio e l'unità d'Italia*. Milan: Istituto Editoriale Cisalpino, 1963.

Pesci, Ugo. "I primi anni di Roma capitale. 1870–1878." In *Memorialisti dell'Ottocento*, vol. 59, edited by Tomo II. Carmelo Cappuccio. Milan: Riccardo Ricciardi Editore, 1958, 475–571.

Pessina, Enrico. *Dei progressi del diritto penale in Italia nel secolo XIX: discorsi di E.P.* Florence: Stabilimenti Civelli, 1868.

———, ed. *Enciclopedia del diritto penale italiano: raccolta di monografie.* Vol. 2. Milan: Società Editrice Libraria, 1906.

Pettiti, Agostino. Generale Agostino pettiti Bagliani di Roreto. *Madonna della Scoperta. Battaglia di San Martino, 24 giugno 1859. Studio storico tattico.* Turin: F. Casanova, 1909.

Pieri, Piero. *Storia militare del Risorgimento: Guerre e insurrezioni.* Turin: Einaudi, 1962.

Pio, Oscar, and Nicola Argenti. *Processi celebri contemporanei italiani e stranieri.* Naples: Ernesto Anfossi, 1889.

Pisetzky, Rosita Levi. *Il costume e la moda nella società italiana.* Turin: Einaudi, 1978.

Piselli, Fortunata. *Parentela ed emigrazione: Mutamenti e continuità in una comunità calabrese.* Turin: Einaudi, 1981.

Piselli, Fortunata, and Giovanni Arrighi. "Parentela, clientela e comunità." In *Storia d'Italia. Le regioni dall'Unità a oggi. La Calabria*, edited by Piero Bevilacqua and Augusto Placanica. Turin: Einaudi, 1985, 367–494.

Pisu. "Luigi Arnaldo Vassallo." Associazone Franco Fossati—Museo del Fumetto e della Communicazione, 2006. http://www.lfb.it/fff/giorn/aut/g/gandolin.htm. Accessed August 24, 2010.

Placanica, Augusto. *Alle origini dell'egemonia borghese in Calabria: La privatizzazione delle terre ecclesiastiche 17684–1815.* Salerno–Catanzaro: Società editrice meridionale, 1979.

———. "La Cassa Sacra e i beni della Chiesa della Calabria settecentesca." *Economic History Review* 28, no. 2 (May 1975): 370.

———. *La Cassa Sacra e i beni della Chiesa nella Calabria del Settecento.* Naples: Università di Napoli, 1970.

Polenghi, Simonetta. *Fanciulli soldati: La militarizzazione dell'infanzia abbandonata nell'Europe moderna.* Rome: Carocci Editore, 2003.

Porciani, Ilaria. *La festa della nazione. Rappresentazione dello Stato e spazi sociali nell'Italia unita.* Bologna: Il Mulino, 1997.

Pretini, Giancarlo. *Antonio Franconi e la nascita del circo.* Udine: Trapezio, 1988.

———. *La grande cavalcata.* Udine: Trapezio, 1987.

Programma della spettacolosa pantomima Napoleone I in Egitto alla battaglia delle primaidi, ovvero la morte del General Kleber. Circo Olimpico delle Due Sicilie, Compagnia Equestre Guillaume (Naples: Tipografia Strada San Giuseppe 37, 1838). Biblioteca Nazionale di Napoli.

Pullini, Giorgio. *Il teatro in Italia. Vol. 3: Settecento e Ottocento.* Rome: Edizioni Studium, 1995.

Quarenghi, Nina. *L'altra battaglia. Solferino e San Martino tra realtà e memoria.* Verona: Cierre Edizioni, 2009. See esp. chapters 4 and 5.

Raccolta delle circolari emanate dal Ministero di Grazia e Giustizia e dei Culti: anni 1871–1880. Rome: Regia Tipografia, 1881.

Radi, Salvo. *Per le donne. a Giosué Carducci.* 24 ottobre, 1879, Biblioteca Casa Carducci, cat. no. 02–101–06.

Ragionieri, Ernesto. *Italia giudicata, 1861–1945, ovvfero la storia degli italiani scritta dagli altri*. Bari: Laterza, 1969.

Re, Lucia. "Passion and Sexual Difference: The Risorgimento and the Gendering of Writing in Nineteenth-Century Italian Culture." In *Making and Remaking Italy*, edited by Albert Russell Ascoli and Krystyna von Henneberg. Oxford: Berg, 2001, 155–202.

Renevey, Monica. *Il circo e il suo mondo*. Bari: Laterza, 1985.

Restucci, Americo. "Cap. 4: il territorio." *Italia moderna: immagini e storia di un'identità nazionale. vol. 1: Dall'unità al nuovo secolo*. Rome: Electa, 1982.

Ricordo della pubblica esposizione del 1883. Società degli amatori e cultori delle Belle Arti a Roma. Roma: Fototipia Danesi, 1883.

Rigotti Colin, Mariella. "Il soldato e l'eroe nella letteratura scolastica dell'Italia liberale." *Rivista di storia contemporanea* 14, no. 3 (July 1985): 329–51.

Rizzi, Giovanni. *Ah, voi credeste che fosse il Parini . . . ?* Cremona: Tipografia Sociale, 1879. Biblioteca Casa Carducci, cat. no. 02–1011–07.

Rizzo, Domenico. "Liberal Decorum and Men in conflict: Rome, 1871–90." *Journal of Modern Italian Studies* 10, no. 3. (2005): 281–96.

Roberts, Warren. *Jacques-Louis David and Jean-Louis Prieur: Revolutionary Artists, the Public, the Populace, and Images of the French Revolution*. Albany: SUNY Press, 2000.

———. *Jacques-Louis David, Revolutionary Artist: Art, Politics, and the French Revolution*. Chapel Hill: UNC Press, 1989.

Rocchi, Nicolò, ed. *Il Palazzo delle Esposizioni a Roma*. Rome: Preprogetti, 2007.

Romanelli, Raffaele. *Il commando impossibile: stato e società nell'Italia liberale*. Bologna: Il Mulino, 1988.

———. *L'Italia liberale. 1861–1900*. Bologna: Il Mulino, 1979.

Romano, Sergio. *Finis italiae: Declino e morte dell'ideologia risogrimentale. Perché gli italiani si disprezzano*. Milan: All'Insegna del pesce d'oro, di Vanni Scheiwiller, 1994.

Rosano, Pietro. *Per la signora Raffaella Saraceni, vedova Fadda, condannata ai lavori forzati a vita. ricorrente alla Eccellentissima Corte di Cassazione in Roma. Udienza 21 gennnaio 1880*. Naples: R. tipografia del Comm. Gennaro De Angelis e Figlio, 1880.

Rosoli, Gianfausto, ed. *Un secolo di emigrazione italiana. 1876–1976*. Rome: Centro Studi Emigrazione, 1978.

Rosselli, John. *The Opera Industry from Cimarosa to Verdi: The Role of the Impresario*. New York: Cambridge University Press, 1984.

Rossi, Paolo, ed. *L'Età del positivismo*. Bologna: Il Mulino, 1986.

———. *Immagini della scienza*. Rome: Editori Riuniti, 1977.

Rossi, Pietro, and Carlo A. Viano, eds. *Storia della filosofia. vol. 5: Ottocento*. Bari: Laterza, 1997.

Rovighi, Cesare. *Storia della Terza Divisione dell'esercito sardo nella Guerra del 1859*. Turin: Unione Tipografico-Editirice, 1860.

Ruffilli, Roberto, and Serena M. Piretti. *L'unità d'Italia e lo stato liberale*. Florence: Le Monnier, 1981.

Russo, Angela. *'Nel desiderio delle tue care nuove': Scritture private e relazioni di genere nell'Ottocento risorgimentale*. Milan: Franco Angeli, 2006.

Rüstow, W. *Guerra d'Italia del 1859. Narrazione politico-militare*. Translated by Col. Roberto Patresi. Milan: Domenico Salvi, 1860.

Sabbatucci, Giovanni, and Vittorio Vidotto, eds. *Storia d'Italia. Vol. 2: Il nuovo stato e la società civile, 1861–1887*. Rome: Laterza, 1985.

Saccenti, Mario, ed. *Opere scelte di Giosué Carducci. Vil. 1: Poesie*. Turin: UTET, 1993.

Sandri, Antonio. *Traduzione in latino di "Alla Regina d'Italia" e della 1 strofa de "A proposito del processo Fadda."* Biblioteca Casa Carducci, Cart. LXXVII, 4a. IX.

Santucci, Antonio. "Positivismo e cultura positivistica: problemi vecchi e nuovi." In *L'Età del positivismo*, edited by Paolo Rossi. Bologna: Il Mulino, 1986.

Sarti, Telesforo. *Il parlamento italiano nel cinquantenario dello Statuto*. Rome: Tipografia Agostiniana, 1898.

Sbarbaro, Pietro. *Parlamento o disciplina militare? Lettera dell'avv. professore Pietro Sbarbaro*. Rome: Tipografia del Commercio, 1886.

Sbarbaro, Pietro, Lopez, Tommaso, and Coboevich, Nicolò, *Via crucis (Per la libertà della stampa)*. Rome: Angelo Sommaruga, 1884.

Sbricccoli, Mario et al., eds. *Ordo Iuris: Storie e forme dell'esperienze giuridica*. Milan: Giuffrè, 2003.

Scarfoglio, Edoardo. *Le più belle pagine di Edoardo Scarfoglio*. Edited by Alberto Consiglio. Milan: Garzanti, 1939.

———. *Il romanzo di Misdea*. Edited by Manola Fausti. Florence: Edizioni Polistampa, 2003.

Scarpino, Salvatore. *La Guerra 'cafona': il brigantaggio meridionale contro lo stato unitario*. Milan: Boroli, 2005.

Schiavone, Aldo, ed. *Stato e cultura giuridica in Italia dall'unità alla repubblica*. Bari: Laterza, 1990.

Schechner, Richard. *Performance Theory*. London: Routledge, 2003.

Schram, Albert. *Railways and the Formation of the Italian State in the Nineteenth Century*. New York: Cambridge University Press, 1997.

Scrivano, Riccardo. "Il verismo nell'Italia mediana: aspetti letterari." In *I verismi regionali: Atti del Congresso Internazionale di Studi, Catania, 27–29 aprile 1992*. Catania: Fondazione Verga, 1996, 189–218.

Sergi, Giuseppe. *Sociologia e nazionalità*. Rome: Rivista italiana, 1916.

Serianni, Luca. *Storia della lingua italiana*. Bologna: Il Mulino, 1990.

Seymour, Mark. *Debating Divorce in Italy: Marriage and the Making of Modern Italians, 1860–1974*. New York: Palgrave Macmillan, 2006.

———. "Keystone of the Patriarchal Family? Indissoluble Marriage, Masculinity and Divorce in Liberal Italy." *Journal of Modern Italian Studies* 10, no. 3 (2005): 297–313.

Sgrelli, Massimo. *Il cerimoniale*. Rome: Master Edizioni, 2007.

Sighele, Scipio. *La folla delinquente: studio di psicologia collettiva*. Turin: Fratelli Bocca, 1895.

———. *La coppia criminale*. Turin: Fratelli Bocca, 1897.

———. *Eva moderna*. Milan: Treves, 1910.

———. *La donna e l'amore*. Milan: Treves, 1913.

Sighele, Scipio, and Alfredo Niceforo. *La mala vita a Roma*. Turin: Forni Editore, 1898.

Siligato, Rosella, and Maria Elisa Tittoni Monti. *Assessorato alla cultura and Quadriennale nazionale d'arte di Roma. 1990. Il Palazzo delle esposizioni: urbanistica e architettura, l'esposizione inaugurale del 1883, le acquisizioni pubbliche, le attivita espositive*. Rome: Edizioni Carte segrete. n.p., 1990.

Silvestre, Le General F. *Etude sur la Campagne de 1859 en Italie*. Paris: Berger-Levrault, 1909.

Soldani, Simonetta, and Gabriele Turi, eds. *Fare gli italiani: scuola e cultura nell'Italia contemporanea*. Bologna: Il Mulino, 1993.

Soldani, Simonetta, ed. *L'Educazione delle donne: scuole e modelli di vita femminile nell'Italia dell'Ottocento*. Milan: Franco Angeli, 1991.

Sommaruga, Angelo. *Crónica bizantina. 1881–1885*. Milan: Mondadori, 1941.

Spadolini, Giovanni. *Firenze capitale*. Florence: Le Monnier, 1967.

Squarciapino, Giuseppe. *Roma bizantina. Società e letteratura ai tempi di Angelo Sommaruga*. Turin: Einaudi, 1950.

Stafford, Barbara Maria. *Echo Objects: The Cognitive Work of Images*. Chicago: University of Chicago Press, 2007.

Starobinski, Jean. *Portrait del l'artiste en saltimbanque*. Geneva: Les Sentiers de la Création, 1970.

Stewart-Steinberg, Suzanne. *The Pinocchio Effect. On Making Italians. 1860–1920*. Chicago: University of Chicago Press, 2007.

Storia dell'arte italiana. Il Novecento. Turin: Einaudi, 1982.

Storia della lingua italiana. Vol. 3: le altre lingue. Turin: Einaudi, 1994.

Storia d'Italia. Annali 12. La Criminalità. Turin: Einaudi, 1997.

Talamo, Giuseppe. *Il Messaggero e la sua città. Cento anni du storia. Vol. 1, 1878–1918*. Florence: Le Monnier, 1979.

———. *Il Messaggero: un giornale laico*. Florence: Le Monnier, 1991.

Tarchetti, Igino Ugo. *Tutte le opere*. Edited by Enrico Ghidetti. Rocca San Casciano: Cappelli, 1967.

Tellini, Gino, ed. *Scrivere lettere. Tipologie epistolari nell'Ottocento italiano*. Rome: Bulzoni Editore, 2002.

Thétard, Henry. *La merveilleuse histoire di Circque*. Paris: Julliard, 1978.

Tobia, Bruno. *Una patria per gli italiani. Spazi, itinerari, monumenti nell'Italia unita. 1870–1900*. Bari: Laterza, 1991.

———. "Una cultura per la nuova Italia." In *Storia d'Italia. Vol. 2. Il Nuovo Stato e la Società Civile, 1861–1887*, edited by Giovanni Sabatucci and Vittorio Vidotto, 427–529. Rome: Laterza, 1995, 427–525.

Toole-Stott, R. *Circus and Allied Arts, A World Bibliography 1500–1957. Vol. 1*. Derby, England: Harpur & Sons, 1958.

Trebbi, Luciana. *La 'ruota' di Via S. Maria a Pisa. 1808–1814*. Pisa: Edizioni ETS, 1997.

Tribunale Civile e Penale di Roma. Archivio Civile e Penale. Circolo d'Assise. AD 3659 fascicolo penale 18958–18959 Procedimento Penale N. 100 del registro generale della Corte D'Assise. Compendio preparato 6 febbraio 1879. Corte di Cassazione di Roma, registro n. 1702.

Tullio-Altan, Carlo. *La nostra Italia. Clientelismo, trasformismo e ribellismo dall'Unità al 2000.* Milan: Università Bocconi Editore, 2000.

Turnbull, Lt. Col. Patrick. *Solferino: The Birth of a Nation.* London: Robert Hale, 1985.

Turone, Sergio. *Corrotti e corruttori dall'unità d'Italia alla P2.* Bari: Laterza, 1984.

Turzio, Silvano, ed. Lombroso e la fotografia. Milan: Mondadori, 2005.

Valera, Paolo. *Milano sconosciuta e Milano moderna.* Milan: Editore Internazionale, 1898.

Vassallo, L. A. (Gandolin). *Gli uomini che ho conosciuto, seguito dalle Memorie d'uno smemorato.* Milan: Fratelli Treves, 1918.

———. *Illustrazione italiana.* 9, no. 4, January 22, 1882.

———. *Processo Cardinali e coimputati per l'assassinio del Capitano Fadda commesso in Roma il 6 ottobre 1878.* Rome: Edoardo Perino, undated (but 1879).

Veo, Ettore. *Processo Fadda in versi romaneschi.* Rome: Tipografia S.A.I.G.E., 1930.

Verdone, Mario. *Il circo.* Padua: Editrice R.A.D.A.R., 1969.

Vidotto, Vittorio, ed. *Roma capitale: Storia di Roma dall'antichità ad oggi.* Bari: Laterza, 2002.

Vigo, Pietro. *Annali d'Italia, Storia degli Ultimi Trent'Anni del Secolo XIX.* Vol. 3, 1879–1882. Milan: Treves, 1909.

Villa, Renzo. *Il deviante e i suoi segni: Lombroso e la nascita dell'antropologia criminale.* Milan: Franco Angeli, 1985.

Villari, Pasquale. *Le lettere meridionali ed altri scritti sulla questione sociale in Italia.* Naples: Guida, 1979.

Violi, Alessandra. *L'immagine informe: Bataille, Warburg, Benjamin e i fantasmi della tradizione.* Forum Avanzato di Ricerca Multimediale, *www.farum.it*, 2004.

Vitali, Lamberto. *Un fotografo fin de siècle. Il conte Primoli.* Turin: Einaudi, 1968.

Vivanelli, Roberto, ed. *La cultura italiana tra '800 e '900 e le origini del nazionalismo.* Florence: Olschki, 1981.

Viviani, Raffaele, "Circo equestre Sgueglia: commedia in tre atti" in *Viviani, 34 commedie scelte da tutto il teatro di Raffaele Viviani*, Ridenti, Lucio, ed. Turin: ILTE 1957.

White, Jonathan. *Italian Cultural Lineages.* Toronto: University of Toronto Press, 2007.

Whittam, John. *The Politics of the Italian Army, 1861–1918.* London: Croom Helm, 1977.

Willard, Ashton Rollins. *History of Modern Italian Art.* London: Longman Green, 1898.

Wong, Aliza S. *Race and Nation in Liberal Italy, 1861–1911. Meridionalism, Empire, and Diaspora.* New York: Palgrave Macmillan, 2006.

Woolf, Stuart. *A History of Italy 1700–1860: The Social Constraints of Political Change.* London: Methuen, 1979.

Yorick figlio di Yorick. Avv. P. C. Ferrigni (or Francesco Leopoldo Ferrigni, according to A. Groppi). *La morte di una musa*. Florence: Tipografia editrice del Fieramosca, 1885.

Zara, Alfonso. *L' assassino del capitano Fadda : Dramma in un prologo e cinque atti*. Rome, 1881. s.l. : s.t. s.n.; Bound with: *I mafiusi*, di Giuseppe Rizzotto, and other works. Inv. 9691 Biblioteca Labronica, Villa Fabbricotti, Livorno.

Index

Italicized page numbers refer to tables and figures.